CU01371285

Lennox Berkeley and Friends

Writings, Letters and Interviews

Lennox Berkeley and Friends

Writings, Letters and Interviews

edited by Peter Dickinson

BOYDELL PRESS

Editorial matter © Peter Dickinson 2012

All Rights Reserved. Except as permitted under current legislation
no part of this work may be photocopied, stored in a retrieval system,
published, performed in public, adapted, broadcast, transmitted,
recorded or reproduced in any form or by any means,
without the prior permission of the copyright owner

First published 2012
The Boydell Press, Woodbridge

ISBN 978 1 84383 785 5

The Boydell Press is an imprint of Boydell & Brewer Ltd
PO Box 9, Woodbridge, Suffolk IP12 3DF, UK
and of Boydell & Brewer Inc.
668 Mount Hope Ave, Rochester, NY 14620-2731, USA
website: www.boydellandbrewer.com

A catalogue record for this book is available
from the British Library

The publisher has no responsibility for the continued existence or
accuracy of URLs for external or third-party internet websites referred
to in this book, and does not guarantee that any content on such
websites is, or will remain, accurate or appropriate

Papers used by Boydell & Brewer Ltd are natural,
recyclable products made from wood grown in sustainable forests

Designed and typeset in Garamond Premier Pro by
David Roberts, Pershore, Worcestershire

Printed and bound in Great Britain by
CPI Group (UK) Ltd, Croydon, CR0 4YY

*This book is dedicated to the memory of
Richard Hickox (1948–2008)
in recognition of his uniquely
authoritative performances and
recordings of Lennox Berkeley's music.*

Contents

List of Illustrations *viii*

Acknowledgements *ix*

Introduction by Peter Dickinson *1*

Part I Reports from Paris, 1929–34 *15*

Part II Letters to Nadia Boulanger, 1929–74 *45*

Part III Selections from Berkeley's Later Writings and Talks, 1943–82 *89*

  1 Britten and his String Quartet [no. 1] (1943) *91*
  2 Modern French Ballet Music (1946) *93*
  3 British Music Today (1949) *97*
  4 Britten's *Spring Symphony* (1950) *105*
  5 Poulenc's Piano Concerto (1950) *108*
  6 Mr Lennox Berkeley on the Composer's Need to Hear his own Works (1959) *110*
  7 Gabriel Fauré (1962) *112*
  8 The Sound of Words (1962) *115*
  9 Concert-going in 1963 (1962) *117*
10 Britten's Characters (1963) *119*
11 Francis Poulenc: Obituary (1963) *121*
12 Truth in Music (1966) *123*
13 Lennox Berkeley Describes his Setting of the Magnificat (1968) *127*
14 Lili Boulanger (1968) *130*
15 Last Week's Broadcast Music [I] (1969) *132*
16 Last Week's Broadcast Music [II] (1969) *134*
17 Charles Burney's Tour (1970) *136*
18 Lennox Berkeley Writes about Alan Rawsthorne (1971) *138*
19 On Criticism (1972) *140*
20 Berkeley as Song-writer (1973) *143*
21 Maurice Ravel (1978) *145*
22 Stravinsky: A Centenary Tribute (1982) *150*
23 Bid the World Good-Night (1981) *152*

Part IV	Interviews with Berkeley, 1973–8	*154*
	1 With Peter Dickinson, 1973 *154*	
	2 With C. B. Cox, Alan Young and Michael Schmidt, 1974 *163*	
	3 With Peter Dickinson, 1978 *172*	
	4 With Michael Oliver, 1978 *176*	
Part V	Extracts from Berkeley's Diaries, 1966–82 *179*	
Part VI	Interviews with Performers, Composers, Family and Friends, 1990–91 *225*	
	1 Performers: Julian Bream, Norman Del Mar, Colin Horsley *225*	
	2 Composers: John Manduell, Nicholas Maw, Malcolm Williamson *243*	
	3 Family: Freda Berkeley, Michael Berkeley *258*	
	4 Friends: Basil Douglas, Desmond Shawe-Taylor *271*	
Part VII	Memorial Address by Sir John Manduell *281*	
	Catalogue of Works *283*	
	Bibliography *297*	
	Index of Works by Berkeley *305*	
	General Index *307*	

Illustrations

FRONTISPIECE

Berkeley, 1950s (Janet Stone, © the Estate of Reynolds and Janet Stone)

PLATES

The plates appear between pages 116 and 117.

1. Lennox Berkeley and his cousin, Lison d'Eppinghoven, 1906
2. Lennox with his dog, Tip, *c.* 1910
3. Berkeley as cox of the Merton IV, Oxford, 1923
4. Berkeley with Ravel, London, *c.* 1925 (Gordon Bryan)
5. Berkeley with sister Geraldine and their mother, France, *c.* 1930
6. Berkeley, 1943 (Germaine Kanova)
7. 36 Rue Ballu today, now Place Lili Boulanger
8. Plaque outside 36 Rue Ballu
9. Nadia Boulanger, 1964 (permission of Julian Berkeley)
10. 1 Cité chaptal today
11. Berkeley and Vere Pilkinton, *c.* 1946
12. A typical cover – in Cambridge blue – used for Berkeley scores from 1945 to 1960
13. The bill for Peter Dickinson's purchase, as a schoolboy, of Berkeley's Piano Sonata
14. *Nelson* at Sadler's Wells, 1954
15. Lennox and Freda Berkeley at their cottage in Norfolk, *c.* 1959 (Derek Hill)
16. Berkeley and Poulenc, *c.* 1960 (Dezo Hoffmann)
17. Berkeley and Bream, 1974 (Sophie Baker)
18. The Berkeley family, *c.* 1973
19. 'The Lord is my Shepherd', op. 91/1, 1975
20. The Seventy-fifth Birthday Concert, 1978
21. Peter Dickinson, Berkeley, Alice Artz and Lady Berkeley outside Keele University Chapel, 1978
22. Letter from Berkeley commenting on Peter Dickinsons' article for *The New Grove Dictionary*, 1980
23. Berkeley at 8 Warwick Avenue, 1981 (Malcolm Crowthers)
24. The Memorial Requiem Mass, 1990

Many photographs courtesy of Tony Scotland, by permission of Lady Berkeley and the Berkeley Estate, and the original photographers where it has been possible to reach them.

Acknowledgements

I should like to make the first of my acknowledgements to Sir Lennox himself. He was always generous and co-operative in being prepared to be interviewed and appreciative of everything done on behalf of his music. It was, quite simply, a privilege to have known him. My connection with the Berkeley family goes back to 1956. I wrote my first articles about his music in 1963; since then I have much enjoyed many associations with the family and have appreciated their encouragement and answers to my queries.

The first edition of *The Music of Lennox Berkeley* appeared in 1988 with Thames Publishing directed by John Bishop. There was just time for me to put a copy of the book into Berkeley's hands before he died the following year, and I think he had some idea of what it was. The whole project was enthusiastically supported by John Bishop from the start, but the rewritten second edition (Boydell, 2003) is now what matters, and the first should be ignored. Nadia Boulanger had generously agreed to write a foreword to my first book, but unfortunately that was not completed until ten years after she died.

Anyone who values the music of Lennox Berkeley cannot fail to have noticed the unique contribution made by the late Richard Hickox in many live performances and recordings over the last two decades. So this book is dedicated to his memory in grateful recognition.

I have acquired an archive of materials about Berkeley over a period of over fifty years, and in doing this I have been indebted to the staff of many organisations. All along I have been grateful for support from Berkeley's loyal publisher, Chester Music – the late Sheila MacCrindle, George Rizza, Christopher Norris and, of current staff, James Rushton, Meg Montieth, Victoria Small and especially Howard Friend, who has seen the *Collected Works for Solo Piano* (2003) and other editions through the press. Katie Connolly at Boosey & Hawkes provided copies of the Berkeley correspondence in their archives. I have been given assistance on several occasions by the staff of the Britten–Pears Library – including the late Rosamund Strode, Jennifer Doctor and most recently Nick Clark and Judith Ratcliffe. I also acknowledge the support of Richard Chesser and the staff at the British Library. Quotation from letters and writings of Benjamin Britten are copyright the Trustees of the Britten–Pears Foundation. Selections from Lennox Berkeley's letters to Britten, letters to Berkeley, and extracts from Berkeley's writings and diaries are reproduced courtesy of the Britten–Pears Library, which holds them, and the Lennox Berkeley Estate.

I am grateful to the BBC for material in what is the fourth of my books drawing on interviews made for radio programmes. Arthur Johnson was the fastidious producer of the Radio 3 documentary 'Lennox Berkeley' broadcast on 31 August 1992 and repeated on 13 September 1994. This gave me the unique series of interviews from which I quoted in *The Music of Lennox Berkeley* but which are now published here complete.

The transcriptions of their own interviews were checked by Julian Bream, Colin Horsley, Sir John Manduell, Lady Berkeley, Michael Berkeley and, on behalf of the subjects no longer living, Jonathan Del Mar, Natasha Maw and Simon Campion (for Malcolm Williamson). Oliver Goulden scrupulously went through my translations.

I am grateful to Jacquie Kavanagh at the BBC Written Archives Centre for permission to print the interviews and to further staff there – Fallon Lee, Samantha Blake and James Codd.

I appreciate permission, through Michael Downing, to print Berkeley's BBC Radio 3 interview with the late Michael Oliver about the Fourth Symphony; Michelle Healey arranged permission from Carcanet Press Ltd for the discussion that appeared in *Poetry Nation 2*; and Peter Phillips has agreed the use of Berkeley's interview with me and other material in *The Musical Times*. There are several acknowledgements needed for Berkeley's own writings. I am grateful to Ben Smith at The Times/NI Syndication for permission to reprint articles Berkeley wrote for *The Times* and the *Sunday Times*, and Chris Payne at Oxford University Press for authorising Berkeley's article on Britten's *Spring Symphony*. It appears that all other permissions were author's copyright and have now come through Lady Berkeley and the Berkeley Estate.

My debt to Tony Scotland, author of the magisterial double biography *Lennox and Freda* (2010), is enormous. He provided material for *The Music of Lennox Berkeley* (2003) and this time read most of the typescript, offered valuable suggestions about presentation and has helped with photographs. He also introduced me to Humphrey Stone and Ian Beck, who kindly provided the frontispiece. Corinne Harrison and the staff at the National Portrait Gallery helped me to reach copyright holders.

I visited the Bibliothèque nationale de France to obtain copies of Berkeley's letters to Boulanger, and arrangements were made for me by Elizabeth Guilini, Director of Music, Laurence Decobert, Anne Michels and other staff in the music library. Robert Orledge kindly provided routes to some of these facilities

There is further material that has not been included. Berkeley's letters to Britten are represented in the volumes of Britten's *Letters from a Life* and in Scotland's *Lennox and Freda*. In any case this book deliberately throws the spotlight on Berkeley without putting him in the shadow of Britten as his centenary approaches in 2013. There are other letters of personal and family interest which I have seen, some referred to by Scotland, but I have not included those in my selection here.

There are several books that have been important. Obviously, *A Lennox Berkeley Source Book* by Stewart Craggs, with its valuable catalogue of manuscripts by Joan Redding. Back in the 1980s it was she who first drew my attention to Berkeley's reports from Paris in *The Monthly Musical Record* and I have used her careful transcriptions here, later confirmed in every detail by consulting the actual magazine.

Allan C. Jones provided many dates of performances and reviews of Berkeley's music in Paris in the 1920s and 30s; Eric Wetherall gave me further information about the 1927 Harrogate Festival programme; Anthony Burton helped with references – and his CD booklet notes to the Berkeley Edition of recordings on Chandos should be consulted; and Mary Bernard, widow of Anthony Bernard, showed me some programmes. I have drawn on the writings and broadcasts of Roger Nicholls, whose

Acknowledgements

book *The Harlequin Years* is a valuable source of information. I was given access to manuscripts by many people including the late Sir William Glock (*Introduction and Allegro* for two pianos and orchestra), the late John C. G. Waterhouse (Toccata written for his father J. F. Waterhouse), Michael Thomas (Prelude and Fugue for clavichord), Angelo Gilardino (*Quatre pièces pour guitarre*), Richard Sandland at the Royal Shakespeare Company (incidental music for *A Winter's Tale*), Colin Horsley (Concerto for piano and double string orchestra, including the otherwise missing cadenza in the first movement), and the staff of the BBC Music Library located for many years at Yalding House. I also acknowledge the generous assistance and enthusiasm of the late William Wynne Willson, who provided many preliminary print-outs for my edition of the *Collected Works for Solo Piano* (2003) and other pieces not yet in print. Kathleen Walker, co-founder of the Lennox Berkeley Society, has been stalwart in tracking down Berkeley performances and sharing new information. John France has also made Berkeley information available on his website, including the Paris Reports.

The publication of this book has been made possible thanks to grants towards its production costs. These have come equally from the Charlotte Bonham-Carter Trust, The Vaughan Williams Trust, the Staypar Trust and the Lennox Berkeley Society.

I much appreciate corrections from my sister, Meriel Dickinson, who read the entire text, and from others who have read the book in whole or in part and made suggestions including Bridget Dickinson and Arnold Whittall. Once again I have been fortunate to work with Boydell & Brewer, where Michael Middeke and Megan Milan handled arrangements, and I was especially pleased to have David Roberts again for copy-editing and layout. There are bound to be omissions in this list of credits and permissions and I can only apologise to anyone left out and undertake to take steps to make corrections at the next opportunity.

Peter Dickinson
Aldeburgh 2012

THE LENNOX BERKELEY SOCIETY

Chairman: Petroc Trelawny

The Society was founded in 1999 by Kathleen Walker and Jim Nicol to increase public awareness of Berkeley and his music; to advance the knowledge of his life and work; and to encourage and support live performances and recordings. Recent projects have included grants towards Chandos CDs of songs, performed by tenor James Gilchrist, Anna Tilbrook and Alison Nicholls, and Berkeley's *Flute Concerto*, with Emily Beynon and the BBC National Orchestra of Wales. Thanks in part to the Society, Berkeley's one-act comic opera *A Dinner Engagement* has been staged around the world, in cities from Rio to Sydney. The Society also helps to fund Berkeley performances by amateurs and professionals at festivals across the UK. There is an annual Journal, and a popular website – www.lennoxberkeley.org.uk – which offers general and specialised information about Berkeley and his music. Publication of this book has been supported by the Society.

Introduction

Peter Dickinson

Sir Lennox Berkeley needs little introduction as one of the most important British composers of the mid-twentieth century. Thanks to the advocacy of the late Richard Hickox, much of his orchestral music is now recorded; so are two of his operas. Hardly a week goes by without his liturgical music gracing the cathedral lists all over the country, and his chamber music has recently found an international public through many performances and recordings.

Lennox Randall Francis Berkeley was born into an aristocratic family at Sunningwell Plain, near Oxford, on 12 May 1903. His father was a naval officer and there were many family connections with France, where Berkeley's parents were living at the time when he was based in Paris.[1]

Berkeley went to school in Oxford and then to Gresham's School, Holt, where he was followed by W. H. Auden and – ten years later – Benjamin Britten. In 1922 he went up to Merton College, Oxford, to read French, Old French and Philology. Whilst there he rowed, took organ lessons and had a few compositions performed. Auden was a contemporary, and Berkeley must have been the earliest composer to set his poetry to music, but these songs are lost. At Oxford Berkeley shared rooms with Vere Pilkington, an outstanding amateur keyboard player who owned a harpsichord and introduced Berkeley to early music.

When Ravel was staying in London in 1925 Berkeley, who knew his hosts, took the opportunity of showing him some of his scores. Ravel said he didn't teach any more but offered to introduce him to Nadia Boulanger, the famous teacher of composition who lived in Paris. That changed Berkeley's life. He gained the professional instruction he could never have found in England and formed a lifelong devotion to his teacher. As a pedagogue Boulanger worked tirelessly and in return demanded everything from her pupils: Berkeley responded with almost total veneration. By 1935 both Berkeley's parents had died and Boulanger remained as a kind of matriarchal figure. As his many letters to her show – Part II below consists of selections from them – she was a cardinal influence for many years.

From 1929 to 1934 Berkeley wrote reports on music in Paris for *The Monthly Musical Record* – published complete in Part I below. Stravinsky was influential, and Berkeley derived much from his friendships with both Ravel and Poulenc. Like Boulanger, Poulenc was a Roman Catholic, and in 1928 Berkeley converted, which appears to have been a gradual decision.

The second major landmark in Berkeley's life and career came in 1936 when he met Britten in Barcelona at the International Society for Contemporary Music Festival where both composers were having works played. Berkeley conducted

---

[1] For full biographical details, see Tony Scotland, *Lennox and Freda* (Norwich, 2010).

his Overture, op. 8, and Britten played his Suite for Violin and Piano, op. 6, with Antonio Brosa.[2]

Berkeley's maturity came slowly, compared with Britten, but by the later 1930s he had achieved a distinctive and individual voice of a completely personal kind. Landmarks at this period include the Serenade for Strings, op. 12 (1939), a classic amongst British works for this medium; the First Symphony, op. 16, the following year; and the Divertimento in B flat, op. 18, in 1943. A third personal encounter of enormous significance was Berkeley's meeting with Freda Bernstein and their marriage in 1946. This lifted Berkeley from the insecurities of the kind of gay world he inhabited into a remarkably happy and stable marriage, a story impressively chronicled in Tony Scotland's double biography *Lennox and Freda* (2010).

Berkeley's music reflects the change. Major achievements of the 1940s include two pairs of works – the *Four Poems of St Teresa of Avila*, op. 27, and the *Stabat mater*, op. 28: the Piano Concerto, op. 29, and the Concerto for Two Pianos, op. 30.

By the early 1950s Berkeley was ready for opera. His grand opera *Nelson*, op. 41, was produced at Sadler's Wells in 1954, and in the same year his one-act comedy *A Dinner Engagement* was premiered. These were followed only two years later by *Ruth*, op. 50. *Nelson* was ambitious and has not been revived onstage, but the other two, especially after the Hickox recordings, have achieved international productions.

In the 1960s, as we shall see, Berkeley's music evolved into the more complex harmonic and contrapuntal idiom of his final period.

On 16 July 1953, as a schoolboy, I purchased a copy of Berkeley's Piano Sonata, op. 20 (completed 1946),[3] at Miller's music shop in Cambridge. Miller's also had branches in Huntingdon, St Ives and Ely, and in those days such shops displayed the latest in sheet music publications. I was soon the proud owner of most of Berkeley's piano music with their light blue covers. What was the almost mesmeric attraction? I had been playing Beethoven and Brahms on the piano for the Performer's Diploma of the Royal Academy and of the Royal College in London and masses of Bach on the organ. I also played Howells, but realised that he offered nothing for the future. Berkeley's music had a refreshingly individual harmonic idiom allied to melody and a pianistic style that has produced some of the finest British piano music. There was nothing quite like it.

The following day – 17 July 1953 – I bought a copy of Hindemith's *Ludus Tonalis*, which came out on the bill as *Nudas Tonatis*. (See plate 13.) The Hindemith

---

[2] Antonio Brosa (1894–1979), Catalan violinist. For details of the ISCM Festival and for Brosa's many connections with Britten, see John Evans, ed., *Journeying Boy: the Diaries of the Young Benjamin Britten, 1928–1938* (London, 2009).

[3] Premiered 22 July 1946 at the Wigmore Hall, London, by Clifford Curzon – not 28 July as given in Stewart R. Craggs, *Lennox Berkeley: a Sourcebook* (Aldershot, 2000), or in my edition *Lennox Berkeley: Collected Works for Solo Piano* (London, 2003). For discussion of the Piano Sonata see Peter Dickinson, *The Music of Lennox Berkeley* (London, 1988; revised and enlarged, Woodbridge, 2003), 73–6 (all page references below are to the revised edition), and Lisa Hardy, *The British Piano Sonata* (Woodbridge, 2001), 168–70.

had been recommended to me by Robin Orr,[4] who, like Berkeley, had been a pupil of Nadia Boulanger. Hugh Davis, the Director of Music at The Leys School,[5] had not known what to make of my efforts at composition, so he sent me to Orr, then a lecturer in the Music Faculty at Cambridge. When I went up to Queens' College as organ scholar, I read music. Orr's orchestration lectures were illustrated by Berkeley's Divertimento.

In those years Berkeley was a prominent figure in British music. A friend of mine introduced me to somebody by announcing impressively: 'He knows Lennox Berkeley!' That was after my tutor at Cambridge, Philip Radcliffe[6] at King's, thought it time for me to consult a real composer. So in 1956 I went to show Berkeley some scores. With trepidation I walked up to 8 Warwick Avenue in Little Venice to meet the composer I admired so much. At that time much of the Bishop's Bridge Road was derelict and about to be demolished in preparation for the building of the new Westway, but Little Venice and the canal were much as they are today.

I played Berkeley my *Vitalitas Variations* for piano.[7] Since not many of Berkeley's pupils have recorded his specific criticisms of their work, I can mention that he thought that the final chord of the second variation ought not to be a dominant major ninth chord since this carried tonal expectations that were not going to be fulfilled. I amplified it with added components. I also played him my *Four W. H. Auden Songs*[8] and probably *Five Early Piano Pieces*:[9] the Auden songs particularly show my admiration for Berkeley. However, the tables were turned the following year when Berkeley received an American commission and set three of the same poems in his own Auden songs. It was typical of the generosity of the man that when I played him a recording of my songs twenty years later, and pointed out that he had set some of the same poems, he said that my setting of 'What's in your mind' was better than his.[10]

---

[4] Robin Orr (1909–2006), Scottish composer, Professor at Glasgow (1956–65) and Cambridge (1965–76).

[5] Peter Dickinson, 'Hugh Scott Davis' [obituary], *Independent*, 15 April 2010.

[6] Philip Radcliffe (1905–86), wrote books on Mendelssohn and Beethoven and spent a lifetime at King's College.

[7] Originally called Piano Variations but renamed for the ballet by Mexican choreographer Gloria Contreras. See CD of my piano music on Naxos 8 572654 (2010).

[8] Recorded on Albany TROY 365 (2000); performed on 15 June 1957 for W. H. Auden at Cambridge.

[9] Recorded on Naxos 8 572287 (2009).

[10] There has been some confusion about the metronome marking for this song, since the original published score had crotchet = 50–54 when it was obvious that it ought to have been minim = 50–54. Meriel Dickinson and I performed these songs for the composer and he confirmed this, even though the manuscript at the British Library has the crotchet marking. A copyist's manuscript used by Mrs Alice Esty in New York has crotchet = 92. However, as recently as the Berkeley Centenary Concert at the Wigmore Hall in 2003 Toby Spence sang this song at half speed. There are two fine recordings: Philip Langridge and Steuart Bedford on Naxos 8 557204 (1998); James Gilchrist and Anna Tilbrook in an all-Berkeley CD on Chandos CHAN 10528 (2009). However, the Auden cycle, like the

The New York singer and patron Alice Swanson Esty (1904–2000), a pupil of Pierre Bernac, commissioned and performed songs by a number of contemporary composers. According to Sidney Buckland[11] Esty also commissioned Berkeley's *Automne* along with other tributes to Poulenc on the first anniversary of his death and she gave the premieres on 13 January 1964 at Carnegie Recital Hall, New York.

After Cambridge I was based in or near New York for three academic years but made contact with Berkeley again when I had a teaching post in London at the College of St Mark and St John, which he visited on 30 November 1965 when Jill Gomez with Alan Rowlands performed his Auden songs. But before that I had written about Berkeley's music in both *The Musical Times* and *Music and Musicians* to mark his sixtieth birthday in 1963.[12] The *Musical Times* article rather patronisingly but perhaps presciently found that Berkeley

> has made a successful fusion of influences and has developed a definite but unobtrusive musical personality ... His musical inheritance, unpretentiously European, finds its centre of gravity somewhere in the English Channel. His technical assurance and adherence to tonality relate him to Britten, with whom he has collaborated, but the music of the older man is more elusive and hence unlikely to achieve meteoric success.

I went on to consider the Second Symphony, the Horn Trio, the Auden songs and some choral pieces including the Donne setting 'Thou hast made me', all with music examples. My much longer article in *Music and Musicians* was called 'Berkeley on the Keyboard' and covered all the piano works up to that time, again with music examples. It started:

> Berkeley is one of very few British composers to show an interest in writing for the piano, and of the generation following Ireland and Bax none can show greater facility in this medium. His treatment of the instrument in solo music, duet, two-piano, concerto and chamber music is highly effective and personal without possessing the radical originality of major twentieth-century composers, such as Bartók, Schoenberg or Stravinsky Berkeley's work stems from a poetic rather than a dramatic or intellectual source. His best works, such as the *Four Poems of St Teresa*, the Divertimento, or the Piano Sonata, and many others, show an elegant and supremely musical personality in successful and satisfying achievements.

Fifty years later there is not much to quarrel with here. In 1965, in another long article for *Music and Musicians*,[13] I began with the piano works, particularly the Sonata, but then turned to the First Symphony and *Nelson* and looked at some of

---

Chinese Songs, was written for female voice. My own *Auden Studies* for oboe and piano (1988) uses both settings of the three poems.

[11] 'Berkeley and Poulenc', *Lennox Berkeley Society Journal* (2011), 4–13.

[12] 'The Music of Lennox Berkeley', *Musical Times* 104 (May 1963), 327–30; 'Berkeley on the Keyboard', *Music and Musicians*, April 1963, 10–11, 58.

[13] 'Lennox Berkeley', *Music and Musicians*, August 1965, 20–23, 54.

Berkeley's writings, and pointed out that what he said about Fauré could be applied to his own work too.[14]

Hardly anyone had discussed Berkeley's music in this kind of detail before but there was one interesting exception. In 1951 H. F. Redlich (1903–68), the Vienna-born British musicologist, wrote about Berkeley in *Music Survey*, the periodical edited by Donald Mitchell and Hans Keller.[15] He brought a different perspective from most British writers to the task of evaluating what Berkeley had achieved at this early stage and found that he

> became a clear-cut artistic individuality in the late thirties ... From 1940 onwards Berkeley produced a wealth of instrumental music, starting with the Symphony [no. 1] and with chamber music for various combinations (including the excellent String Trio of 1944). This music has gone a long way to establish him as one of the prominent and most promising British composers. The decade between 1940 and 1950 ... yielded to Berkeley a full harvest of symphonic and concerto music, quite apart from a crop of delightful miniatures such as the Nocturne, for orchestra, the De la Mare Songs, the Preludes and Three Mazurkas for piano ...

Redlich went on to discuss, with music examples, the Piano Concerto and the Two-Piano Concerto, where he even found common ground between the theme of the second-movement variations and Wagner's early Symphony in C, and then admired the *Stabat mater*. Redlich noted the textural contrast between the three-voice canon in the sixth section and the homophony of the eighth, which he compares with the 1881 choral settings of Hugo Wolf.[16] This was high praise from a critic nurtured in the Austro-German tradition, and Redlich concluded that Berkeley 'has certainly earned the right to expect universal sympathy and attention when embarking on the period of his full maturity.'

Frank Howes, the influential chief music critic of *The Times* from 1943 to 1960, wrote sympathetically about Berkeley in his survey *The English Musical Renaissance*.[17] Howes recalled the impact made by Berkeley's First Symphony at the Proms in 1943 where it 'made a great impression by its abstention from any attempt to impress. The economy of scoring and the spare texture were precisely fitted to the logic and lucidity of an argument that was not unduly pressed to a conclusion but was delightfully and stylishly expounded.' Howes went on to admire the Piano Concerto and, of the operas, *A Dinner Engagement*, and concluded that 'it comes as something of a surprise on surveying the output of a composer whose manner of speech is so modest to discover what a substantial corpus of work has come from his pen since he rather belatedly found his style.' Howes ended by finding that Berkeley had more in common with Rawsthorne than Walton or Britten. In

---

[14] See Berkeley's BBC talk on Fauré, p. 112 below.

[15] H. F. Redlich, 'Lennox Berkeley', *Music Survey* 3 (1951), 245–9. Mitchell and Keller also edited *Benjamin Britten: a Commentary on his Works from a Group of Specialists* (London 1952), to which Berkeley contributed 'The Light Music', 287–94.

[16] *Sechs geistliche Lieder* (Eichendorf).

[17] Frank Howes (1891–1974), *The English Musical Renaissance* (London, 1966), 274–7.

the articles included in Part III of this book Berkeley writes sympathetically about both Rawsthorne and Britten, but more passionately about the latter. Howes had been present at the main Berkeley performances in London for more than thirty years, much as Desmond Shawe-Taylor, one of Berkeley's most sensitive critics, was later.[18]

Other writers have reported on the symphonies, which are an indication of Berkeley's progress, even if not his most characteristic genre. A year after the First Symphony's premiere, Robin Hull recalled that 'Its four movements express with classical purity some of the most original thoughts yet conceived in contemporary style. The music is essentially of our time while maintaining, without a trace of archaism, all the ready accessibility, the genial spirit, and lyrical grace more customary during the eighteenth century.'[19] Ten years later Wilfrid Mellers was surprised that Berkeley should have written a Symphony at all and felt it was 'a turning point in his career'.

> His Symphony is a big work, though neither its duration in time nor its instrumental resource is extravagant. While the influence of the later Stravinsky remains dominant in the elliptical treatment of classical form and in the transparent orchestral texture, the music has acquired much greater melodic force than is observable in the Parisian works. Lyricism is now impressively integrated with the harmony ...[20]

All this is true and, as I have demonstrated in my own studies, arises from the character and sheer memorability of the musical ideas themselves.[21] Berkeley had started work on a symphony as early as 1936; he discussed it with Boulanger; and had plenty of time to polish his material and gain orchestral experience before completing it.

The career of the Second Symphony is less straightforward and the result more questionable. Berkeley came to it after his triumphs during the 1950s. Three operas had been produced; the concertos for one and for two pianos; and outstanding chamber works such as the Horn Trio and the Sextet. Although *Nelson* was not an unqualified success, it was a high-profile event and Berkeley was at the height of his powers with the major works of the 1940s and 50s behind him.[22]

---

[18] See interview with Shawe-Taylor, p. 276 below.

[19] Robin Hull, 'The Music of Lennox Berkeley', *Listener*, 16 March 1944, 309.

[20] Wilfrid Mellers, 'The Music of Lennox Berkeley', *Listener*, 24 June 1954, 1113. Wilfrid Mellers (1914–2008), prolific writer and composer who in 1964 founded the influential music department at the University of York. See his article on Berkeley in *Grove's Dictionary of Music*, 5th edn, ed. E. Blom (London: 1954).

[21] See Peter Dickinson, *The Music of Lennox Berkeley*, 53–60.

[22] For a choice of recordings of works from this decade, see Peter Dickinson, 'Lennox Berkeley in the 1940s', *Gramophone*, January 2012, 88–9. These were: *The Berkeley Edition*, vols. 1, 5 and 6, BBC National Orchestra of Wales/Hickox on Chandos CHAN 9981, CHAN 10265, and CHAN 10408. *Piano Works by Lennox and Michael Berkeley*, Margaret Fingerhut on Chandos CHAN 10247; *Sacred Choral Music*, Choir of St John's College, Cambridge/Robinson on Naxos 8 557277; *Lennox Berkeley*, Schirmer Ensemble on Naxos 8 557324; and *String Quartets nos. 1–3*, Maggini Quartet on Naxos 8 570415; *Berkeley conducts Berkeley*, London Philharmonic Orchestra on Lyrita SRCD 226; *Piano Concerto and Concerto for Two*

Martin Cooper, the authority on French music, introduced the Second Symphony before the broadcast by the City of Birmingham Symphony Orchestra under Andrzej Panufnik.[23] Cooper looked at Berkeley's background, finding *Jonah*, op. 3 (1935), lacking in melodic interest and individuality, but admired the concertos with piano and Berkeley's move to vocal music in the Teresa of Avila songs and the *Stabat mater*. He felt that the epic subject of Nelson had been beyond Berkeley's grasp but recognised the 'remarkably successful' string trio and other chamber music as well as vocal works to religious texts. Overall Cooper felt: 'It is characteristic of Berkeley that he demands of his listeners the mind of musical awareness that accepts a hint, an almost disguised reference to what has gone before, in place of unambiguous repetition.' This aspect of Berkeley was identified by Andrew Porter, reviewing the premiere of the Sinfonia Concertante for oboe and chamber orchestra at the Proms fifteen years later.

> As in all Berkeley's works, our attention is held by the play of rhythmic and melodic fancy – a fancy perhaps the more fascinating for being temperate and unextravagant. The character of Berkeley's music is hard to describe; anyone unprepared to listen to a quiet voice saying things subtle but not tortuous, gentle even in assertion, and still courteous at its most confident, may miss the merits altogether.[24]

This is the approach that makes some of Berkeley elusive, especially at a first hearing, and I shall refer again to his distaste for literal repetition. Cooper described the layout of the Second Symphony in factual terms – he was going by the score – whereas by 1963 I had heard the broadcast premiere and greeted the new style in the original version with unqualified enthusiasm: 'the Second Symphony profits enormously from the taut later style and achieves a most convincing symphonic cohesion.'[25] Noel Goodwin, reviewing the premiere felt that 'the symphony proved to be a work of rewarding quality and distinction ... [it] achieved a compelling style of expression for Berkeley's predominantly lyrical impulse.'[26]

The Times reported on the Prom performance on 9 September under the composer: 'It is coherent, purposeful and clearly and attractively scored – yet at a single hearing the actual impulse behind the musical invention seems not to be very strong.'[27]

However, after the Birmingham premiere and the Prom, the Symphony was probably not performed again until a recording was planned, which took place in

Pianos, David Wilde, Garth Becket and Boyd McDonald, New Philharmonia Orchestra/Braithwaite, London Philharmonic Orchestra/Del Mar on Lyrita SRC 250; and *Chamber Works for Wind, Strings and Piano*, Tagore Trio, Sarah Francis, Judith Fitton, Michael Dussek on Regis RRC 1380.

[23] Martin Cooper, 'Lennox Berkeley and his New Symphony', *Listener*, 19 February 1959, 351. Andrzej Panufnik (1914–91), leading Polish composer and conductor who came to the England in 1954 and became a British citizen.

[24] Andrew Porter, 'Berkeley', *Financial Times*, 4 August 1973.

[25] Dickinson, 'The Music of Lennox Berkeley', 327.

[26] 'Berkeley's Second Symphony at Birmingham', *Musical Times* 100 (April 1959), 215.

[27] 'Mr Lennox Berkeley's Second Symphony', *The Times*, 10 September 1959.

August 1976.[28] At that time Berkeley told his diary that he had spent 'much of the last year rewriting' the Symphony, although the third movement was unchanged.[29]

In his sleeve-note for the LP, Berkeley explains:

> My reasons for the revision were chiefly connected with scoring; I was much preoccupied at the time I originally wrote it with keeping the various orchestral colours distinct. Later, I felt I had overdone this and that the work would gain from a freer and more robust treatment. I have introduced no new thematic material in this revised version, though certain passages have been somewhat extended.

However, this work originally had problems. Richard Stoker was a pupil of Berkeley's when he was writing it in 1958 and remembers that he suffered from a period of creative block lasting about three weeks: apparently he even asked Stoker how he would proceed at certain points.[30]

The original Lento introduction opens with low woodwind over a bass drum roll; the second bar has a dissonant triad held in trombones below the harp's reference to the first theme of the allegro; and there are tremolando strings. In the revision the bass drum, trombones and tremolando strings have all gone. The harp is more prominent and the context is now clear D major, the tonal centre of the work – confusingly in the opposite direction from the new style. But, apart from the slow movement, the Symphony was completely rewritten and Berkeley committed a considerable amount of time to trying to get it right. Of the two recorded performances, Braithwaite is often too slow and Hickox, unafraid of faster tempi, as in his live performances of Berkeley, makes far better sense of everything.[31]

A totally unknown work premiered in the same month of February 1959 is the Concerto for Piano and Double String Orchestra. Colin Horsley, who commissioned it and gave the first performances, has described the unfortunate circumstances of the premiere.[32]

In spite of Horsley's indisposition, *The Times* found that 'The composer has hit on felicitous ideas for both solo and the special texture of his orchestra ... it is invariably poetical, the piano writing dextrous, the material well organised into shapely movements.'[33] The composer's manuscript shows the signs of haste

---

[28] London Philharmonic Orchestra under Nicholas Braithwaite, Lyrita SRCS 94 (1978); long delayed reissue on CD SRCD 249 (2007), where the first and second symphonies are now coupled.

[29] In a letter to me of 29 February 1976 Berkeley said: 'I'm glad to be at home a bit after all our travels and to be able to do some work. My immediate task is the revision of my Second Symphony which is going quite well. I've never been satisfied with it and have hated the idea of leaving it as it was.'

[30] 'Lennox Berkeley: John France interviews Richard Stoker', *Lennox Berkeley Society Newsletter* 18 (Autumn 2005), 9–16.

[31] *Berkeley Edition*, vol. 4, BBC National Orchestra of Wales/Hickox, Chandos CHAN 10167 (2004).

[32] See interview with Horsley, p. 236 below.

[33] 'Poetical Piano Concerto', *The Times*, 11 February 1959.

mentioned by Horsley and the style of the music is not as colourful as the earlier Piano Concerto, giving some signs of what was to come. It is a pastoral piece but with a strong cadenza almost at the end of the first movement. The central Lento opens with some neatly spaced chords and this theme recurs after another cadenza at the end. Alternations between soloist and double strings are neatly handled in the lighter last movement, subtitled 'Capriccio'.

In *The Music of Lennox Berkeley* I discussed at length, with music examples, what this transition meant. In 1948 Berkeley was unsympathetic to serial music, but by 1959 he admitted he had benefited from studying it and had used serial themes.[34] The technique was fashionable. Britten had used a twelve-note theme in *The Turn of the Screw* (1954); some of Berkeley's pupils, such as Richard Rodney Bennett, were deeply committed serialists; and Berkeley felt behind the times. I have pointed out the note-rows in Aria I from the Concertino, op. 49 (1955); Boaz's recognition aria in *Ruth* (1955–6); and in the ground bass employed in the slow movement of the Violin Concerto, op. 56 (1958). There's a brief reference to twelve notes at the start of the Sonatina for Oboe and Piano, op. 61 (1962), but serial derivations are more important in the Third Symphony, op. 74 (1969), and the Third String Quartet, op. 76 (1970).[35] However, Berkeley's more dissonant later style, approaching atonality, coexisted with his freer melodic aspect. For example, the catchy tune of the D major Canzona in the Sinfonia Concertante for oboe and orchestra, op. 84 (1973) – a retrospective oasis of diatonic calm – and, of course, completely tonal material in light works such as the *Palm Court Waltz*, op. 81/2 (1971). This ambivalence is present in Copland from 1950, and even Schoenberg himself, whose later American works included the Suite for Strings in G major (1934) and the *Theme and Variations* for band (1943) in G minor.

The evidence confirms that Berkeley suffered a crisis at the time of the Second Symphony. He realised his new style was not yet stable so he went back to the Symphony after some successful works employing the later style.[36] In an interview with the Canadian composer Murray Schaffer in 1963, Berkeley explained:

> It's natural for a composer to feel a need to enlarge his idiom … Once you feel you have said everything you have to say in your old style, you want to alter it somehow, expand it, revitalise your thinking … My style today is less diatonic, I might say harmonically less ordinary than it was before … I've managed to gain a greater freedom.[37]

What Berkeley had sacrificed was the easy flow of melody over highly characteristic harmonies that had made the period from the later thirties to the later fifties into a golden age. Berkeley's use of tonality intentionally became

---

[34] See Dickinson, *The Music of Lennox Berkeley*, 161.

[35] See the revelatory recording of all three quartets by the Maggini Quartet on Naxos 8 570415 (2007).

[36] The Second Symphony – and the Third – was taken seriously by Peter Evans in the *Blackwell History of Music in Britain: the Twentieth Century*, ed. Stephen Banfield (Oxford, 1995), 231, and also by Arnold Whittall in 'Berkeley and the Twentieth-Century Symphony', *The Lennox Berkeley Society Journal* (2008), 8–13.

[37] R. Murray Schaffer, *British Composers in Interview* (London, 1963), 85.

less direct; he began to work with dissonant chords; and became obsessed with counterpoint in a way that made it responsible for both texture and harmony. Although some impressive pieces emerged later on, my *Musical Times* article for Berkeley's sixty-fifth birthday in 1968 still contained some special pleading: 'By the time the post-Webern mania had gripped the young, composers of Berkeley's generation appeared ultra-conservative, clinging to traditional means in the face of onslaught; they sometimes seemed unable to develop beyond the earlier work which had established their reputation.'[38]

In the same issue of *The Musical Times* there was a copy of Berkeley's *The Windhover*, op. 72/2 (1968), a SATB setting of Gerard Manley Hopkins's mystical text. Berkeley's vocally demanding ecstatic treatment clearly demonstrated that he had developed far beyond his earlier achievements.

The first four *Chinese Songs*, op. 78 (November 1970 – January 1971) employ the new mildly atonal idiom fluently. Berkeley's diaries show that, from the inspirational angle, everything was going well.[39] With his Auden cycle some twelve years earlier only the fourth one used the new style, but in the *Chinese Songs* the first two end on a chord combining major and minor thirds; the next two use a dissonant chord as a structural point of reference, as in Schoenberg's *Stefan George Lieder*; but the last one, where Berkeley felt the poem 'could have been made for me' is in pure D flat major.[40] By comparison, the three De la Mare poems set in *Another Spring*, op. 93 (February/March 1977) – the third time he set this poet – are a pale reflection of the *Chinese Songs*: the slow final song is again in clear D flat major.

Orchestral pieces in the late period include two atmospheric works – *Antiphon* and *Voices of the Night*, both premiered in 1973, and the final concerto – for guitar, op. 88 (1974), but in the last few years there was a perceptible falling off. The harmonic materials are less distinctive and the gestures, often involving sequences, have become routine in a detached objective fashion. There's a kind of neo-classical austerity about the Quintet for piano and wind, op. 90 (1975), which succeeds through its resourceful and idiomatic instrumentation, and Berkeley has not lost his harmonic acumen, as is shown by the treatments of the A major theme in the fourth movement – a relation of the theme of the last movement of the Violin and Piano Sonatina in the same key over thirty years earlier. By the time of the Flute Sonata, op. 97 (1978), written for James Galway, these tendencies are more pronounced.[41] It was at this point, approaching old age, and the Alzheimer's that came with it, that Berkeley embarked on the revision of the Second Symphony. Will some future generation want to revert to the original version?

Ironically the impersonal quality of these later pieces was turned to advantage in some of the sacred works. There, almost in the tradition of Palestrina, the

---

[38] Peter Dickinson, 'Berkeley's Music Today', *Musical Times* 109 (November 1968), 1013–14.

[39] For a discussion of this compositional process, see Jonathan Harvey, *Music and Inspiration* (London, 1999).

[40] See Berkeley's diary for 8 December 1970, p. 190 below.

[41] Recorded with the Flute Concerto and Sonatina for flute and piano on *James Galway plays Lennox Berkeley*, RCA Red Seal RS 9011 (1983).

personality of the composer becomes less obtrusive through the use of a rather anonymous style. There is quiet counterpoint in the service of the text and truly spiritual qualities can emerge. Berkeley has confirmed this: 'In writing music to be performed in church as part of the service ... I have found that I wanted to make it somewhat more impersonal, so that it would merge into the liturgy, and not create a violent contrast or cause too much distraction.'[42]

In the now popular *The Lord is my Shepherd*, op. 91/1 (1975; see plate 19 for a page from the autograph score), the G major melody under a moving accompaniment pattern is an ancestor of the central section of *A Festival Anthem*, op. 21/2, thirty years earlier. That melody had been kept alive by Berkeley's arrangement for cello and piano as *Andantino* in 1955 and Jennifer Bate's arrangement for organ in 1982 for her recording, including the Fantasia, op. 92 (1976) and the *Three Pieces*, op. 72/1 (1966).[43] Notice that the lyricism of G major seems to have a special association for Berkeley as in the ninth variation in the second movement of the Two-Piano Concerto and at the words 'esurientes' in the *Magnificat*.

In *The Music of Lennox Berkeley* I was, by implication, dismissive of the Fourth Symphony, op. 94 (1976–8), although the pace of everything is surprisingly well under control. There's sustained energy in the opening Allegro following the Lento introduction and two well placed climaxes. The minor thirds of the theme for the central movement colours some eloquent variations even if others meander.

As a whole the symphony retreats from Berkeley's newer idiom as though he felt the need to go back – this time on an expansive scale – but he could no longer find distinctive melodic and harmonic materials. Further, in his interview with Michael Oliver[44] Berkeley states, as he had done earlier, that the exact repetition of themes in the classical and romantic periods was no longer possible. This was not new in Berkeley. Back in 1947, the second subject in the first movement of the Piano Concerto is a delightful bluesy melody announced by the soloist; the orchestra follows suit; but in the recapitulation, although obediently now in the tonic, the melody has been changed and, after the first four notes, the orchestra has still another version. This makes for the wayward quality in Berkeley that Julian Bream found attractive, but it causes some of the works in his later style to seem virtually athematic.

The causes of Berkeley's stylistic changes in the late 1950s are worth further examination. Copland's employment of serial techniques in works like the Piano Quartet (1950) anticipated Stravinsky's move to serialism after *The Rake's Progress* which lasted the rest of his life. More significant was the example of Britten, with Berkeley considering *The Turn of the Screw* his greatest masterpiece. Other British composers of the older generation had responded. The opening theme of the finale of Walton's Second Symphony (1960) was much discussed as a twelve-note series;[45] Rawsthorne was much more serious in using a note-row in his Third Symphony

---

[42] See Lennox Berkeley, 'Truth in Music', p. 123 below.

[43] Organ Music by Lennox Berkeley and Peter Dickinson, Hyperion LP A66061 (1983).

[44] See interview with Michael Oliver, p. 176 below.

[45] See Michael Kennedy, *Portrait of Walton* (Oxford, 1989).

(1964);[46] and Berkeley knew Humphrey Searle who, along with Elisabeth Lutyens, was one of the first British twelve-note composers.[47]

The context was the enormous prestige of serial techniques in the so-called serious music world of the 1960s. Even middle-of-the-road composers in Europe and America were affected, not wanting to be outdone by Boulez and Stockhausen, leading a younger generation. Every American university had its serial composers, all anxious to impress each other and able to disregard the wider audience – thanks to their university salaries. In 1952 Boulez had thrown down the gauntlet: 'I assert that any musician who has not experienced – I do not say understood, but in all exactness experienced – the necessity for the dodecaphonic language is USELESS. For his whole work is irrelevant to the needs of his epoch.'[48]

All this was at a time when the professional musical establishment through radio stations and concert promotion was still powerful enough to call the tune. Pop idols like Elvis Presley and even the Beatles were regarded as something else, and the tremendous inroads that would be made by pop music into mainstream culture were still in the future. The intellectual climate made serialism fashionable, although the wider public now has little interest in late Stravinsky and its always tentative appetite for Schoenberg and other twelve-note composers has diminished in the face of assaults from the minimalists. However, as Arnold Whittall has claimed: 'From its earliest years, when the twelve-tone method showed itself able to relate to aspects of neo-classicism on the one hand (Schoenberg's Piano Suite) and late-romanticism on the other (Berg's Violin Concerto) serialism of one kind or another has proved to be a constant presence within the wider dialogue between the progressive and the conservative that has shaped music since 1900 as it extended, exploded and reinstated tonality.'[49]

Where does this leave Berkeley? When I wrote my first articles about his work and later in *The Music of Lennox Berkeley* I was too inclined to take him at his own valuation, in particular that his music was demonstrably inferior to that of Britten. Berkeley had, after all, told Britten in a letter[50] that he liked his music better than his own and – in typical fashion – Berkeley regularly apologised for what he had just composed, explaining that it was not as good as what he hoped to be able to do later. In a sense that was a personality problem that should never have been imposed on the work. Further, Julian Bream, Norman Del Mar and Colin Horsley, in their interviews here, fail to find a strong influence of Britten, and Desmond Shawe-Taylor felt the two composers enriched each other.

Going further with this comparison, I am reminded of Bernard Shaw's preface to *Three Plays for Puritans* (1900) where he has a section entitled 'Better than Shakespear' (he spelt it like that). How about 'Better than Britten'? Obviously not

---

[46] See John McCabe, *Alan Rawsthorne: Portrait of a Composer* (Oxford, 1999), 247–63.

[47] See Humphrey Searle, *Quadrille with a Raven: Memoirs*, www.musicweb-international.com/searle/titlepg.htm.

[48] Originally in *Revue musicale*, reprinted in Pierre Boulez, *Notes of an Apprenticeship*, trans. Herbert Weinstock (New York, 1968), 148.

[49] Arnold Whittall, *The Cambridge Introduction to Serialism* (Cambridge, 2008), 238.

[50] 30 September 1937, see Dickinson, *The Music of Lennox Berkeley*, 48.

in opera, where Britten, alongside Strauss and Puccini, was one of the three most successful opera composers of the twentieth century, an astonishing achievement for an English composer from a background with no lengthy operatic tradition. But in the field of chamber music, keyboard works, songs and religious choral pieces, Berkeley does more than hold his own – to the extent that he stands up to the inevitable comparison with Britten as well as any British composer of that generation. And on a larger scale in the concertos, beginning with the Cello Concerto (1939) which waited forty years for a first performance, Berkeley expands the sheer attractiveness of orchestral pieces like the Serenade for strings and the Divertimento. They show Berkeley at his best where he is not troubled by the cut and thrust of logical development traditionally associated with symphonies. The engaging interplay between soloist and orchestra suited him better and this aspect continued into his later style with the Sinfonia Concertante – in effect an oboe concerto – and the final Concerto for guitar.

In *The Music of Lennox Berkeley* my primary aim, as in my earlier articles, was to look at the music in some detail, with over a hundred music examples and a certain amount of analysis, to show that the music rewarded this kind of scrutiny. It does. Fortunately, performers in many countries are now playing and recording the chamber music; the sacred choral works have entered the repertoire; even the operas *A Dinner Engagement* and *Ruth* have achieved international productions since the availability of recordings. Sixty years after that schoolboy encountered Berkeley's music for the first time, its future now seems assured.

– Part I –
Reports from Paris, 1929–34

INTRODUCTION

Between the wars Paris reigned supreme. Harold Acton proclaimed: 'Intellectually Paris was the capital of the world, and the judgement of Paris was final. The Entente Cordiale in the fine arts had never been stronger.'[1] The appalling casualties and deprivations of the First World War had left Paris anxious to forget the Germans and to concentrate on French art and ideals. It was in that spirit that in 1915 Debussy announced his Six Sonatas and signed the title pages 'musicien Français' – but he lived to complete only three and never saw the end of the conflict.

Purely French theatrical traditions were invoked when, starting before the armistice, the Opéra reopened with thirty-three performances of Rameau's *Castor et Pollux*.[2] On 20 January 1919 the song-cycle *Clairières dans le ciel* by Lili Boulanger, Nadia's sister, was given its premiere by the enterprising Société musicale indépendante, which would later present several works by Berkeley. In his letters to his teacher he would refer regularly to the anniversaries of Lili Boulanger's premature death in March 1918 at the age of only twenty-four.

With the entry of the United States into the war in April 1917 and the influx of Americans into Paris, early jazz arrived and the city would remain host to many jazz musicians. It was a cultural shock which the New World injected into the Old – and the Old World has never recovered. These American jazz musicians and entertainers – black and white – were presented in many Parisian night-clubs as well as concert halls. One of the best-known venues was *Le Bœuf sur le toit*, founded in 1921 and named after a Brazilian popular song and a ballet by Milhaud. In jazz, Ravel and the young composers of Les Six found a new stimulus thoroughly in keeping with Jean Cocteau's manifesto *Le Coq et l'arlequin* published in 1918.[3] Cocteau preached a gospel of simplicity as embodied the year before by Erik Satie in the ballet *Parade*, which brought Cocteau and Satie together with Picasso under the auspices of Diaghilev's Ballets Russes. Stravinsky knew Satie, and in many ways his new direction of pieces based on ragtime followed by neo-classicism emerged from this climate. Cocteau said: 'The music-hall, the circus and America negro-bands, all these things fertilise an artist just as life does.'[4]

In 1921 the American Conservatory was founded in Fontainebleau. It was in the first year that Aaron Copland arrived there and started his lessons with Nadia Boulanger. Over fifty years later he recalled his arrival:

---

[1] Harold Acton, *Memoirs of an Aesthete* (London, 1948), 149.

[2] According to Roger Nichols.

[3] Jean Cocteau (1889–1963), influential French writer and artist who collaborated with leading figures in all the arts.

[4] Jean Cocteau, *Le Coq et l'harlequin: notes autour de musique* (Paris, 1918), trans. Rollo Myers as *Cock and Harlequin* (London, 1921), 23.

Paris, of course, was the centre of renewed excitement in the arts. Arriving at twenty on French soil, my expectations were dangerously high, but I was not to be disappointed. Paris was filled with cosmopolitan artists from all over the world, many of whom had settled there as ex-patriots. It was the time of Tristan Tzara[5] and Dada; the time of André Breton and surrealism; it was when we first heard the names of James Joyce and Gertrude Stein, T. S. Eliot and Ezra Pound, and also of the French writers Marcel Proust and André Gide. The painters were enormously active, with Picasso taking centre stage and interesting figures like Georges Braque and Max Ernst working in Paris at that time.[6]

Another American, the composer and critic Virgil Thomson, arrived in 1925 and became aware of Paris as a literary centre too:

> ... the presence of Joyce and Stein, orbiting and surrounded by satellites, gave to Paris in the 1920s and 30s its position of world centre for the writing of English poetry and prose. Hemingway, Fitzgerald and Ford Madox Ford ... Ezra Pound, e. e. cummings and Hart Crane worked out of Paris and depended on it for judgement, as often as not for publication too.[7]

Countless Americans followed. So many young American composers came to study with Nadia Boulanger that Thomson saluted her on her seventy-fifth birthday by claiming that 'for more than forty years she has been a one-woman graduate school so powerful and so permeating that legend credits every US town with two things – a five-and-dime store and a Boulanger pupil.'[8]

Matters were different for Berkeley, who was not a naïve American encountering European civilisation on the spot for the first time. He had a French grandmother; his parents were living in the south of France, although he had been to English schools; and he was bilingual. But, as his letters to Boulanger show, he still had to try and break into the musical scene in Paris dominated by cliques and patrons and with an influx of competing talents from all over the world.

Many new concert organisations and ensembles were founded in Paris during the 1920s. There was also activity in early music with the prominence of Bach, the discovery of Monteverdi, and interest in English Elizabethan composers – all associated with Boulanger. Berkeley was served best by the Societé musicale indépendante, but there were also the Concerts Straram. In 1928 their conductor Walter Straram launched Berkeley's orchestral Suite and the composer conducted it at the Proms in London the following year.[9] In 1933 Berkeley said the Straram Orchestra was 'perhaps the best in Paris at the moment' – and it gave the most first performances.

---

[5] Tristan Tzara (1896–1963), Romanian poet, one of the founders of the Dada movement in Zurich in 1915.

[6] Aaron Copland and Vivian Perlis, *Copland, Volume I: 1900–1942* (London, 1984), 56.

[7] Virgil Thomson, *Virgil Thomson by Virgil Thomson* (London, 1967), 77.

[8] Virgil Thomson, *A Virgil Thomson Reader* (Boston, 1981), 389.

[9] Dickinson, *The Music of Lennox Berkeley*, 12–14.

The presence in Paris of Stravinsky was enormously influential, as Berkeley's reports confirm. Stravinsky's three early ballets – *The Firebird* (1910), *Petroushka* (1911) and *The Rite of Spring* (1913) – had been a sensation in the productions of Diaghilev's Ballets Russes which brought together the finest talents in all art forms. Stravinsky and his family, after wartime exile in Switzerland, moved to France in 1920 and his connections with Paris continued: the Opéra, which had presented *The Nightingale* just before the war, staged *Pulcinella* (1920), *Renard* and *Mavra* (1922), *Les Noces* (1923), *Le Baiser de la fée* (1928) and *Perséphone* (1928). The Opéra had also put on Stravinsky's Octet in 1923, regarded as the start of neo-classicism, and there were Paris premieres of his Piano Concerto in 1924 and the Capriccio for piano and orchestra in 1929, the last two with the composer as soloist. Then Berkeley reviews later premieres.

Since the end of the war young French composers embodied a new spirit during the 'silly' twenties, although Milhaud, one of the group called Les Six, disliked the term:

> I am always very angry ... when I read about the 'silly' twenties, because I think it has been the most marvellous period that I have been through. At this time everything was possible, we could try everything we wanted: it was a period of experiment, of liberty of expression in the widest sense of this word.[10]

Les Six were reacting against the influence of Wagner as well as the refinements of impressionism in Debussy and Ravel. This was in tune with Cocteau's manifesto, and Berkeley used five of his poems in his set of songs called *Tombeaux* (1926) written in a taut style not far from Cocteau's ideals.

Les Six was a journalistic label used by a critic in 1920,[11] but the composers really had little in common, although they met weekly for two years at Milhaud's apartment, and most of them admired Satie.[12] Honegger had dual nationality, both Swiss and French, and soon made an imposing contribution to the symphonic and choral repertory, as Berkeley chronicles; Milhaud, with his development of polytonality and his interest in Latin-American music and jazz, was the most avant-garde; and Poulenc moved on from apparently light-weight frivolity into songs, orchestral music and opera – and became a good friend of Berkeley.

After Debussy's death in 1918, Ravel became prominent as the leading French composer – and a strong personal and musical influence on Berkeley. Ravel's post-war works included *La Valse* (1920), the opera *L'Enfant et les sortilèges* (1925), and *Boléro* (1928), mentioned more than once in Berkeley's reports. Ravel wrote his Piano Concerto for the Left Hand (1929–30) immediately before his Piano Concerto (1930–31) just as Berkeley would write his Piano Concerto (1947) closely followed by his Concerto for Two Pianos (1948). Ravel's Violin and Piano Sonata

---

[10] BBC Third Programme talk, 4 February 1962, quoted in Roger Nichols, *The Harlequin Years* (London, 2002), 276.

[11] Henri Collet, *Commedia*, 16 January 1920.

[12] Darius Milhaud, *Notes sans musique* (Paris, 1949), trans. Donald Evans as *Notes without Music* (London, 1952), 83.

(1927) has a slow movement entitled 'Blues' – Berkeley also succumbed to this kind of sublimated jazz influence in several works of this period and the major classic in this cross-over idiom was Milhaud's *La Création du monde*, premiered by the Ballet Suédois in Paris as early as 1923, and now known almost to the detriment of everything else this prolific composer wrote.

Berkeley was an astute observer and his reactions to the Paris scene are consistent and often chime with his views in his diaries forty years later. He admired everything to do with Stravinsky and was present at significant premieres such as the Capriccio for Piano and Orchestra, the *Symphony of Psalms* and the Violin Concerto. He tried to spot winners – Bohuslav Martinů, Igor Markevitch at the age of seventeen, and, more surprisingly, the Swiss Conrad Beck. There were odd reactions too in that he always preferred early Ravel to the post-war works and was often doubtful about Poulenc. This is surprising when they were both such good friends – and history has proved Berkeley wrong. He found little interest in Paris in Vaughan Williams and, together with Britten, would later make fun of his scores.[13] Mahler was unfashionable in Paris and Berkeley never overcame his indifference to both Mahler and Richard Strauss, probably because his own tastes and inclinations were formed when he was young and impressionable in a Francophile context. As a reviewer Berkeley was never afraid to condemn feeble works in print – safely, of course, because the composers were not likely to read a British journal. He was aware of writing for readers familiar with the concert life of London and many of his judgements have stood the test of time. In his final report he wrote about Stravinsky's *Perséphone*: 'It is music that has been ruthlessly stripped of every element that is not purely musical.' That accords with Cocteau's manifesto, Stravinsky's neo-classicism, and even much of Berkeley's own music.

These reports were published in *The Monthly Musical Record*, an influential British music magazine published in London from 1871 to 1960. At the time Berkeley sent them from Paris the editor was the critic and Schubert scholar Richard Capell, who in 1933 handed over to J. A. Westrup, later Heather Professor of Music at Oxford. These are all the reports Berkeley contributed and appear as published with occasional corrections. For further details about *The Monthly Musical Record* see Richard Kitson's detailed survey online in *Retrospective Index to Music Periodicals, 1800–1950*.

Footnotes have been added to cover composers now little known.

---

[13] Humphrey Carpenter, *Benjamin Britten: a Biography* (London, 1992), 84.

THE REPORTS

June 1929

There is always such a profusion of concerts and recitals in Paris that it is impossible to do more than give some account of those that have presented a special interest or novelty during the last months.

One of the most remarkable of these was a concert of Honegger's works, with the composer conducting throughout. I think it is of particular importance to mention this concert, as Honegger's symphonic works are too little known in England. The novelty of this program was the new *mouvement-symphonique Rugby*. It is interesting to note in passing that the movement-symphonique is in some sense a new form that Honegger has invented for himself; it resembles the overture, but is much freer, having sometimes several main subjects, and not necessarily any recapitulation.

Pacific 231, which is also of the type, was played at this concert, but it is too well known to need any comment. *Rugby* is in my view a masterpiece. No attempt is made at an exact reproduction or imitation of sounds connected with the subject; but the general atmosphere of exhilaration, speed and physical energy is reproduced with wonderful vividness and power. The work is scored for normal full orchestra, but there is no percussion; it is much more tonal than many of Honegger's earlier works, being very definitely in D major, and ending unashamedly with a good solid common chord. The rest of the programme consisted of the magnificent *Prelude to The Tempest*, the incidental music to *Phèdre*, the *Chant de joie*, and the Concertino for Piano and Orchestra. *Phèdre* is a particularly fine work, showing Honegger in that sombre and heavy mood he has expressed so often. This concert was a demonstration of the composer's robust strength of feeling and good workmanship.

Another concert by the Orchestre Symphonique de Paris gave us the first concert performance of Nicholas Nabokov's ballet *Ode* for choir and orchestra, and Stravinsky's *Les Noces*. *Ode* does not seem to me a very satisfactory work; in trying to recreate an older style the composer has only achieved a tiresome and incredibly noisy pastiche of the Russian music of 1860.[14] *Les Noces* is, of course, an acknowledged masterpiece; the performance on this occasion was not very satisfactory; but it is a work of great difficulty. The concert was conducted by Ansermet.

More recently we had a concert of works by Stravinsky, in which the composer took part. The program consisted of the Octet for wind instruments, the Serenade and Sonata for piano – played by the composer – and *L'Histoire du soldat*. The Octet is delightful music, wonderfully scored and beautifully constructed; it is, perhaps, Stravinsky's best work of that period. The remorseless logic of the two

---

[14] Nicholas Nabokov (1903–78), American composer of Russian origin who came to attention with his ballet *Ode*, commissioned by Diaghilev in 1927. Nabokov said: 'The music of *Ode* was essentially tender, gentle and lyrical … akin to the music of Russian composers like Glinka, Dargomijsky and Tchaikovsky'. *Old Friends and New Music* (London, 1951), 77.

piano works was well expressed by the composer, and *L'Histoire du soldat* was given a good performance. The spoken parts were recited by Jacques Copeau.

During April two orchestral concerts and one chamber concert were devoted to the works of Albert Roussel. This composer deserves to be better known abroad than he is; his later work in particular is very strong and personal. The *Suite in F*, written in 1926, is particularly fine and vigorous. This, together with *Le Festin de l'araignée*, *Les Evocations*, and a new setting of the eightieth psalm, were given at a concert at the Opéra in celebration of the composer's sixtieth birthday. *Psalm 80*, a very interesting but rather complicated work, is written to the English version, though on this occasion a French translation was used.

On May 3 we heard the first performance of Poulenc's *Concert champêtre* for harpsichord and orchestra, conducted by Pierre Monteux; the solo part was played by Mme. Landowska.[15] This is certainly the most important composition that Poulenc has produced for some time. He has lost none of his extraordinary power of melodic invention and, though the work is perhaps not very satisfactory as regards unity of style and form, it has a great deal of charm. The harpsichord was a little lost in the Salle Pleyel – one wished that its tone could have been in some way amplified; apart from this, it combined very well with the orchestra.

Lastly, I must mention the first performance in Paris of Walton's *Façade*. The wit and colour of this delightful work made an instant appeal to the audience, and the composer, who conducted, together with Miss Edith Sitwell and Mr. Constant Lambert who recited the poems, was warmly applauded.

August 1929

Since I last wrote, the most interesting of the bigger concerts have been those given by the Hofburg Kapelle of Vienna and by the Berlin Philharmonic Orchestra conducted by Furtwängler. The Choir of the Imperial Chapel of Vienna, in which Schubert sang as a boy, gave two concerts, one of which consisted of a magnificent performance of Mozart's *Coronation Mass*, and the other of short choral works, chiefly by old Italian masters. Both concerts were of exceptional interest, consisting, as they did, in works which one very seldom hears, beautifully performed.

Furtwängler gave two concerts in which he confined himself to classical works – Brahms, Schumann, Beethoven and Berlioz. He can well afford to do so, for his extraordinary technique and subtlety of feeling give one the impression of hearing well-known masterpieces for the first time.

There have been two interesting chamber music concerts. The first was given by the Société musicale indépendante which exists for the primary purpose of performing the works of the lesser-known contemporary composers. On this occasion we had a sonata for cello and piano by the young Hungarian composer,

---

[15] Wanda Landowska (1879–1959), Polish keyboard player who lived in Paris, where she founded her École de musique ancienne, and was widely influential in the revival of the harpsichord, starting early in the twentieth century. The Poulenc was written for her, and so was Falla's Harpsichord Concerto. She moved to the US in 1940.

Tibor Harsányi.[16] Harsányi is a fine musician, but this sonata seemed a somewhat dreary work. It may not have been well played; anyhow, the general effect was somewhat turgid. Conrad Beck's sonata for violin and piano was excellent. Beck is a young Swiss composer whose string quartet aroused interest at the International Society for Contemporary Music a few years ago. Since then his output has been considerable; his style is severe and contrapuntal, but his music is full of energy, feeling and intelligence.[17]

Three Bulgarian folksongs, arranged for voice, piano, flute, and cello by Lyubomir Pipkov[18] are worthy of comment, as are two very clever pieces for string quartet by Simon Laks.[19] Laks is a young Polish composer; his music has a subtle and ironical flavour that reminds one of Ravel, though the style is utterly different.

The second chamber concert was devoted to works by young American composers; most of them are, or were, students here. The most striking of them is Aaron Copland, an ex-pupil of Mlle. Nadia Boulanger. Copland, who is already fairly well known in America, is an interesting composer.[20] He possesses an extraordinary rhythmical power, a good deal of which is probably due to the influence of jazz. If this is so, it is an instance of the good influence that jazz can have on serious music. Copland's actual technique is outstandingly good. Another promising young American is Roy Harris, whose Sextet for clarinet, piano, and string quartet was played at the same concert. He has less charm and less éclat than Copland, but there is fine feeling in his music.

We have also had a season of Italian opera – or rather a season of Rossini – by the Teatro di Torino. These performances made a great impression. We have been given so much mock Rossini by a certain school of modern composers that it is extraordinarily pleasant to hear the real thing.

Finally, there has been the season of the Russian Ballet at Théâtre Sarah Bernhardt. They produced three new ballets. *Le Fils prodigue*, with music by Prokofiev and scenery by Rouault, is among the best things they have given us for some years. The music is extremely simple, yet strong, personal, and, in some places, very moving. Prokofiev is not afraid to be romantic, and there is an entire absence of orchestral affectations. It is straightforward good music. The principal part in the ballet was superbly danced by Serge Lifar.

The music of Stravinsky's *Renard* was not new, but was given in a fresh arrangement. It belongs to the period of *Les Noces* and, though it is perhaps not

---

[16] Tibor Harsányi (1898–1954), French composer, conductor and pianist of Hungarian birth and early training as a pupil of Kodaly but subsequently based in Paris.

[17] Conrad Beck (1901–89), prolific Swiss composer resident in Paris 1924–34, He was music director of Swiss Radio 1939–66.

[18] Lyubomir Pipkov (1904–74), Bulgarian composer and teacher, Boulanger pupil, who became prominent in various administrative posts in his own country.

[19] Simon Laks (1901–87) was one of a group of young Polish composers studying in Paris at this time. He spent some years in concentration camps during the war, but survived and wrote a book about his experiences.

[20] Aaron Copland (1900–90) was well established in America by this time. Boulanger had premiered his Organ Symphony in New York in 1925 and Koussevitsky had conducted *Music for the Theatre* and the Piano Concerto.

one of Stravinsky's finest works, it is full of life and originality. The ballet was most exhilarating, very grotesque, excellently staged and performed.

Le Bal, which was the third new ballet, was also a success. The scenery in particular, by de Chirico, was admirable – in fact, the best part of it. The music, by the young Italian composer Vittorio Rieti, is of a very light order, and is full of reminiscences, though one is not quite sure whether they are intentional or not; its chief merit is its orchestration, which is extremely good.[21] It is certainly just what is wanted to go with the rest of the ballet, and the whole performance is another example of Diaghilev's wonderful power of combining music, scenery, and choreography into a coherent and aesthetic whole.

December 1929

The most interesting Paris concerts are generally reserved for the 'season'; at this time of year it is rare that anything at all sensational takes place in the musical world. However, the usual orchestral concerts are in full swing, and, if they have given us nothing very extraordinary, they have at least maintained their standard of performance.

Pierre Monteux continues to conduct the Orchestre Symphonique de Paris, though he has invited many distinguished foreign conductors to direct his orchestra from time to time, among them Sir Henry Wood, who conducted on November 8. His programme consisted of a Suite by Purcell, an Andante by Mozart, Beethoven's Violin Concerto, and Vaughan Williams's *London Symphony*. The Purcell Suite, arranged by Sir Henry, was delightful, and was received with enthusiasm by the audience, as was also the Mozart Andante. The solo part of the Concerto was admirably played by Mischa Elman. The *London Symphony* was quite well played, but seemed to hang fire a little. It was received with interest, but without much enthusiasm; one feels that Vaughan Williams will never be very much appreciated in France. There is a certain vagueness in his thought with which the French mind is impatient. Is this the fault of Vaughan Williams or of the French mind? Both, perhaps are at fault; nevertheless, one feels it a pity that a man who has done such fine work with purely English material should have failed to carry his art a step farther by diminishing the importance of that very material on which he has built his style, thereby making his music more universal in its appeal. Perhaps this will happen – indeed, it may have happened already. One hears so little English music in Paris that one is often unacquainted with the latest developments.

Mengelberg has also conducted the Orchestre Symphonique lately, and maintained his reputation as one of the greatest conductors of our time.[22]

At the Pasdeloup Concerts we had a concert of Honegger and Milhaud. The two composers conducted their respective works. Nothing new was revealed, but many fine things were played, including Honegger's *Pacific 231* and *Rugby*, and *La*

---

[21] Vittorio Rieti (1898–1994) American composer of Italian descent who worked in Paris and Rome between the wars and moved to the US in 1940. He wrote ballet music for Diaghilev and for Balanchine.

[22] Willem Mengelberg (1871–1951), influential Dutch conductor, a strong advocate of Strauss and Mahler.

Création du monde and *Six chants populaires hébraïques*, by Milhaud. Several works by the same composer never seem to be quite so satisfactory when played at the same concert as when heard separately. One notices certain tricks of orchestration which come over and over again, and are apt to become very irritating. An instance of this is Honegger's habit of cutting the main rhythm by explosions on the brass; a device which is certainly very effective, but which he is inclined to overdo. However, the concert was most enjoyable, and the two composers were warmly applauded.

Mrs. E. S. Coolidge gave two invitation concerts of modern chamber music during the last week of October.[23] Several works by young and comparatively unknown composers were given. By far the most interesting of these was a string quintet by the young Czech composer Martinů, which seems to me a work of the first order. It is robust and broad in feeling – influenced both in its type of emotion and its style by the modern German school, but nevertheless very personal. One hesitates to affirm that a modern work, heard only once, is great music, but in listening to this I felt the joy that only such music can give. From the technical point of view, Martinů's workmanship is admirable; there is no trace of the beginner or the amateur. The next best things, in my view, were Arthur Bliss's Oboe Quintet and Albert Roussel's Trio for flute, viola and cello. Bliss's work was received with much interest, and the general impression was that it was the best piece of English chamber music that had been heard here for some time. Roussel's Trio is a work of great charm and accomplishment, the difficult combination of instruments is very well treated. A work by Malipiero [*Sonata à 3* for piano trio, 1927] was also played; it was disappointing, being rather incoherent, and in spite of much animation, did not seem to get anywhere. The first movement is for cello and piano, the second for violin and piano, and the third for all three together. This method of treating the trio is interesting; unfortunately, the work itself is not. Another composition was a *Divertissement grotesque* for wind instruments and piano by Josef Hüttel.[24] The work, in spite of the fact that it won the Coolidge Prize this year, is not good; it is superficial and the grotesqueness is stereotyped. The result is unpleasant and dreary.

May 1930

The winter season has been very rich in good concerts. Among new works one of the most striking was Stravinsky's Capriccio for piano and orchestra. This was given at a concert of the Orchestre Symphonique de Paris, with the composer playing the solo part. Stravinsky continues to renew himself in the most amazing way, and though for each work he chooses a different style, each bears the imprint of his personality. He proves to us that in reality style matters very little. Good music can be written in any style, and any style can be made new and interesting if the composer's ideas and technique are equal to the task. The Capriccio, as its

---

[23] Elizabeth Sprague Coolidge (1864–1953), American patron who commissioned many of the leading international composers and started the festival which became Tanglewood.

[24] Josef Hüttel (1893–1951), Czechoslovakian composer and conductor.

title implies, is rather light music, and the composer has used to a large extent a style that calls to mind Liszt's Rhapsodies – one that adapts itself admirably to the combination of piano and orchestra. The work is in three movements, of which the last is the most brilliant; but all three are full of vitality and interest. The composition forms a striking contrast to the austerity of *Apollon musagète* and to the style of the last few years, but in other respects is very typical of Stravinsky.

Another novelty was also a work for piano and orchestra – Poulenc's *Aubade*. This is a series of pieces originally written for a ballet, in which the piano takes a leading part and is accompanied by a small orchestra.[25] At the first performance the composer, who is a fine pianist, played the solo part. Although it has considerable charm in places, the *Aubade* is not very satisfactory music – there is a great diversity of styles and a lack of continuity of thought and feeling, which leave one disappointed with the work as a whole. Poulenc seems to have reached rather an uncomfortable stage, having lost something of the freshness and originality of his earlier works, and failed to find any more solid qualities with which to replace them.

A third new work given recently was Hindemith's overture to his new opera, *Neues vom Tage*, which made an instant appeal by its splendid vigour and originality. We have also been given the first concert performance of Ravel's *Boléro*, which is a veritable tour de force, the whole work being nothing less than an enormous crescendo, using one theme repeated over and over again, but with great subtlety of orchestration. The fact that the work lasts twenty minutes will give some idea of the technical mastery that such a feat demands. The *Boléro* is profoundly Spanish in character, without using any of the ordinary means, such as castanets, to produce local colour. From the very beginning it has a somewhat sinister atmosphere, and the final fortissimo is positively diabolical.

The Straram concerts have also had good programmes, but there has been nothing very striking to report.[26] The most interesting new work there so far has been Conrad Beck's Concerto for Orchestra. This work is a Concerto in the sense in which Bach used the word; there is no solo instrument, but all the instruments have important solo parts – it is the old classical method of concertini and ripieni. Beck is certainly a musician of importance, but one is inclined to feel that he is too remorseless a contrapuntist – he seems to disregard any other aspect of music. Counterpoint is the order of the day, and rightly; but this composer thrusts it down one's throat, and consequently his music lacks charm, though it is by no means devoid of emotion.

Among the best concerts of the season were the three Beethoven concerts conducted by Bruno Walter, whose magnificent renderings of the great Beethoven symphonies aroused much enthusiasm. At the second of his concerts the programme included the *Emperor Concerto*, the solo part being superbly played by Gieseking.[27] The extraordinary intelligence and feeling of Gieseking's playing have

---

[25] *Aubade: concerto chorégraphique*, for piano and 18 instruments (1929).

[26] See n. 44, p. 41 below.

[27] See also Berkeley's remarks in a letter to Boulanger, p. 47 below.

won great popularity for him in Paris, where he is regarded as the greatest pianist of the younger generation. On this occasion he excelled himself; the piano seemed to have more variety of tone colour than the orchestra.

Another interesting musical event has been the production of Johann Strauss's operetta *Die Fledermaus* at the Théatre Pigalle. The soloists, who included Lotte Schöne, were all extremely good, and the gaiety and dash of the music, culminating in the famous *Blue Danube* waltz, delighted the audience. We have rather lost Johann Strauss's *joie de vivre*. If some of our modern composers would give us works of this sort they would be very welcome.

August 1930

The season has been particularly rich in good music of all sorts, and the big orchestras have maintained their usual standard of interesting and varied programmes.

During May the most notable musical event was a concert of the works of Manuel de Falla conducted by the composer. This was the first time that Falla had conducted his big orchestral works here, and he was welcomed with much enthusiasm at the Salle Pleyel. The programme consisted of *El amor brujo*, *Seven Spanish Folksongs*, *Nights in the Gardens of Spain*, and *El retablo de maese pedro*. It was most interesting to hear the composer's own reading of the much-played *El amor brujo*. What struck one most was its restraint; the tempi were slightly slower than those one usually hears, with the result that many details of Falla's extraordinarily rich and subtle orchestration stood out very clearly. The *Spanish Folksongs* were superbly sung by Vera Janacopoulos, accompanied at the piano by the composer. These songs cannot be too highly praised; they constitute a perfect example of Falla's art – a strongly national and popular character disciplined by technical mastery and personal inspiration. *Nights in the Gardens of Spain*, beautiful as it is, has not perhaps quite the originality of Falla's later works. It was given a very fine performance, with Ricardo Vines, to whom the work is dedicated, as solo pianist. *El retablo* was the most interesting item of the programme. In this work the composer sets out on a new and more personal line; the national element is as strong as ever, but apart from this the music is more modern and harder in outline. Here we have no longer the voluptuous harmonies of *El amor brujo* – on the contrary, there is something almost ascetic and bare. The evening gave one a clear idea of Falla's position in contemporary music. His great vitality and fervour, combined with good workmanship, have won for him an important and well-deserved place.

Another orchestral concert which took place at about the same time gave us some interesting modern works. Some songs for voice and orchestra, by Germaine Tailleferre, were very spontaneous and charming, and very delicately orchestrated.[28] At the same concert we heard Hindemith's overture *Neues vom Tage*, of which I have already spoken, and Ravel's brilliant and ironical *La Valse*.

---

[28] Germaine Tailleferre (1892–1983), the only female member of Les Six. This work could have been her *Six chansons françaises* (1929).

At the last concert of the Orchestre Symphonique de Paris for this season, the most important work was the new Cello Concerto by Honegger. This is a fine work. At a first hearing it seemed a little disjointed, but that may be a false impression. It is much simpler than most of Honegger's previous works, and very far removed from the polytonality of *Pacific 231*, *Judith*, and the music of that period. A calm and peaceful atmosphere prevails almost throughout, which recalls in some ways the early *Pastorale d'été*. The solo part was played with great virtuosity by Maurice Maréchal. The programme also included a prelude to one of the acts of Milhaud's opera *Les Euménides*. This prelude is tremendously powerful and, though brutal, has the merit of being a fine piece of musical construction.

Quite a sensation was caused in the musical world by the first performance of Igor Markevitch's Cantata, written in collaboration with Jean Cocteau.[29] It is no exaggeration to say that this is a piece of first-class music that can be favourably compared to the best music of today, and as Markevitch is only seventeen, the work is an extraordinary achievement. The really odd thing is that it gives one an impression of maturity, and it is difficult to trace any influence except that of Hindemith, and even that not to any great extent. One may legitimately entertain the highest hopes that Markevitch will be one of the great composers of the future. At the same concert a work by Rameau, the manuscript of which was only recently discovered in the Bibliothèque Nationale, was given, and also Satie's *Mercure*.

Pavlova gave a short season of ballets here recently. From the musical point of view they were most disappointing for the music mainly consisted of a few well-known and rather hackneyed pieces, and such unknown music as was played was of so poor a quality that it is likely to remain so. However, I did not see all the ballets, and may have been unlucky. Pavlova herself is magnificent, and has lost none of her grace and charm, but one good dancer – one great dancer even – does not make a good ballet, and one fears that the art of making good ballets has died with Diaghilev.

March 1931

There has been a good deal of discussion in the musical papers lately about the Paris orchestras and orchestral concerts. The conditions here are very different from those in England. Each orchestra is run by a 'société' as it is called, with regular subscribers or season-ticket holders, and each is self-supporting and independent.

The Concerts Lamoureux, the Concerts Colonne, and the Concerts Pasdeloup each give two concerts a week on Saturdays and Sundays, and more or less at the same time, for about eight months of the year – from July to October there are no orchestral concerts. In addition to this, the Orchestre Symphonique de Paris gives a concert on Sunday, and sometimes on a weekday as well, and from January to June the Concerts Straram take place every Thursday. There are also two more orchestral societies which give occasional concerts. It is not difficult to imagine

---

[29] Igor Markevitch (1912–83), French composer and conductor of Ukranian descent who turned to conducting rather than fulfilling his extraordinary early promise as a composer.

the disadvantages of this state of affairs. People have been complaining that the orchestras give indifferent performances and are continually playing the same things. The players say that they are overworked and underpaid. The only remedy would seem to be to effect some sort of amalgamation and have fewer concerts and more rehearsals: it would then be hoped that more people would attend, that the musicians could be better paid, and there would be time to rehearse new works. One good concert is better than many bad ones. There have not, so far, been many outstanding musical events this season. The Opéra Russe à Paris has perhaps scored the greatest success, and it has certainly given some wonderful performances, the singing and acting being of a particularly high standard. Chaliapin has appeared several times in *Boris Godounov*: he is as great an actor as he is a singer, and scenes of indescribable enthusiasm take place every time he performs. The same company is also giving ballets under the direction of Nijinska. Two pieces of the Diaghilev repertory are announced: *Les Biches* and *Petroushka*.

An interesting concert, conducted by Roger Desormière, one of the ablest of the younger men who had charge of the orchestra of the Russian Ballet during the last years of its existence, consisted of an unknown Haydn symphony which, unlike most neglected works of great composers, turned out to be extremely good, a Concerto Grosso by the young Russian composer Igor Markevitch, a ballet suite *La Nuit* by Sauguet, and Stravinsky's *Renard*. I have spoken of Markevitch before; he continues to astonish the musical world by his precocity. This work, written on the classical model with each instrument in turn having an important solo part, took one's breath away by the brilliance of its orchestration, the untiring vitality of its rhythm, and the almost diabolical cleverness of its counterpoint. Nevertheless, one feels it to be more exhilarating than moving, and one is a little doubtful whether Markevitch is capable of real depth of feeling – this, however, may come later. Sauguet's *La Nuit* is colourless but quite pretty; he has developed the style for which Erik Satie is largely responsible and his music is quite well written and has a certain vogue, but one fears that it is too anaemic to live long. Stravinsky's *Renard* requires the ballet to give its greatest effect, but the music remains full of life and originality.

Alfredo Casella, conducting the Orchestre Symphonique de Paris recently, gave a concerto by Vivaldi (for a long time wrongly attributed to W. F. Bach), Rossini's delicious overture to *Cenerentola*, Saint-Saëns's rather tedious but well-written Cello Concerto in A minor, played by Baroult, his own Serenata for small orchestra, Stravinsky's second Suite, Debussy's *L'Après-midi* and Ravel's *Boléro*. The Serenata is an arrangement of a work for violin, cello, trumpet, clarinet and bassoon; though well orchestrated, it suffers from a disconcerting mixture of styles, and does not give one a feeling of continuity.

Casella also lectured on the modern Italian school of composers. He pointed out that the modern Italians were not of the Bolshevik school, but sought, as in his opinion did the best of the moderns, including Stravinsky and Hindemith, to adhere to the classical form, while using modern feeling and modern developments. The lecture was followed by a concert of chamber music. No new talents were revealed, but Malipiero's quartet *Rispetti a strambotti* and Casella's Second Cello Sonata had good moments. These, combined with a group of songs, showed that if the modern Italian school has not produced a great composer as yet, it has at least some capable and gifted musicians.

May 1931

The most important musical event of the past weeks was the first performance in Paris of Stravinsky's *Symphonie de psaumes*. The work has made a profound impression in musical circles here and is considered to be one of Stravinsky's finest achievements. He has chosen verses from the Latin version of the Psalms. The work is divided into three movements. The text of the first is from a psalm of supplication, the second of contemplation, and the third of praise – Psalm 150.

The whole work is extremely religious in character, the feeling being deep and yet restrained. From the technical point of view it well repays a careful study – the economy of thematic material is most remarkable throughout; the second movement is a double fugue, and though all the well-known contrapuntal devices are employed it seems extraordinarily new and original. The orchestration too is full of innovations – there are no violins, no violas and no clarinets, but two pianos are added, forming another instance of Stravinsky's predilection for the piano as an orchestral instrument. One feels that this work is the culmination of Stravinsky's third period, which began with such works as the Sonata and *Oedipus Rex*, and its austerity is tempered by that tremendous ardour and power by which we recognize the composer of *The Rite of Spring*. The *Psalm Symphony* expresses the Christian spirit as strongly as *The Rite* expressed the spirit of paganism. If one looks back from this work on the whole of Stravinsky's output, one cannot help being struck by the extraordinary variety of styles that it contains, and one comes to the conclusion that it matters little what style a composer uses so long as he adheres to it consistently during the same work; and not only this, but that the same composer can use a different style for each work without ever losing his own individuality. I suppose this has never been done to such an extent before, and it is a fine thing to see an artist despise the success that is so easily obtained by repeating himself after one successful work, and boldly striking out afresh each time at the risk of being misunderstood by his late admirers.

Two piano recitals given by Walter Gieseking deserve special mention. This magnificent pianist differs so much from the ordinary virtuoso that it would be most difficult to give an idea of his playing to anyone who had not heard him. The utter absence of show and exterior effect and the concentration on the music itself make his art a refreshingly different thing from what one is used to. He played at his first recital twelve preludes by Chopin and Debussy's twenty-four preludes, and at the second, four Beethoven sonatas. Several times during both concerts one had the feeling of listening for the first time to things that one knew by heart.

Pierre Monteux has given some interesting works with the Paris Symphonic Orchestra, amongst which Beck's Fifth symphony, Markevitch's Piano Concerto and a portion of Alban Berg's opera *Wozzeck* are worthy of note – the latter especially containing some very brilliant and original orchestration.

There has also been an orchestral concert of the works of Ravel, the programme including the early *Rapsodie espagnol*, the whole of *Daphnis et Chloé*, a work that is rarely heard in its entirety, and *Boléro*. Although *Boléro* is a wonderful idea brilliantly executed one feels that such a method of composing is too arbitrary to lead anywhere, and its final paroxysm is so calculated that it can only thrill one once – however, it is better to be thrilled once than not at all. Ravel's early works are undoubtedly his most original, and this concert made one feel how much modern music owes to him.

Honegger's operetta *Les Aventures du roi pansole* continues to have great success, though it is in some respects disappointing from a purely musical point of view. In his desire to write an ordinary operetta and to avoid any savour of the high-brow, Honegger seems to have gone too far. The result is that a good deal of it is frankly banal, which is a pity, as it has life and gaiety, and if only he had managed to be a little more original, it would have yet more.

Various concerts have been given, notably by the Schola Cantorum and the Colonne orchestra, to celebrate Vincent d'Indy's eightieth birthday on March 27. The composer has been promoted Grand Officer of the Legion of Honour.

July 1931

The months of May and June, which roughly constitute the season here, have been particularly brilliant this year from the musical point of view. A regular invasion of virtuosos of all sorts has made it almost impossible to keep pace with the musical events. I cannot do more here than mention those concerts which particularly impressed me.

One concert that remains in my mind was the recital given by Roland Hayes in the Salle Pleyel on May 8.[30] It was one of the most successful of the season. Roland Hayes is an artist of the first rank; one is at a loss to say what one admires most in him – the extraordinary beauty of his voice or the consummate art with which he uses it. His programme ranged from seventeenth-century Italian music to negro spirituals; and especially striking was the difference between his rendering of the latter and of the rest of his programme. It is, of course, obvious that one cannot sing Schubert and spirituals in the same manner, but Hayes understands the differences, and assumes what seems to be a different voice for the spirituals. His admirable enunciation greatly enhances his singing – one heard every word, whether it was French, English, German, or Italian.

Another recital that aroused great enthusiasm was Segovia's concert at the Opéra.[31] I think it is superfluous to praise Segovia's guitar playing – it will suffice to say that he was at the top of his form, and amply justified his choice of the Opéra to perform in. His programme included some interesting eighteenth-century lute music – a *Préambule et gavotte* by Chilesotti and a Partita by Silvius Weiss. He also played Turina's delightful *Fandanguillo*, of which there is an excellent recording on

---

[30] Roland Hayes (1887–1977), American tenor who initially sang with the Jubilee Singers and became one of the first African American singers to make an international career.

[31] Berkeley wrote *Quatre pièces pour la guitarre* and dedicated them to Andrés Segovia (1893–1987), who made his Paris debut in 1924. Angelo Gilardino found the manuscript when he was going through Segovia's library in Spain in 2001; his edition was published in 2002 by Bèrben, Ancona, Italy.

His Master's Voice. The fact that one heard perfectly every sound bears witness not only to Segovia's power of tone-production, but also to the acoustic properties of the Opéra.

Paderewski announced two concerts, but at the last minute was prevented from giving the second, owing to the illness of his wife. The first concert was a triumph. Though over seventy, he has not lost his amazing powers. Paderewski gave his share of the proceeds to the fund for the erection of a monument in memory of Debussy. Kreisler, Horowitz, Heifetz and other well-known virtuosos have also played here lately.

There have also been numerous outstanding orchestral concerts – Mengelberg, Furtwängler, Weingartner and Bruno Walter have all conducted here within the last two months. Mengelberg, in addition to the Prelude to *Tristan* and an electrifying performance of the *Meistersinger* Overture, gave Mahler's *Das Lied von der Erde*, which, in spite of a masterly performance, was not received with great enthusiasm. Mahler has the fashion of the day against him – his ultra-romanticism does not commend itself easily to the modern ear – nevertheless, no musical person could fail to admire the originality and variety of his orchestration.

We have also had some interesting first performances. Two important new works by Honegger, one by Milhaud and one by Conrad Beck were among the most noteworthy. Of these, in my opinion, Beck's work was the finest. It was a Concerto for String Quartet and Orchestra, and was very well performed by the Berlin String Quartet and Straram and his orchestra. This Concerto has a richness of material and a depth of thought and feeling of which very few composers of today are capable. The one thing with which one can reproach Beck is his excessive austerity. One feels that he is afraid of pleasure in music – there is plenty of life, and even of joy, at moments, in his music, but he never makes the slightest concession to the senses. Pleasant sound or charm is perhaps not an essential ingredient of good music, but I feel that its absence prevents Beck from being as complete an artist as he might be.

Milhaud's Concerto for Viola and Orchestra has an original flavour and is characteristic of its composer, but it seemed a little patchy – which is also, I fear, rather a characteristic of its composer. In the first movement one had, instead of an impression of speed, a feeling of fuss and bustle and then it was all over. It was like a lot of people all scrambling to get on a bus or into a train, and when they had got there nothing happened. This, of course, may not be the composer's fault – on the other hand it may be intentional, but if it is, I feel that it is not quite a success aesthetically.

The same must be said of Honegger's *Cris du monde*. This is a setting for soloists, chorus, and orchestra of a poem by René Bizet. The idea expressed in the poem is that modern man is pursued by the noise of machines, gramophones, loud-speakers and so on to such an extent that he can find no rest, nor any tranquillity in which to commune with his own soul – should he wish to do so. Unfortunately the words are very undistinguished, and one can only suppose that they have infected the composer, for much of the music is frankly banal. I do not mean that there are no beautiful passages, but the general impression is unsatisfactory. Honegger's new Symphony [no. 1] is, in my view, better than the choral work – it has a fine and vigorous opening, and many moments of considerable beauty, but there is a certain lack of unity of style, which prevents it from being in the first rank.

December 1931

There is nothing in Paris corresponding to our Promenade Concerts, and consequently there is no music worth thinking about during August and September. In addition to this the season finishes earlier than in London, and thus there is practically no music in July either. People often complain that the distribution of concerts throughout the year is very uneven; everything is crushed into the few months that constitute spring and early summer, with the result that in May, for instance, there is an interesting concert every night, whereas between July and December they are few and far between.

It appears, however, that the concert agents are urging musicians to give concerts during October and November, and they maintain – I think rightly – that they will get a larger public during these months than during the season, when they risk passing unnoticed and when the enthusiasm of even the most indefatigable concert-goers is beginning to flag. On the other hand, I doubt very much whether a system similar to our Promenade Concerts would prove successful in Paris. The audiences of the Concerts Pasdeloup, Lamoureux, Colonne, and so on are for the most part regular subscribers of the upper middle-classes who hold season tickets and who are away in the summer. I do not think that the man in the street is as musical in Paris as in London, and the audience of the Promenade Concerts is essentially one of men in the street – if I may say so without disrespect.

To write about music in Paris during the summer being thus no easy task, I will take the opportunity created by the lack of concerts to give an outline of the state of contemporary music in Paris.

I say contemporary music in Paris and not contemporary French music, because among the young composers in Paris – I mean those of outstanding merit – the French by no means predominate – and this fact is one of supreme importance in studying present-day tendencies. In the old days artists went to a certain place to study their art because there was a school there. In Paris this is no longer the case. The French school seems to have died with Fauré; for it is obvious that the so-called school of Les Six was composed of musicians of great talent but who beyond that had nothing whatever in common, or at all events not enough to create what is known as a school in art. It would be difficult to find, in the same generation, two composers more different than Honegger and Poulenc, for instance. Therefore those musicians who go to Paris to study go there rather to be in a centre, if not *the* centre, of modern art than to study any particular school of composition. It is difficult to say whether this state of affairs is a factor for good or ill in the development of contemporary music in general, but it is perhaps a pity for the French themselves, since the modern Russian and German masters seem to have taken possession of Paris and to have temporarily usurped their natural position.

As regards teachers, however, the French certainly retain their pre-eminence. One has only to think of Nadia Boulanger, Charles Koechlin, Paul Dukas, Alfred Cortot, and Isidore Philipp to see one of the reasons why so many young composers of all nationalities go to Paris to complete their musical education. Another reason is that the French are in general excellent technicians and amazingly hard workers, thus creating the right atmosphere for anyone who wishes to study seriously.

As regards the general attitude of the public towards music, I think that that too is favourable to students and young musicians. I have just said that the French are not a particularly musical race; but they have other qualities that make up for it. First of all, their love of and interest in anything new – in which they differ so strikingly from the English – ensures a fair hearing for the young composer or executant and stimulates his efforts; then, secondly, their feeling that art is a thing to be encouraged, and that it is in no way abnormal to be an artist. A third point may be added – the fact that the French prefer individuality to uniformity, and expect some degree of originality in an artist. This preference is a fundamental thing, and, as André Siegfried[32] has pointed out, is at the root of the difference between French and English politics. These reasons make for a more sympathetic attitude towards modern music on the part of the critics than is the case everywhere – an additional advantage for unknown composers. Thus, though Paris lacks a school proper, such as those of Hindemith or Schoenberg, it has not ceased to be a place favourable to the formation and development of the young musician.

February 1932

To the Editor of *The Monthly Musical Record*
(Our correspondent's letter was written before the beginning of the autumn concert season)

Sir,

With regard to the remarks in your December issue about the concerts of English music at the Paris Colonial Exhibition, I feel that I must protest against the accusation of contempt for English music which you bring against the French. The real reason for the apparent lack of interest on this occasion was that the concerts were held at a time when the musical public is away. The season ends much earlier here than in London, and it is quite hopeless to expect to arouse any interest in a concert which takes place later than June. I was told, also, that the concerts were insufficiently advertised – as I was away myself at the time, I cannot vouch for this.

It is true that the French do not take easily to English music; but they are quite open-minded about it, and ready to give anything a fair hearing. Let us therefore not ask too much of them, nor expect that their esteem for contemporary English music should be such that they will abandon their wives and children at the seaside, and rush back to Paris on their summer holidays.

L.B.

---

[32] André Siegfried (1875–1959), distinguished political commentator whose subjects included politics in France, North America and the United Kingdom.

March–April 1932

A very large audience assembled at the Salle Pleyel on December 17 for the first performance of Stravinsky's Violin Concerto. As this work has already been played in London it is unnecessary to attempt any description of it here; it will suffice to give an account of the impression that it made in musical circles in Paris. All the critics agree that it is a real concerto in the more specialized sense of the term, and all comment upon the extraordinary brilliance of the violin writing. One feels grateful to a composer who has taken the trouble to make such an exhaustive study of the resources of the instrument for which he is writing. As for the music itself, most people consider the new concerto a big work and think that Stravinsky is very much on the right lines in setting his face against all sensuous and sentimental appeals, in bringing music back to the sterner classical style, and in making for pure aesthetic feeling only. Some critics, however, consider that Stravinsky is too much preoccupied with technical problems, and that he lays too much stress upon the execution of musical conjuring-tricks. The concerto was received with great enthusiasm, and the solo part was admirably played by Samuel Dushkin.

Some time before this we had an orchestral concert of the works of Prokofiev. His Fourth Symphony, performed then for the first time, is particularly interesting to those who saw his ballet *Le Fils prodigue*, as he has here made use of the same themes, developing them at greater length than was possible in the ballet. The other novelty was an arrangement for string orchestra of the Andante movement from his new string quartet [no. 1], and the programme was completed by the delightful *Classical Symphony*, a suite from the ballet *Le Pas d'acier*, and the First Piano Concerto – the solo part being played with great brilliance by the composer himself. Without having any startling originality Prokofiev's music continues to have a strongly personal flavour, and is full of life and colour.

A new musical society called La Sérénade has been founded in Paris with the object of giving performances of modern chamber works. Its first concert was certainly nothing if not modern. The programme consisted mainly of first performances of works by the younger school of composers, who were represented by Milhaud, Rieti, Sauguet, Markevitch and a young and, I think, hitherto unknown Italian composer, Leone Massimo. Rieti's work was perhaps the most successful of these, and Sauguet's had considerable charm and lightness of touch. Markevitch's harsh and dissonant style does not seem to adapt itself well to chamber music, and when he is deprived of the weight of the orchestra and its variety of colours, his music is very arid. Massimo's Serenade for two violins may look well on paper, but it was most tedious to listen to.

Earlier in the season, three concerts given under the auspices of Mrs. Coolidge attracted a great deal of attention. Two chamber concerts revealed new works by Prokofiev, Frank Bridge, Tansman, Malipiero, Raymond Petit, and Hindemith. Of these Prokofiev's String Quartet and Hindemith's Concerto for piano, two harps, and brass were the most striking. The former would seem, as far as one could tell at a first hearing, to be a work of the first order, as happy in its inspiration as in its technical accomplishment; while the latter is most original and interesting from every point of view – particularly from that of instrumentation. A third concert was entirely devoted to the music of Monteverdi and Lully – the first part of the programme consisting of madrigals, for one or for two voices with the accompaniment of strings and harpsichord, by Monteverdi, and in the second part, a performance of fragments from Lully's operas *Cadmus* and *Alceste*. The concert was wholly delightful, consisting as it did of music that one so seldom hears, but that one hopes will now be more frequently performed, thanks to Malipiero's editing of Monteverdi, and Henry Prunières's work on Lully. The centuries have certainly not robbed Monteverdi of his freshness and purity, nor have they tarnished the extraordinary vigour and richness of Lully, and one feels ashamed of the unwarranted neglect which they have suffered in the past.

In giving Milhaud's *Maximilien* the director of the Opéra took an important step; for this is the first time that that august institution has had anything more than a flirtation with one of the real moderns. The Opéra here is run by the State, and its artists are State fonctionnaires so that any innovation is a serious matter and may create a political situation. It is largely for this reason that the production of a really modern opera had not been attempted before, and it is probable that had Milhaud not been obliged to go to Berlin to get his last opera, *Christopher Columbus*, performed, it would not have been done yet.[33] However, having decided to do *Maximilien*, they at least did it thoroughly, for the work was well staged, well sung, and fairly well played by the orchestra; and if it was a failure, as it certainly was, it was not due to inefficiency on the part of those who produced it. Whether it was due to the shortcomings of the work itself, or to lack of comprehension on the part of the public, is a more difficult question to answer. It was probably due to both.

The libretto deals with the tragic story of Maximilian of Austria, who, having become Emperor of Mexico, made an heroic struggle against the rebellion led by Juarez. He was at first assisted by French and Austrian troops, but these discreetly retired to Europe when things began to go badly, and the Emperor, refusing to fly, was taken prisoner and shot by the revolutionaries. In Act I we are shown Maximilian's court at the beginning of the revolution; Act II shows us the revolutionaries gaining strength, and in Act III the Emperor is seen in prison before his execution.

Milhaud has made good use of the dramatic material contained in the story, but the music itself was too modern to please the public, and too imperfect to please the specialists. The orchestration is often clumsy, the vocal parts not always well laid out for the voice, and a great deal of the music sounds unnecessarily confused. But with all its faults it is a work of magnificent power and emotion, and of outstanding originality. It also has the merit of containing some real tunes and not 'motifs', which are so often a camouflage for melodic poverty. The military march which opens and closes the whole work is extraordinarily poignant with its harsh discords and insistent rhythm. André Pernet played and sang the part of Maximilian magnificently, and even managed to he convincingly heroic in a top hat and frock coat – no mean achievement. *Maximilien* was given six performances,

[33] *Christophe Colomb*, produced at the Berlin Staatsoper on 5 May 1930.

but judging from its reception at the hands of the critics (most of whom were not only stupid, which they cannot help, but definitely malevolent, which they need not be) and the public, one fears that it will not be given again, unless it is revived sometime in the future.

Ravel's new Piano Concerto is a very different affair. Technically it is almost perfect; it has been hailed as a masterpiece by many critics, and received universal approbation. It is made in the classical model: Allegramente – Adagio – Rondo. The slow movement is perhaps the most striking; a calm and reflective theme is exposed by the piano, the orchestra joining in by degrees and adding very subtle shades of tone-colour. The rondo has considerable dash and brilliance, and rounds off the work admirably. Nevertheless, in spite of its technical perfection and the many passages of real beauty in the work, one feels that Ravel is not as happy in his new style as in his earlier manner. There is a certain lack of spontaneity – something a little forced, which makes one think regretfully of the delicious freshness of the opening bars of his String Quartet, for instance, or of the pathos and luxuriance of *Daphnis et Chloé*. However, it would be ungracious to grumble. The Concerto is an interesting work, and perhaps one only needs to hear it again to enjoy that unmixed pleasure that Ravel has so often given us in the past.

June 1932

Alfred Cortot's concert in celebration of the Haydn bicentenary was much appreciated by the musical public here. An interesting feature was that two of the works performed had never been played in Paris before. These were the Sinfonia Concertante for violin, cello, oboe, bassoon and orchestra, and orchestral fragments from the *Seven Last Words of our Saviour*. The former work is particularly delightful, and one wonders why it has been so seldom performed. The latter is something of a musical curiosity – it was written at the request of the Chapter of Cadiz Cathedral for the Good Friday services there. Haydn made different versions of the work, and an interesting feature of this performance was that the manuscript, from which Haydn himself conducted when he gave a performance of the instrumental version in London, is at present in M. Cortot's possession, and was used on this occasion.

At the same concert Mme. Wanda Landowska played, with amazing virtuosity and perfection, one of the piano sonatas, and also the solo part of a concerto for harpsichord and orchestra. A new singer who is rapidly making a name for herself, Mme. Modrakowska, sang with great feeling and wonderful purity of tone an air from *The Seasons*.[34] Cortot conducted the whole concert. He is perhaps not the ideal interpreter of Haydn, but his wonderful all-round musicianship secured an excellent performance. As a conductor he is a pleasure to watch, his gestures being sober and restrained, and yet precise and authoritative.

The Société musicale indépendante gave two concerts of modern chamber music, the first of which consisted of three string quartets and a piano quintet.

---

[34] Maria Modrakowska (1896–1965), Polish singer and writer devoted to Boulanger, with whom she studied at the École normale and privately and performed professionally. She gave recitals with Poulenc in North Africa and in France in 1935.

Two of these works, a quartet by Conrad Beck and another by Martinů, were of outstanding merit. Beck's quartet [no. 3] is already known to the musical public; it was played at one of the International Festivals [Frankfurt, 1927] and has since been heard many times in Paris. It is solidly constructed, a little on the heavy side perhaps, but with a beautiful and profound slow movement. Martinů's Quartet [no. 3], which opened with an astonishing effect obtained by a combination of col legno and pizzicato, is also a fine work with an individual flavour; it held one's attention throughout. I think that Martinů is almost unknown in England and it is a pity, as he is certainly one of the most striking of the younger composers. The two other works, a string quartet by Mihalovici[35] and a quintet for piano and strings by Harsanyi, made a less powerful impression. At the second concert we were given a larger and more varied programme. Roussel's Second Violin and Piano Sonata is perhaps not one of his best works; it is rather colourless music, though the slow movement is good. Jean Cartan[36] was one of the most promising of the younger French composers; his Sonatina for flute and clarinet was played at this concert in memoriam since he died recently. Another accomplished essay in the modern style was a Sonata for flute and piano by Jacques Beers.[37] The programme was completed by songs by Szymanowski, Poulenc and Labunski, a young Polish composer.[38]

September 1932

The Debussy memorial was unveiled on June 17, and official honours were paid to the greatest French composer of modern times. The ceremony was presided over by the President of the Republic, speeches were made, and extracts from Debussy's music were played by the band of the Garde républicaine. The monument itself, which is situated in the Boulevard Lannes, near the Bois de Boulogne, is very well done: a series of bas-reliefs portrays Saint Sébastian, Mélisande, the Faun, and the *Cathédrale engloutie*, and the whole thing is given a charming and most appropriate delicacy by the reflection in the water which forms an important part of the whole conception. In the evening, on the same day, an orchestral concert was given at the Théâtre des Champs Elysées. M. Philippe Gaubert conducted part of *Le Martyre de Saint Sébastian*, M. Pierné conducted the *Nocturnes* and M. Inghelbrecht a selection from *Pelléas*. All three gave very satisfactory performances, but the most striking thing of the evening was Toscanini's rendering of *La Mer*. This was a magnificent performance of a work that is notoriously difficult. The only other item of the programme was an interesting experiment which must be acknowledged as a failure: *L'Après-midi d'un faune* was received by wireless from Easel, conducted by Weingartner. Unfortunately the transmission was poor, the timbre of the instruments being so much impaired as to be rendered at times unrecognizable.

[35] Marcel Mihalovici (1898–1985), French composer of Rumanian origin.
[36] Jean Cartan (1906–31).
[37] Jacques Beers (1902–47), Dutch student of Boulanger.
[38] Felix Labunski (1892–1979), Polish composer, student of Boulanger and Dukas, emigrated to the US in 1936.

The season of Russian opera and ballet at the Opéra Comique was a great success, the chief attraction being Chaliapin, who sang in *Boris Godunov*, *Prince Igor* and *Mozart and Salieri*. The ballet under the direction of Mme. Nijinska included a revival of *Les Biches* and a new ballet danced to Casella's suite *Scarlattiana*.

We have been very well provided for in the way of ballet lately, for simultaneously with the ballets at the Opéra Comique the Ballets Russes de Monte Carlo gave a short season at the Champs Elysées. They produced some remarkably good new ballets, the best we have seen here since the death of Diaghilev – in fact they were very much in the Diaghilev tradition, and critics spoke of 'the renascence of the Russian ballet'. Boris Kochno's ballet *Jeux d'enfants* was particularly successful; the ballet was made to a series of delightful pieces by Bizet (written originally for piano duet), the scenery was by Miro and the choreography by Massine. The other new ballets were *La Concurrence* – ballet and scenery by Dérain, music by Auric and choreography by Balanchine; *Cotillon*, another ballet by Kochno to a selection of Chabrier's music and with very clever scenery and costumes by Christian Bérard, and *Le Bourgeois gentilhomme*, after Molière, to Strauss's music. All the ballets were good and the dancing excellent throughout. Great excitement was caused by the fact that the première danseuse was a prodigy of only sixteen – Tamara Toumanova. She has a technique of extraordinary virtuosity, and a gracefulness and charm that make her already a great dancer. The troupe also includes Leon Woizikovsky, who is an old friend of all lovers of ballet, and an excellent young dancer David Lichine who shares with him the most important parts.

The Salle Pleyel is perhaps a little large for a trio, even when the trio is made up of Cortot, Thibaud and Casals, nevertheless the three concerts at which they played all Beethoven's trios were unforgettable, and drew enormous and enthusiastic audiences.

There has not been very much new music, but some interesting new things were played at a chamber concert of works written for the Vicomte de Noailles. The composers represented were Markevitch, Nabokov, Poulenc and Sauguet. Sauguet's work for voice and small orchestra was pleasing, and is probably the best thing that he has done so far; Markevitch's *Galop* for piano and small orchestra is clever and strikes a personal note. Poulenc's *Le Bal masqué* (poem by Max Jacob), for voice and a small number of instruments, was perhaps the most enjoyable work of the evening. It is very typical of Poulenc, tuneful and witty, and carried along with great brio from beginning to end. It is extremely well orchestrated, and one notices particularly the progress that Poulenc has made in this side of his art.

December 1932

Nothing very remarkable has happened in the musical world here so far this season, but we are promised good things. It is to be hoped that the concert agents will succeed in avoiding having all their star turns at the same time – last year there were many unfortunate clashes.

A new orchestra has been formed by the Pathé-Natan film company which is to be specially employed in music for the screen. This orchestra gave a concert at the end of September by way of announcing its existence; it proved an excellent body of players, a great many of whom are drawn from the other orchestras. Part of the programme was conducted by Vladimir Golschmann, who is already well known here, and part by Maurice Jaubert, who made a successful debut. But his very slow tempo in the Gavotte of Bach's Suite in D turned a lively dance into a very solemn affair. It is right to treat Bach with reverence and awe, but why should he not be allowed his lighter moments? It is to be hoped that this excellent orchestra will have opportunities of exercising its particular function and that we shall have some really good music to accompany new films, for so far, with a very few exceptions, one has heard no film music that was worthy of a full orchestra.

A new society for the performance of chamber music, Le Triton, has also been formed. Whether there is a large enough musical public to supply audiences for yet another musical society is a matter of doubt. There are certainly enough composers living here to provide new works, and almost enough to provide a good-sized audience. I have been to concerts in which the audience appeared to be entirely made up of them. However, the committee of the new society includes Honegger, Milhaud and Prokoviev, so a good standard of new music may reasonably be hoped for.

The Paris Symphonic Orchestra has already given several concerts under Pierre Monteux, at one of which a new symphony by a young French composer, Jean Françaix, was played.[39] Unfortunately the audience was quite the wrong one on which to try very modern music by a very young and rather inexperienced composer, for it consisted mainly of admirers of the singer Georges Thill (of the Opéra), who sang at the same concert. It manifested its disapproval in no uncertain manner, until the conductor requested people to refrain from making those odd noises in which French audiences indulge when confronted with music they do not understand (unless it be written by a well-known composer, in which case it is, of course, acceptable). As a matter of fact this symphony, by a composer aged only nineteen, is a remarkable work. It lacks breadth and melody somewhat, and probably has not much permanent value, but it gives great promise, and such an early mastery of form and orchestration is astonishing.

Another new series of concerts this season is being organized by Alfred Cortot at the École normale. It is a semi-educational series given mainly for the benefit of students. At the first concert Cortot conducted part of the programme himself. Brahms's Serenade, op. 16 – a work almost unknown in Paris – was given, and the rest of the programme included Ravel's *Hebrew Songs*, two works by Prokoviev (Overture for seventeen instruments and *Waltzes on themes by Schubert* for two pianos), and *Three Pieces* for five wind instruments by Jacques Ibert.

Several virtuosi have already made their appearance. Horowitz played Rachmaninov's Third Concerto with the Paris Symphonic Orchestra, Mischa Elman gave a recital, and Segovia played at the first of a series of concerts organized by the *Revue Musicale*. Also a regular epidemic of infant prodigies seems to have

---

[39] Jean Françaix (1912–97), prolific French composer and brilliant pianist, who studied with Boulanger who conducted several of his works. The early symphony that Berkeley heard was withdrawn, but Françaix's international career had already been launched with his *Eight Bagatelles* for string quartet and piano at the ISCM Festival in Vienna that year.

broken out – two violinists and a pianist, all, I think, under ten, have played or are to play during this season, not to mention Menuhin, who, however prodigious, is now hardly an infant.[40]

March–April 1933

The most sensational concert that we have had here recently was undoubtedly the one given by La Sérénade at which Kurt Weill's operas *Mahagonny* and *Der Jasager* were performed. These works are interesting in the highest degree. In the first place they are remarkable in that they represent a successful attempt to adapt opera to modern conditions, for they require an absolute minimum of scenery, costumes and lighting. The fact that they were given in a concert hall is a proof of this. They are short, and only need a small body of singers, and are scored for small orchestra.

Mahagonny, which was given in its original form, is the lighter of the two, and the style throughout is that of the popular music of today. Jazz effects are continually used – in fact, the orchestra resembles a jazz-band rather than a normal theatre orchestra, being composed of trumpets, trombones, saxophones, percussion, guitar, banjo, and a few strings. And yet the music is very far removed from ordinary jazz – it is simpler, more melodic, and much stronger in harmony; also there is something profoundly German about it, as there was in the same composer's music to the film *Die Dreigroschenoper*; which removes it still further from what one associates with the word jazz.

Der Jasager is in a very different style, being nearer to the neo-classicism of Hindemith and other modern composers. This opera was written to be performed by schoolboys and was performed by them here. There are only two grown-up parts, the other principal roles and the chorus being taken by boys. The story is taken from the Japanese, and translated into German from Arthur Waley's English version. The orchestra consists of two pianos, harmonium, three violins, cello and double-bass, percussion and three wind instruments, the latter being ad libitum. This opera is certainly one of the most successful attempts to simplify modern music that has yet been made, for it is not only easy to understand but also to play and sing, and yet it is new and original, so that one feels that Weill has to a large extent solved one of the greatest difficulties with which the modern composer is faced.

At the same concert Manuel de Falla's magnificent but extremely difficult Concerto for Harpsichord was played. There was also the first performance of a Piano Sonata by Auric which was very tedious to listen to. One felt that the composer was forcing himself to write in the grand manner, as though he wished to prove that he could use a more serious style than that which he usually adopts; but apart from some successful exploiting of piano technique, he proved, I think fairly conclusively, that he couldn't.

One of the most interesting new works that have been played here lately is Stravinsky's *Duo concertant* for violin and piano, which was performed by Samuel

---

[40] Yehudi Menuhin (1916–1999), one of the outstanding violinists of the century and a child prodigy, was born in New York. He recorded Elgar's Violin Concerto under the composer in 1932; he commissioned Berkeley's Violin Concerto, op. 59, in 1961.

Dushkin and the composer himself. The work is profound in feeling and, though it is impossible to give any critical appreciation of it after one hearing, Stravinsky's consummate mastery of form and unity of style afford a sense of aesthetic satisfaction that perhaps no other living composer can give one as strongly. The movement called Eglogue II and the Gigue are particularly striking, the former on account of its great melodic beauty, and the latter by reason of its rhythmical power, and the fact that, in spite of its speed, it makes an impression of calm and serenity.

The new chamber-music society Le Triton gave its first concert on December 16. The programme consisted of a String Quartet by László Lajtha,[41] a Sonata for two violins by Prokoviev, Fauré's *L'Horizon chimérique* magnificently sung by Mme. Croiza,[42] a Sonatina for violin and cello by Honegger and Roussel's Quartet, op. 4. Of the new works Prokoviev's Sonata was the most successful, and was characteristic in its vigour, freedom and richness of invention. The Honegger was disappointing and was noticeably lacking in new ideas. Roussel's Quartet is very well written, but, like a good deal of his music, seems always to be on the verge of being very good, and leaves one with a feeling of dissatisfaction.

Two important new orchestral works by Prokoviev have been given here lately – the ballet *Sur le borysthène*, produced by Lifar at the Opéra, and a new piano concerto [no. 5] played at the Pasdeloup concerts with the composer as soloist. The ballet I was unfortunately unable to hear, but it is said to be disappointing. In the Concerto, Prokoviev seems to have been carried away by his amazing virtuosity as a pianist. The work, though powerful, lacks the simplicity of his best compositions, and he seems 'inebriated with the exuberance' of his own technique.

Of Ravel's new Piano Concerto for the left hand there is no need for me to speak, since it has already been given in London. It was performed here for the first time on January 17 by Paul Wittgenstein, with the composer conducting.

A concert of the orchestral works of Charles Koechlin was given recently.[43] It was interesting to hear the works of a musician who is so well known and so much respected as a teacher; but as a composer he seems to lack some necessary and indefinable quality. One rarely hears music which is so well constructed and in a way so original, and yet which fails to satisfy. The programme included a setting for voices and orchestra of poems, translated into French, from Kipling's *Jungle Book*, two Fugues, and five *Chorals dans le style des modes du moyen-âge*.

June 1933

The regular orchestral concerts are now at an end, but the season is in full swing, and the usual series of concerts given by foreign conductors and recitals by virtuosi is announced. Indeed, the latter seem to regard a recital in Paris during May or

---

[41] László Lajtha (1892–1963), Hungarian composer, conductor and ethnomusicologist, whose music was banned by the communist regime after 1956.

[42] Claire Croiza (1882–1947), influential French mezzo-soprano and teacher.

[43] Charles Koechlin (1867–1950). *La Course de printemps: symphonic poem after Kipling's Jungle Book*, op. 95. The concert was given on 29 November 1932 during a Koechlin Festival.

June as essential to the maintenance of their reputation, with the result that there are so many concerts that all but the most stout-hearted concert-goers may well feel inclined to give up the unequal struggle.

The usual winter season of orchestral concerts (Pasdeloup, Lamoureux, Colonne, Straram, etc.) finished shortly before Easter. They maintained on the whole their usual good standard of playing, and also, with the exception of the Straram programmes and one or two furtive excursions into the works of contemporary composers in the others, their usual sameness and lack of originality in the choice of music. However, French musicians have the faculty of throwing themselves wholeheartedly into whatever they are playing, even when a work is so familiar to them that they could play it in their sleep.

The Straram orchestra is perhaps the best in Paris at the moment, and that which gives the greatest number of first performances. M. Straram has done more for young and unknown composers than any other conductor here.[44] In almost every programme he finds room for one new work. Moreover, his programmes are always excellently composed, and have the merit of not being too long – an important point here, where the lack of sufficient ventilation in theatres and concert halls reduces one to a state of partial suffocation long before the end of the average performance. The first Straram concert illustrated very well the type of programme: it consisted of Bach's *Third Brandenburg Concerto*, Beethoven's Fifth Symphony, a *Prélude chorégraphique* by Claude Delvincourt,[45] and Stravinsky's *Firebird*. Delvincourt's work is really an overture for his ballet *Le Bal vénitien*, which has been accepted for performance, though not yet given, at the Opéra Comique. It is a clever and brightly-coloured score, and would certainly make good theatrical music, though on the concert platform it rather lacks originality.

Another interesting first performance here was that of an orchestral suite taken from Casella's new opera *La Donna serpente*, played by Albert Wolf's orchestra and conducted by the composer. Casella's music is always clever, and if his ideas are not always of the highest order, he excels in the manner of presenting them. This work has perhaps more breadth of feeling and spontaneity than most of his music, though it is difficult to form any opinion from an extract. At the same concert Casella's Partita for piano and orchestra was played – a lively and in some ways an attractive work, but spoilt by a lack of unity of style.

A great impression was made here by the two concerts given by the Greek conductor Dimitri Mitropoulos, who is also an excellent pianist, and performed the unusual feat of playing, and at the same time conducting, a piano concerto. At his first concert he began with an admirable transcription for full orchestra of Bach's Prelude and Fugue in B minor for organ. The Fugue was particularly magnificent, and the unexpected countersubject towards the end was brought out with a force that was perhaps not intended by the composer, but was extraordinarily

---

[44] Walter Straram (1876–1933) founded his orchestra in 1926 and it occupied a prominent position in Parisian musical life until his death. He gave many important premieres; performed Berkeley's Suite (1927) at the Salle Pleyel on 16 February 1928; but no other British works.

[45] Claude Delvincourt (1888–1954), Director of the Paris Conservatoire during the German occupation.

effective. After this, Schoenberg's *Verklärte nacht*, written for string sextet in 1899 and arranged for string orchestra in 1917, was given in the latter version. It was interesting to hear this rarely performed work, in which, though the influence of Wagner is clearly felt, the harmony already shows traces of the composer's later style. The programme continued with Brahms' Second Piano Concerto, in which Mitropoulos played the piano part, conducting, or rather controlling, the orchestra at the same time. It was a remarkable performance, for he not only played the solo part with great vigour and efficiency, but secured at the same time a very good ensemble from the orchestra. The concert ended with Beethoven's overture *Leonora* no. 2.

December 1933

The three concerts given recently by the Orchestre Straram are undoubtedly the most important musical events that have taken place so far this season.

Two concerts only were announced, but such a large number of people could not get seats that the second had to be repeated. The first concert consisted of modern, or comparatively modern, French and Italian works only. Italy was represented by Pizzetti and Respighi – a curious choice, for though both composers have a very sound technique – Respighi, as everyone knows, is a master of orchestration – their lack of originality made them compare unfavourably with the French composers. Pizzetti's *Concerto dell'estate* is a well-constructed but peculiarly unattractive work, while Respighi's *Pines of Rome*, in spite of the composer's great skill and imagination, remains second-rate and vulgar; at the moment when a door was opened at the back of the platform, and a record of a real nightingale singing was incorporated into one of the movements, the audience had some difficulty in refraining from laughter. The rest of the programme consisted of Berlioz's Scherzo from *Queen Mab*, Debussy's *Prélude à l'après-midi d'un faune*, Dukas' *L'Apprenti sorcier*, and Ravel's *Daphnis et Chloé* (second suite). Toscanini's conducting on this occasion confirmed the general opinion here that no conductor in the world can surpass him; the perfect clearness and exactitude of every phase was amazing. I was unable to go to the second concert, which was an all-Wagner programme, but I had the privilege of attending one of the rehearsals, and realized that part of his power lies in the fact that nothing escapes him.

Two concerts of considerable interest were those given by the Kammerchor of Basle. The lack of good choirs in France is well known and much deplored, so that the musical public was glad of this opportunity of hearing some choral music. Unfortunately the Kammerchor was disappointing. The tone was woolly, and there was an absence of attack, which made everything sound alike. On the other hand the intonation was good and the actual music which was sung was of the greatest interest. The first concert was entirely given up to religious music, beginning with plainsong melodies, continuing with excellent examples of the polyphonic school, and ending with Stravinsky's *Symphonie de psaumes*. Some of the most beautiful works of the old Italian masters, including Palestrina's 'Sicut cervus' and 'Pueri hebraeorum' and the magnificent *Crucifixus* of Antonio Lotti, were given, and also, in a later style, Schütz's 'Ich danke dem Herrn'. Another interesting work was a beautiful 'De Profundis' by Gluck. Stravinsky's *Symphonie* was in keeping with the other works; it was curious to lay alongside them, as it were, a modern expression of the religious spirit. At the second concert the Kammerchor gave a performance of Mozart's *Idomeneo*. It is difficult to understand how it is that this work has always been a failure, for it contains some of the loveliest and most characteristic music that Mozart ever wrote. The performance was not all that one could have wished, but one was grateful for the opportunity of hearing this rarely-given work.

Honegger's *Troisième mouvement symphonique* is practically the only new work that has been heard so far this season. It has already been played in Berlin and in London. Great things, however, are announced by Mme. Ida Rubinstein for her season at the Opéra which will probably take place in March. Stravinsky's new work *Perséphone* written specially for her, is, I understand, finished, while Ravel is still at work on a composition which she has commissioned.

June 1934

Madame Ida Rubinstein's performances at the Opéra, which are now in full swing, constitute the most important musical event of the early part of the season.[46] Curiously enough, the opening night coincided with the first night at Covent Garden and drew the same type of audience, though to a very different programme. It is difficult to find a word which describes these performances, for they are neither operas nor ballets; here they call them 'spectacles', and indeed, with their gorgeous scenery and elaborate lighting, they are nearer the 'spectacle de Music Hall' than anything else. If Mme. Rubinstein's performances are not very much to the taste of those who would prefer to see real ballet, one cannot be too grateful to her for commissioning music from such composers as Stravinsky, Ravel and Honegger.

The outstanding work in this year's programme is undoubtedly Stravinsky's *Perséphone*. The Greek myth has been arranged by M. André Gide for theatrical performance. His poem contains three principal elements: the story itself which is sung by a solo voice, commentaries and descriptive passages which are sung by the chorus, and the part of Persephone herself to be recited 'against the music', to use that rather unfortunate but apt phrase. It is presented in one act and three tableaux without any break. Besides this, there is a certain amount of action on the stage illustrating the story and consisting mainly of rhythmic movement and poses. To those who are familiar with Stravinsky's later works, the style of *Perséphone* will not be a surprise, for it is a continuation and development of that used in such works as *Oedipus rex*, the *Symphonie de psaumes*, the Capriccio, the Violin Concerto, and the *Duo concertante*. It is music that has been ruthlessly stripped of every element that is not purely musical, and it is this austerity and restraint that many people find so disconcerting. There are no orchestral effects in this score, and one would listen in vain for those purple passages so dear to conductors – and to audiences. Every note is an essential part of the music itself and the orchestral colour is never a mere embellishment. The vocal writing recalls the Italian bel canto, but the

---

[46] Ida Rubinstein (1885–1960), Russian ballerina, actress and celebrated patron. After appearing with Diaghilev's Ballets Russes from 1909–11 she formed her own company.

accompaniment is treated in a very different and most original way, for it frequently forms free counterpoints round the vocal parts in the manner of an obbligato, and although it accompanies the vocal part, it seems itself to spring from a melodic rather than a harmonic basis. Though certain phrases may remind one of the old Italian composers such its Alessandro Scarlatti or Pergolesi, that work is in no way a pastiche, for Stravinsky has the power of using style for his own purposes, and *Perséphone* is as characteristic of him as *Petroushka*.

Honegger's music to *Semiramis* is a very different matter; in fact it represents the opposite tendency in modern music. It is almost entirely atonal (whereas with Stravinsky the tonality is always clearly felt), it is a succession of heavy crushes of sound, as opposed to clear contrapuntal lines, and it is romantic in spirit rather than classical. An interesting innovation in this score is the use of M. Martenot's Instrument à ondes.[47] This instrument, invented some years ago, has often been described, but very few people have heard it, and I think this is the first important orchestral work in which it has been employed. Its tone somewhat resembles that of the human voice, and it has tremendous powers of crescendo and diminuendo in addition to a very extended compass. In this work it is chiefly used for melodic purposes with an orchestral background; one unison passage with the violins produced a very striking effect. Both in *Perséphone* and in *Semiramis* there are important passages of recitation with orchestral accompaniment. In neither work were these passages very satisfactory: the music prevented one from hearing the words, and the voice made it difficult to listen to the music. It is bad enough not to hear the words in singing, but when they are spoken it becomes absurd.

The other new work staged by Mme. Rubinstein was *Diane de Poitiers*. For this, music by the French composers of the Renaissance, very cleverly orchestrated by Jacques Ibert, was used. M. Ibert had added certain dances of his own composition which, although modern in treatment, harmonized very well with the rest of the music. The work was much appreciated by the public. Mme. Rubinstein had also commissioned a new work from Ravel, who unfortunately fell ill and was unable to complete it. *La Valse* and the rather overworked *Boléro* were given in place of the new ballet, which it is to be hoped will be heard on another occasion.

---

[47] The Ondes Martenot, named after its inventor Maurice Martenot (1898–1980), used by Honegger in *Jeanne d'Arc au bucher* and in many works by Messiaen.

– *Part II* –
Letters to Nadia Boulanger, 1929–74

INTRODUCTION

Nadia Boulanger (1887–1979) had an enormous influence as one of the leading teachers of composition in the twentieth century, especially on her American students, who included Aaron Copland, Walter Piston and Elliott Carter. Her father, Ernest Boulanger (1815–1900), was a successful composer and teacher who won the Prix de Rome in 1836, and her mother, who was a pupil of his, was a domineering woman of obscure Russian origins forty years younger than her husband. Raïsa Boulanger, who claimed unsubstantiated aristocratic origins, seems never to have been satisfied with anything and this demanding approach was transferred to her daughter's attitude to education. Léonie Rosenthal concludes that 'no one could entirely please Nadia Boulanger'.[1] As Boulanger was growing up, musical training in Paris was rigorously conventional and deviously political – nepotism and lobbying were rife. Aspiring students had to go through an elaborate series of labyrinthine contests that might end up with the coveted Prix de Rome. Nadia, who entered the Paris Conservatoire at the age of ten, just missed it, coming second, but her ailing younger sister Lili (1893–1918) was the first woman to win it in 1913 at a time of strong prejudice against women composers.

As a composer herself, Nadia soon preferred to fall under the shadow of her precocious younger sister and she took many opportunities to promote her work. Nadia bitterly resented her sister's early death; almost always thereafter she dressed in black, and marked the anniversary every year, as the letters from Berkeley show.

To say that Boulanger was a dedicated teacher is a serious understatement. She drove herself relentlessly and would often teach from 7.00 in the morning until after midnight. She continued teaching into her final years when she was virtually blind and deaf. Although she was a pioneer in promoting early music – her recordings of Monteverdi in the 1930s were a revelation – her range was not as comprehensive as might have been expected. She was not enthusiastic about Bartók and took permanent offence when he sent what she regarded as an inadequate reply to her letter of enquiry in 1924. Although initially interested in the Second Viennese School she soon passed over Schoenberg and later on even Messiaen, who was organist at the Trinité, which was her own parish and where she must have heard his music countless times. She idolised Bach, the Viennese classics and Stravinsky. It is hard to find a Boulanger pupil who has not absorbed neo-classical Stravinsky at a profound level – the best of them then moved on to find their own personalities. She conducted the premiere of Stravinsky's *Dumbarton Oaks Concerto* in America in 1938 and even had a role in its commissioning.

As a performer Boulanger was active as pianist, organist and conductor in Paris and elsewhere. She substituted for Fauré at the Madeleine and developed a career with the eminent pianist Raoul Pugno (1852–1914), often in two-piano repertoire,

[1] Léonie Rosenstiel, *Nadia Boulanger: a Life in Music* (New York, 1982).

which lasted until he died – in Moscow on a concert tour with Boulanger which was cancelled when Rachmaninov refused to stand in. It was an odd relationship with Pugno, where Boulanger was invariably regarded as a mere assistant even though they wrote an opera together which has never been staged. Pugno had a country house in Gargenville outside Paris which became the setting for summer events. Inevitably tongues wagged about the relationship between Boulanger and Pugno, but Gabriele D'Annunzio observed it and concluded: 'it is certainly the first time that a virgin has inseminated an old impotent'.

Boulanger lived with her mother and, after her father's death, she provided the funds to maintain their large fourth-floor apartment with their elaborate soirées at what was then 36 rue Ballu but was later renamed Place Lili Boulanger (see plate 7). These demands lasted until her mother's death in 1935.

Boulanger made headlines in the 1930s as the first woman to conduct major orchestras in London and in the USA, and in 1938 she gave what may have been the first British performance of the Requiem by Gabriel Fauré, her old teacher. Her lectures in heavily accented English were increasingly in demand, especially in America, where she spent six years during the war – with some misgivings. On 17 March 1941 she wrote to Stravinsky: 'I didn't know how much I loved France, how much I need her, and how much, in her weakness, I would feel her greatness. How we have served her poorly, we Frenchmen, whose flesh and spirit were formed by her, her traditions, her faith ...'[2]

She believed in American composers and thought that American music was taking off just as Russian music had done in the mid-nineteenth century. She was right and she recognised the involvement of jazz as an ingredient in creating a specifically American idiom.

Boulanger was generous to impoverished students and frequently helped them with introductions to aristocratic sponsors. She was a founder member of the Conservatoire Américain at Fontainebleau in 1921, where Copland came that year, and she became Director in 1948. An outstanding example of her generosity to her best students was when she gave the premiere of Copland's *Symphony for Organ and Orchestra* with the New York Symphony Orchestra under Walter Damrosch on 11 January 1925 – and she introduced Copland to Koussevitsky with extensive consequences just as he took up his post with the Boston Symphony. These letters show how she conducted works by Berkeley and helped to introduce him to performers. In return he dedicated pieces to her and constantly told her how much he owed to her encouragement.

The letters have been selected and annotated from the collection at the Bibliothèque nationale, Paris, by kind permission of Dominique Merlet, President of the Centre internationale Nadia et Lili Boulanger, and Lady Berkeley for the Berkeley Estate.

Some of the letters are undated but other evidence has confirmed some dates – those in square brackets are editorial. Most of the letters are in French but later on they are mixed. Translations are by the editor with assistance from Oliver Goulden.

[2] In Kimberly Francis, 'Nadia Boulanger, Igor Stravinsky, and the Symphony in C', *Musical Quarterly* 94 (2011), 250.

Footnotes have been provided to explain the context behind the letters and the people involved. Most of the letters from Boulanger to Berkeley have not survived. Quotations from the few that have, and from other correspondents, are courtesy of the Britten-Pears Library.

Berkeley wrote to Boulanger as Mademoiselle until 30 October 1969, when he addressed her as Nadia. He signed himself simply as Lennox rather than Lennox Berkeley from 1934.

LETTERS 1929–74

19 rue du Mont Cenis, Paris XVIII
4 December 1929

I forgot to give you my address in London … I shall be c/o John Greenidge Esq., 28 Great Ormond Street, London W.C.1.[3]

I was very excited about Gieseking[4] the day before yesterday: he is a great musician. I think you were not there, and that troubles me, because you have missed something extraordinary. He played the *Kinderszenen*[5] unforgettably – everything with him is so inward, true and simple that one loves the music even more, and in a new way after hearing it.

I hope that Madame Boulanger is well. I often think of her – because of my mother I understand the position a little, and what it means for you[6] …

19 rue du Mont Cenis, Paris XVIII
15 November [1930]

I forgot to tell you the other day that I have written, at the request of the editor of an English musical periodical, an article where I have discussed you as a teacher – they have just asked for a few words about my impression of your attitude to music – the teaching of music.

I have discussed you quite impersonally, naturally. I hope you won't mind since I do not want the article to appear without your consent. Do not trouble to reply if you agree.[7]

I rehearsed my songs with M. Sautelet[8] yesterday and I am very pleased with his

---

[3] John Theodore Waterman Greenidge (1899–1953), architect and lifelong friend, who painted a portrait of Berkeley.

[4] Walter Gieseking (1895–1956), German pianist who made his Paris debut in 1928. See also Berkeley's reports for the *Monthly Musical Record*, 1 May 1931, reprinted at pp. 24 and 28 above.

[5] Schumann: *Scenes from Childhood*, op. 15.

[6] Both their mothers were ill.

[7] Berkeley's article follows below. It is typical of the many tributes he wrote or broadcast over the years.

[8] Charles Sautelet sang the five songs of *Tombeaux* (poems by Jean Cocteau) with Berkeley at the piano at the Société musicale indépendante in the Salle Gaveau on 1 June 1927. (In the same programme Ravel was the pianist in his own Violin and Piano Sonata.) A version

interpretation – he has a very interesting programme – with quite a lot of English music which is rare here. God knows there is not much good English music, but it exists all the same – and I think that instead of complaining that there isn't any, it is better to benefit from what there is. So few musicians know Purcell and Byrd and the English composers of that period.

Nadia Boulanger as Teacher by Lennox Berkeley, *The Monthly Musical Record*, January 1931

In considering a great teacher of composition, one wonders to what extent composition can be taught at all; for examples spring to one's mind of musicians of great knowledge and impeccable technique who fail completely as composers, and of others full of talent and ideas who fail equally for lack of training and musical workmanship. One can only conclude that teaching in composition is useless in the case of people who have insufficient natural ability, but indispensable to those who have talent. Although a certain amount can be achieved by a man of great musical gifts without study, I know of no great composer whose talent alone has sufficed. All have had to go through the mill and master a certain amount of musical theory. Nor is this all: a young composer requires somebody who is capable of guiding his faltering steps, and of showing him how to develop his ideas and to present them in an intelligible form.

Nadia Boulanger is more than a teacher of counterpoint and fugue, and by this I do not mean merely that she also teaches the piano and the organ and lectures on musical form and interpretation, but that she is a teacher of the art of music as a whole, and has a positive genius for the training and development of the aesthetic sense of a composer. She infuses into her pupils that power of self-criticism and discipline which is so essential to the composer.

Let us consider her attitude towards music in general. The first thing that strikes us is the extreme catholicity of her taste. She loves passionately all good music, whether it be light or heavy, simple or complicated. A good waltz has just as much value to her as a good fugue, and this is because she judges a work solely upon its aesthetic content. To judge a work of art from other than the purely aesthetic standpoint is a failing to which I think English people are particularly

---

of *Tombeaux* with orchestra, dedicated to the conductor Anthony Bernard, was given in Paris the following year; the first British concert performance was on 10 February at the Aeolian Hall with Jeanne Dusseau; and Sophie Wyss gave the first BBC broadcast on 11 March 1929 – all under Bernard. Other performances of Berkeley's music in Paris at this period included: *Prelude, Intermezzo (Blues) and Finale* for flute (Gaston Blanquart), violin (Jeanne Isnard), viola (Boulay) and piano (Gordon Bryan) at the Salle des Agricultures on 27 January 1928; Sonatine for violin solo (Jeanne Isnard) at the Salle Chopin on 26 February 1929 (reviewed in *Le Menestral* on 8 March 1929 where Marcel Belvianes considered it well thought-out and charmingly written, though he found a tango for solo violin a challenge!); *Morceaux* for string quartet on 2 May 1930 – no venue listed, but the performers included the American composer Quincy Porter (1898–1966) who was studying in Paris for three years. Information from Michel Duchesneau, *L'Avant-garde musicale et ses sociétés à Paris de 1871 à 1939* (Sprimont, 1997), courtesy of Allan C. Jones.

prone. I therefore stress purposely this point in considering Nadia Boulanger's attitude towards music in general. Some people think that because you like Stravinsky you cannot also like Beethoven, or that an admiration of Johann Strauss is incompatible with a love of Bach. To Nadia Boulanger such an attitude would be incomprehensible. Different composers are different people, and their music has a different use. You cannot say that a comic opera is not as good as a Mass, any more than you can say that a saucepan is not as good as a top-hat, or that a tea-pot is not good because you cannot have a bath in it. In other words, the only thing necessary is to know whether or not a work is good music, and not to allow any other consideration to trouble your judgement.

As regards Nadia Boulanger's method in general, the chief points are: the study of the works of great masters (chiefly for form and orchestration), the writing of musical exercises, and the submitting to her of compositions. With regard to the first point, her system is to lecture at the piano on some work or series of works which the pupils have previously analysed by themselves. For instance, we have studied recently in class Beethoven's piano sonatas and string quartets, a large number of Bach's church cantatas, some early polyphonic music, Stravinsky's *Les Noces*, and works by Debussy and Ravel.

The musical exercises are the ordinary series involved in the study of counterpoint and fugue. These have to be done with absolute correctness, and if wrong, have to be done again until they are right.

It is, however, the advice given for actual composition that is the most valuable part of her teaching. Here the important thing to note is that she is very severe, but extremely impartial – that is to say, she is severe in condemnation of the least technical flaw or failing in unity of style, but impartial in that she admits any innovation that will come off. It does not matter what style you use so long as you use it consistently. This question of style is indeed a vital point, and it is the bugbear of the beginner or amateur composer. Anybody with talent can have good ideas, but very few can write a work on a big scale and yet preserve that unity of style which is essential to any good work of art.

Nadia Boulanger teaches that the composer must first be a good workman who knows his job, and that then only is he free to write what he likes, and to realize whatever ideas he has: that it does not matter how much drudgery you go through to gain that freedom, for a man must lose his life in order to find it, and in music he must lose his originality and personality in order to find them. Moreover, there is no risk in the case of a man who has really got something to say that he will become dry and pedantic through a severe technical training. It is true that a certain period of difficulty is often experienced by a composer who, having written a certain amount by the light of nature, applies himself to the study of theory. Whereas everything that he wrote seemed good to him before, now nothing does; and he stops and asks himself: 'What would the books say I ought to do now?', and the natural flow of the music is impeded. But this is only a phase. Little by little he begins to do the right thing subconsciously, and his acquired knowledge becomes a second instinct. Thus, in the experience of most people, the process is justified.

There is little more that one can say. It is extremely difficult to give an adequate idea of a great teacher, or to summarize those qualities which make any particular teacher a great one. The fact is that the chief quality is something indefinable, and unless one goes into the question of the psychology and moral character of the person concerned, one is obliged to leave it at that. I suppose you may say that a great teacher is one who possesses the power not only of imparting knowledge to people in such a way that they retain it, but also of making them catch a positive enthusiasm for the acquiring of that knowledge.

I think that the word enthusiasm gives us the key to Nadia Boulanger's power – it is a most infectious enthusiasm, and it is supported by an immense erudition, a keen intelligence and an open mind.

19 rue du Mont Cenis, Paris XVIII
[early 1931]

... I want to thank you for your kind note about my article – I was very touched. Thankyou for writing.

19 rue du Mont Cenis, Paris XVIII
22 September [1931]

I hope you received my Sonata.[9] I had the luck to try it out with an excellent violinist at Cannes before sending it to you – it generally sounds well, but there are some passages where I shall need your advice before making a final copy. ...

19 rue du Mont Cenis, Paris XVIII
21 November [1931]

I visited Dushkin[10] yesterday and played him my Sonata. He gives the impression of being interested and as soon as I have made the final version he wants me to take it to him so he can play it with Webster[11] to see how it sounds. He thinks it is very successful as violin music which is very encouraging. I told him that it was to be played at the S.M.I.[12] but I had not yet got a performer – but naturally I did not dare to ask him. If you see him, or if you have occasion to telephone him – would you speak to him about it? It would be so marvellous if he and Webster could give the premiere. I get the impression that Dushkin would do it if you asked him, and if his engagements allow.

[9] Violin Sonata no. 1 (1931) would be premiered 4 May 1932 at the École normale de musique by Yvonne Astruc and Madeleine Grovlez for the Société musicale indépendante. Another performance on 28 May at the same venue is listed in Duchesneau, *L'Avant-garde musicale et ses sociétés à Paris*.

[10] Samuel Dushkin (1891–1976), American violinist who studied with Fritz Kreisler; he made his European debut in 1918. In 1928 he worked with Stravinsky and gave the premieres of his Violin Concerto (1931), with the composer conducting, and the *Duo Concertante* (1932) for violin and piano with the composer at the piano.

[11] Beveridge Webster (1908–99), American pianist who studied at the Paris Conservatoire, winning a Grand Prix on graduation in 1926. He returned to the US in 1934.

[12] The Société musicale indépendante where Berkeley's First Violin and Piano Sonata would be performed – not by Dushkin and Webster – on 4 May 1932.

19 rue du Mont Cenis, Paris XVIII
10 December [1930 or 1931]

Please excuse me for not having come to the class this afternoon, but I have not quite finished the new version of my Concerto[13] and I have to send it on Friday at the latest to London for the jury of the International Festival of Contemporary Music.[14] I hate missing the class which is a real musical nourishment for me – but it was very important for me to send off my Concerto.

19 rue du Mont Cenis, Paris XVIII
17 December 1931

… My Symphony for Strings[15] went well in London. It was mostly very well received by the public. However, I am not so pleased because, although the form is good, the instrumentation is not very successful. Anyway – I have learned an enormous amount about stringed instruments and that is very useful.

I send you all my best wishes for the New Year and for Madame Boulanger's better health. …

19 rue du Mont Cenis, Paris XVIII
17 August [1932]

Let me first congratulate you with all my heart on your Legion d'Honneur[16] – I did not know until recently because I do not read newspapers when I am here. I was so delighted when I was told about it, above all to realise that people know something of what you have done for music and musicians and that all your work has been officially recognised.

Following your suggestion I am working on a second Sonata for Violin and Piano.[17] I had reached the last movement and would have finished it by now but I

---

[13] This could be a revised version of Berkeley's Concertino for Chamber Orchestra (now lost) premiered 6 April 1927 at a British Music Society concert in London under Anthony Bernard, and given again on 22 September at the Harrogate Festival – on the progamme as Concertino for Small Orchestra. On 23 September *The Times* claimed this as the 'first public performance', but the reviewer might have been star-struck by the fact that Elgar was there and conducted his Violin Concerto (with Albert Sammons as soloist), *Introduction and Allegro* for strings, and *Pomp and Circumstance March* no. 1. The review does not reveal who conducted the Berkeley, although it was probably Basil Cameron, who started the Festival. I wonder if Elgar heard it – and what he thought.

[14] The work was not selected. Berkeley's Overture, op. 8, was chosen for the ISCM in Czechoslovakia in 1935 but cancelled owing to local difficulties and it was included in the Barcelona Festival in 1936 where Berkeley met Britten, and his psalm *Domini est terra* was in the ISCM at London in 1938.

[15] Symphony for String Orchestra (1930), now lost. It was performed on 14 December 1931 at Queen's Hall, London, by the London Chamber Orchestra under Anthony Bernard.

[16] Boulanger was award the Chevalier of the Légion d'honneur in 1932 and the Grand Officier in 1977.

[17] Violin and Piano Sonata no. 2, Berkeley's official op. 1, published by Chester in 1934.

fell ill on getting here. I had to spend almost two weeks in bed – that held me up a bit. Now I am quite well and I bathe in the sea as often as possible. ...

I am very pleased with the Sonata so far – I dream of getting Dushkin to play it; do you think that would be possible? He has always been very nice to me and has often told me to show him my First Sonata – anyhow I am sure that if you ask him he would do it. Shall I send it to you when it is finished or would you rather I show it to you when you return to Paris?

19 rue du Mont Cenis, Paris XVIII
5 October 1932

... Your letter about my [Second] Sonata was a profound joy – you know that your approval means more than anything to me. So I regard that seriously as an order for if I wrote a hundred sonatas for you I could never repay the debt I owe you – and since, if you like this sonata, I hope you will allow me to dedicate it to you.

Have you been able to talk to Dushkin?

As I said to Mademoiselle Dieudonné,[18] if you do not need the sonata before I see you I should very much like to take it to England because I know many musicians over there and may be able to arrange a performance in London[19] ...

19 rue du Mont Cenis, Paris XVIII
27 February [1933]

I had to leave the concert before the end yesterday and I could not tell you how impressed I had been by the *Psalms*.[20] I find that there is an extraordinary grandeur and force in this music, and how well I understand the mixture of feelings – joy and sadness – you must have felt in hearing it!

I hope you found the performance adequate – everything sounded admirably, the orchestration is so secure.

28 Great Ormond Street, London W.C.1[21]
14 March [1933]

I am writing this little note to tell you that I shall be thinking of you tomorrow and that I am sorry not to be with you.[22] Since I have heard some of your sister's music

---

[18] Annette Dieudonné, Boulanger's assistant and devoted friend.

[19] Sonata no. 2, op. 1, was premiered 6 June 1933 at the Contemporary Music Centre in London by Orrea Pernel and Kathleen Long. The Paris premiere followed six days later – see n. 26 below.

[20] Stravinsky: *Symphony of Psalms*. See also Berkeley's 'Music in Paris' for *The Monthly Musical Record*, 1 May 1931, reprinted at p. 28 above.

[21] Berkeley shared this flat with his old friend John Greenidge until it was bombed during the war.

[22] Lili Boulanger (1893–1918), Nadia's sister, died on 15 March. Berkeley regularly referred to this anniversary in his correspondence with Boulanger.

it seems to me that I know her a little, and I understand more what this day of remembrance must be for you and Madame Boulanger.

Yesterday Stravinsky and Dushkin played almost the same programme they gave in Paris[23] – the *Duo Concertant* moved me deeply: it's a real chef d'œuvre – how can anyone think the music of Stravinsky is cold?! It is certainly bare, but justly stripped of all that does not come from the heart.

They played the *Duo* twice, which was good because one felt the audience had grasped it better the second time. Dushkin played admirably – it must have been difficult for him with M. Fairchild in his present state.[24]

I am going to visit Lord Berners next week.[25]

Domaine du Rayet, Falicon, Alpes Maritime
14 April [1933]

I am very sorry to have left Paris without being able to make definite arrangements with a violinist for my [Second] Sonata – but I cannot do anything myself, not knowing Soetans.[26]

I apologise for the trouble I am giving you in asking you to make an approach to Soetans – but I do not see any other way. It is the last chance. Dushkin certainly knows him because he played the Prokofiev Sonata for Two Violins with him in a concert at the Triton. But I shall write to Dushkin and ask him if he could speak to him about it – in case you are not able to do it yourself, but I think it would be better if it was you who asked him, if, of course, that is possible. ...

Olvido, Falicon, Alpes Maritime
[summer 1933]

... I want to thank you again for having made the performance of this [Second] Sonata possible – it was very encouraging for me.[27] And perhaps for you too, for

---

[23] They played the *Duo concertant* at the BBC on 13 March and again at their Queen's Hall recital the following year when *The Times* (28 February 1934) lamented that Stravinsky's works were now 'much less spontaneous than those he wrote in the carefree days of the Diaghilev ballet' and found his piano playing 'monotonous and toneless' in the half-empty Queen's Hall.

[24] Blair Fairchild (1877–1933), American composer who had supported Dushkin in his studies and died the following month.

[25] Lord Berners (1883–1950), fourteenth baron, composer, writer, painter and famous eccentric. Berkeley told me that it was probably in 1933 that he went to dinner with Berners in London, where Boulanger was also a guest and after that meeting Berners introduced Berkeley to his own publisher, J. & W. Chester. See Dickinson *The Music of Lennox Berkeley*, 44–5.

[26] Robert Soetans, French violinist who commissioned Prokofiev's Second Violin Concerto. Soetans did give the French premiere of Berkeley's second sonata with Jacques Février on 14 June 1933 at an SMI concert. It was favourably reviewed in *Le Ménestral* on 23 June 1933: 'a sonata which appeals through its abundance and scope, both compelling and profound. A truly beautiful peroration crowns this passionate and strong work.'

[27] The Soetans and Février performance in Paris.

you were very patient with me – and if what I do begins to resemble real music, I owe it very much to you. ...

> Villa Melfort, avenue centrale, St. Jean Cap Ferrat, Alpes Maritime
> 3 January 1934

I thought this book would please you because I know you love Valéry.[28] I am sending it now with my best wishes for the New Year. ... I can never tell you what your influence has meant to me – not only for music but for life. ...

I have no news about my oratorio [*Jonah*], except that Beecham has it.[29] He will certainly have received your letter, but I fear he does not read French well – we shall have to wait. If you ever come across anyone who knows him you might perhaps speak to them about it. It is perhaps foolish to write a thing of this importance (material importance, not aesthetic!) when one is not known, but I think sometimes you have to play for high stakes. ...

> Villa Melfort, avenue centrale, St. Jean Cap Ferrat, Alpes Maritime
> [January 1935]

[Berkeley wishes Boulanger and her mother a happy New Year]

... I am working hard all the time. Do you think it would be possible to get my Overture played in Paris?[30] I can send you the score if you think that would help. As for these recitations on the poems of Pindar,[31] I fear that we shall never get them performed in their present form – perhaps I could make a new version for voice and orchestra. What do you think of that? If you feel it is worth the trouble I must ask you to be kind enough to send me back the manuscript. When are you going to be able to come and spend a little time on the Côte d'Azur? How happy I would be to see you here. Vere Pilkington[32] is here for Christmas ... we have played two-piano music. ...

[first surviving letter to Boulanger signed simply Lennox]

---

[28] Paul Valéry (1871–1945), poet, essayist and critic.

[29] Sir Thomas Beecham (1879–1961). This obviously got nowhere, but on 19 January 1948 Beecham conducted Berkeley's film music for *The First Gentleman* with the Royal Philharmonic Orchestra. See interview with Norman Del Mar, p. 230 below.

[30] Overture, op. 8, given on 1 October 1935 at Queen's Hall, London, with the BBC Symphony Orchestra conducted by the composer. Berkeley conducted it again when the Overture was done at the ISCM in Barcelona on 23 April 1936 – then he withdrew the work.

[31] See n. 40 below.

[32] Vere Pilkington (1905–83) was a fine amateur musician who much later became chairman of Sotheby's. He was the first of only two pupils of the influential early music pioneer Violet Gordon Woodhouse (1872–1948). His father gave him a harpsichord for his twenty-first birthday; Berkeley, who shared rooms with him in his last year at Oxford, wrote a five-movement suite for him in 1930 and began an association with early music instruments that lasted throughout his career. The suite survives but is still unknown.

Villa Melfort, avenue centrale, St. Jean Cap Ferrat, Alpes Maritime
19 January 1936

[following the death of Berkeley's mother on 17 December 1935]

Heartfelt thanks for your good and affectionate letter. You understand so well having suffered so much yourself. It is hard for me to get used to her absence, but I know that until my own death I shall need her every day. Yet I realise I ought not to grieve too much, because it is infinitely better for her – she suffered more and more – it was so frightful, and now her soul is liberated from her body which suffered so cruelly. Now I must not be too sad, for there is an element of 'self-pity' in that, as we say in English, and I feel that I ought to rejoice at this deliverance. It is now that faith is put to the test. I must not doubt for a single instant that her soul lives, and that one day I shall be able to rejoin her – for that is what I want more than anything in the world.

Strangely enough I feel that her influence on me is even stronger than when she was living, and that I have to try to be worthy of her. ...

I am trying to sell this house – it is useless for me to stay here now; I am staying for the moment to deal with business and also to finish my oratorio *Jonah* which the BBC are going to give in June, and which I have completely redone. They are already asking for the chorus parts to begin rehearsals and I am late, because of this sad event.

One of my mother's last joys was to hear my Quartet [no. 1] marvellously played by the Pro Arte Quartet – she had never heard my music well played.[33] She liked music and was pleased that I may be a musician...I think of you a lot – my mother's death brings me closer to you and we both live a little in another world, invisible but very real.

28 Great Ormond Street, London W.C.1
17 June [1936]

Just a word to tell you they are broadcasting *Jonah* on Friday 19th at 22.20. Try to listen if possible – it is on London National. How I wish you could be there! I think you have received the vocal score. Do not look too hard at the piano part – it is so difficult to make something playable.

The rehearsals are going well – the choirs are excellent.

The Princess de Polignac is going to come to the concert, and I think also to the rehearsal on Friday.[34]

I am fortunate to be performed in such favourable conditions. My oratorio is full of imperfections but I think there is also some good music and in any case it is in hearing it that I shall learn to do better. I hope you can manage to listen to it.

---

[33] The Pro Arte Quartet gave the premiere on 19 November 1935 at the Cowdray Hall, London: the BBC broadcast Berkeley heard with his mother was on December 9. The first quartet waited for a recording until 2006, when the Maggini Quartet recorded all three on Naxos 8 570415.

[34] Winaretta Singer, Princesse Edmond de Polignac (1865–1943), heir to the American Singer sewing-machine fortune and an important patron of contemporary composers.

28 Great Ormond Street, London W.C.1
[summer 1936]

Just a word to tell you that I've found a text that suits me, that what I've started will turn out well. It is Psalm 23 *Domini est terra*[35] – it is not very original to choose a psalm but it seems to me that with this text I can do more-or-less what I like.

As usual I am in frightful difficulties about getting going – my thoughts are always so confused at the start but sometimes I find a way forward all the same. So let's hope!

I hope to pass through Paris in the first week of August and I shall tell you as soon as I know exactly, so I can see you and show you what I have done.

1 Cité Chaptal, continued from 28 Great Ormond Street
Monday [autumn 1936]

... No point in telling you that I shall be entirely at your disposal during your visit, and that I count on you to tell me what I can do for you that would be helpful.[36] If you would simply like to tell me where you are, that would be easy. ...

Bernac[37] came yesterday. His pronunciation was already almost perfect, but I was able to help him with the few words he was not sure about.

28 Great Ormond Street, London W.C.1
Tuesday [17 November 1936]

I have not been able to tell you how good your talk was – I don't mean the material but the pronunciation. I heard it here and everything was perfectly clear and understandable. Undoubtedly people will already have told you, but your Professor of English congratulates you![38]

I've written to Mr Van Wyck[39] saying he needs an extra musician for the percussion at the concert at the Embassy.[40] I suppose there is still no possibility of augmenting the strings? Even two more violinists would make such a difference,

---

[35] *Domini est terra*, op. 10, dedicated to Boulanger and performed at the opening concert of the ISCM, on 17 June 1938 at Queen's Hall, London, and again on 8 September 1938 at the Three Choirs Festival in Worcester, revised and conducted by the composer.

[36] Boulanger visited London in November 1936 and late October and November 1937.

[37] Pierre Bernac (1899–1979), French baritone frequently accompanied by Poulenc. They gave a BBC recital together on 1 December 1936.

[38] Whilst Boulanger was in London she gave at least four talks for the BBC in November.

[39] Arnold van Wyck, concert agent, and sponsor along with the Princesse de Polignac and Robert Mayer of Boulanger's first visit.

[40] Berkeley's work was *Deux poèmes de Pindar* (initially called *Dithyramb and Hymn*) for chorus and small orchestra, dedicated to the Princesse de Polignac. Boulanger, making her debut in London conducted the official premiere on 24 November 1936 with the Oriana Madrigal Society Choir and the London Symphony Orchestra at Queen's Hall, London. *The Times* (25 November) applauded Boulanger for her 'complete concentration on the musical purpose of the work whatever its date or style' but failed to understand the Berkeley. However, she obviously thought highly enough of the work to conduct it again at Queen's Hall in 1937.

and frankly I fear the balance will be very poor with nothing but five string players. ...

The request to the Ambassador has succeeded – he authorises me to invite four people, providing their names.

Until tomorrow. ...

What a ravishing piece by Jean Françaix![41]

[The French Ambassador cancelled this concert on the day – 20 November – because of the funeral of the Minister of the Interior, Roger Henri Charles Salengro, who had committed suicide after having been falsely accused by the right-wing press, and the explosion at the State Powder Factory at Saint-Chamas, near Marseilles where many people were killed and injured.]

28 Great Ormond Street, London W.C.1
[21 November 1936]

I've just left the extra parts at the hotel. It hasn't been easy but we managed all the same. ...

I have decided to return [to London] on Monday to be able to attend the rehearsal.[42]

I think that at number 10 it ought to be in 3/4 – I forgot to mark it. The reprise of 6/8 a few bars later is marked[43] ...

28 Great Ormond Street, London W.C.1
18 December 1936

I am so pleased to know that you have performed my *Poèmes* at the Cercle[44] – it must have been good in a smaller hall. My friend Raffalli[45] has told me that you sent him an invitation – you are very kind, it gave him great pleasure. ...

I plan to come to Paris on January 15. I am in the process of arranging the third poem, *Ode*. I shall send it to you in a few days and then you can see if you would like to perform it with the others at the concert on the 26th.[46]

---

[41] Jean Françaix (1912–97), composer and pianist, child prodigy who studied with Boulanger, who had a high opinion of him.

[42] The French Embassy concert was rescheduled for 22 November. Britten had been due to play the piano part on 20 November but could not manage the new date and arranged a replacement with Millicent Silver. See John Evans, *Journeying Boy: the Diaries of the Young Benjamin Britten, 1928–38* (London, 2009), 390.

[43] *Deux poèmes de Pindar*. The manuscript score needs this adjustment: it has not yet been published.

[44] The Cercle interallié where Boulanger organised concerts during the winter season in Paris.

[45] N. José Raffalli, Berkeley's Corsican friend who shared his flat in Paris and was killed fighting in the resistance in about 1941.

[46] The issue seems unresolved. The *Ode* is a separate score and both that and the *Deux poèmes de Pindar* were left with Boulanger and emerged only after her death in 1979 after which her executors sent a collection of forgotten scores back to Berkeley.

Your concert at the Queen's Hall made a very profound impression, above all the Fauré – people are still talking about it a lot.[47]

Tuesday morning [probably 1937]

... The more I think about what you said about my Symphony [no. 1] the more I am sure you are right – there's no line.[48] I shall begin again – it is exactly what Walton has done very well, even if one does not like that sort of music.

I hope that you will be able to record *La Poulette grise* – I would be very pleased! I think it would sound well on a record – it is very clear. It seems to me that the Bourdariat would be good too, and since the tunes are well known, that would encourage people to buy the record.[49]

I cannot leave without sending you these flowers – I couldn't find words to tell you what you mean to me, and how grateful I am.

[no date or heading, but probably 1937]

... here is Walton's Symphony[50] – I do not think you will like it but because of our conversation on Saturday I would be very interested to know what you think. ...

Rudge House, Painswick, Gloucestershire[51]
4 January 1937

I was so touched that you thought about me and my dear mother. It is true that time does not lessen the separation: it is a sorrow one has to live with – that is all.

But it is also something that helps me and leads me to everything that is good, for when one has understood the grandeur of a mother's love all the rest becomes so small by comparison and only spiritual matters are important. You have known this for a long time, but previously I only knew it theoretically, so to speak, and this suffering was necessary for me. I also know now that I can live *for* my mother much as when she was with me, if not more: it is a thought which frightens me a little, but at the same time is the only thing that makes me feel like living. You must feel the same way and I know that it brings us much closer together.

I cannot tell you how much the extent of your confidence in me musically encourages me. It is infinitely precious, above all because I have so little fluency – I find more and more that music is horribly difficult. You support me in this struggle, as you do in the struggle of living. ...

---

[47] 24 November 1936. Boulanger's performances of the Fauré Requiem were widely praised.

[48] In a letter to Britten on 25 August 1936 Berkeley said he was starting on a symphony which it would take many years to write.

[49] *La Poulette grise* is an unpublished three-minute setting of a poem set for children's voices, trumpet and two pianos. As a folksong there are various versions in circulation. Les Bourdariat may refer to the source of tunes or lyrics. On 30 January 1952 in her letter to Berkeley Boulanger mentions the work and a possible performance in America.

[50] Sir William Walton (1902–83): Symphony no. 1 (1931–5). First performed with its first three movements on 3 December 1934, then complete on 6 November 1935, both with the LSO under Hamilton Harty.

[51] Berkeley was staying with Gladys Sophia Bryans.

28 Great Ormond Street, London W.C.1
17 March 1937

I must tell you how much I am thinking of you at this time[52] – how much I should like to be able to find words to say to what extent I share the sorrow that the separation brings you. But how does one speak of something so mysterious and so profound? One does not dare. In any case it is not with words that I could express myself; we understand each other better in our language; and it is through all the beauty that you have revealed to me – for I only understood half of it before knowing you – that I think of you. May it give you the courage to continue and to be happy in spite of everything.

28 Great Ormond Street, London W.C.1
23 July 1937

… I have finished my *Psalm* – I am in the process of copying it and I will send it to you in a few days. …

28 Great Ormond Street, London W.C.1
18 October 1937

Could you arrange to send Vadot the final version of my *Psalm* for him to make a photographic copy?…I want to make a version with orchestra and submit it to the ISCM next year, but this is very urgent – it has got to be ready before November 7. I do not know if you have succeeded in putting my Psalm into one of your programmes here [London] but I hope so.

Stravinsky is here for the first performance in London of *Jeux de cartes* – what a marvellous piece.[53] I have been to all the rehearsals and I see Stravinsky every day. One can learn so much about this truly astonishing man.

I am delighted to think that you will soon be here. Tell me if I can do anything for you before your arrival.[54]

Jonah went well at Leeds – very well received by the public but a frightful press.[55]

---

[52] Anniversary of Lili Boulanger's death.
[53] Berkeley attended the concert on 19 October with Britten.
[54] On Sunday 31 October Berkeley took Boulanger to the BBC Maida Vale Studio to hear Britten's *Variations on a Theme of Frank Bridge*.
[55] 7 October 1937. On 23 June 1936 Berkeley wrote to Britten, who had heard the BBC broadcast of the first performance: 'I can't tell you how pleased I was with your letter. It is the greatest encouragement to know that you appreciated *Jonah*.'

28 Great Ormond Street, London W.C.1
Friday [5 November 1937]

I didn't want to telephone you this morning because I thought so many people would.[56]

I didn't think that it would be possible to be so moved a second time, and yet I also know what the Requiem [Fauré] means to you and you know that it is the same for me.

You make people understand that real beauty is something very simple, which is a little disconcerting. I wish you could conduct more often – how good it would be if you could give all those people what you have given to us!

1 Cité Chaptal, Paris IX
29 December 1937

I am so touched that you thought of me.[57] Separation from those we love most continues to be just as painful. For me there is only the faith – the certainty of being together again one day, which makes it tolerable – also the understanding and affection of a small number of friends like you. It was so good to spend the day at Solesmes[58] – I must tell you about it – so could I ask you to telephone me when you have a free moment? We could talk even if only for a few minutes.

My *Psalm* has been accepted by the ISCM and will be given at the next Festival. I am very pleased about it because I must admit I have a special affection for this particular work, which *you* made me write.

I was moved by the death of Ravel,[59] as all musicians must be – he has given music something so personal – I've always loved this indefinable quality.

1 Cité Chaptal, Paris IX
10 January 1938

I am very late in sending you my wishes for the New Year – but if they are late they are no less sincere for that. I think of you so often, and of all that you have done for me for which I can never thank you enough.

I am in Paris for a short time and when I pass by rue Ballu I am very sad to think that you are far away.[60] I am working a lot – but I find it becomes harder and harder – the more one knows about music and life, the less one is satisfied with oneself. When I started I knew nothing, I found what I wrote very good

---

[56] Berkeley is writing the day after Boulanger's Queen's Hall concert on 4 November, where her programme included Rameau, Monteverdi, Haydn and, as in the previous year, Fauré's Requiem. Her conducting was again widely praised.

[57] Anniversary of his mother's death.

[58] Berkeley spent Christmas at the Benedictine monastery.

[59] 28 December 1937.

[60] Boulanger left Paris on 25 January to sail to the US, a few weeks after she had given a two-piano recital with Clifford Curzon including Berkeley's *Nocturne and Polka*, op. 5: the latter was encored. According to Tony Scotland, she played all three pieces with Jean Françaix in the US.

(!) and couldn't understand why everybody wasn't of the same opinion; now it's the opposite – I have had many encouragements, and it is I who am not satisfied. Anyway – I think it is always better to know what is good, even if one cannot achieve it.

I hope you are well – I am certain that you are killing yourself with work as usual, but I don't think anything can be done about that!

28 Great Ormond Street, London W.C.1
15 March 1938

Just a word to tell you that I am thinking of you – what more can I say?[61] I don't know what to say about such deep matters, but I can feel them, and that is how I can, in a way, share your memory. How I should like to be with you – unfortunately I can't come to Paris at the moment.

I have written the third piece for two pianos, as you requested, but it is not yet copied – would you like to send me your address in America so I can send it to you there?[62]

I should much like to hear from you, but you mustn't write: I know that you will be very busy. As for me, all goes well. I am working very hard, not always very well, but I'm doing my best. There are times when I ask myself if what I am doing is interesting enough for all the trouble I give myself, but I think everyone feels this way, apart from those who are very pleased with themselves and that is not a very good sign either!

I resent America for keeping you so long away from us, but no doubt you feel the change as beneficial since Paris has so many sad memories. I hope the Mass of Remembrance will be comforting.

28 Great Ormond Street, London W.C.1
25 June 1938

What a pity you weren't here yesterday. Copland has had a real triumph with his orchestral piece *El Salón México* which is astonishing.[63] Certainly along with Britten's Variations, a beautiful cantata by Krenek, and fragments of an oratorio by Burkhard it was the best – at least in my opinion.[64]

It was a pleasure to hear something that was not pretentious and cerebral – and Copland himself is a delightful man whom I was very pleased to see again.

---

[61] The anniversary of Lili Boulanger's death on 15 March 1918.

[62] Polka (published in 1934, also as a piano solo), Nocturne and Capriccio (both published in 1938), op. 5.

[63] Aaron Copland (1900–90) was probably Boulanger's greatest pupil, who, like Berkeley, never wavered in his wholehearted admiration for her.

[64] The 1938 ISCM Festival in London. Britten: *Variations on a Theme of Frank Bridge*; Ernst Krenek: Cantata for soprano, chorus and piano; Willi Burkhard: excepts from *The Vision of Isaiah*.

And let me say again how glad I was that you were there on the 17th[65] – it would be nice if we could look at the score of the Psalm together – I was not very satisfied but I don't know if it was my fault or a poor performance.

Domaine de Rayet, Falicon, Alpes Maritimes
24 July [1938]

Could you send me the copies you have of my Nocturne for two pianos?[66] I have just had a letter from Chester who tell me they now want to publish it and ask me to send it to them as quickly as possible because it is to be played at a recital in London in September and they want it to come out first. They also want to publish the Capriccio which I sent you in America – by the way, I don't know if you received it?

I was so pleased to be able to spend a moment with you. I hope to come to Paris again in October or November – there are so many things I should like to talk to you about and so many things I have written lately that have been played, but which you have never seen. Alas – life becomes such a struggle against time.

I think it would be better, if you don't mind, to send me the Capriccio too, because the other copies are with Rae Robertson and Ethel Bartlett who are away on holiday and I don't know where.[67] Forgive me, dear Mademoiselle, for this inconvenience but it's unavoidable.

I shall be at this address until August 10.

The Old Mill, Snape, Saxmundham, Suffolk[68]
30 September 1938

… I hope you are well. What a terrible moment we have passed through![69] One breathes again but I fear we can never feel safe while the present regime exists in Germany.

So, if we are left in peace, I expect to spend a fortnight in Paris around October 15 – 16 and I hope to see you. I think you are to come to London in November but I shall already have returned by then.

I am now spending most of the time here – it is so much better for working in the country – and for everything else. I share this house with Britten. I know it is dangerous to live with another composer, but so far, by an inexplicable miracle, we haven't come to blows.

---

[65] Performance of Berkeley's *Psalm 24* at Queen's Hall with the London Select Choir under Arnold Fulton.

[66] The second of the *Three Pieces*, op. 5.

[67] Ethel Bartlett (1896–1978) and Rae Robertson (1893–1956), well-known two-piano duo for whom Berkeley wrote his *Three Pieces*, gave the premiere of the set of three on 4 February 1938 at the Wigmore Hall. However, they played the Polka much earlier in New York Town Hall during their American tour, according to *The Musical Courier*, on 11 February 1934.

[68] The house Britten had bought in 1937 and shared with Berkeley.

[69] The Munich conference was on 29 September at which the Sudetenland in Czechoslovakia was transferred to Germany, thus postponing war for a year.

I heard from Jean Françaix the other day. He told me that you asked him to learn English – 'something really monstrous'! Having done that he'd have to learn American, which is even more monstrous.

I now have the proofs of my Capriccio and Nocturne – they will soon come out, and I shall send you copies quickly.[70]

[no date or heading, but must be 26 October 1938]

… Tomorrow afternoon (Thursday) on Radio London National Britten is going to play his Concerto[71] – I have very much wanted you to hear this work, which is why I am pointing it out, although I realise it may be impossible. It goes out at about 3.30 in a concert at Bournemouth directed by Sir Henry Wood. Finally, they are not playing my Overture on Monday – I am not disappointed because the competition was really formidable![72]

The Old Mill, Snape, Saxmundham, Suffolk
10 November [1938]

I much regret not having come to [London to] see you one last time, but my meeting with Goossens[73] was cancelled, and as well as that I have work to finish for next week and I am late. So I thought it was more sensible to give up the idea.

All the same we have been able to see each other a little more than usual – and that has been a great joy for me.

I told you that there was a vague plan for Britten and me to go to America next winter – Britten would play his Concerto and he and I would play together the piece I have shown you.[74] It is Mr Hawkes, the publisher, who is trying to arrange something.[75] If, when you are there, you have the opportunity to talk about it when you think it might be useful, I should very much appreciate it.[76] I am a little ashamed to ask you but I know that a word from you could do a great deal.

When you think of your mother and your sister, think sometimes of my mother and me too. I should like so much to be able to live as she would have wished – and I can't do it, but it's through feebleness – at least I know that I am wrong! I feel that

---

[70] The *Three Pieces* for two pianos were published separately.

[71] Benjamin Britten (1913–76): Piano Concerto, op. 13 (1938), premiered at the Proms on 18 August 1938 by Britten with the BBC Symphony Orchestra under Sir Henry Wood. The second performance with the Bournemouth Municipal Orchestra was broadcast on 27 October.

[72] With Britten's Piano Concerto in the same programme.

[73] Eugene Goossens (1893–1962), composer and conductor from the prominent musical family, knighted in 1955.

[74] Berkeley's *Introduction and Allegro for Two Pianos*, op. 11, dedicated to Britten, whose Piano Concerto, op. 13, is dedicated to Berkeley.

[75] Ralph Hawkes, joint owner of Boosey & Hawkes, based in New York.

[76] Boulanger was in the US for three months from 2 February 1938.

your thoughts at moments like that could help me to change things, for on my part I think so often of you.

The Monteverdi was so beautiful the other evening.[77]

28 Great Ormond Street, London W.C.1
Saturday [November 1938]

I am certain that your concert has done a lot of good and what a joy for those who understand.[78] Here we are suffocated with Sibelius, Delius, Ireland, Vaughan Williams (VW is better – but still not right). How marvellous to breathe freely! If only we could have a whole series of concerts like that.

If you have a few minutes to spare tomorrow do telephone me … for otherwise I shan't see you again until after next summer and that's really too long. You have no idea how much good it does me to spend even a short time with you – not only musically. I should also like to show you, and if possible play you, the last thing I have done, about which we spoke yesterday. Lord Berners told me I could come and see you whenever I wanted – he is so kind, I only know him slightly.[79]

I found the Szalowski so good.[80] I didn't know he had so much talent – and so much craftsmanship – it was so well made.

Brussels
1 April 1939

Your letter was a real joy for me. I was on the point of writing to you. Do I need to tell you how much I have been thinking of you in recent days? Each year I feel more united with you in your remembrance of your mother and sister because the longer I live the more I see that it is only things of that sort that matter, and which have real value. And everything beautiful is close to this kind of feeling.

I was delighted that you have played my pieces with Jean Françaix – how I should like to have heard you! I should very much like you to make a recording. I still have nothing recorded. Would it be possible?

I have got Mademoiselle Dieudonné's letter about [a minor British composer]. Since I know nothing about him, except that he has some things published by Chester, I have asked them to send me some of his works. I have now read four songs, a piano piece and a cantata for children, and I regret to tell you that it has absolutely no interest – a banal melodic line harmonised somewhat in the manner of Delius, but less well done (!), all lifeless and without the least originality. I'm not

---

[77] Presumably her BBC concert of 8 November.

[78] Boulanger was in England for BBC engagements and concerts with her Vocal Ensemble in late October and early November 1938, when three talks and four concerts were advertised.

[79] Boulanger was presumably staying with Lord Berners in London at his London house, 3 Halkin Street, SW1.

[80] Antoni Szalowski (1907–73), Polish-French composer, pupil of Boulanger. Three of his works were performed at ISCM Festivals. Overture (Warsaw, 1939); String Quartet no. 3 (New York, 1941); Sonatina for oboe and piano (Amsterdam, 1948). Boulanger included a first performance of one of his works at her Wigmore Hall recital on 15 June 1949.

very surprised – I have never heard him spoken of as having the slightest interest. It may not be kind to be so little indulgent about a colleague – but really you have only to see one page of his music to get the picture.[81]

I am visiting relations here. Then I shall spend a fortnight in Paris – but it's sad to go there and think of you in America. America takes everything from us!

[Boulanger was in America from January to June 1939. She gave 102 lectures in 118 days and was a great success in breaking new ground as a woman conducting major orchestras.]

1 Cité Chaptal, Paris IX
12 October 1939

I have just arrived in Paris (yesterday evening) and got your letter just as I left. I haven't written to you sooner simply because I was hoping to be able to come, but I didn't know when. After many applications I got permission to come for two weeks, and I am determined to see you, because later I may perhaps be called up, and God knows when we could meet again. At present they leave me in peace and I go on working – in England they are discouraging people from volunteering. That only adds to the confusion – we now have conscription and as a result they will call us up when we are needed. Besides, I confess I am in no hurry to launch myself into a military career for which I have no aptitude! Although I'm ready to do my duty.

As you say – we can't help feeling lost. As if there wasn't enough suffering already!

I am so touched that you thought of me.

Will you send me a word here to tell me when I can come and see you?

1 Cité Chaptal, Paris IX
Thursday [October 1939]

I am so sad to leave without having seen you that I must write once again to tell you. In fact – I know very well that you can do nothing about it. It's just bad luck!

If I am called up, what I shall resent most will be not being able to create music. That and the idea of having to have to kill anyone. I shall never manage to believe in 'war for the sake of peace' – the use of force cannot produce peace. We have already been told all that, and we know it is not true. The result of a war for peace is a peace for war. On the other hand I must admit that I really cannot see how we can do anything else, or how England and France could have acted differently.

If I am not called up, I very much want to come back to France, but for that I shall need a reason. So I thought that if concerts begin again after the New Year, and if you had the opportunity to perform my pieces for two pianos, I could perhaps play, and this would be a valid reason for my being allowed to come. I should much appreciate it if you could think of that if the occasion arises. ...

I wonder what has happened to Jean Françaix. Has he been called up? I often think of him.

---

[81] This is unusually trenchant for Berkeley. The composer is now dead but since this was a confidential report his name is withheld.

[Written on the top of the letter]
4 o'clock. I have just got your pneu.[82] What rotten luck! – obliged to bring forward my departure, I'm going immediately – 5.30 at the Gare du Nord. Not even time to send you a pneu. I was to leave only tomorrow morning – and now the boat is leaving at 8.00 in the morning and I have to leave Paris the evening before. I am furious.

28 Great Ormond Street, London W.C.1
28 December 1939

How are you? I think you must be well again because I know you conducted a concert the other day. What a fine programme! – how I would love to have been there. I am still furious at having missed seeing you by so little when I was in Paris. I very much need to see you and I should so much like to show you a few of the things I have done recently. They are nothing extraordinary – so much better than what I did before that I think you would be pleased. I want to see you, if there is any way of getting to Paris, in February (I can't come before) – but I don't know if I'll get permission. Generally there has to be a more or less serious reason – that's why I allowed myself to ask you not to forget me if ever you have the chance to play anything of mine at a concert – that would be a reason to ask for permission to make the journey.

I've recently finished a Serenade for Strings which is going to be played in London on January 30th.[83] I am lucky because there are so few first performances at present. Now I'm working at some Concert Studies for piano.[84] It seems to me that there is so little modern music that is really 'for piano' and I am very excited about this work, although I find it very difficult. I can't really see how I can get it played. Horowitz would be needed – (you see I don't go in for half measures!) it's absolutely made for him.[85] Perhaps that might not be his opinion; and in any case

---

[82] Pneumatique rapid communication.

[83] Serenade for Strings, op. 12, premiered 30 January 1940 at the Aeolian Hall, London, by the Boyd Neel Orchestra, in the same concert as the premiere of Britten's *Les Illuminations*, op. 18. In a letter to Britten on 21 April 1940 Berkeley said: 'Boosey & Hawkes lent me a proof of your *Illuminations*. ... I couldn't get Nadia to be very keen – she doesn't seem to take to your music easily. We had a terrible argument about it. She much admired the string writing, but thinks you haven't found your real musical language yet – she doesn't feel that the harmony is sufficiently personal. I can see what she means, but it doesn't worry me so much – in fact I definitely disagree ...' The extent of British cynicism about Britten was revealed in a review of the score of *Les Illuminations* in *The Monthly Musical Record*, September 1940: 'The imagination displayed in this series of settings is predominantly technical and not musical. Indeed the latter element in the work is so restricted and so thin that it is exhausted at a single reading, and one is left to marvel at the virtuosity displayed in the medium employed. This virtuosity is the composer's bane, for he relies on it to puff out ideas that have little interior significance. O for a trace of clumsiness somewhere.' British amateurism at its worst? I am afraid it was written by Edmund Rubbra.

[84] *Four Concert Studies*, op. 14/1.

[85] Vladimir Horowitz (1903–89), American pianist born in the Ukraine. A supreme virtuoso, he specialised in the standard repertoire but introduced Prokofiev sonatas to the US and inspired Samuel Barber's Sonata (1950).

I don't know him, and if he is like most virtuosos he's probably not dying to play modern music. …

I think a lot about the war, but I have become less of a pacifist, for it seems to me that there are principles for which it is sometimes necessary to fight when one has exhausted every other means of resistance.

Dear Mademoiselle – I wish for you all that we can wish now. Happiness – one can't have much of that while the war lasts. At least one can hope that this war may finish before the end of this year, which is starting so sadly.

I am writing from the country where I am spending part of the time with some very good friends – the Davenports.[86] I think you know John Davenport – he is an extremely cultivated man who knows music marvellously well. …

> 28 Great Ormond Street, London W.C.1
> 2 April 1940

I telephoned Chester's this morning and they tell me they have sent you the parts of my Serenade. As for a second score, they'll send it to you in a few days but they have to make another photographic copy of my manuscript. … I asked them to do it as quickly as possible. Can you tell me if the concert on the 16th is broadcast and if so on what station? Also, if it is not too much to ask, would it be possible to send an invitation to two of my friends?[87] …

I was so pleased to have been able to spend a little time with you at last.[88] Thankyou for all you are doing for me – the thought that you have confidence in me musically is an enormous encouragement and will help me – I am sure of it – to do better.

I hope that the other concerts in the north went well.

> 28 Great Ormond Street, London W.C.1
> 12 April 1940

Could you send one of the scores of my Serenade to Mme Casella, 7 Rue Mesnil, Paris XVI, as soon as you don't need it any more?[89] She has spoken to Munch[90] and it looks as if he would like to see the score. It's a nuisance to have only three scores

---

[86] John Davenport (1908–66), writer and critic, Berkeley's host at Marshfield, Gloucestershire. Other residents around this period included Dylan and Caitlin Thomas, Humphrey Searle, Arnold Cooke, Henry Boys, and William Glock, who later married Davenport's wife, Clement.

[87] N. José Raffalli, in the army at Montreuil-sous-bois, Seine, and Manuel Frère. This concert included the French premiere of the Serenade under Boulanger.

[88] It looks as if Berkeley got back to Paris a second time after war was declared.

[89] Hélène Kahn-Casella, ex-wife of Italian composer Alfredo Casella, administrator at the Société musicale indépendante.

[90] Charles Munch (1891–1968), French conductor associated with many significant premieres: nothing came of this approach, although he heard the French premiere of the Serenade.

in total, but since I hope it will soon be published this is only temporary. I shall try to hear the concert on the 16th – I imagine it is broadcast.

Excuse a word in haste. ...

Marshfield, Gloucestershire
25 April 1940

What joy your letter has given me! I have told you so often that your approval is more precious to me than any success, and if I repeat this it's because it is quite simply true, and I feel the need to say so again. In my heart everything I write is dedicated first to my mother and to you, for she gave me life, and it's you who have shown me what to make of it.

It seems to me that it's not only your technical teaching that is inestimable, but that you show everybody how, and to what point, they can love music. I find that with many musicians of today, this love of music is submerged by considerations of career, of fashion, or else by theories and systems.

It must be through love that one doesn't permit an unsatisfactory bar. I am sure that part of the genius of Mozart was to *love* music that much. ...

Schott want to publish my *Four Concert Studies* – I should have liked to show them to you, but I did not have time to copy them in Paris. Perhaps you could just glance through the proofs – we'll see if that's possible. ...

Could you tell me, as soon as you can, on what date you plan to play my Serenade again? I don't expect to be able to come to Paris again, but I am very much tempted, and there is just a chance it might be possible. However, for that it would be necessary to know a long time in advance.

[On 14 June 1940 the Germans entered Paris and on the 22nd an armistice was concluded. Boulanger arrived in New York, via Lisbon, on 6 November 1940]

28 Great Ormond Street, London W.C.1
21 November 1940

What joy to have news of you at last! No need to tell you how much I have thought of you over these last months. I have not had any news of my French friends – it's as if France no longer existed – it's terrible, and of course it's not true, thank God. I feel that we can't talk of these tragic events yet, we are too close to be able to judge, and in any case the drama is not yet finished. I think that here in England, if we have one quality it is tenacity – and it's clear that it is now a matter of holding on. It is going to be very long and very disagreeable, but what can we do?

As for me I am still not a soldier but I am engaged in Civil Defence, being what we call an Air Raid Warden. It's a question of going round at nights during alerts, visiting the shelters and calling the emergency services when there's a bomb. I don't do it all night – just till midnight, every other night, and during the day if they need me. I have only had to help pull out the wounded and the dead once – it was dreadful, and it made me ill for three days. Since I am a volunteer (that's to say I'm not paid) I can go away when I want and I've just taken a holiday in the country for two weeks.

In spite of everything I manage to write a little music. I can even say that I love music more than ever. What is sad is that we have almost no concerts, and it is going to be more difficult than ever to get performances. However, I have been lucky, for the day before the bombing really started, my Introduction and Allegro for two pianos was performed at the Queen's Hall. It was one of the Promenade Concerts – they had to be abandoned two days later. I played one piano myself (without catastrophe) and with me I had William Glock, an excellent pianist.[91] I have some new things published now which I am going to send you. Since there is so little happening here, I hope to be able to get some performances in America. I am sure that you won't forget me if an opportunity comes up. Maurice Eisenberg has the score and the piano reduction of my Concerto for Cello and Orchestra.[92] He wants to give the first performance, but so far I think he hasn't found the concert he wants. If you are in contact with him, you might be kind enough to encourage him a bit.

I have written recently a new string quartet which is infinitely better than the first. I think it is by far the best thing I have done. Unfortunately there is no question of its being published at the moment, but all the same I'll try and send you a copy.

I am so sad when I think that I shall have to spend a long time – years perhaps – without seeing you. I've frequently spoken about the enormous influence you have had on my life. Never shall I forget what I owe you. Just thinking of you does me good and gives me strength.

When you have time to write to me, please give me news of Poulenc and Jean Françaix; what has become of them? And the Polignacs? I often saw the Princess when she was in London, I think she is usually in the country – for good reason!...

Au revoir – (till when?) dear Mademoiselle

24 Coulson Street, London S.W.3[93]
6 October 1942

I was so pleased to get your letter, because I often think of you and if I have not written to you, it's because there are so many things I'd like to talk to you about, it would be too long, and that discourages me – and then I finish by not writing at all.

In spite of everything my life has not changed very much – I now have to work in an office, but my work concerns music which is quite something.[94] As for

---

[91] William Glock (1908–2000), pupil of Artur Schnabel: see n. 114, p. 75 below.

[92] Maurice Eisenberg (1902–72), German-American cellist, student of Boulanger and Casals. After a decade based in Paris, Eisenberg moved to the US, the Cello Concerto was forgotten and he never played it. The premiere was eventually given on 17 July 1983 at the Cheltenham Festival by Moray Welsh and the Hallé Orchestra under James Loughran. Publicity was made of the fact that Berkeley had forgotten he ever wrote it, which was not strictly true. Eisenberg's only London recital at the Wigmore Hall on 20 February 1947 was advertised as including a piece by Nadia Boulanger.

[93] According to Tony Scotland, Berkeley was lodging with Douglas Gordon at this address following the bombing of John Greenidge's flat in Bloomsbury.

[94] Berkeley worked for the BBC 1941–5, mostly as an orchestral programme builder.

composition, I keep going, but it goes slowly because I can only work in my free time. I am a Sunday composer! Well, that's something.

I am very pleased that you have received my Piano Studies and that you like them. I fear that they are not very original but all the same I think they are successful. I have written a new String Quartet which I think is pretty good – it's been played several times here, and a Symphony which has not yet been performed.[95]

[continues in English for the first time]

I find it very difficult to do without France – it is a part of one's life that has suddenly ceased to exist. What you must feel, I can't think! – but I hope that things will soon begin to change. It is terrible to think of what lies ahead but it has got to be.

I have not heard anything new that I thought much of in the last year or two. In fact, I can only think of two works that have really impressed me as being in the first class – one is Bartók's Divertimento and the other Britten's *Sinfonia da Requiem*. Stravinsky's Symphony has not been played here yet, nor Hindemith's, and I'm most impatient to hear both.[96] It is rather difficult to get hold of new music (I mean the actual material) nowadays – and a great deal of French music is unobtainable over here, but in spite of everything there is a great deal of music going on, and it is encouraging to see that people seem to need it more than ever – the concert halls are packed.

I can't begin to tell you how much it would mean to me to be able to see you again, and I won't give up hope that the day will come when we shall be able to meet – it is so difficult to do without those few people who are so necessary to one.

I can't give you any news of the people you mention in your letter. How many people one has lost touch with …

I spoke just now of Britten who is back in England. He has done some settings of Michelangelo's sonnets, which are of the utmost beauty, and though I know you do not like all his work, you would find it impossible not to be moved by these.[97]

Everything is much the same. We are of course very tired of wartime conditions, but the people here seem not to waver in their determination to go on to the end, at whatever cost. We have had no air-raids for a long time which is a mercy as they are unpleasant things. I was in London all through that terrible time when they never stopped. How horrible it all is!

I have heard a rumour that you were going to leave America, but as you say nothing about it in your letter – I imagine it is not true.

Madame de Polignac is living in this country, or rather she has been, but I hear that she may be coming back to London. Berners I haven't seen for

---

[95] String Quartet no. 2, op. 15, premiered 5 June 1941 by the Stratton Quartet at the Cambridge Theatre, London. Symphony no. 1, op. 16, premiered 8 July 1943 at the Royal Albert Hall, with the London Philharmonic Orchestra under the composer.

[96] Stravinsky, Symphony in C, premiered 7 November 1940 in Chicago. Presumably Hindemith's Symphony in E flat (1940). Both composers were in the US.

[97] *Seven Sonnets of Michelangelo*, op. 22, premiered 23 September 1942 at the Wigmore Hall, London, by Pears and Britten.

ages – I don't think he ever comes to London.[98] I can't think of anyone else you know.

Good-by dear Mademoiselle. I hope that you are well and not overworking.

24 Coulson Street, London S.W.3
10 August 1943

[In English]

I am horrified to find that I have your letter so long unanswered, but my life at present is almost like yours used to be! I work in an office all day, and have to do my composing in the evenings and at weekends with the result that letter-writing is almost an impossibility. And when I do start to write a letter like this, there is so much to say that I don't know how to begin!

You say nothing about yourself, dear Mademoiselle, which is a pity, because that's what I want to know about; but I realise what this exile from your country and friends and so many people and things that you hold dear must be. Nothing can compensate for that, and I am sad to think how much it must make you suffer. I hope at least that you are well and as happy as possible in the circumstances.

I have seen Mme de Polignac several times lately. She is well, but feels this long separation from her family and belongings very much – at her age it is a great trial, and she longs to get back to France. What a wonderful character she has – I admire her immense culture and her tolerance and understanding of others so much. We always speak about you – how we wish we could speak to you and with you and not merely about you! I also see the Chaplins from time to time.[99] Anthony has behaved so splendidly, because he hates every minute of his present life, and he could easily have done something more congenial – and less dangerous – but he is obviously one of those who can only be content with what is best and finest. I have long discussions with him about music. I think he has rather extreme views – although I'm devoted to the sixteenth-century composers and Scarlatti, I can't see that it is therefore necessary to consign Beethoven and the romantics to the rubbish-heap! However we do agree about most things. ...

There is a composer here called Michael Tippett[100] who is doing very fine work – it is very original and you would be most interested. He is thirty-eight and has been writing for a long time, but it is only his recent things that are so remarkable. I think it is in some ways a good thing to develop slowly in this way.

Britten's String Quartet is very beautiful – have you heard it?[101]

I conducted the first performance of my Symphony last month.[102] It went quite

---

[98] Lord Berners was living in Oxford during part of the war.
[99] Anthony Chaplin, 3rd Viscount (1906–81), amateur zoologist, composer and former Boulanger pupil, officer in the RAF who joined Bomber Command as a gunner. He commissioned Berkeley's Third String Quartet, op. 76, and the *Four Piano Studies*, op. 82.
[100] Sir Michael Tippett (1905–98), knighted 1966.
[101] Berkeley's article about Britten's String Quartet no. 1, op. 25, appears on p. 91 below.
[102] Premiered 8 July 1943 at the Royal Albert Hall with the London Philharmonic Orchestra, conducted by the composer.

well but I am not altogether pleased with the work – I wrote it two years ago and I think I can do better now. I have just finished a String Trio which was played on Saturday.[103] I think you would like it – I'll try and send you a copy of it sometime. Edwin Evans[104] wrote an article in which he spoke of my Symphony and your influence on modern music.

Please write again soon. Perhaps the war will not last so very long now and we shall be able to meet again ... I often think of you.

PS [in French]

Just as I was taking your letter to the post I received yours. Thank you dear Mademoiselle, I'm so pleased that you haven't forgotten me, and that you sometimes think of my mother. I'm adding nothing – this letter is already too long.

24 Coulson Street, London S.W.3
25 January 1944

[Now in English]

You must forgive me for having left your letter unanswered for some weeks but I have been writing the music for a film, and it all had to be done in my spare time from my BBC work, so that letters just had to be postponed – when I tell you that I had to write the full score (forty-seven minutes' music) in three weeks having only a few sketches before, you will understand that it was rather a scramble.[105] I don't think it is good to write as quickly regularly but it does no harm – except make me very tired – to have to do it occasionally. You speak in your letter of the problem of writing for the cinema – my view about this is that it is not necessary for us to lower the standard when writing film music, but merely to use a rather easier idiom – at least that is what I do. Like the difference between the idiom of poetry and that of ordinary speech – and that provided this difference is allowed for, we ourselves can keep the standard up. Also I find that to have to write pieces that have to be timed to the second, and yet satisfy one's sense of form, is excellent discipline. Also, I often wonder whether the old patrons had so much taste as people think – apart from Rasumovsky and Esterhazy – the rest merely obeyed a convention and occasionally, rather to their embarrassment, found themselves landed with a genius! I think the worst aspect of the question is that the only people now in a position to pay for music are the film companies, and they only require music that is part of something else, and not an end in itself.

You will have heard the very sad news of the death of the Princess de Polignac. It was a real shock to me as I had got to like and admire her greatly. I know what a blow this news will have been to you. I was just speaking of patrons – was she not the perfect patron? It is sad that her last years should have had to be spent in a kind

---

[103] Premiered 7 August 1943 at the Wigmore Hall, London, by Frederick Grinke, Watson Forbes and James Phillips.

[104] Edwin Evans (1874–1945), influential English critic who promoted contemporary composers, especially French and British.

[105] *Hotel Reserve* (RKO, 1944), adapted from Eric Ambler, *Epitaph for a Spy* (London, 1938).

of exile. I understand that her death was extremely sudden – she had been about all day and had dined with Lady Colefax a few hours before.[106] It is difficult to realise that she is gone.

We have had two performances of Stravinsky's Symphony [in C] and I was much moved by it – it is a fine and noble work full of genius. I think the first movement is a masterpiece and I like particularly the second movement which has a most tender and beautiful feeling. I did not care for the last movement quite so much, though the end is very fine. The whole thing is so intensely personal and individual – he is, as you say, a great man.

I have telephoned to Chester about *Tilimbom* and the *Symphonies of Wind Instruments* and they are making enquiries about them.[107] They tell me there is certainly a score of *Tilimbom* somewhere, so that, or a copy, can be sent to M. Stravinsky, or rather to you – as I don't know his address. As for the Symphony they are very doubtful about whether there is a copy in this country, but they are making further enquiries.

Some of my music is being published quite soon – a String Trio, a Divertimento for small orchestra, and a Sonatina for Violin and Piano.[108] I will send you copies of them when they appear and also if I can get hold of a spare copy – a score of my Symphony. I miss so much being able to talk to you about music, and often long to ask your opinion of something that puzzles me. However, I am so happy to get your letter, to know that you remember my mother, as I remember yours – how clearly and vividly! – and to feel that we are not quite cut off from any contact.

Please write again soon, dear Mademoiselle, and do not forget.

58 Warwick Square, London S.W.1
18 November 1945

[Now in French]

What a joy to know that you are coming back; it's the best news I've had for a long time. Try to return through London – you have so many friends here who so much want to see you – me above all ... – we love you so much, and no one could fill the gap that your absence has left. They have great need of you in Paris too; I recently saw Marie-Blanche who is waiting impatiently for you.[109]

I am leaving the BBC at the end of the year. I am going to try and concentrate entirely on composition. If you want to do something really well, you have to devote yourself to it entirely. How I should love to have been present at the series of concerts of Fauré of which you sent me the programme. We are beginning, even

---

[106] Sybil Lady Colefax (1874–1950), assiduous London society hostess who established a business in interior design which became Colefax and Fowler.

[107] 'Tilibom', the first of Stravinsky's *Three Children's Tales* (1917), revised for voice and orchestra (1923), published by Chester.

[108] J. & W. Chester remained Berkeley's publisher for the rest of his life.

[109] Countess Jean de Polignac, Marie-Blanche (née Lanvin), a fine singer who performed professionally with Boulanger's ensembles.

in England, to realise the grandeur of Fauré, and he's being performed more often now.

David Ponsonby[110] has returned after some extraordinary adventures during the occupation in France – things which could only happen to him and which he tells with his usual modesty – never taking himself seriously – and with his sense of humour which is so characteristic and unique. I have seen so many friends again recently, but it's you I miss, chère Mademoiselle, do not delay.

[on the top of this letter]

I very much like *Four Norwegian Moods* – they have a fine pure beauty.[111] They were performed recently on the BBC. Did I thank you for the score?

[Boulanger returned to Paris in January 1946]

58 Warwick Square, London S.W.1
12 April [1946]

I am so pleased to hear of your return – it's the best news for a long time. I am hoping to pass through Paris on the way to Strasbourg where I am going to conduct my Symphony in a concert of English music.[112] I shall probably be with Alvide Chaplin[113] and I expect to be there from Thursday the 18th to Monday 22nd [April]. I'm afraid that since it's Easter you won't perhaps be there but I hope (and how!) that you will. It has been so long – it would do me so much good to see you.

58 Warwick Square, London S.W.1
5 May [1946]

[Now in English]

I must tell you how wonderful it was to see you after all this time, and how much I enjoyed having dinner with you – above all how badly I needed your attitude towards music which of course I had not forgotten, but which I needed to be in contact with once again. I feel I can now 'get away' with things rather too easily, mainly because my music happens to be more pleasing to the ear and more easily understood than most contemporary music, and because of this I am perhaps more tempted to think that it is good than if it were written in a more difficult idiom. But you bring me back to reality in a moment! And I find myself already looking at my work with a more critical eye since I have seen you. I think that certain natures easily confuse beauty with pleasure and have to make a continual effort to keep

---

[110] David Brabazon Ponsonby (1901–86), Oxford contemporary of Berkeley, pianist and composer, student of Boulanger, and resistance fighter in France. The first of the *Four Concert Studies*, op. 14/1 is dedicated to him.

[111] Stravinsky, *Four Norwegian Moods* for orchestra (1942).

[112] Berkeley's first visit to France since the war where he conducted his First Symphony at a British Council Concert.

[113] Alvide Chaplin, ex-wife of Viscount Chaplin, later married to James Lees-Milne. She lived at Le Mé Chaplin, Jouy-en-Josas, near Versailles, in the house she inherited from the Princess de Polignac.

them apart – I think that Poulenc for instance is apt to do this, but though it is dangerous to people like him and me, it is perhaps a good thing that the element of pleasure should return to music after all the grim and false austerity of the 1920s. Stravinsky has the true austerity, and at the same time pleasure is by no means absent from his music.

William Glock tells me that you are going to write some articles for his new magazine which is good news. Glock is the most intelligent critic in England (that's not saying much, but he is intelligent, has absolutely the right ideas).[114]

I am always sorry that you do not care for Britten's music more than you do – I think he is so unusually musical and his music is written with such meticulous care, but he is too romantic for you. I would, however, like you to read his Serenade which I think is beautiful – I'll send it to you. ...[115]

58 Warwick Square, London S.W.1
3 November 1946

[Now in French]

I definitely don't have luck with your trains – I went to Victoria this morning thinking the train left at 9.20 and it appeared to have left at 9.00. I think it's 9.20 on a weekday and 9.00 on Sunday! I am desperate because I would have loved to see you again before you go away.[116]

I heard your talk on Stravinsky – which gave you so much trouble – and I'm sure it will have done good. I tried to listen to it as if I didn't know this music, and it seems to me that one got a very clear impression which really gave food for thought. And how beautiful the music was! – naturally I knew it by heart, but it seemed more beautiful than ever. It's strange that one has so much difficulty in understanding it, but I think that in fact one needs an education – the pure state of music is disconcerting – one no longer knows how to listen.

The new works by Jean Françaix have impressed me, above all *La Bête de la mer*[117] which is extraordinary from all points of view; in fact one can no longer regard him as a frivolous composer when one has heard that! I also very much enjoyed the *Chants du rossignol* by Préger.[118]

But apart from music, what a pleasure to see you again – and what benefit; you put everything back into its place – the things of real value as opposed to those of relative value.

---

[114] William Glock (1908–2000), editor of *The Score* (1949–61), Founder of the Bryanston Summer School (1949), Director of the Dartington Festival (1953–79), Controller of Music at the BBC (1959–72) where he revitalised the music programmes, knighted in 1970. He was the other pianist with the composer in Berkeley's *Introduction and Allegro for Two Pianos and Orchestra*, op. 11, at the Proms on 6 September 1938.

[115] *Serenade for Tenor, Horn and Strings*, op. 31 (1943).

[116] Boulanger had been in London for a concert of French music with her vocal ensemble at the Wigmore Hall on 30 October.

[117] Part of the third section of Françaix's oratorio *L'Apocalypse selon Saint-Jean* (1939).

[118] Léo Préger (1907–65), Corsican composer, pupil of Boulanger, who specialised in choral music.

I hope to see you again soon. I shan't be able to come to Paris at the moment, but I know that you are due to come back here.

[Berkeley married Freda Bernstein on 14 December 1946]

8 Warwick Avenue, London W.2
13 September 1947

I should very much like you to hear a pianist – Natasha Litvin[119] – or at least meet her. Actually she's going to be in Paris from the 21st to the 26th of this month and I took the liberty of telling her to telephone you. She has an excellent technique – she is a real musician and I am sure you will like her very much. She is the wife of Stephen Spender – one of our best poets, whose name you may know. She is staying with Mr & Mrs Julian Huxley at 17 Avenue Foche.[120]

I very much regretted not seeing you again, but you know what it's like when one has only a few days. The British Council finally sent me to Zurich for the first performance of the *Stabat Mater*, which really went very well. They are performing it here next week conducted by Britten.[121]

Are you coming to England this winter? I have to say that things are pretty bad here; it seems that things aren't going any better in France either, but while with you it's a political and moral crisis, here it's economic. We're going to be short of everything this winter. Still we mustn't complain, we didn't suffer during the war like some countries; but this is largely the fault of the present government.

I know you're too busy to write, so don't answer – you know I often think of you. I hope it will be possible to see you during the winter.

8 Warwick Avenue, London W.2
30 November 1947

I am so pleased to know that you are coming to London, and I am writing to implore you to keep a moment free to come and see us. I don't know what your address will be in London, but perhaps you can telephone me to arrange something. I have good news to give you – it is that we hope to have a baby in May … we are very happy about it.[122]

It seems that Soulima[123] has written a very beautiful sonata – which I should like to hear. I am trying to persuade the BBC to bring him here to perform. They appear to welcome the idea and I hope it will happen.

---

[119] Natasha Litvin (1919–2010).

[120] Sir Julian Huxley (1887–1975), influential biologist, evolutionist, first Director of UNESCO.

[121] *Stabat mater*, op. 28, premiered 19 August 1947 at the Tonhalle, Zurich, by the English Opera Group conducted by the composer. The performance conducted by Britten was a BBC broadcast of 27 September 1947 from the Concert Hall, Broadcasting House, London.

[122] Michael Berkeley, composer and broadcaster. See interview with him, p. 265 below.

[123] Soulima Stravinsky (1910–94), pianist and composer, youngest son of Igor Stravinsky, with whom he gave recitals, pupil of Boulanger. Born in Switzerland, he moved with his family to Paris; unlike his parents, he remained in Europe during the war, serving in the French army. He moved to the US with his family in 1948.

The news about France is very disturbing – things aren't brilliant here, but it's a purely economic crisis, whilst with you it's much more serious. Will you even be able to travel?

8 Warwick Avenue, London W.2
25 July 1948

Thankyou! If you knew what pleasure I had in being able to talk about you in that little article – it seems to me that ever since I met you, I have felt the need to say that. As ever I am bad at writing words – it's not our language – but this time I was able to do it very quickly, almost without stopping[124] …

[Boulanger was at the Bryanston Summer School of Music, announced as lecturing every morning in August 1948, and she went again in 1949. After the Summer School had moved to Devon as the Dartington Summer School she went to Dartington Hall in 1957.]

8 Warwick Avenue, London W.2
19 January 1949

[In French]

I have just heard from the BBC that you are going to conduct my Concerto for Two Pianos and Orchestra on February 27. I am so pleased about it – it's the best thing that has happened to me for a long time! By chance Mr Gibson, my publisher, is just leaving for Paris this morning, so he will bring you the score.[125]

Only one thing worries me – it's that this work is not worthy of you, and still so far from what I should like to do! I am proud of the confidence that you have had in me by accepting this without having seen the music – at least I can say that it is music which is (I hope) in the right direction, and there is not much today about which one can even say that! Anyway, I hope that you will not be too disappointed.

[Berkeley then explained that the seventh variation of the second movement should have its tempo changed from a minim to a dotted minim but still 'one beat in a bar' and not too fast]

Please let me know the day of your arrival in London so I can see you right away
The pianists are good – they played very well at the premiere.[126]
I am studying Stravinsky's *Orphée* which I find staggeringly beautiful and novel.[127]

---

[124] Berkeley wrote regular tributes to Boulanger and also gave BBC talks. For what is probably the earliest of these tributes, see p. 48 above.

[125] Douglas Gibson at J. & W. Chester, who loyally looked after Berkeley and his music for many years. The performance was on 27 February 1949.

[126] Concerto for Two Pianos and Orchestra, op. 30, premiered 13 December 1948 at the Royal Albert Hall by Phyllis Sellick and Cyril Smith with the London Symphony Orchestra under Malcolm Sargent, and given again at the Proms in the following year.

[127] *Orpheus*, ballet (1947).

8 Warwick Avenue, London W.2
26 October 1949

I very much regret not having seen you again. As it happens I came to your train only to find that I was not allowed to cross the barrier because you had been through customs! I insisted that I had no intention of giving you a bag of diamonds – all in vain. It appears that you tried to telephone me on Saturday. Still, let's hope it will not be too long before we can see each other again. I always have so many things I would like to ask your advice about in my work ... alas, when we meet only over dinner that is impossible.

At the moment I'm studying Stravinsky's Mass which I like more and more.[128] Not only is the idea beautiful but the choice of notes is so extraordinary. I find it's this quality of 'choice' (or taste) that is important, because it is above all taste that most composers and almost all the public have lost. I often tell myself now – Stravinsky has no other notes, or no more notes to work with, than I have, or anybody else. We all have to choose between the same ones. So the important thing is the exercise of choice.

8 Warwick Avenue, London W.2
4 February [1950]

Gibson has told me that you were ill – for about ten days I have wanted to write to say that I hope it was not serious and that you are now much better. I am delighted at the thought of seeing you very soon.

They have sent me the Soulima's Sonata[129] – it is very beautiful – freshness and above all taste everywhere. What a marvellous achievement! There's very little music as good.

8 Warwick Avenue, London W.2
[July 1950]

... It seems ages since we had news of you, but I know you don't have time to write. It's the same with me, I have to say. I am very busy and am lazy about letters! About you I have only hear-say – that you were to come to conduct Bach cantatas, and then that you were not coming after all (a real pity since I am certain that there is no-one in the world who can perform them like you) – still, all that may not be true – let us hope not. Whatever the truth of it, it is too long since we saw you.

I think you must be at Aix now, because I have seen that you are going to conduct some Purcell (bravo) – how I should like to be there. Unfortunately, we cannot make long journeys this year – perhaps next year, but it's complicated because of the children.

---

[128] *Mass* for SATB, wind and brass (1948).

[129] High praise, but the work seems to have disappeared.

Lyulph's Tower, Ullswater, Nr Penrith, Cumberland
3 September [1950]

We are here for a little holiday; I had never been to the Lake District before and I think it's really beautiful. It is one of the rare places in England which is not ruined by too many houses ... too many people. I am still working a lot, but music doesn't become less difficult![130]

As from 8 Warwick Avenue, but actually in Jersey
6 January 1951

[Now in English]

... I was so very distressed to hear of Dinu Lipatti's death[131] – he was one of the few one could call a great musician; the more experience of music one has, the more one realises how seldom one can use those words. ...

8 Warwick Avenue, London W.2
25 February 1951

[Now in French]

Your letter gave me great joy! To know that my music really pleased you encourages me enormously. I was delighted to know that they performed that in Paris – I didn't know until afterwards. I should very much like them to perform my *Stabat Mater* which is, I think, better than the *St Teresa Poems*[132] – at least it's what I like best of the things I have done up to now. I think you have a score (it's for six solo voices and twelve instruments) and my dream would be to have you conduct it. Don't forget if there is ever an opportunity. ...

---

[130] Berkeley wrote to Douglas Gibson on 17 August: 'This is an extremely pretty place, with wonderful views – so far it has poured with rain without ceasing but one expects a good deal of that.' Then he asked, as often, for manuscript paper to be sent so he could write out the score of his Sinfonietta, op. 34, to be premiered on 1 December with the London Chamber Orchestra under Anthony Bernard.

[131] Dinu Lipatti (1917–50), Romanian pianist and composer, pupil of Boulanger.

[132] *Four Poems of St Teresa of Avila*, op. 27, for contralto and strings. The premiere was a broadcast of 4 April 1948 from the Concert Hall, Broadcasting House, London, by Kathleen Ferrier (1912–53) with the Goldsbrough String Orchestra under Arnold Goldsbrough (on CD Gala GL 318, released 2000). The first concert performance was also by Ferrier with the LSO under Hugo Rignold, 5 September 1949 at the Freemason's Hall, Edinburgh. They performed it again on 6 April 1952 at the Festival Hall, and this performance was broadcast on 8 October 2003 by BBC Radio 3 in Kathleen Ferrier Night as a recent discovery. There was a further BBC broadcast on 23 November 1949 with Ferrier and the Hallé Strings under Barbirolli (on CD Pearl GEM 0229, released 2006). After these performances Berkeley revised the vocal line in bar 22 of the first song to reach up to an F natural – a distinct improvement – used from now on.

8 Warwick Avenue, London W.2
19 June 1951

[Berkeley explains that he had to cancel his trip to Paris to serve on the jury of the Marguerite Long prize through pressure of work]

I see that Préger has won the Prix de Biarritz – I'm sure that he has done something splendid. The plot of the ballet (which was sent to me) seems charming. It's a long time since I heard anything about him. ...

8 Warwick Avenue, London W.2
23 October 1953

I was very touched by your letter. In fact the death of Kathleen [Ferrier] has made us very sad – this was an extraordinary artist and soul. As you can imagine, music is in mourning here. Almost at the same time I lost my old friend John Greenidge who was with me at first in Paris, as perhaps you may remember. That too has caused us great sorrow.

I was on the point of writing to tell you that I have had a long talk about you with the Director of Music at the BBC Third Programme. He would like you to come to London in the spring because it is a long time since you were heard on the radio. I continue in English – it's so much quicker!

[Now in English]

He would like you to give a talk on any musical subject you like, and then in the same week – perhaps within a few days – a concert with some ensemble or chamber orchestra. He would like you to make some suggestions. If the idea appeals to you, would you first write a line to me, and let me know if there is anything you would particularly like to speak about and perform, also when you would be free – I can then discuss it with him and if it looks like working, he will write you an official letter. I do hope you will feel able to do this. I know that you are always extremely busy, but this is quite a long way ahead – I doubt whether they would be able to put it in before March or April – and it would give you time to prepare it gradually. And what a good excuse for me to be able to see something of you.

8 Warwick Avenue, London W.2
[1953]

I have spoken again to Leonard Isaacs of the BBC about your possible visit here. He very much wants you to perform Monteverdi – Rameau too – more or less what you like of early music. But not Charpentier's *Medée* because it has been performed here recently. I think it would have to be done with singers from here, but, by a lucky chance, Cuénod[133] will be in London at the beginning of May – then, with him as soloist and a small choir, that should go well.

---

[133] Hughes Cuénod (1902–2010), esteemed Swiss tenor who studied with Boulanger and took part in her early music performances and recordings, notably of Monteverdi.

They would also like you to talk on the Third Programme – on whatever you like, but they have suggested to me something about French contemporary music. I don't know if that would suit you. Let me know what you think and if the beginning of May would fit in.

8 Warwick Avenue, London W.2
25 January 1954

[Now in French]

... What we want above all is to see you again, and I hope that this project with the BBC will come off. It's something I would really like, not only because it would be a pretext to see you again but also because I would like it musically. If you would really like to do it, the best thing is to write directly to Leonard Isaacs[134] at the BBC [address given] who really wants you to come and will understand the type of programme you would like to give – do it, Mademoiselle, I implore you – it would be a great thing for me, and for music here, which has great need of you!

I am reading the *Journal* by Julien Green[135] and find it marvellous. It seems to me that I have never read anybody who could express so exactly what I feel myself. ...

8 Warwick Avenue, London W.2
8 April 1954

How pleased I am – what a joy to think we shall see you again soon.[136]

I telephoned the BBC about the work by Dufay, and I hope it can be arranged. When it comes to a composer recommended by you who has also received the Prix de Rome, it is not a question of submitting the work to the panel who decide in general between unknown works but, I am told, it is still necessary for someone to have seen it. However, I have done all that I can and they have promised me to re-examine the question.

Yes, in fact our age is one of committees – the result is that nobody dares to have an opinion any more – soon we shall be incapable of choosing anything for ourselves. Fortunately the end of the world is predicted for 1999. (Nostradamus)[137] ...

8 Warwick Avenue, London W.2
29 September 1954

How kind of you to think of me! Well, the premiere of *Nelson* has gone well[138] – it was well received, and the critics have been rather favourable. It was given twice last

---

[134] Leonard Isaacs (1909–97), Head of Music at the BBC Third Programme, 1950–54, then at Home Service 1954–63.

[135] Julien Green (1900–98), American novelist who wrote mainly in French. He published three volumes of *Journals* (1938–46).

[136] Boulanger came and conducted French Renaissance choral music on the BBC Third Programme on 3 July 1954.

[137] Nostradamus (1503–66), French astrologer and physician famous for enigmatic prophecies.

[138] Sadler's Wells Theatre, London, 22 September 1954.

week and twice again this week. It will be performed in Manchester on October 8th and at Birmingham on the 14th, and then again here.

I don't know what to think of it myself – as we say 'it comes off' and I really think there are some nice things, but I should like to find a more personal musical language. I think I'm making progress from this point of view, but it's very slow – and since I'm already fifty-one, I haven't much time left for someone who moves ahead so slowly!

So, I have had some success with the opera, but I am not very satisfied with it myself – there it is. Perhaps if I was satisfied that would be a bad sign. ...

8 Warwick Avenue, London W.2
8 November 1954

[To Mademoiselle Dieudonné]

I am going to try and find the text of my little talk on Mademoiselle Boulanger – if I can't find my draft here (which I can copy) I think the French Section of the BBC, which asked for it, will probably have kept a copy.

How I should like to be there on the 23rd. Yes, please, tell me how it goes.

In reading your address I am filled with nostalgia – Rue Ravignan![139] In the past I lived in Montmartre, and it seemed that Rue Ravignan was very typical.

I hope to come to Paris one of these days and have the opportunity to see you again.

8 Warwick Avenue, London W.2
11 January 1955

[Now in English]

... How I longed to come to your Anniversary Concert – alas, I am committed to so many things here that it is difficult for me to get away.

My opera went well and has been favourably received. I thought it good in parts, but there was a good deal I was not satisfied with. I have been re-writing parts of the first act before they do it again in March.[140]

The best new work we have had here was Britten's *The Turn of the Screw*.[141] I know you have not liked his earlier music but this, far the best thing he has ever written, you could not fail to like. How I wish I could see you and talk about this and so many other things![142]

---

[139] Rue Ravignan was a famous artists' quarter for painters and poets in the years immediately before World War I. Picasso had his studio there.

[140] There were further performances of *Nelson* on 22, 26 and 29 March 1955.

[141] *The Turn of the Screw*, op. 54, premiered 17 September 1954 at La Fenice, Venice, under Britten.

[142] Boulanger wrote to Berkeley on 30 January 1955 asking impatiently for a score of *Nelson*. She said that he was always the same, talking more about others than himself. She did want to see *The Turn of the Screw* but *Nelson* too.

8 Warwick Avenue, London W.2
30 January 1955

[Now in French]

Yes – I accept with the greatest pleasure – fortunately there is no obstacle, and I can easily be away for ten days.[143] Above all it will be a great joy for me to be with you – we see each other so rarely. And then it will be interesting from all points of view.

I think they will give me information later concerning the journey and where we are to meet. You are very kind to have thought of me for a task to be performed in such pleasant circumstances!

PS I'll try to have a score of *Nelson* so you can have a look at it.

Hotel de Paris, Monte-Carlo
[April 1955]

[Now in English]

This is just to give you some details on the subject of which we were speaking.

I *Nelson* is a full-length opera in three acts. It is of normal proportions and requires six principal soloists with two subsidiary parts, chorus and an orchestra of the usual size. It must have a first-rate tenor, as it is a very big part. I long to have a continental production of it, as one could improve in many ways on the London one. It does not require a particularly big stage. There is at present no French translation but that could easily be done. This is, I gather, what the Prince was interested in.[144]

II *A Dinner Engagement*. This is a comedy in one act. It requires only seven singers and an orchestra consisting of flute, oboe, clarinet, bassoon, horn, harp, percussion and string quintet.[145] The ideal thing would be to get the English Opera Group to do it, as they could give performances of the Britten operas, and they also have something that can be put with mine. Otherwise it could be given by the opera here by arrangement with the English Opera Group. (I think I could persuade them to waive their exclusive right if necessary).

III Just before I left England, Basil Douglas, the manager of the English Opera Group, told me that someone who has an official position here made some tentative enquiries about whether the group would be willing to accept an engagement to come to Monte Carlo to give a performance of Purcell's *Dido and Aeneas*, together with a new work (one act), for the Prince's birthday in November next, if such an offer were made to them.[146] He asked me whether, if the offer were made, I would be prepared to write a new one-act opera to go with the Purcell (which takes about

---

[143] The invitation, suggested by Boulanger, for Berkeley to join the jury of the annual Prince Rainier of Monaco International Award, which became the main opportunity for them to meet for many years.

[144] Prince Rainier III of Monaco (1923–2005) was crowned in 1950 when he married the American film star Grace Kelly following the abdication of his father.

[145] The piano part for the recitatives is played by the conductor.

[146] The Prince's birthday was on 31 May.

an hour). I said I would think about it but that I feared the time was too short. Meanwhile he has heard nothing more from Monte Carlo. Do you know anything about this? I couldn't ask anyone here as nothing official has yet been said.

I am sorry to inflict this long letter on you, but in view of the Prince's remarks to me yesterday, I thought I had better tell you how matters stood. Perhaps you could ring me up tomorrow morning to say what you think about it, as I doubt if we shall have an opportunity for private conversation. I have to leave tomorrow evening.

PS I can in any case send you piano scores of my two existing operas.

Hotel de Paris, Monte-Carlo
[April 1955]

[Now in French]

I haven't said goodbye, thinking to see you again – sadly, I can't – since I've got to leave here soon.

I want to thank you – for it's through you, mainly, that I owe such an interesting and pleasant week. I am above all pleased to have been able to spend some moments with you. ...

8 Warwick Avenue, London W.2
24 February 1957

You are too kind – you shouldn't have troubled to write![147]

Obviously we know that honours have little connection with real merit, but I admit that this has nevertheless pleased me – being always in need of encouragement – and even more in that it was a complete surprise.

I am going to ask Mr Gibson to send you one or two things which have come out lately, not because I am proud of them, but because I hope that they may be a bit better than what I have done for some time.

8 Warwick Avenue, London W.2
13 March 1958

[Now in English]

I have promised a pupil of mine who is at the Royal Academy that I would ask you if you could take him as a student for a short time if he gets a scholarship to go to Paris in the autumn. I don't know whether you will like what he is doing, but I am convinced that he has real talent and a genuine musical individuality. ... It may be that you cannot take on any more pupils, but if you feel you could, I should be so grateful if you would let me know. His name is Nicholas Maw.[148]

---

[147] The Award of the CBE.
[148] Nicholas Maw (1935–2010), a leading British composer of his generation who moved to the US in 1984. In 1959 he won the Award of the Lili Boulanger Memorial Fund for his Nocturne for Chamber Orchestra. The formidable panel of judges consisted of Boulanger,

I hear you are going to America – how I wish you were coming here!

[Boulanger visited the US again, arriving in April 1958.]

8 Warwick Avenue, London W.2
2 November 1959

[Now in French]

Freda and I were thrilled to spend the evening with you – thankyou a thousand times. For me it was something more than a pleasure – I was moved by so many memories. ...

And I was conscious that I was often dreaming at the moment when I ought to have joined in the conversation! ...

Hotel de Paris, Monte-Carlo
17 February 1960

[Now in English]

I had hoped to see you again – and Freda was not even able to say goodbye, but we must not complain, because it was a wonderful opportunity to spend a little time in your company and, for me, that is from time to time, a necessity!

I think, as regards the prizes, that we made the right decisions. I was a little doubtful at first about the Finkheimer Trio, because, although it had great accomplishment and real musical talent, I find it difficult with dodecaphonic music to get rid of a feeling that I have heard it all before. It reminds me of the Greek legend of the people who had only one eye between them which had to be passed to each in turn before they could see! Nevertheless, it represents one of the styles that must be considered valid today, and as the opera was in such a very difficult style, I am certain that your suggestion was the right one. It was a pity that we had so few interesting works to read. I'm glad to say that I can now read music with far greater facility than I could when I was a student, and I get a great deal of pleasure from reading new scores. I think one can hope for a better standard in the future.[149]

[There are gaps in the letters now because they mostly concern family matters]

8 Warwick Avenue, London W.2.
1 February 1963

... I'm very sad about the death of Francis Poulenc – such a very old friend of mine. I knew him when I came to France for holidays when I was at Oxford – even before I met you! He was always a very loyal friend, and I used to see him regularly when he came to London. ...

Copland, Alexei Haieff, Piston and Stravinsky. See the interview with Nicholas Maw, p. 248 below.

[149] No information to hand about Finkheimer now.

8 Warwick Avenue, London W.2
1 June 1965

[Now in French]
I must tell you that I was extremely touched that you thought of me to join your Committee of Honour and I accept with pleasure! Although I didn't know your sister, I feel close to her through you, for I know what she has meant to you.[150]

I am sorry to hear how much sadness and anxiety you have had. So often painful things come one on top of the other. ...

8 Warwick Avenue, London W.2
21 July 1965

[Now in English]
Could you spare a moment to see John Tavener and his father who are going to be in Paris next week? Knowing that you found the boy's work interesting, I told him he could ring you up.[151] It occurs to me that you are perhaps already at Fontainebleau, but they would certainly come and see you there if you could spare the time – I should be grateful, as John is hoping to spend most of the winter in Paris and would like to come to you.

8 Warwick Avenue, London W.2
18 May 1967

Very many thanks for your charming note.[152] The great thing about the Monaco Prize from my point of view is that it enables me to spend a little time with you every year – otherwise I know I should never see you!

I'm very keen to do anything I can to get a better entry for next year – I'm quite sure that as far as this country is concerned, not enough of our younger composers know about it. If by any chance you have time to come on and see us next month please do not fail to do so. We shall be at Aldeburgh for the rehearsals and first performance of my opera from May 31 to June 5 but otherwise here. ...[153]

---

[150] See Lennox Berkeley, 'Lili Boulanger', *Listener*, 21 November 1968, reprinted at p. 130 below.

[151] John Tavener (1944–). His *Cain and Abel* (1965) had been awarded the Prince Rainer of Monaco International Award in 1965 when Boulanger chaired the jury; its premiere in London attracted considerable attention. Tavener and his parents did go to see Boulanger at Fontainebleau but he decided not to study with her. He was knighted in 2000.

[152] Boulanger was ill and unable to go to Monaco. On 18 November 1967 Prince Rainier III named Berkeley as Commandeur de l'ordre du mérite culturel.

[153] *Castaway*, premiered 3 June 1967 in the Jubilee Hall, Aldeburgh.

8 Warwick Avenue, London W.2
17 September 1967

You must be receiving so many letters that I hesitate to add to their number, yet I cannot let your birthday go by without sending you a personal message of love and affection from all of us.[154] What you have been and still are for me I need hardly say again – my whole life was changed by your influence and example, and though I've not been able to live up to the ideals, musical and otherwise, that you set before me in my student days, I still can, and do, thank God for them. It is such a great happiness to see such a vast number of people who know about your work for music – something that we have known for so long is now known to the whole musical world.

I greatly regret that I can't be with you later this month to join in the celebration of your birthday, but present circumstances make it impossible. You know that I shall be with you in thought. ...

8 Warwick Avenue, London W.2
25 June 1968

I heard reports of your visit to Oxford and of how you made your way there strikes and upheavals notwithstanding! You didn't tell me that you were being given an honorary degree – I am delighted – it was long overdue. I'm particularly happy that it was Oxford – my university and my home town – that has shown such good taste and judgement![155]

8 Warwick Avenue, London W.2
30 October 1969

[In French]

Your letter gave me so much pleasure – to know that you have found my [Third] Symphony rather good, in general, is the greatest encouragement. I didn't even know that French Radio had broadcast it. I wonder if it was a recording of the concert at Cheltenham, or if they played it again. Anyhow the orchestra is excellent in every way.[156]

---

[154] Boulanger was eighty on 16 September.

[155] Boulanger was awarded a DMus by Oxford University (*The Times*, 27 May 1968). In 1959 she had been given an Hon. DMus by Birmingham University, where the Professor was her old student Anthony Lewis. Another doctorate came from Leeds University in 1972.

[156] Symphony no. 3, op. 74, premiered 3 August 1969 at the Cheltenham Festival by the RTF Orchestra under Jean Martinon. See interview with John Manduell, p. 243 below. On 24 October 1969 Boulanger wrote to Berkeley: 'What a superb achievement. Fortunately the radio had the intelligence to broadcast your symphony, and I would really love to comment but you know how it is, and you must wait for our next meeting for clearer precision. Mais pourquoi en Anglais?'

8 Warwick Avenue, London W.2
June 1973

[In English]

I must tell you – since I was not able to see you again before you left London, how much it meant to me that you came to the concert given by my publisher last month. I was much moved to have you there beside me – to have the support of your presence, and I thought of the immense moral support you gave me many years ago through which I was able to become a composer at all, even if only a minor one. You know that I will never forget what I owe to you.

I realised that you were not well during your visit here – I hope this was only momentary and that you are in good health again. ...

[Boulanger attended a seventieth birthday celebration recital for Berkeley at the Goldsmith's Hall, London EC2, on 22 May 1973.

Sonatina for piano duet – Susan Bradshaw and Richard Rodney Bennett
Songs: Tant que mes yeux; How love came in – Meriel and Peter Dickinson
Sonatina for oboe and piano – Janet Craxton and Alan Richardson
Three Mazurkas for piano – Janet de Roet
Five Poems of W. H. Auden – Meriel and Peter Dickinson

As an encore Berkeley and I played his *Palm Court Waltz*, op. 81/2a, for piano duet. In his diary for June 11 that year he admitted: 'I was a little frightened about playing this frivolous extravaganza in front of Nadia but I think she took it in good part.' In his earlier diary entry of 2 December 1971 he wrote: 'It's pure light music in which I could indulge my taste for rather sentimental harmony to the full']

8 Warwick Avenue, London W.2
4 July 1974

It was so kind of you to write – Freda and I were deeply touched by your letter.[157] I think many people are happy to see an honour go to music or the arts – whatever they may think of the actual recipient! I've had many kind letters and messages.

You know that you are often in my thoughts. Freda joins me in sending our love and every good wish.

---

[157] Berkeley had been given a knighthood in the recent honours list.

– *Part III* –
Selections from Berkeley's Later Writings and Talks, 1943–82

INTRODUCTION

Berkeley wrote occasional articles and reviews for newspapers and periodicals, invariably expressed with style and discrimination. This selection starts with Berkeley anxious to share his enthusiasm for Britten's music. Britten had heard early works of Berkeley in London five years before they met.[1] One can understand Britten admiring the objective neo-baroque movements of Berkeley's Suite for oboe and cello, steeped in Bach and so different from the provincial English folksong school. The two composers met in April 1936 when they were both represented in the International Society for Contemporary Music Festival at Barcelona on the eve of the Spanish Civil War. They immediately became close friends and worked together on the orchestral *Mont Juic Suite*. It was premiered in a BBC broadcast on 8 January 1938. From then onwards Berkeley followed every work of Britten's with the greatest interest, and in 1943 wrote the first article included here, about his String Quartet no. 1. Britten figures prominently in Berkeley's 1949 lectures given in France, which provide a panoramic and judicious survey of British composers at that time; he continued with an article on Britten's *Spring Symphony*; but I have not included his chapter on the light music written in 1952.[2] As with Boulanger, Berkeley paid tribute to Britten on many occasions – they were the two constants in his professional musical life.[3]

Of course, the French aspect is well represented here, with a 1946 BBC talk on ballet music, and contributions about Poulenc and Ravel, both of whom were friends. Berkeley comments perceptively on Fauré, who taught both Ravel and Nadia Boulanger, and therefore is the source of a tradition to which Berkeley himself can be attached. In 1968 he drew attention to the slender output of Lili Boulanger, whose tragic early death had such an effect on her sister, as Berkeley well knew. His tribute to Alan Rawsthorne, marking the composer's death in 1971, shows a complete and generous understanding – in depth – of what Rawsthorne's music is about and why it had been neglected. And when Berkeley

---

[1] The *Petite Suite* for oboe and cello (1927) was recorded by the Endymion Ensemble on Dutton CDLX 7100 (1999) and other works of this period are surfacing, such as the Suite for flute, oboe and string trio (1930), with Judith Fitton, Sarah Francis and the Tagore String Trio on Regis RRC1380 (2011). See the CD booklet and Dickinson, *The Music of Lennox Berkeley*, 10; also *Letters from a Life: Selected Letters and Diaries of Benjamin Britten: Volume One, 1923–39*, ed. Donald Mitchell and Philip Reed (London, 1991), 436.

[2] Donald Mitchell with Hans Keller, eds., *Benjamin Britten: a Commentary on his Works by a Group of Specialists* (London, 1952), 287–94.

[3] Berkeley's diary entry for December 1966 rates Britten alongside Mozart.

writes sympathetically about Fauré some of what he says can be applied to his own music.[4]

Thirty years after those reports from Paris were published in *The Monthly Musical Record*, Berkeley emerges again as a perceptive reviewer, with a far greater range and sophistication than Britten's limited output in words. Berkeley wrote and spoke informatively about his own music[5] and was acutely aware of the problems that composers experience. His broadcast talk about musical criticism is an unusually lucid and penetrating discussion of the issues involved – a classic statement that ought to be widely known. However, in 1972, he was not up to date about the contribution that musical scholars had been making to the literature of music.

Berkeley also opens a window in the most endearing way into the wide range of books he reads, his spiritual concerns and his attitude to church music. His religious faith is the core of the man and goes a long way to account for the integrity and continuing presence of his liturgical music in cathedral lists today.

In 1982 Berkeley paid tribute to the greatest master of his period – Stravinsky – although he found it difficult to come to terms with his later conversion to serialism. As Berkeley wrote in 1949: 'I have never been able to derive much satisfaction from atonal music …'[6]

The article which I have placed at the end is a moving reflection on the problems of old age and it sums up Berkeley's serene philosophy of life.

---

[4] Dickinson, *The Music of Lennox Berkeley*, 52. Berkeley arranged some pieces by Fauré for two pianos to go with the ballet *La Fête étrange* in 1940 and orchestrated them in 1947 for Sadler's Wells. The ballet was revived at Covent Garden in 2005 by the Royal Ballet. See Scotland, *Lennox and Freda*, 405.

[5] See also Dickinson, *The Music of Lennox Berkeley*, 52–3, for the only source of Berkeley's BBC introduction to his String Quartet no. 2.

[6] Quoted complete in Dickinson, *The Music of Lennox Berkeley*, 161.

1 Britten and his String Quartet [no. 1]

The Listener, 27 May 1943

The difficulty of assessing the value of contemporary works of art is well known. We always seem to be either too close or too far away to see them in their true perspective. If we can understand or perhaps even speak their language, we are too close, too grateful for their expression of what we ourselves would express, while if we can only feel at home with the idiom of earlier periods, we fail to grasp their meaning. This is one of the reasons why such diverse and even contradictory opinions prevail on the subject of modern art. In music this divergence of opinion is perhaps not quite so apparent as in the other arts because people find themselves more easily out of their depth in discussing it, and are more prepared to leave the matter in the hands of experts. And yet, the desire for music and for a music that can adequately speak the language of today, is felt by many people at the present time.

Among the new works that have been played recently, Benjamin Britten's String Quartet has aroused great interest by reason of its striking originality of idiom and the individuality of its musical thought. It is one of his most recent works, commissioned by Mrs. Elizabeth Sprague Coolidge, whose generosity has been responsible for the creation of so much new music.

Britten's mastery of the technique of composition has for some time now been admitted by all; he has (incomprehensibly enough) even been reproached by some critics for the apparent ease with which he solves technical problems, as though a high standard of professional competence were undesirable. This criticism was based on the suspicion that Britten's astonishing technique was nothing more than slickness, and that his music lacked depth. The idea that clever technicians are necessarily superficial, and that there is something not quite gentlemanly about the professional, is a curious aberration to which the English mind is particularly prone. Nevertheless, if it was true that for some time Britten's technique was in advance of his mental and emotional development, it is no longer true today. The *Sinfonia da Requiem*, the *Michelangelo Sonnets*, and perhaps most of all the String Quartet have revealed a fully mature artist whose work is not merely exceptionally clever but exceptionally significant.

The work is in four movements. The first movement is constructed with such clarity and economy of material that, as far as the form is concerned, it is very easy to follow. It is made up of two episodes, the one slow and the other quick. The slow one, a cluster of notes very high up which move in a pattern of great beauty, punctuated by pizzicato notes in the cello indicating the tonality and providing a rhythmical background, begins the movement. This is followed by the quick section: a rhythmical figure with which a vigorous theme is combined. These two episodes alternate, but each time they appear they are telescoped until finally the first episode is reduced to three bars, and the second to two. The scherzo comes next, and here we see how far removed Britten is from those who think that progress can only be made by throwing overboard the tonal system; for the movement is entirely based upon changes of tonality.

The third movement (Andante calmo) is perhaps the most easily accessible. Its restrained and yet passionate feeling is maintained from the first bar to the last and always with the simplest and most effective means. Emotionally this movement bears a very unexpected but undeniable resemblance to late Beethoven, though the form is much more compact. The last movement with its brilliantly contrived counterpoint, its breath-taking speed, and its very typical central tune, reminds one of the composer's earlier works, but bears the stamp of his personality much more strongly. This movement is made out of a short phrase caught up by one instrument after the other, and conveys an impression of great dexterity. Later, a robust and vehement tune played by the two violins and the viola in unison appears over a running figure in the cello.

Much more important, however than the success with which the material is handled, is the meaning of the music itself. Britten is in a sense an extremely traditional composer. The novelty of his music does not consist in any new discovery of musical language or form. He relies on the freshness and individuality of his musical thought rather than on deliberate innovation. True originality in an artist does not consist in his being peculiar, but in his being peculiar to himself. There is no new system here, but a personal and new use of an established one. It is sometimes said that certain composers, even some of the great ones, are a law unto themselves, outside the main stream of music. This can certainly be said of Stravinsky and to some extent of Debussy. Britten, on the other hand, belongs very much to the main stream. This music could only have been written by someone who had a profound understanding of the classical masters. The new element in his music is generally a development or new treatment of something that was there before, but he infuses into it a freshness and life that are all his own. Auden gives us a clue to the understanding of this type of originality in his *Hymn to St Cecilia*:

> Where hope within the altogether strange
> From every out-worn image is released ...[7]

It is this release from the out-worn image that Britten brings us: the release from every kind of cliché, from those too easy gestures that have become meaningless. And though appreciation of his more recent music makes certain demands on the listener, there is nothing forbidding about it. The String Quartet is full of unusual qualities but the really surprising thing is its beauty.

---

[7] W. H. Auden, *Anthem for St Cecilia's Day* (July 1940), dedicated to Benjamin Britten, who was born on St Cecilia's Day, 22 November 1913.

2 Modern French Ballet Music

Illustrated radio talk broadcast 19 July 1946 by the BBC Overseas Programme Eastern Service under the title of 'Descriptive Music: the Ballet'. The producer was Basil Douglas.[8]

The ballet has always played an important part in French cultural life, since the days when Louis XIV danced in ballets composed and devised by Lully,[9] right up to this year, when a French ballet company came to London having formed itself and created an entirely new repertoire of ballets in spite of the war and the occupation of the country.[10] That, I think, shows that the tradition is very strong. During the early part of this century, however, it received a new stimulus from Diaghilev's Russian Ballet which began its career in Paris in 1909; it had an immediate and enormous effect on composers and painters in all European countries and the French were the first to react to its influence.[11] Diaghilev on his side was anxious to use French talent and in 1911 he commissioned *Daphnis et Chloé* from Ravel.[12] I want to spend a little time considering this ballet because it's not only Ravel's largest orchestral work, but it is also one of the most considerable pieces of ballet music in existence. At this point, I feel obliged to ask myself how often one can call a ballet of this kind descriptive music. Well, I think one can say that the music acts as a kind of landscape; the mood and emotional climate is created by a musical description of the idyllic scene in which the action is set.

The scenario of the ballet follows fairly closely the story as told by Longus.[13] It is the prototype of the shepherd and shepherdess story that became so popular in the eighteenth century. Daphnis, a young and beautiful shepherd-boy, falls in love with the shepherdess Chloé. Both are innocent and at first hardly realise the nature of their feelings, and the story, which includes episodes such as an attack by pirates, who attempt the abduction of Chloé, and a dancing competition between Daphnis and the cowherd Dorion is really nothing other than the development of this simple theme. Here is an extract which in the orchestral suite is called Nocturne.

Music example: Orchestre de la société des concerts, HMV DB 4930A, 2′30″

Now here is part of the music to the scene in which the pirates make their

---

[8] See interview with Basil Douglas, p. 271 below.

[9] Jean-Baptiste Lully (1632–87), Italian-born French composer who entered the service of Louis XIV from 1652 as dancer and composer, and in 1661 became Surintendant de la musique de la chambre du roi. With his operas, ballets and church music he became the most influential French composer of the period.

[10] Les Ballets des Champs-Elysées, formed in 1945 by Roland Petit and Boris Kochno: their London visit was acclaimed.

[11] Sergei Diaghilev (1872–1929), Russian impresario whose Ballets Russes brought together the leading talents in all the arts with a sensational impact. He launched Stravinsky and commissioned ten works.

[12] Maurice Ravel (1875–1937). See also Berkeley's article on Ravel, p. 145 below.

[13] Second- or third-century Greek writer of the romance *Daphnis and Chloé*, set on the Isle of Lesbos.

incursion. It is seemingly vigorous and rhythmical – a style that was rather new to Ravel at this time and which I think shows the influence of Russian music.

Music example: HMV DB 4930B, 1′20″

Although it is very well known I cannot resist playing you the opening of the second suite because it is one of the loveliest sounds that a composer has ever devised. It certainly is a peak of descriptive music. I know of no other composition in which the sounds of nature have been used with such ravishing effect. It represents the dawn: absolute stillness but for the almost imperceptible murmur of a stream. Little by little, day breaks.

Music example: Boston Symphony Orchestra, HMV D1826, 4′15″

I think you'll agree that this achieves in a supreme degree the object of all descriptive music, which is not merely to give a musical picture of something, but to use the descriptive idea in such a way that it becomes as important as a theme would be in more abstract music.

Ten years later Ravel wrote a choreographic poem which he intended for the stage, but which in fact was not used for a ballet until long after it had become famous as a concert piece. This was *La Valse*.[14] I think it is legitimate to class this work as descriptive music; there is a note by the composer on the score in which he tells us that he has in mind a ball at an imperial court in the 1850s, but it is, of course, a different kind of description from what we have just had – here it is not a question of natural sounds, for it would be difficult to go further from nature than a court ball in the mid-nineteenth century, it is description simply by using material based on the style with which such a scene is associated. The tunes, although they closely resemble those of the period, are all Ravel's invention and bear the stamp of his personality. There is an element of parody in *La Valse*, but it is mixed with genuine appreciation, as the French proverb says: 'on se moque de ce qu'on aime' – we laugh at what we love – and in consequence it is touched with a very subtle and attractive irony. Several notions probably lay behind the creation of the work – the foremost and simplest being a love of the Viennese waltz for its own sake and a desire on the part of the composer to recreate it in his own language.

But then there was also, I think, for Ravel a psychological appeal in the mixture of sentiment and superficiality that characterises the waltz; the sensuous charm and pathos combined with a rather empty glitter – all that fascinated him, for he was a man to whom the finer shades of feeling made a greater appeal than the more powerful emotions. Another motive that may have contributed is that the shape of Ravel's melody falls very easily into waltz time anyway, and that his harmony adopts itself very well to this style. Here is an extract which will show you what I mean.

Music example: San Francisco Symphony Orchestra, HMV DB 5964, 1′15″

---

[14] *La Valse, poème chorégraphique* (1919–20), stage premiere 2 October 1926 at the Flemish Opera, Antwerp.

Now here is some music from another French ballet from about the same time as *Daphnis*. It is the opening of Roussel's *La Festin de l'araignée*[15] – *The Spider's Banquet* – which was produced at the Théâtre des Arts in 1913. Roussel was then at the beginning of his career as a composer and his style had not developed the individuality it had later, nevertheless this opening passage is very charming and evocative.

Music example: Orchestre de les concerts Straram, Col LFX 47, 4′ 15″

I should not leave the period before World War I without mentioning Paul Dukas' ballet *La Péri* and Florent Schmitt's *La Tragédie de Salomé*, both of which enjoyed some popularity.[16]

The transition between 1913 and 1920 is abrupt; in 1920 we find that an entirely new aesthetic theory has taken the field – it is the return to simplicity, the avoidance of the romantic and the picturesque, preached by Jean Cocteau[17], and practised in music by Erik Satie and the group known as The Six. This movement was seized on by Diaghilev who was always hot on the scent of anything new, and the result was several French ballets with music by Satie, Poulenc, Auric, Milhaud and a little later Henri Sauguet.[18] Unfortunately I can give you no adequate musical illustrations of this period, as a good deal of the music proved to be somewhat ephemeral. Very little has been recorded and almost none is now available. Here, however, is a piano version of the Andantino from Poulenc's *Les Biches*[19] – one of the few examples of this period to have survived. The piano is played by the composer.

Music example: Andantino, Poulenc, COL D 15094A, 1′ 53″

The next piece I want to play forms part of a ballet called *L'Éventail de Jeanne*, the music of which was written by several composers each writing a movement; it was given for a special function at the opera in Paris and ten composers took part.[20] This movement called *Pastourelle* is a piano version of Poulenc's contribution. It contains much of what was best in the style of Les Six – an engaging simplicity, freshness and tunefulness.

Music example: Pastourelle, Horowitz, HMV DB 2247, 2′ 15″

There are many other French ballets of recent times that I should like to talk about – those commissioned by Ida Rubinstein, for instance, like Ibert's *Diane de*

---

[15] Albert Roussel (1869–1937).

[16] Paul Dukas (1865–1935), *La Péri: poème dansé* (Paris, 1912). Florent Schmidt (1870–1958), *La Tragédie de Salomé*, op. 50, ballet, 1907, revised as a symphonic poem in 1910.

[17] Jean Cocteau (1889–1963), writer, designer, film-maker and propagandist who provided the text for Stravinsky's *Oedipus rex* (1928), and whose poems were set to music by several of the leading French composers.

[18] Erik Satie (1866–1925), godfather to Les Six – including Francis Poulenc (1899–1963), George Auric (1899–1983) and Darius Milhaud (1892–1974); Henri Sauguet (1901–89).

[19] *Les Biches* (ballet avec chant), Monte Carlo, 1924.

[20] *L'Eventail de Jeanne* (Paris, 1927). The other composers were Ravel, Roussel, Ferroud, Ibert, Roland-Manuel, Delannoy, Milhaud, Auric and Schmitt.

Poitiers, Ravel's *Boléro*[21] and those performed by the new Ballet des Champs Elysées which have recently been given in London – alas, there is no time nor are there yet any records to play but I should like in conclusion to play you the end of Poulenc's *Aubade*.[22] This work is a kind of choreographic divertissement scored for piano and eighteen instruments. I think it is interesting because it sums up very effectively the various influences that have been at work in the period between the wars. One can recognise here the influence of Stravinsky and the development from the very light style of the French ballet music of the 1920s into something rather more solid. Music and dancing have always been very close together, they have continually reacted upon each other, for although we may not connect a slow pulse like this with dancing, to my mind it was very obviously inspired by the dance, and in turn the music brings to the stage a restraint and clarity that only a French composer could have given it.

Music example: Aubade, Orchestre des concerts Straram, Col LF35, 2′35″

---

[21] Ibert: *Diane de Poitiers* (Paris, 1934); Ravel: *Boléro* (1919–20), ballet (Paris, 1928).

[22] *Aubade: concerto choréographique* (Paris, 1929).

3 British Music Today

In March 1949 the British Council arranged a lecture tour for Berkeley to promote British music. He started at Roubaix, near Lille, on 21 March and went on to Nancy, Strasbourg and finally Paris on 30 March.[23] The typescript is at the Britten-Pears Library: it has been translated from French by the editor with assistance from Oliver Goulden.

Mesdames, Messieurs,
When I came to Paris twenty-four years ago to study music,[24] I found that people were astonished to learn that composers existed in England: it was felt that England was a country of businessmen and sportsmen, and that apart from literature, the arts had little importance in our life. At that period there was nothing surprising about this attitude. During the last part of the nineteenth century, and the start of the twentieth, painting and music which were of major importance in France, were with us almost dead. To find the causes of this I think it is necessary to go a long way back. The spiritual and cultural isolation which the Reformation produced is perhaps one:[25] the nineteenth-century industrial revolution is perhaps another. What is sure is that at the time when France produced painters like Cézanne and Renoir, composers like Fauré, Debussy and Ravel, England, as far as painting and music are concerned, counted for nothing. She lacked a tradition, and her few composers, submerged by waves of Wagner, failed because their works were completely lacking in personality and freshness. A single composer at the beginning of the twentieth century – Edward Elgar[26] – succeeded in giving his music a specifically English quality, and this, added to a very solid technique, allowed him to go further than the others. We must admit that the influence of German music is very perceptible with Elgar, but all the same he was the first composer of what can be called the renaissance of English music. For, since the end of the First World War – since about 1920 – not only have we got numerous composers but the quality of what they are producing is much superior to what there was before.

It is the same thing in painting: without exaggeration, I think we can say that the works of English painters and composers today are at least comparable in interest to those of painters and composers of other countries. You see there a great change which has come about in a relatively short space of time. It is in some ways

---

[23] According to Scotland, *Lennox and Freda*, 416.

[24] In 1926 Berkeley settled in Paris, where he began his studies with Nadia Boulanger.

[25] As a pious Roman Catholic, Berkeley was perhaps ruefully referring to the Act of Supremacy (1534) whereby Henry VIII severed the link with Rome and became supreme head of the Church of England. The Dissolution of the Monasteries (1535–9) that followed was a social and cultural disaster of far-reaching proportions.

[26] Sir Edward Elgar (1857–1934). In his diary for 5 January 1973 Berkeley wrote: 'Elgar's First Symphony is a fine work – expert and effective scoring, but the sound is very thick and over-elaborate. One can't think of any other English composer of the time who could have achieved anything nearly as good.' However, on an occasion late in his life when Alzheimer's meant he could no longer speak but could still enjoy music, I played the piano to him. I started on the Prelude to *The Dream of Gerontius* and he left the room!

the opposite of the nineteenth-century situation – complete decadence in the arts but immense success in commerce. Now, painting and music are developing rapidly and it is business that does not go so well. But one can't have everything!

So, as I was saying, we now have a living music. It is difficult to place an artist who is in mid-career, and I would even say it is impossible to judge definitively a composer, painter or writer who is still living: one cannot see the complete output, and one cannot always understand trends before seeing where they are going to lead.

That is why critics prefer dead composers, a preference I have never understood better than while I was preparing this lecture, because I am going to talk to you only about living composers.

When Elgar died there were already several composers who occupied an important place in English music. The most outstanding was one who is now the doyen of English musicians: Vaughan Williams.[27] With him we are already far from Elgar.

From the start of his career he turned to English folksong. Being conscious of the lack of tradition in English music, he thought that the best way to remake one would be to draw on folk music. He succeeded in liberating English music from the German influence and he found a way of using folk music to build a very personal style. Vaughan Williams, who is now seventy-seven, is the best-loved composer in England. We recognise something in the quality of his thought and feeling which is profoundly English. His music has a kind of contemplative serenity, a state of mind which is extremely personal. I should like you to hear the opening of his Fifth Symphony.

Music example: Vaughan Williams, Symphony no. 5 (1938–43)

The structure of this music is strange: we could say that the themes grow naturally, independently, so to speak, of the wish of the composer. It seems that a development is not imposed on the music, but that it develops of itself. However, you mustn't think that all the music of Vaughan Williams resembles what you've just heard. So I want you to hear a piece of a very different character. Here is the opening of the finale of the Fourth Symphony.

Music example: Vaughan Williams, Symphony no. 4 (1931–4)

I wanted to play you that because we find here one of the characteristic traits of English music – I mean the tendency to avoid chromatic harmony. You have perhaps noticed that, in this movement, the composer harmonises his main theme with a succession of common chords. He often uses this procedure, as in our traditional melodies.

I think one can say that, in Vaughan Williams' music, the interest lies in melody and counterpoint. Theme and harmony are much less important.[28] With some exceptions, this seems to me to be true of English music in general, particularly that which is based on folksong, for in our popular music rhythm is not very marked.

---

[27] Ralph Vaughan Williams (1872–1958).

[28] This is what Berkeley wrote, but the logic is elusive.

The essential thing is always the melody, and it is the melodic curve that gives the music its character, and fulfils the function performed by rhythm in Spanish popular music, for example.

However, it seems to me that Vaughan Williams is the only composer who has been able to use English folksong – at least the only one who has made such a success of it. Has he drawn from it all that could be extracted, or are the other composers afraid of falling into a style too close to his? I'm not sure. Anyhow, most other English composers have looked for their inspiration elsewhere.

After Vaughan Williams, among composers no longer young but whose names are well known with us, are Arnold Bax, John Ireland and Arthur Bliss.[29] Bax, an extremely gifted musician, belongs to what might be called the impressionist school, often inspired by the visual as indicated by the titles of many of his works. For him music, far from being an abstract and subjective thing, should always be the direct expression of an emotion.

Ireland is known above all for his piano music. More simple and clear than that of Bax, it gets very close to French music, which is obviously an influence.

As for Bliss, I believe he is a composer already well known in France. He has written a lot for the theatre. A few years ago Sadler's Wells Ballet gave his *Checkmate* at the Théâtre des Champs Elysées.[30] He has written two other ballets and plenty of orchestral music, and he has just finished an opera where I am sure we shall find the qualities of vigour and imagination which have always distinguished his music.[31]

I come to a very much younger composer, but one who has had great success in England: William Walton is forty-six.[32] Success came to him very young, his first works showing great competence and a natural feeling for the orchestra. Although he uses a contemporary musical language, Walton is more of a romantic. By that I mean that his music has a tendency to express either a feeling or an emotional state, rather than finding beauty through form or sonority. It is difficult to define exactly what one understands by 'classic' and 'romantic' in music, but I believe that one can, to some extent, define composers in these terms. As an example, I would say that Debussy had more of a romantic mentality and Ravel more classic.

However that may be, Walton certainly speaks a contemporary language.

You will see what I mean if I play you the beginning of his Concerto for Viola and Orchestra. This is one of his first works, written when he was in his mid-twenties, but I think it remains one of his best.

Music example: William Walton, Viola Concerto (1928–9)

This music has a very English melancholy, an atmosphere one recognises in our poets of the eighteenth and nineteenth centuries, for example in Wordsworth. The

---

[29] Sir Arnold Bax (1883–1953), Master of the King's (later Queen's) Music, 1941. John Ireland (1879–1962). Sir Arthur Bliss (1891–1975), Master of the Queen's Music, 1953. Director of Music at the BBC when Berkeley was working there during the war.

[30] *Checkmate*, with choreography by Ninette de Valois, was premiered 15 June 1937 at the Champs-Elysées, Paris.

[31] *The Olympians*, with a libretto by J. B. Priestley, was premiered 29 September 1949 at Covent Garden.

[32] Sir William Walton (1902–83).

second movement of this concerto resembles the contemporary music of other countries with a very marked rhythm and clear, dry orchestration.

Music example: William Walton, Viola Concerto, Vivo con moto preciso

Walton works slowly, which means his list of works is not long. Most are for orchestra; there is a symphony, two overtures and a violin concerto; also a cantata on biblical words called *Belshazzar's Feast* (1931). This last created a sensation fifteen years ago at its first performance: it's a very robust work, more remarkable for the effect it produces than its musical content, but it marks all the same a stage in the renaissance of British music. Walton is an extremely gifted man whose music is of a high standard which merits the place it occupies in the music of today.

I think everyone will agree that Benjamin Britten is the greatest talent among the young English composers.[33] At thirty-five his name is known among musicians throughout the world. How has he managed to overtake his colleagues in such a short time? I think there are several reasons. First of all, he possesses magnificent craftsmanship, and a profound knowledge of all the theory and technique of composition. He is one of those artists who loves his work, and who, in their youth, instead of wasting time on grandiose projects and ambitious dreams, applied himself to acquiring technical mastery. The attitude of the musician towards music is very important – there are composers who use music to express their ideas and their emotions, there are others who love music for itself. Britten is one of these.

With him we sense pleasure, ease, and a concern for elegant writing. But he should not be thought of as a mere theoretician; his music is always clever, but never dry; there is an exquisite sensibility, and in all his best works a truly remarkable freshness and invention. He has written music in all genres but has specialised in music for the stage, and above all is known for his three operas: *Peter Grimes*, *The Rape of Lucretia* and *Albert Herring*.[34]

Peter Grimes is a grand opera with chorus, orchestra and about ten principal roles. The first performance took place on 7 June 1945 at Sadler's Wells in London. Since then it has been produced in almost all the countries of Europe and America. The subject of the opera comes from a poem by George Crabbe, an eighteenth-century writer, and the action takes place in a small fishing town on the English coast in about 1830.[35] I'd like you to hear an orchestral piece, taken from the beginning of the opera, where the composer describes the countryside where the action unfolds. It's on the coast overlooking the North Sea, flat and arid country which resembles certain parts of Holland, but with a marked character that Britten depicts admirably.[36]

Music example: Benjamin Britten, *Four Sea Interludes* no. 1

---

[33] Benjamin Britten (1913–76), made a life peer in 1976.

[34] *Peter Grimes*, op. 33; *The Rape of Lucretia*, op. 37, premiered 12 July 1946 at Glyndebourne, Sussex; *Albert Herring*, op. 39, premiered 20 June 1947 at Glyndebourne.

[35] George Crabbe (1753–1832). His poem *The Borough* (1810) includes the tales of Peter Grimes.

[36] Britten and Berkeley both knew this part of Suffolk well. Britten was born in Lowestoft, Suffolk, and Berkeley shared The Old Mill at Snape with Britten between 1938 and 1939.

I think you'll agree that this music has a plenty of atmosphere. I'd very much have liked to play you other parts of this opera which is so well known and so loved in my country – unfortunately it would be too long.

After *Peter Grimes* Britten has written two operas for the English Opera Group, a theatre company of which he is one of the founders. This group has been formed with the intention of performing operas requiring only a small orchestra, which allows them to travel with their own musicians. In fact they have played more-or-less everywhere in England as well as in Switzerland and Holland. The orchestra consists of only twelve musicians and, in the two operas he has written for this ensemble, Britten uses the small number of players with a truly astonishing virtuosity. His other works include a *Sinfonia da Requiem* for full orchestra, Piano Concerto, Violin Concerto, two string quartets, a cantata for a capella choir,[37] another for choir and organ,[38] and *A Ceremony of Carols* for children's voices and harp.

I should like you to hear part of one of his most beautiful things: it's the *Serenade for Tenor, Horn and Strings*. This consists of six poems, all about evening or night, but by different poets. Britten has achieved an extraordinary unity in the six movements of the work. Here is the second, called Nocturne, on a well-known poem by Tennyson.

Music example:
Benjamin Britten: Serenade for Tenor, Horn and Strings, op. 31

I should now like you to hear an aria from the opera *The Rape of Lucretia*. On the stage, Lucretia is asleep: the voice is accompanied by only four instruments – bass flute, muted horn, bass clarinet and harp, which doubles the voice part at the octave.

Music example: Benjamin Britten: aria from *The Rape of Lucretia*

For me this is truly beautiful. So much contemporary music comes exclusively from the brain and, for that reason, cannot touch the heart, but here it seems that we have a music which brings us the freshness of a new personality capable of moving us.

There is no new system here, but the result is new. As André Cœuroy called it, when writing about French music: 'Innovation within tradition.'[39] I think one can say that of Britten. It shows us it is still possible to find something new whilst retaining a modified conception of tonality. The most recent music by Stravinsky proves this even more. In Stravinsky we are always conscious of a tonal centre, around which the music moves, nearer or further away. We notice the same thing in the music of Hindemith, and that doesn't stop the music of these two masters being very different. Britten remains closer still to tonality, but he also has a very

---

[37] Presumably the *Hymn to St Ceclia*, op. 27 (1942), words by W. H. Auden.
[38] Presumably *Rejoice in the Lamb*, op. 30 (1943), words by Christopher Smart.
[39] André Cœuroy (1891–1976), French critic and writer on music, co-founder of *Revue musicale* and editor 1920–37.

personal way of moving away from it. For example, he often uses two keys at once – in the piece you have just heard that is very clear.

I realise there is nothing new in this, but there's a new way of doing it which corresponds to the needs of a new personality. Finally, I should like to underline this characteristic: the power of recreating traditional procedures by giving them a new life – from this point of view Britten is fundamentally 'classic'. Britten is never afraid of adapting the methods of other composers because he knows that there will be no resemblance to the model in the finished work.

Another composer, a little older than Britten, is starting to gain an important place in English music today: Alan Rawsthorne.[40] With Rawsthorne we find ourselves in the presence of a very different musical mentality from those of the composers I have already discussed. Here we are dealing with a musician rather of the classical genre, whose music is carefully written, and more abstract than is usual amongst the English. He generally works with a phrase of a few notes, develops it in a very logical fashion, adding a sort of commentary which makes it progressively more meaningful. His style is closer to that of most contemporary music in other countries. He chooses the themes rather for what he can do with them, for their contrapuntal and rhythmic possibilities, rather than for the beauty of the idea itself.

For a man of forty-three, Rawsthorne has written little. That is partly because of his extreme care in writing (he loves to think carefully about what he has to say) but also to the fact that war broke out just at the moment when his music was becoming interesting and he found himself in the army for the duration. Further, his house was destroyed by a German bomb and he lost the sketches of his Violin Concerto as well as other important manuscripts. His principal works are: *Theme and Variations* for two violins;[41] Bagatelles for piano; *Symphonic Studies*; two overtures; Piano Concerto; Violin Concerto; Quartet for clarinet and string trio.

Rawsthorne particularly likes variation form – the set for two violins is one of his best works.

The *Symphonic Studies*, written in 1938, is Rawsthorne's most important work. Here we are again very near variation form. In fact the work is a type of suite in five movements, where each one is a variation of the theme heard at the beginning. The orchestration is done with remarkable certainty and imagination. Here is the first part.

Music example: Alan Rawsthorne, *Symphonic Studies*[42]

Apart from Britten, I think that Rawsthorne is the most exportable of our composers. He speaks a language that approaches that of several European composers at the present time.

With Michael Tippett[43] we have a very abstract, pure music. He came to music late, at least to composition: that is to say he composed in his youth but what he

---

[40] Alan Rawsthorne (1905–71). See Berkeley's article on Rawsthorne, p. 138 below.
[41] Premiered 1938 at the London festival of the International Society for Contemporary Music.
[42] First performed in 1939 at the Warsaw festival of the ISCM; British premiere in London the following year.
[43] Michael Tippett (1905–98), knighted 1966.

did then did not satisfy him. With a modesty which, one must say, is very rare he waited for the moment when he felt truly ready.

For a long time he studied early English music – that is to say music of the sixteenth century. For we mustn't forget, that the greatest glory of English music was at that period. In fact the music of Morley, Gibbons, Byrd, Purcell and the other composers of the period of Henry VIII, Elizabeth and James I, otherwise called the age of Shakespeare, was a point of departure for Tippett. It's an interesting case but quite understandable.

Imagine a contemporary English composer with a deep knowledge of this ancient music and aware of the absence of a living tradition. He wondered whether he could manage to find the equivalent of this technique in a modern style – and he succeeded. His style is entirely contrapuntal, much more than the others, and you could even say that the music is conceived on an absolutely horizontal plan. Of course, the same could be said of the music of Hindemith and several others, but what is interesting is that Tippett managed to adapt the style and rhythms of the sixteenth century to a present-day language.

So it is not surprising that he has written mostly choral and chamber music. In particular, there are three string quartets and I am sure that it will interest you to hear part of the last movement of the second – the only one recorded.

Music example: Michael Tippett, String Quartet no. 2, finale

I find the ending beautiful and moving.

Undoubtedly, you'll have noticed the rhythmic liberty of each voice. Each instrument has an independent life, a melodic line which mixes with the others but keeps its own character. One senses that harmony doesn't interest him. Of course, it is necessary in all music that the meeting of the parts should produce harmony and the composer has to take this into account. But with some composers, and certainly with Tippett, harmony exists only as a result of horizontal movement.

Tippett has written an oratorio, *A Child of Our Time*, for which he also wrote the words. Here he followed traditional design: recitative, arias, choruses, and he has even retained the chorale form one finds in the Bach cantatas.[44] There is also a symphony[45] – very beautiful and original – and he is at the moment working on an opera.[46]

Another composer who developed slowly, but who now has a considerable place in English music, is Edmund Rubbra.[47] He is dedicated to writing large orchestral works and has written five symphonies. Like Tippett, it's the structure that interests him. He's exceptional among contemporary composers in needing the large spaces of a symphonic framework for the development of his ideas. For him, colour has much less importance than line. Very traditionalist by nature, his symphonies are

---

[44] *A Child of Our Time* (1939–41), premiered 19 March 1944 in London. A significant difference between Bach's chorales and those of Tippett is that he uses Negro spirituals.

[45] Symphony no. 1 (1944–5).

[46] *The Midsummer Marriage* (1946–52), premiered 27 January 1955 at Covent Garden.

[47] Edmund Rubbra (1901–86) eventually wrote eleven symphonies. Berkeley said eight, corrected to five at the time of his talk.

usually in classical form which he adapts according to his requirements. There is perhaps no striking originality in his music but it is very satisfying through the clarity of structure and logic of musical thought.

As for other young composers, it is hard to know what to say, for there are so many gifted ones that it is impossible to name them all. I am simply going to say a few words about five or six of them.

First, a young woman: Priaulx Rainier,[48] whose music is very serious and often very beautiful. There is a string quartet of hers which has already been played in France and in other countries. We have two other women composers of remarkable talent: Elizabeth Maconchy and Elisabeth Lutyens.[49] The latter, along with Humphrey Searle,[50] usually writes in an atonal style. Gerald Finzi[51] – quite the reverse – is much more traditionalist and has concentrated on songs and choral music. The names of Alan Bush, William Alwyn and Bernard Stevens,[52] still young, appear from time to time on our programmes. Among the youngest composers, it seems to me that the element of nationalism is very slight, far slighter than with their elders. At the moment, it seems to me, all this music reflects the period rather than the country.

Now that we have so many barriers between nations – one cannot even visit another country without formalities and documents – it would be a good thing if the arts became again what they always have been – a manifestation of the human soul and mind which goes beyond political dogma and renders it superfluous. Mesdames, Messieurs, if you will permit me, I am going to finish this lecture by playing on the piano five Preludes of my own.[53]

---

[48] Priaulx Rainier (1903–86), neglected South African-English composer. String Quartet (1939).

[49] Elizabeth Maconchy (1907–94), whose six string quartets have been recorded; Elisabeth Lutyens (1906–83), writer of film music but in her concert and stage works was a British pioneer of serial techniques.

[50] Humphrey Searle (1915–82), another serial pioneer, pupil of Webern, writer on music and authority on Liszt. He worked at the BBC in Bristol; overlapped with Berkeley when they were living at Marshfield; and Berkeley apparently scored his First Symphony (completed in 1953). See Scotland, *Lennox and Freda*, 289–90.

[51] Gerald Finzi (1901–56), whose work has enjoyed continuous popularity in the categories Berkeley cites and more widely, supported by the Finzi Trust, established in 1969.

[52] Alan Bush (1900–95), lifelong communist whose operas were produced in East Germany; William Alwyn (1905–85), successful film composer, many of whose works have been recorded under the aegis of the William Alwyn Trust; Bernard Stevens (1916–83), represented on CD.

[53] From *Six Preludes*, op. 23 (1945). Berkeley would have found the exacting figuration of the third Prelude rather taxing, so presumably decided to leave it out.

4 Britten's *Spring Symphony*

Music & Letters 31/3 (July 1950)

Benjamin Britten's *Spring Symphony*, op. 44, which is dedicated to Serge Koussevitzky and the Boston Symphony Orchestra and was performed for the first time at Amsterdam in July 1949, was given in London at the Royal Albert Hall by the London Philharmonic Choir and Orchestra, conducted by Eduard van Beinum, on March 9.

Seldom can the acoustical shortcomings of that building have been more unfortunate. The publication of the symphony (by Boosey & Hawkes) will be particularly welcome to those who, like myself, have heard it only there. The extremely contrapuntal nature of the music makes it essential for the listener to hear the part-writing clearly; the moment the parts are blurred or indistinct it loses its meaning. Only on reading this beautiful but rather disconcerting work did I realise how little I had heard and how inaccurately.

The *Spring Symphony* is by no means an easy work, and one can understand that, at first hearing, if many people appreciated it at once, others were somewhat bewildered. This was due to various reasons but chiefly, I think, to the fact that recently the composer has greatly developed his style, and his admirers have to make an effort to keep up with him. This always happens with an artist whose personality is rich enough to permit of development. When he always carries his public with him it generally means that he is standing still, rewriting, albeit with more assurance and accomplishment, what he has already written. It is when he is progressing that he is most likely to be misunderstood. For example, Stravinsky's refusal to repeat himself, his habit of starting all over again with each new work, is surely the reason for the otherwise incomprehensible neglect and underrating of his later compositions.

But if I am right in thinking that a development of Britten's technique and personality has been a difficulty, there are others. The spirit of the work and its climate are highly unconventional. It is about the spring; but it does not correspond to most people's preconceived ideas on the subject – derived, as they so often are, rather from pictures they have seen and poems they have read than from a direct, personal apprehension of Nature. The feeling for Nature here is of an unusual kind; it is far removed from Wordsworth's appreciation of Nature's moral or religious significance, and it is equally distant from the serene classical landscapes of Claude and Poussin. To my mind it is more nearly akin to Breughel than any other artist; there is something of the same full-blooded identification of Nature with ordinary human life, the same sympathy with humanity. This breadth of feeling has always been an important part of Britten's music, and largely accounts for his success as an operatic composer.

The work is scored for soprano, alto and tenor soloists, boys' chorus, mixed chorus and orchestra, the words being taken from various poets ranging from the anonymous author of 'Sumer is icumen in' to Auden. There are twelve movements. The orchestra is large; but it is used all together in only four movements, the others being scored for various sections only. Thus 'The Merry Cuckoo' is for tenor and three trumpets; 'The Driving Boy' for soprano, boys' chorus, woodwind, tuba, percussion and violins. (The boys' part, which includes whistling, looks very effective on paper and would, no doubt, be so when performed in better conditions than those of the first London performance. Where I was sitting the boys were almost inaudible, and they seemed to be singing, I thought, too much like choir-boys and not enough like street-boys. The ecclesiastical associations of the medium are evidently difficult to shake off!)

Other movements are scored for tenor accompanied by the violins alone; alto with woodwind, harps and the lower strings; chorus with brass, timpani and percussion. This last, a setting of Milton's 'Now the bright morning star', is music of a dignity and beauty comparable with the poetry itself. Such use of the orchestra in sections is rare, but a similar tendency is found in other contemporary composers and would seem to indicate a desire for purer tone-colour and avoidance of the heavy, over-loaded scoring of so many romantic composers. Much comment has been caused by the cow-horn used in the last movement. This instrument, resembling in tone the Swiss cow-horn but having three notes instead of one, was specially made for the composer by Boosey & Hawkes, and it fulfils its function admirably, producing that curiously awkward, rustic and rather blaring sound that no regular orchestral instrument can make in that particular register. One may doubt whether it has much of a future as a member of the orchestra; but it is the only instrument I have heard that sounds really well in the Albert Hall.

I have said that the *Spring Symphony* shows a further development of Britten's idiom, but there is little in it that was not implicit in his previous works. His genius has always lain not in innovation but in masterly and valid adaptation of traditional methods to his own purpose. He has never rejected tonality, but his use of it becomes increasingly removed from diatonic harmony. Even in this work the tonal centres are very clearly defined. If the impression of bitonality or polytonality is often felt it is produced more by the simultaneous use of different scales having the same root or key-note than by such use of two or more different keys. This very free employment of notes that are foreign to the key in an idiom that is nevertheless tonal is pushed farther here than in Britten's previous music, and the ear has to get accustomed to it.

The methods of construction are as firmly classical as ever, and are used with the customary dexterity. The setting of George Peele's poem 'Fair and fair', for example, is not only a lovely tune but also a wonderful piece of craftsmanship. The melody has a rare freedom of rhythm; it is in 6/8 time, with the natural accent of the phrase appearing in each bar in a different place and forming a subtle and delightful rhythm. To this is added a counter-melody having a shape of its own but falling very neatly into place. At the recapitulation both the main melody and the counter-melody appear in canon, so that the piece moves in double canon through the whole of this section. This is but one example of the composer's skill. A detailed analysis of any movement would yield as much of technical interest.

To me the most moving piece in the whole work is the all too short 'Spring, the Sweet Spring' by Thomas Nashe. Here a melody of the utmost simplicity and freshness is supported by a regular rhythm swinging lazily backwards and forwards between two chords. The three sections, punctuated by the soloists' bird-calls, give the impression of being nearly the same, and yet tune, harmony and rhythm are each time different. Chorus and soloists throw the tune one to the other, the chorus mainly doubled by the woodwind and the soloists by the solo string quartet, while rhythm and harmony are supplied by horns, trombones, harps and timpani. The more one gets to know this movement the more its emotional subtlety grows upon one, its mixture of languor and astringency reflecting so exactly the combination of tender softness and joyous urgency brought by the first appearance of spring. It seems to have the property of evoking something already experienced, in the way that a certain smell, or the texture of some fabric, will bring back a scene of one's childhood.

In general shape, too, the work is original. I can think of nothing similar. It is divided into four parts, each part except the last being subdivided. The first part is framed by the slow introductory movement 'Shine out, Fair Sun' (Anon., sixteenth century), depicting the numb and frozen earth waiting for spring's awakening, and 'The Morning Star' (Milton), to which I have already referred. In between are three moderately fast movements. The most important movement of the second part, forming the slow movement of the work, is the setting of Auden's 'Out on the lawn I lie in bed'. This is preceded by two shorter pieces. The third part begins with the allegro impetuoso, 'When will my May come?' (Barnfield), and is followed by two allegretto movements. The last part consists of a single poem, 'London, to thee I do present', from Beaumont and Fletcher, towards the end of which is incorporated 'Sumer is icumen in', sung by the boys' chorus.

The whole weight of the work is borne by the voices; indeed, the orchestra's function is chiefly to accompany and it is seldom heard alone, a fact that has caused some people to boggle at the title, the word symphony having generally been used for instrumental compositions or, in the seventeenth and eighteenth centuries, for instrumental movements occurring in vocal works. The word, however, has already served to describe music of such utterly different character and form that its use here is likely to upset none but the pedantic. Britten, for that matter, has surely earned the right to his own interpretation of words, for he has here re-created in a new and entirely individual language the very spirit of the poems of his choice.

5 Poulenc's Piano Concerto

Programme note for the first performance in England, 8 November 1950, with the BBC Symphony Orchestra and Poulenc as soloist

In looking back over Francis Poulenc's output during the thirty years in which he has been writing, one is struck by two things: the intensely individual flavour of his music, and the way in which he has been almost completely unaffected by the various musical trends and fashions that have sprung up during that time. Indifferent to the frowns of those for whom an intellectual approach is all-important, he has gone his own way, developing those qualities that make him stand out so sharply from his contemporaries. His success may be said to be largely due to his understanding of the nature of his talent; he excels in the smaller forms – songs and piano pieces – into which he infuses a lyricism and human warmth for which one may look in vain in much contemporary music. He has therefore tended to avoid large works, and the list of his orchestral compositions is small in comparison with that of other composers of his standing. Nevertheless, he has shown himself capable of encompassing works on a large scale. Of these, perhaps the most important is the grave and moving cantata *Figure humaine*, while his orchestral works include the charming *Aubade*, the Concerto for two pianos and orchestra, the *Concert champêtre* for harpsichord and orchestra, and the more recent Sinfonietta. In these, though the scale is different, the style remains the same; he does not try to alter the type of musical expression that is natural to him in order to produce something that might be superficially more impressive. Indeed, the absence of any desire to impress is one of his most endearing characteristics – he is content to charm and to refresh, as well he may be, for such a power is rare today.

The Piano Concerto was written in 1949, and received its first performance last January by the composer with the Boston Symphony Orchestra under Charles Munch. In form, it is an adaptation of the classical concerto to modern needs. That is to say that some of what may be termed the excrescences, such as the orchestral introduction, the cadenza, and the full-length recapitulation, have been omitted. The form is otherwise traditional. Thus, the first movement, Allegretto, contains the usual elements – somewhat episodically treated, but with the various components flowing so naturally from each other that a feeling of unity is achieved. The first theme, followed by its answering phrase, is typical in its conciseness and symmetry. Later, a motif marked più mosso, which seems to hark back to an earlier manner, plays an important part in the development. Towards the end of the movement a recitative-like passage recalls the style of a former work for piano and orchestra – the *Aubade*.

The slow movement, Andante con moto, is in three sections. It begins with a broad and tranquil melody, played by the violins, to a very soft rhythmical accompaniment on the horns; the melody is then taken up by the piano, marked très doux et baigné de pédale. This is succeeded by a quicker section, followed by a bridge-passage leading the music gently but firmly back to a restatement of the initial theme. This movement is very characteristic of the composer's later manner.

In the third movement, *Rondeau à la française*, we have a slightly modified form of the rondo found so frequently in the last movements of Hadyn and Mozart; the repeats of the principal theme punctuate the other episodes as in the classical form.

The role of the piano, throughout the work, is complementary to the orchestra rather than in opposition to it. Neither piano nor orchestra seeks to dominate the other. It is a friendly dialogue – a conversation which the soloist does no more than enliven and embellish. The scoring is discreet but telling; attractive, as is the whole work, by its restraint and clarity.

6 Mr. Lennox Berkeley on the Composer's Need to Hear his own Works

The Times, 2 April 1959

From our Special Correspondent

When a composer completes a new work, he thereafter hopes two things of it: first, that it may communicate to other people the impulse that obliged him to write the music; and second, that he may be led, by hearing it in public performance, to appraise its qualities self-critically, and so understand more clearly how his art must go on developing. He wants to give pleasure, and he wants to learn.

These at least are the hopes of Lennox Berkeley, one of our most active composers, whose second symphony and second piano concerto recently came to first performance. He says: 'I don't know if I'm old fashioned in wanting my works to give pleasure. So often with new music one feels that the composer isn't interested in communicating to anybody but a small circle of colleagues. So many of these composers are obsessed with technique, and the sound of the music is of quite small importance. The public is bound to fight shy of this highly intellectualised music. I'm not at all opposed to serial music; I've benefited from studying it, and I have sometimes found myself writing serial themes – though I don't elaborate them according to strict serial principles, because I'm quite definitely a tonal composer. And there are some exceptions to the gospel of intellectualisation – I enjoyed listening to the record of Boulez's *Le Marteau sans maître* very much, because there the timbres of the music were attractive in themselves'.[54]

For the apparent absence of public interest in new music Berkeley would apportion blame fairly evenly between composers, performers, concert managers, and the public. 'Conductors and soloists are very much to blame. One would expect them to feel it a duty to promote the music of their own time; and one would expect, too, that having troubled to learn a work for a first performance they would make the effort worth while by performing it several times. But most of them fall back, after one performance, on the easy popular successes. With most modern music you can't hope that an audience will like a work after only one hearing. I've been fortunate, of course, in Colin Horsley who likes my piano music; has played it time and time again abroad as well as in Britain; and it was he who commissioned my second piano concerto.'[55]

'The shortage of opera companies in Britain has meant that only one company has been able to mount each of my operas in this country; the two chamber operas *A Dinner Engagement* and *Ruth* would probably suit the resources of Sadler's Wells, but they haven't had enough money to put on much modern opera – they produced my *Nelson*, of course. In another country a composer would hope that several of the smaller provincial opera houses would produce all these operas, and

---

[54] Pierre Boulez (1925–): *Le Marteau sans maître* (1954), premiered at the ISCM, Baden-Baden, in 1955 and recorded by Marie-Thérèse Cahn under the composer on mono LP Westminster Hi-Fi XWN 18746.

[55] See interview with Horsley, p. 236 below.

the composer would learn enormously from these different productions. But we haven't got them here; there isn't the operatic tradition in existence.'

'It's the process of getting people accustomed to modern music that's so difficult. In the theatre they have the visual element to help them; Stravinsky has reached a wide public that way. I'd like to write for the ballet but the chief interest at the moment is for three-act ballets, and I don't know whether even after the experience of *Nelson*, I could sustain invention over such a large space of time. Britten told me he was exhausted by composing *The Prince of the Pagodas* – and the fact that he found it so difficult did not encourage me.'

'Records and the radio, I'm sure, make it much easier nowadays for a composer to make himself understood by the public at large. Here again I'm lucky, because the British Council has sponsored a long playing record of some of my vocal music.[56] But the British Council has to work on a tiny budget, and they can't do much of this extremely helpful work. Broadcasting helps, but the curtailment of the Third Programme has been a serious setback for all of us.'

'Many composers have more difficulty in getting through to the public than I have: I know quite well that I'm only a minor composer, and I don't mind that. What worries me is that I find I'm writing more slowly now than ever before, and I've been dissatisfied with my latest works. If I heard them more often I should find out why they dissatisfy me, and perhaps see what I have to do in the next ones. I had something of the same difficulty in the 1930s; I was thinking too much about technique, and Benjamin Britten helped me a lot then. He used to say: "If you want to do that, do it; don't think all the time about whether Nadia Boulanger (with whom I studied) would approve!" And as a result of his encouragement my style somehow expanded.'

'I feel the same urge now to expand my style – I don't know at present in what direction. I've had several commissions to fulfil: a set of songs to poems by Auden – they're included in this British Council record – a two-piano sonatina for Sir Ashley Clarke, our Ambassador in Rome, and an Overture for the B. B. C. Concert Orchestra. When I've finished that, I shan't start another definite project; I need some time to experiment.'

In his middle fifties, Berkeley is plainly on the threshold of a statutory third period, and it will surely be a decisive one. Many would deny that he is only a minor composer; and this urge to expand the frontiers of his art may yet prove him wrong.

---

[56] Presumably the *Four Poems of St Teresa of Avila*, with Pamela Bowden, the *Six Preludes*, with Colin Horsley, and the *Three Greek Songs* and *Five Poems by W. H. Auden*, with Thomas Hemsley and Ernest Lush, on HQM 1069 in the HMV 20 series. The Trio for horn, violin and piano came out earlier on HQM 1007.

7 Gabriel Fauré

BBC Third Programme, 4 August 1962

To many music lovers it may seem unnecessary to stress the importance of Fauré. His music is widely known, its individual character universally recognised, and yet there remains a feeling among many musicians that he has never quite achieved the recognition that is his due. It's not difficult to see the reasons for this. Towards the end of his long life – he lived to be nearly eighty – revolutionary changes began to take place leaving him apparently unaffected, other composers drawing more attention to themselves, and in addition to this it must be admitted that he was a composer of somewhat limited scope, his best works tending to be in the smaller, more intimate forms. He was to some extent eclipsed by Debussy, the originality of whose musical thinking is more obviously striking and whose output covers a wider range of feeling. But the fact remains that the more closely one examines his music the more one is brought to realise that the extreme sobriety of his manner hides a talent of a highly individual kind. There's an element of understatement in his music which has limited his public appeal, and that demands a correspondingly greater effort on the part of the listener than does music of a more extrovert character. One must remember, too, that he came to maturity at a time when Wagner had reached a position of undisputed ascendancy, and that nothing could be further from the spirit of German romanticism than is his music. So it is not surprising that it took some time for him to attract popular attention. His music is essentially of the more intimate kind and, to him, any form of ostentation or exuberance was clearly abhorrent.

In spite of this, it would be a great mistake to think of Fauré as a miniaturist: that much is clear to anyone who has studied his chamber music alone, for it consists of movements laid out on a big scale, and which abound in long sweeping melodies, in vitality of rhythm and in leisurely thematic transformations. At a time when orchestras were growing to enormous proportions, when the large-scale canvases of Wagner and Liszt were the examples to which composers turned, Fauré stood apart, out of step with the times, for he concentrated almost exclusively on chamber music and songs. It is of course true that other composers didn't neglect these fields but I can't think of any other composer at this particular time who concentrated on them to such an extent. Just as the popular image of him as a miniaturist is false, so is the picture of him as a wistful, faded sentimentalist.

The two piano quartets show his breadth of range as well as the vigour of his invention. The opening of the finale of the Piano Quartet in C minor, op. 15, has real rhythmic impetus and a joyful buoyancy that has too often been overlooked in Fauré's music. The first movement of the Piano Quartet in G minor, op. 45, from his early maturity, has many new features such as the continuous melodic line that perpetually renews itself, and the subtle changes of harmony, held together by a single note on which they pivot. These things were new to music, and constitute a true originality in the use of thematic material.

These qualities are very much to the fore in his piano music. Though it hasn't the scope of Schumann or Chopin not yet the brilliance of Liszt, Fauré brought to his piano music a limpidity of sound and a lightness of touch that are rarely to be found. Moreover, his gift for inventing deft and pianistic accompanying figures is most happily used in these works, which, though they vary somewhat in quality, are often haunting and evocative, and in the best of them, such as the sixth and seventh Nocturnes, op. 63 and 74, the fifth Barcarolle, op. 66, and the *Theme and Variations* in C sharp minor, op. 73, are splendid piano music as beautiful in context as they are technically accomplished.

Perhaps the most famous of Fauré's compositions are his songs. He had to an outstanding degree the gifts that a song-writer needs – melodic invention, a feeling for words, and the art of writing effectively for the piano. In his songs, Fauré stands supreme among French composers, and is one of the greatest masters of song in the whole of music. He wrote songs all through his life: the first to be published were in 1865 and the last nearly sixty years later in 1922. They can be roughly divided into three groups: the early songs which range from something very like the drawing-room ballad of the time to a wonderful melody like 'Après un rêve', op. 7/1; then comes a middle period in which the harmonic richness emerges in all its glory; and then the last songs in which he has reached that austere simplicity which characterises all his later work. But already in the early songs are some that foreshadow what is to come, like 'Au bord de l'eau', op. 8/1, with its sliding chromatic harmony.

These early songs were succeeded by some of the best known and most popular such as 'Nell', op. 18/1, 'Les Berceaux', op. 23/1, and 'Clair de lune', op. 46/2, after which come those of what I have called the middle period, which are mainly the famous settings of Verlaine – the *Cinq mélodies*, op. 58, written in Venice in 1890 and dedicated to that great patroness of music, the Princesse de Polignac, and the cycle of nine songs called *La Bonne Chanson*, op. 57. Although Fauré's vocabulary comprises few chords that are new – he certainly did not forge a new language as did Debussy – he is every bit as personal. His subtle harmonic sleights of hand and his original use of already existing means reveal a profoundly original outlook. This music has an identity that is unmistakable.

In the last songs there is less chromaticism, the harmony is simpler, more diatonic, and yet remains intensely personal, the succession of keys through which the music passes being one that only Fauré could have devised. Vocal lines and accompaniment merge into each other as before, but the texture is simpler and more transparent, as in the first song of *L'Horizon chimérique*, op. 118.

Apart from the songs, the most representative and also the most widely known of Fauré's works is without doubt the Requiem, op. 48, a setting of the Latin text of the Requiem Mass. He omits the Dies Irae – all except the last verse – no doubt because its nightmarish and horrific quality, which has so much attracted other composers, was totally alien to his temperament. Instead, he adds two movements at the end that don't belong to the Mass itself. These are the Responsory, 'Libera me', which is part of the Absolution, and the Antiphon, 'In Paradisum', from the Burial Service. This is the work in which Fauré's influence has been most strongly felt by other composers, for it has led them to see how a theme as grandiose as that which deals with the central mystery of human existence can be as movingly expressed by calm and restraint as by a more dramatic language. The spirit of the work is very close to that of the traditional music of the church, and though Fauré was not by all accounts a strict practising believer, the Requiem is profoundly Christian in feeling and unmistakably Catholic. One has only to hear his setting of the Offertory, for example, to see how he has been able to incorporate into his normal idiom something that is very close to the great polyphonic composers of the sixteenth century.

This is an idiom that also strikes one as being close to some tendencies in music today – it seems that already in 1888 Fauré was using a much sparser and more linear style than was common at the time, and pointing the way to a manner that we see reflected in the music of Satie, and even in the neoclassical style used in the 1920s and 30s by Stravinsky.

This brings me to consider Fauré's position in music and what influence he has had in shaping its development. It must be admitted that his large-scale works are not his best, apart from the Requiem. He destroyed his only Symphony, his Violin Concerto was never completed, and his works for the stage never really got known outside his own country, although the incidental music to *Shylock*, op. 57, and *Pélleas and Mélisande*, op. 80, is still heard. There is much beautiful music in *Pénélope* (1913) but few, I think, would claim that it is a really successful opera, and though this may be partly due to the fact that it was written at a time when composers were positively hag-ridden by the shade of Wagner, it is also caused by the fact that all that is best in Fauré's music does not survive the rough and tumble of the operatic stage. One must also remember that he lacked a natural flair for the orchestra, another important sense in which he differs from most of his contemporaries.

In spite of certain limitations, Fauré's musical personality remains strong and shows signs of having that durability that only very good music can have. Moreover, his influence was a decisive one in pointing the way in which French music in particular would develop. Debussy gave it an immense stimulus by his break with the past and his invention of a new idiom, but Fauré inaugurated a purifying of the musical language already in use and a new way of using such specifically French qualities as clarity of mind and subtlety of feeling. There can be no doubt that he influenced the composers who came immediately after him, in particular Ravel, who was his pupil. In certain aspects of Roussel's music we find his influence, too, while Poulenc, also a prolific song-writer, surely also owes much to him. It is difficult to see any connection between him and the younger generation of composers, most of whom write in one or other of the various forms of atonality that are fashionable at the moment, because with Fauré tonality is everything – modulation from one key to another is the very heart of his music. Nevertheless, in his very late works one sees much that looks forward to a style that is still very much alive. The String Quartet, op. 121, written right at the end of his life shows this. Here is music stripped bare of inessentials, using very few notes, but in which each note has a structural importance. One feels that here Fauré was going towards a style taken much further by Bartók and even having a relationship with Stravinsky. Fauré had travelled a long way from the drawing-room music of his early years and reached a truly classical detachment, austere in the logic of his musical thought, but with still a touch of that sensuous enjoyment of sound that is unmistakably French.

8 The Sound of Words

The Times, 28 June 1962

I think I always read purely for pleasure, or rather my intention in reading is always to find pleasure. I used sometimes to struggle on with a book I disliked because I felt I ought to read it, but I do this no longer. I have no scholarly impulse and lack the perseverance, or perhaps simply the intellectual capacity, to read for the purpose of acquiring knowledge; also, being a slow worker, and because my work is of the kind that can be done at any time, reading has become an almost guilty pleasure, indulged in when I feel I should be working – or is this an excuse for having read so little?

It accounts, anyhow, for lacunae that I hardly dare admit, and yet to read later in life something that one ought to have read long ago can be doubly rewarding. For example, until recently I had never read Hardy – the novels, I mean. Reading them now I find something that I might well have been unable to assimilate earlier. It is more than pleasure, for they are concerned with things that are universally human and common to all mankind, completely transcending, as does Shakespeare, any feeling of period. It is the absence of this quality that worries me about so many contemporary novels. It cannot be replaced, I feel, by studies of psychological cases, and I lose interest in the complex interrelationships of characters who never really come alive. I feel this less about the novels of my own generation and it would be ungrateful of me not to record the sheer enjoyment provided by writers such as Evelyn Waugh,[57] Nancy Mitford, and Anthony Powell.

A good deal of my reading has been in French, most of it during my student days when I lived for some years in France. I can think of many books that I liked then, and wonder how I should get on with them today, books like those of J. K. Huysmans, for instance, which then had a great fascination for me. I wonder whether people read Huysmans now; I think I could read *La Cathédrale* again if only to make me recall the beauties of Chartres, but with a book like *À rebours* I should find its hot-house aestheticism, which I then thought decadent and therefore interesting, boring and hardly readable today. We all greatly admired Gide in those days, perhaps because he was alleged to have a pernicious influence on youth, but also on account of his style, which remains as elegant and musical as that of any writer I know.

My favourite contemporary French author is Julien Green. That his novels are gloomy one cannot deny, but though an atmosphere of unease, and even anguish, pervades them, it is clear that his feeling for his characters is chiefly one of compassion. His writing gives me great delight; it is curiously sober and restrained, but his use of words is so telling that he seems to need very few. I have read through his *Journal* more than once; unlike the work of many diarists it is not so much about events and people in themselves as about the effect they have on him and on

---

[57] Berkeley was a contemporary of Waugh at Oxford and wrote music for his film *The Scarlet Woman*. See Scotland, *Lennox and Freda*, 76–93.

his interior life. This sounds tiresomely egocentric, but in fact it is done with great subtlety, the author's company, as it were, never being thrust upon one.

It may seem odd to include books about religion among those read for pleasure, yet I see no reason why enjoyment should not accompany edification. Many religious authors of all periods have appealed to me, from St Augustine to the late Msgr Ronald Knox, whose *Let Dons Delight* – to name only one among the many books by this writer of dazzling wit and lightly-carried learning – has become a great favourite. Other religious writers who have made a lasting impression on me are von Hügel, C. S. Lewis, and Teilhard de Chardin. But I have not always been lucky; mystical experience does not necessarily go hand in hand with talent and some books on this and kindred subjects have seemed to me among the most tedious ever written. The liveliest writer of all in this category is surely St Teresa of Avila; even in translation the vigour of her writing, her imagination, humour, and directness are captivating. Her personality would emerge even if she were writing wholly, as she is sometimes, about purely mundane matters.

I have recently been strongly drawn to classical literature, and feel that I could have taken pleasure in a great deal of it. It is unfortunate that this urge did not make itself felt earlier. I wish I had not been so lazy at school; it is now one of my greatest regrets that my Latin never got farther than the elementary stage, and that when given the choice between Greek and French I chose the latter because I knew it already! I am deeply ashamed of having made this lamentable decision, and now, aware of what I have lost by it, can only snatch through translation an occasional whiff of what I could have so greatly enjoyed.

I have, of course, read many books about music, some of which have helped me in my work, but I have always found that the greatest stimulant comes from music itself and the study of the scores of those composers to whom I have felt most drawn. In the same way the books which give me the most pleasure are those in which I feel an affinity with the author, for then it matters little what they are about. It is perhaps in poetry that I feel this most strongly. In contemporary poetry, for example, uncertainty about the actual meaning of a line, or, indeed, of a whole poem, can defeat, or at least seriously discourage, the reader, but there can be something in the very rhythm of the words or in the quality of the imagery used that can by itself awaken a sympathetic response and lead one to an understanding that may be on a more vital plane than the purely intellectual. This is, after all, the level on which we appreciate music, for in it nobody, not even the most eminent of our music critics, can tell us the exact meaning of a single phrase. Words, it is true, have a definite connotation which notes have not, but one can get a lot out of them apart from, or in addition to, their literal meaning. Is not a great part of pleasure in reading derived from the sound of words, their rhythm and order, when put together by a writer of talent?

1 Lennox Berkeley and his cousin, Lison d'Eppinghoven, 1906

2 Lennox with his dog, Tip, *c.* 1910

3 Berkeley as cox of the Merton IV, Oxford, 1923

4 Berkeley with Ravel, London, *c.* 1925

5 Berkeley with sister Geraldine and their mother, France, *c.* 1930

6 Berkeley, 1943

7 36 Rue Ballu today, now Place Lili Boulanger

8 Plaque outside 36 Rue Ballu

9 Nadia Boulanger, 1964

10 1 Cité chaptal today

11 Berkeley and Vere Pilkinton, *c.* 1946

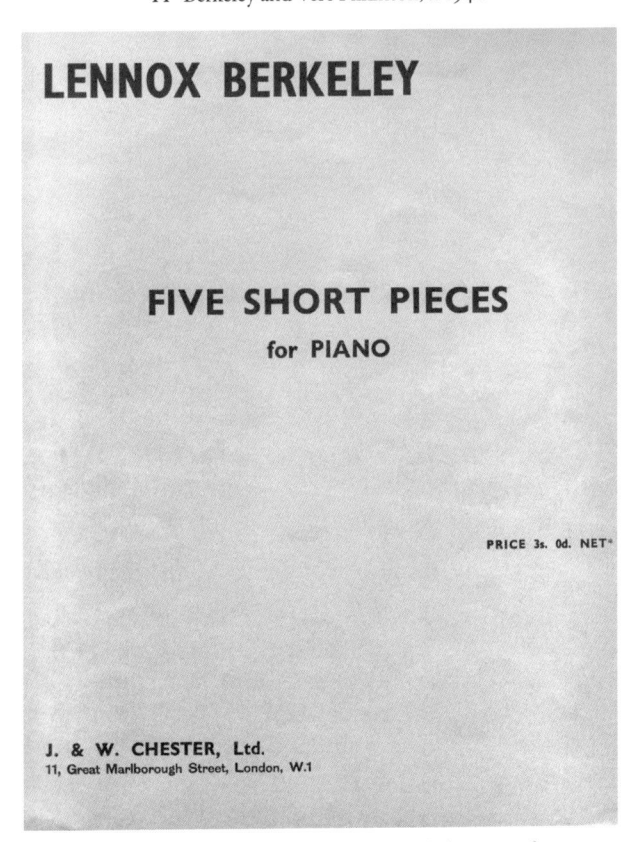

12 A typical cover – in Cambridge blue – used for Berkeley scores from 1945 to 1960

13 The bill for Peter Dickinson's purchase, as a schoolboy, of Berkeley's Piano Sonata

14 *Nelson* at Sadlers Wells, 1954

15 Lennox and Freda Berkeley at their cottage in Norfolk, *c.* 1959

16 Berkeley and Poulenc, *c.* 1960

17 Berkeley and Bream, 1974

18 The Berkeley family, *c.* 1973

19 'The Lord is my Shepherd', op. 91/1, 1975

Park Lane Group
1977-78 Season: Concert 32

Seventy-fifth Birthday Concert for Sir Lennox Berkeley (b. 12 May 1903)

in the presence of
HRH Princess Alexandra

Greater London Council
Queen Elizabeth Hall
Director: George Mann OBE

Friday 12 May 1978
at 7.45 pm

Programme
Berkeley
Antifon for strings
Ravel
Introduction and Allegro
Berkeley
Dialogue for cello and chamber orchestra
Berkeley
Stabat Mater for six voices and instruments
(*arranged for small orchestra by Michael Berkeley*)
first performance of the new version

Park Lane Music Players
leader Richard Layton

Nicholas Braithwaite
conductor
Christopher van Kampen
cello
Teresa Cahill
soprano
Diana Montague
mezzo-soprano
Meriel Dickinson
mezzo-soprano
Brian Burrows
tenor
Richard Jackson
baritone
Stephen Varcoe
baritone

Tickets:
£3.00 £2.50 £2.00 £1.50 £1.00
from Royal Festival Hall Box Office
London SE1 8XX telephone : 01-928 3191
*Free admission and 50% reduction to Friends
and Ordinary Members of PLG
tickets obtainable only from PLG
1 Montague Street, London WC1
telephone : 01-637 9778*

20 The Seventy-fifth Birthday Concert, 1978

21 Peter Dickinson, Berkeley, Alice Artz and Lady Berkeley outside Keele University Chapel, 1978

8 Warwick Avenue London W2 1XB Telephone 01-262 3922

My dear Peter,

I was thrilled to get the proof of your article for Grove. You've been very clever at getting so much information into a not very big space – though I was surprised that so much space had been alotted, because although people on the whole seem to like my music, I have never thought of myself as an important composer! Be that as it may, I feel most grateful to you for all the work you must have put into the article and indeed for all you have done in the past to perform and stimulate people to take an interest in my work.

Give us a ring when you are in London – it would be nice to see you if you have time – and please give love to the family, I hope Bridget and the boys are well

P.S. I can't remember what prevented us from coming to your recent concert – J'n ever Lennox – things have been rather hectic. Sorry to miss it.

22 Letter from Berkeley commenting on Peter Dickinsons' article for *The New Grove Dictionary*, 1980

23 Berkeley at 8 Warwick Avenue, 1981

WESTMINSTER CATHEDRAL

MEMORIAL REQUIEM MASS

FOR

LENNOX RANDAL FRANCIS BERKELEY
1903 – 1989

PRINCIPAL CELEBRANT
HIS EMINENCE CARDINAL GEORGE BASIL HUME OSB
ARCHBISHOP OF WESTMINSTER

Tuesday 20 March 1990
11.00 am

9 Concert-going in 1963

The Sunday Times, 30 December 1962

Dissatisfaction with the repetitious nature of our concert programmes has been frequently expressed of late by critics and other writers in the Press. To these, Mr T. E. Bean, the General Manager of the Royal Festival Hall [1951–65] has recently replied in an interesting and spirited article giving facts and statistics concerning the effect of programmes on concert attendance. He shows that while the largest audiences are still drawn by programmes containing only frequently performed works, others which include one less familiar, or even one contemporary piece, have been better attended in the last year. This is good news, but the fact remains that the proportion of contemporary works in public concerts is still lamentably low.

It is hardly fair to lay the whole blame for this upon concert promoters and managers whose business is to fill the hall. Since the majority of concertgoers show a marked reluctance to attend performances of new or modern music, they themselves are in some measure responsible, for it is largely their refusal to make the effort of getting to know the unfamiliar, and their lack of any desire to savour a new musical experience that result in its exclusion from most programmes.

This has surely not always been so; an eighteenth-century audience, or even one of a hundred years ago expected to hear, and did hear, the music of its time; its reactions may have been variable, but it did not rely exclusively on music of the past. Is the music of today more baffling than was that of an earlier age at the time it was written, and if so, is the present state of affairs the fault of our composers?

Music, like the other arts, is always in a state of development, often involving startling innovations, but the changes that have taken place in the last fifty years have perhaps been more rapid and more radical than at any other period in its history. Moreover, the direction that musical development has recently taken has entailed an emphasis on its intellectual and technical aspect, and it may well be felt that some composers of to-day have been led away by this from the obligation they should feel to make contact with the listener, and are using their newly acquired technique as an end in itself instead of a means of communication.

It is natural that when this is so, people feel cheated by the absence of something wider and more human that great music of the past has always had. It is significant that those composers whose music is not of this esoteric kind, but whose idiom is nevertheless one that has been accepted as valid today, can still attract a big public. An example of this is the fact that the Albert Hall was sold out twenty-four hours after the booking opened for the forthcoming performance of Britten's *War Requiem*.

Apart from a case like this, which indicates a very definite popular response, it is difficult to know what the public really feels about new works, or rather what it would feel if it were more aware of them. Earlier in this century, audiences were much more violent in their reactions; one would be unlikely now to witness a scene like that which took place in 1913 at the first performance of Stravinsky's *Rite of Spring* in Paris, when a riot broke out between those for and against, and elderly gentlemen, their pince-nez awry, were seen belabouring each other with umbrellas. Without suggesting that such behaviour in the concert hall is in any way desirable, one cannot help contrasting the intense feelings that must have occasioned it with the apathy in which present day audiences seem so often to be sunk.

The much wider scope of programmes devised by Mr William Glock[58] for the Proms has been welcomed by the public, but the Proms are a law unto themselves, and bear little relation to ordinary orchestral concerts. Mr Bean is in agreement with those who hold that the only way to improve the present situation is for some new system of concert-planning and programme-building to be devised whereby the various concert-giving organisations would work together, thus avoiding redundancies and ensuring a reasonable proportion of contemporary music. But nobody has so far discovered how this is to be done.

Apart from the problem of how to attract a large enough audience with a more widely inclusive type of programme, there is the difficulty of the time needed for the rehearsal of new works, for they need much more preparation than does the performance of music already in the repertoire. Indeed, first performances are nearly always under-rehearsed, the orchestra only having time to get the actual notes right, and none at all to study interpretation or to get to know how individual parts fit into the whole design. If some of the many hours of rehearsal often demanded by conductors for a Beethoven symphony that every member of the orchestra knows by heart could be used to prepare a really good performance of a contemporary work, a great step forward would have been taken.

Can the composer do anything to help the listener? He clearly cannot modify what he feels to be his true musical language in order to please the public, but he can make sure that his intention is to communicate something that is of vital importance to him, and that he is not indulging in a purely cerebral exercise. Though the ear of the listener may not be ready for it at the time it is written, if the composer gives expression to something genuinely heard in the ear's imagination, he will in the end awaken a response.

---

[58] Controller of Music, BBC Radio 3, 1959–72.

10 Britten's Characters

About the House 1, no. 5 (1963)

In considering the subjects that Britten has chosen, one is struck by the fact that no fewer than four of his operas are about the persecution and death of someone who personifies goodness. Indeed, the betrayal of innocence might be said to be their underlying theme. It is true that Grimes' behaviour towards his apprentices is hardly consistent with goodness, and yet there is no doubt that we are meant to regard him as fundamentally an idealist, hounded by the forces of respectability and convention, and driven, by their hatred of anyone apart and different, to take his own life. In *The Rape of Lucretia* we have the very prototype of innocence and virtue also finding in suicide the only escape from the consequences of lust and brutality. In *The Turn of the Screw*, the forces of evil are let loose upon a child, and once again 'the ceremony of innocence is drowned'. Billy Budd, young, handsome, and good, is brought to the scaffold by the wicked machinations of Claggart, though here we are faced with the cruelty of fate as well as that of man, for Claggart did not presumably intend to bring about Billy's death by forfeiting his own life.

In view of this continually recurring theme, it is interesting to see how Britten sets about making his music depict the struggle between good and evil. Characterisation is well to the fore in *Peter Grimes*. There is an excellent example of it at the beginning of the opera, in the court scene, where Grimes takes the oath he repeats in long calm phrases the same notes that have been rapidly barked out by the lawyer, Swallow, who is accompanied by short sharp chords on the brass, whereas Grimes has sustained chords on the strings. Swallow is very strongly characterised throughout the opera, his leaping sixths suggesting pomposity and fuss quite unmistakably. *Peter Grimes*, with its big cast and abundance of type figures, gave Britten an opportunity for character drawing which he exploited to the full. There was less need for characterisation of this kind in *The Rape of Lucretia*; the different personalities of the three women are clearly felt without any particular musical phrases being attached to them, but in *Albert Herring* it was clearly called for. Here rather than giving the characters note-patterns peculiar to themselves, they are given set pieces in which their characteristics are clearly revealed. The schoolmistress, for example, and Lady Billows are wonderfully portrayed types – how vividly one remembers the superb performances that Margaret Ritchie and Joan Cross gave of these parts! There is, of course, an element of caricature in *Albert Herring*, but it is a gentle, almost affectionate satire.

In none of the Britten operas is characterisation more subtly used than in *Billy Budd*. In the very first bar, introducing Captain Vere's opening soliloquy, is a two-part motif hovering between a minor third in the upper part and a major third in the lower (B natural and D above, and B flat and D below); this creates a feeling of unease, of ambiguity and doubt, that portrays the Captain's dilemma, and also perhaps the nature of his feelings for Billy. Though there is no actual theme associated with him – Britten never uses leitmotif in the Wagnerian sense – Billy Budd himself has curtain musical characteristics, as, for example, the rising fifth with which all his opening phrases begin, and the general brightness and feeling of confidence that his music gives. In Claggart we have a good example of the villainous bass so dear to the heart of every operatic composer, but his music is more consistently sombre than that of most of his kind. His constantly recurring downward fourths produce an impression of heaviness and darkness – he is a much more depressing villain than Iago, to whom Verdi lends the vivacity and charm of manner that give him his ascendancy over Othello; even Sparafucile, hardly a likeable fellow, is accompanied, in his first recitative with Rigoletto, by one of the loveliest melodies in the opera. But in portraying Claggart, Britten set himself the task of presenting a character whose gloomy misanthropy was to be unrelieved throughout the opera. Whenever he appears, the music becomes heavy and despondent.

This characterisation by atmospheric rather than thematic means is much in evidence in *The Turn of the Screw*. It is true that Quint has a three-note figure that always announces his appearance, but it is the unhappy eeriness of his music that makes one even more aware of his presence; he is indeed a soul in hell, forever longing for something forever lost. Moreover, the themes in this opera are more associated with successive situations than with the characters themselves, probably because in an opera with a cast of only six, four of whom consist of two children and two ghosts, there is not much room for characterisation in the usual sense.

Thus we have seen that the manner in which Britten portrays his characters depends upon the nature of the subject and the method of treatment upon which he has decided, but the power to use it as he does is one of the reasons for his success as an operatic composer.

11 Francis Poulenc: Obituary

The Musical Times 104 (March 1963)

By the death of Francis Poulenc we lose a composer of a type that is rare today, for his talent was above all natural and spontaneous. He never sought to bring anything new to music other than the novelty of his own personality, and wrote unashamedly as he felt, paying little heed to musical fashion in so far as his own work was concerned. All through his life, he was content to use conventional harmony, but his use of it was so individual, so immediately recognisable as his own, that it gave his music freshness and validity. It was as a song-writer that he was at his best. He wrote something in the region of 150 songs; in them his melodic invention, his power of expressing subtle and intimate feeling, together with a natural ability for the musical treatment of words and prosody, are everywhere in evidence; also the fact that he was an excellent pianist enabled him to make his piano parts exceptionally interesting and effective. His favourite poets for setting to music were Apollinaire, with whom he had a special affinity, Eluard and Louise de Vilmorin. Even his best songs are too numerous to refer to individually, and it is sad to think that they are as yet so little known in this country.

Apart from his songs, his most significant compositions are perhaps his religious works. He was deeply attached to the Christian faith, and religious texts stimulated his imagination. His only full-scale opera is based on a religious theme, and such works as the *Litanies de la vièrge noire*, the Mass, the *Four Motets* and the *Stabat mater* are among his major compositions. His very harmonic style – counterpoint plays hardly any part in his music – gives a curious character to his choral writing, and presents some difficulty in the matter of intonation, but it remains effective. There are many passages in his religious music that are strangely haunting – moments that reveal a touching tenderness and simplicity of heart, and that remain in the memory.

The gaiety and frivolity of much of his early music gained him a reputation as a wit and parodist, but his music of this period was written at a time of reaction against romanticism and impressionism, and represents only one side of his musical character; nevertheless, the exuberance and vitality of some of these early pieces have kept them alive. Later we find more frequently a prevailing mood of serene contentment, varied by a gentle nostalgia, and a reaching towards a wider emotional range, but he lacked the power of large-scale musical construction, and wrote little symphonic music.

To those of us who knew him well, his death deals a double blow, for apart from his music, he was a most lovable character and a very loyal friend. Moreover he was very good company, he had immense charm, gaiety, and a zest for life that was infectious. As in his music, he was uninhibited in conversation, and his social gifts enabled him to carry off any situation with ease. Unlike some artists, he was genuinely interested in other people's work, and surprisingly appreciative of music very far removed from his. I remember him playing me the records of Boulez's *Le Marteau sans maître* with which he was already familiar when that work was much less well-known than it is today.

Poulenc was fond of England, he had many friends here, and used to come regularly to give concerts with Pierre Bernac. Though a Parisian by birth, Touraine was the part of France he loved best, and he spent part of every year in his house near the banks of the Loire, attracted, one feels, to this peaceful and fertile countryside by qualities that in some ways resembled his own.

12 Truth in Music

The Times Literary Supplement, 3 March 1966

It has been observed that contemporary composers have made much use of religious subjects, either by setting sacred texts to music or by using words or subject matter that are religious or have religious implications. This is somewhat surprising when we consider that we live in a secular age, and that only a minority adheres to any fixed belief or practises any form of institutional religion. The reason for it may partly lie in the fact that music has had such strong ties with religion in the past. Indeed, the beginnings of western music are indissolubly linked with the Church, and it may well be that present-day composers feel a kind of nostalgia for the Christian spirituality that inspired so many of their predecessors, if only because they have found nothing but a rather vague humanism to put in its place.

A great part of our early music was church music, and it was of a quality that still influences us today. Any musician who has heard Benedictine monks sing the office would be bound to feel the impact of a musical, as well as a spiritual, experience. No music has ever been more deeply religious than the plainsong chants – single melodic lines of magnificent shape and subtle expressiveness that seem eternal in their restrained yet unpredictable contours. Moreover, as Mr. Alec Robertson[59] has pointed out in his book *Music of the Catholic Church*, many later developments such as the da capo aria, are found in some of the Kyries and Introits, the rondo forms in some of the responsories, or the ornaments with which final cadences are often embellished, are foreshadowed in plainsong. The music of the polyphonic composers of the sixteenth century derives directly from it and though of the highest value simply as music, is an extension of the liturgy and essentially a part of it. Here rhythm is more exact than in plainsong, since counterpoint must have a definite beat, and has to be considered in its vertical as well as in its horizontal aspect. It is the importance of rhythm in the music of this period that has brought it so close to music of recent times. Contemporary composers have been attracted by its rhythmical vitality, and this may have been a contributory factor in drawing their attention to its religious meaning, and interesting them in the setting of liturgical texts, to which they could bring a new idiom, reinterpreting them in the spirit of the present.

In this country, the Anglican Church has a noble heritage of music and a fine tradition of performance. One has only to think of the long line of organist-composers from Purcell to the present day, or of the many musicians who have been trained in English cathedrals, to realise the deep influence that religious music has had, and in spite of the fact that it suffered a degeneration in the late nineteenth century that many of our composers of fifty years ago found difficult to shake off, English composers still show a marked tendency to use religious themes, whether they are practising members of the church or not. The case of Vaughan Williams, who may for present purposes be counted as contemporary, is

---

[59] Fr Alec Robertson (1892–1982), pre-war chaplain at Westminster Cathedral, BBC producer of music talks.

particularly interesting in this context, for all through his life he continually had recourse to religious texts to which he gave fervent and deeply felt expression, yet it seems that he was a lifelong agnostic. This shows that a man may act and think in accordance with Christian ethics without feeling himself able to give assent to formal belief in Christian doctrine, and therefore that, as a creative artist, he may be as well able to use a religious theme, in all sincerity, as an orthodox believer. He will not be able to give that feeling of personal devotion to Christ, that complete and passionate commitment that we find in Bach, but he may be capable of being inspired by a Christian theme. In this sense Vaughan Williams was a truly religious composer, and one whose music was in great part formed by the Anglican tradition, though he used it in a very individual manner. That he also found inspiration in the liturgy and music of the Catholic Church is evident in his beautiful and truly religious *Mass in G minor*.

Among the many English contemporary composers who have concerned themselves particularly with religious themes are Herbert Howells, Edmund Rubbra, Bernard Naylor and Anthony Milner. Milner has made a special study of the use of contemporary music within the framework of the liturgy, apart from his many religious but non-liturgical works. Benjamin Britten, the most widely known English composer of today, has repeatedly used religious themes; indeed his preoccupation, one might almost say his obsession with human suffering in its relation to moral values is in itself religious. Even in his operas, it is the ever-recurring theme of the betrayal of innocence that releases his strongest feelings. Peter Grimes, Lucretia, Billy Budd, Miles and Flora, are all in different degrees personifications of innocence attacked and laid low by the forces of evil, and the fact that evil triumphs over them in the material sense, but that moral victory is implicit in their apparent defeat brings their story close to the central drama of Christianity. Britten's *War Requiem* is unique in its combination of a liturgical text with secular poems. In this work he has combined poems by Wilfred Owen with settings of the Kyrie, the Sanctus and the Agnus Dei, together with parts of the proper of the Requiem Mass – these include the Introit, the sequence Dies Irae, the offertorium Domine Jesu Rex gloriae – and from the Absolution, the Libera Me and the antiphon In Paradisum. The poems are interspersed between the various parts of the liturgical text with extraordinary skill, so that the music passes imperceptibly from one to the other. Thus, four of the poems come in between verses of the Dies Irae, and at the end, the poem 'It seemed that out of battle I escaped' is merged into the In Paradisum. The immense impact that this work has had on the public shows that not only a composer but also his audience can respond to the appeal of a religious subject as much today as ever before.

I have indicated something of the importance that religion has had for many composers in this country. It would be impossible, within the scope of this article, to discuss in any detail its influence on contemporary music in general, but a few European composers stand out as having responded to it, and it is significant that their religious works tend to be among their most popular. Honegger's *King David,* for example, achieved great popularity forty years ago, and is still frequently performed, as is Stravinsky's *Symphony of*

Psalms.[60] Stravinsky, who has dominated the musical scene since the 1920s, has written a good deal of religious music, much of it liturgical in spirit if not in intention. Apart from the *Symphony of Psalms* and the Mass for choir and wind instruments, his *Canticum Sacrum* and *Threni* are both religious works, and have Latin texts taken from the scriptures. Stravinsky has very definite views about religion and music, as, indeed, about everything else. He holds (as we learn from Robert Craft's *Conversations with Igor Stravinsky*) that church music should only be written by one who believes in the person of Christ, in the devil, and in the miracles of the church. 'Music', he continues, 'is as well or better able to praise than the building of the church and all its decoration: it is the Church's greatest ornament … religious music without religion is almost always vulgar.'

Another contemporary whose name springs to mind in the connection between religion and music is Messiaen. Here is a composer whose creative imagination has been chiefly activated by religious themes, though his preoccupation is not so much with the human condition as with Christian mysticism. He is concerned with the mystic's contemplation of God as revealed in the Incarnation and the various mysteries of the Faith, or as manifested in nature. His is religious music of a different order from any that we have considered so far, for it is largely unconnected with traditional forms, and his best-known works, highly individual in content and form, are instrumental.

Poulenc, more often thought of as a lightweight composer, wrote many religious works. Uninhibited, as is all his music, they are distinguished by a sincere and touching piety: he attached more importance to them than to many of his more widely known pieces.

How, it may be asked, does a composer approach the task of writing religious music? Does he adopt a different tone of voice, or use a special idiom? I would say that in the case of music that is religious in subject matter but intended for the concert platform there is no problem. I cannot imagine that any composer in these circumstances would want to modify his ordinary musical idiom. The great masters of the past certainly did not. But, in writing music to be performed in church as part of the service, some modification might be desirable. Speaking for myself, I have found that I wanted to make it somewhat more impersonal, so that it would merge into the liturgy, and not create a violent contrast or cause too much distraction. The danger of taking this line is that one might easily fall into a pastiche of some form of traditional church music, but a composer of sufficient experience and individuality should be able to avoid this, even when setting well-known liturgical words. Being a Roman Catholic, I have been naturally drawn to the Latin liturgy and felt at home with it; it is part of my life, and I have wanted to bring to it what I have to offer, however unworthy. But it is not easy to use words that are very familiar, particularly when they are already associated with music in one's mind. It is therefore all the more encouraging to observe how widely both the Catholic and the Anglican liturgies have been used by English composers.

[60] See Berkeley's reports from Paris for his admiration of the Stravinsky, p. 28 above.

We have considered so far only music that is explicitly religious in the sense that it is about a religious subject. When we come to think about music in general, that is to say abstract music, as we find it in the sonata or the symphony or other forms, we may wonder whether it has any connection with religious feeling. Here we are up against a grave difficulty, for nobody, not even the composer, can tell us what pure music is about. This is presumably what Stravinsky meant when he uttered his famous dictum that music cannot express anything. The composer cannot tell us in so many words what his music means, the most he can do is to explain the process of his musical thought, but this is inextricably mixed up with the technical means by which he has achieved his end, and we shall be no nearer being able to relate it to anything outside music itself. It can, of course, if he is writing the kind of music that demands it – opera for example – illustrate in terms of the various emotions that his characters are experiencing, but even here it will be the music's construction, shape, and thematic significance that give it value.

It is impossible therefore to assert that any abstract music is religious, yet we feel that the greatest music is concerned with a kind of truth close to religious truth. I suppose one thinks first of Bach in this connection, because with him genius seems at the service of the highest kind of thought and feeling; but then we know him to have been a deeply religious man, and his style is connected in our minds with works like the Passion Music, the Church Cantatas and the *Mass in B minor*. Mozart provides perhaps a better example of what I have mind, for in his later music he reaches an almost superhuman level of order and perfection, a pure unclouded heaven to which he alone had the key, where everything falls into place as though it had been divinely pre-ordained; nor does he leave out the senses, for it ravishes the ear as well as satisfying the mind. This latter point is of great importance, because all music is first apprehended by the senses, and the intellectual approach – all too common today – excludes an essential part of it. This is surely what John Donne meant when he wrote about the senses, in a quite different context:

> So must pure lovers soules descend
> T'affections, and to faculties,
> Which sense may reach and apprehend,
> Else a great Prince in prison lies.[61]

One notices with the great masters, and especially with Mozart, that they often start a work with something that is not particularly memorable; it is what becomes of this material in the course of composition that makes it beautiful and significant. It may be because of this, the transformation of a phrase when in its place within the full design, or the merging of a part into the greater whole, that music can almost become another facet of religious truth.

---

[61] John Donne (1572–1631), 'The Ecstasy', stanza 17.

13 Lennox Berkeley Describes his Setting of the Magnificat[62]

The Listener, 4 July 1968

The Magnificat, from time immemorial the central canticle of Vespers in the Catholic Church, has a formidable musical ancestry. The original plainsong, one of the most ancient melodies, is still in use, and on it are based many of the earliest settings of the text. These generally use the plainsong tune as it stands, in verses alternating with a faux bourdon or descant version, written by the composer. They are thus on the way to becoming independent compositions, but are still firmly tied to the liturgy, and to the traditional music of the Church. More evolved versions of this type are those of the sixteenth and early seventeenth centuries, which include examples by Palestrina, Monteverdi and Victoria. Later come the entirely original works (in the sense of having no connection with plainsong) by innumerable composers; among these looms the mighty figure of J. S. Bach. Then, in this country, we have the vast number of settings of the Anglican version, mostly for choir and organ, designed to be sung as part of the service of Evensong. It might be thought that a composer today would do well to avoid a text that has been so frequently set, but when the suggestion was made to me that I should use it for the opening concert of this year's City of London Festival, in which the choirs of St Paul's Cathedral, Westminster Abbey and Westminster Cathedral were to combine with the London Symphony Orchestra, its suitability to the occasion seemed compelling. I saw at once that it was the right length, that it gave opportunities for a great variety of speed and dynamics, and that, though the Latin text would be unfamiliar to two of the choirs concerned, they would know what it was about, and be aware of the place it had held for so long in Christian worship. I chose the Latin because of its universality, because the Anglican version is too familiar to English people and has lost some of its freshness in consequence, and because permission to use the vernacular in the Catholic Church has been widely interpreted as a virtual proscription of Latin, to the great impoverishment of its liturgy.

    I have often been asked whether, in approaching a liturgical text, a composer feels it necessary to modify his normal style, and to write a kind of music that would be more specifically religious. I think most composers would answer that there is no such thing as religious music, and that all good music is in a sense religious. This surely is only half true. There is, in my view, a difference between music designed to be sung during performance of the liturgy, and music which, though using a religious text, is written for the concert hall: the difference, for example, between a Palestrina Mass and the Verdi Requiem. In writing a purely liturgical work, a composer may, and perhaps should, feel it necessary to make his style more impersonal in order that it should be an accompaniment to the liturgical action, and not a distraction, whereas in a concert work he need have no such inhibitions.

---

[62] See Berkeley's diaries for his report on the unsatisfactory nature of the performance, p. 184 below.

This Magnificat is essentially a concert piece in which I have made no attempt to write liturgical music. It is scored for a large choir, mainly in four parts, and for full orchestra. The organ is also used from time to time. In planning the layout of the work I decided that it should be in separate movements, but that the music should be continuous, the movements being joined by orchestral interludes. Ultimately I modified this plan slightly by making two short breaks. The text comprises ten verses, and the Gloria Patri. It was clear at once that to have a separate piece for each verse would make too many short movements: I therefore decided to combine some of them. Thus there is a fairly extended first movement, which covers the first four verses. This consists of an introduction and opening Allegro, a slightly slower middle section, and a return to the speed, and to some of the material, of the first part. I had from the start intended to make one of the movements an unaccompanied piece for the choir, and the verse that follows – 'Et misericordia ejus' – since it has a more reflective character, would, I felt, lend itself to this treatment; the splendid phrase 'a progenie in progenies' making me want to find expression for something long-sustained and immutable, for which unaccompanied voices would be effective. Though in the greater part of the work I have written for a four-part choir, I have, towards the end, split them up into eight parts.

The Magnificat lays great stress on the contrast between the values of this world and those of eternity, when the great and powerful shall be brought low, the humble exalted, the hungry filled and the rich sent empty away. No less than three verses are concerned with this idea. I felt I must provide music that would mark this contrast without repeating itself. The first of these verses, 'Fecit potentiam in brachio suo', called for rigorous music, and gave me the opportunity, coming as it did after an a cappella piece, to make the most effective use I could of the orchestra in an interlude that links the two. In this third movement I included the next verse, 'Deposuit potentes de sede: et exaltavit humiles', marking the contrast by a change in the orchestral and vocal sound, the men's voices with low woodwind and tuba symbolising the mighty, while the boys' voices and strings depict the humble who shall be exalted. The next verse, 'Esurientes implevit bonis: et divites dimisit inanes', demanded a similar contrast but needed to be presented differently. Here I have used only the boys' voices, sometimes in unison, sometimes in three parts. There are three sections – the first calm and serene, the middle fast-moving and restless, followed by a return to the opening. The music for the first part came to me quickly, but I found it difficult to hit on the atmosphere of frustration and emptiness that had to be set against it. It must, I felt, be fast in order to make the contrast with the slow section, and yet should have an undercurrent of pathos. It would have been easy to introduce a note of satire into the picture of the wealthy in disarray, but this, I felt, would be out of place, and in questionable taste.

After the conflicting emotions of these verses, I thought that something more formal was required. I therefore set the next verse, 'Suscepit Israel', as a fugue; the first exposition being given to the choir with orchestral accompaniment, while later the roles are reversed, the voices continuing a free development while the fugue subject enters instrumentally. The last verse, unashamedly melodic but still contrapuntal, leads straight into the Gloria Patri. At this point I got badly stuck, knowing what I wanted but unable, as happens to me so often, to find the right musical idea. A fairly massive ending using the large forces at my disposal was indicated, but I was anxious to avoid anything heavy or pompous; I wanted it to be lively and bright rather than forceful. Eventually, I found what I had spent a long time looking for – something that would have the character I wanted, and also merge into some of the material I had used in the first movement. I had decided that at a certain point the orchestra should start a partial recapitulation of the music with which the work began, and that the choir should join in at the words 'et in saecula seculorum', repeating the music used for 'quia fecit mihi magna' near the beginning. After a good deal of trial and error, I got this to fit together; there then only remained a short coda using the Amen.

A liturgical text has many advantages to offer a composer, provided that he is in sympathy with religious feeling. There is, first, the time-honoured association between religion and music, the words seeming to invite singing and ritual; then, although divided into verses, it is unlikely to be actually in verse, unless it is a hymn; more important still, it is likely to be about something universal rather than individual. (These things, naturally, are advantages only if the composer is required to write a work involving a large number of performers; they would not necessarily be so in a song, or a piece for solo voice and small ensemble, where the more intimate nature of the performance permits a more personal approach.) The Magnificat has all these advantages and a good deal more; it is a text of remarkable directness, each verse going straight to the point. It attracted me particularly by qualities seldom found in the world we live in now – a joyful forgetfulness of self in the expression of faith in God, and acceptance of his will.

14 Lili Boulanger

The Listener, 21 November 1968

Although the name of Lili Boulanger and the story of her brilliant musical ability and tragically early death are known to music-lovers in this country, the opportunities for hearing her music have been regrettably few. It is because of this that even those who know her name tend to think of her as a composer of great but unfulfilled promise. In fact, she was more than this: a study, or even a hearing of any of her few published compositions convinces one that they are not the work of someone in process of forming a style, but of one already in full possession of a distinctive musical personality. One is equally struck by the impeccable craftsmanship they reveal. Written in the few years of her adult life, they show a maturity and wholeness beyond what one would think possible at that age. There is about them a certainty, a quiet authority that establishes itself immediately.

The works by which she is chiefly known are settings of religious texts. Of these, the most considerable is the psalm for contralto solo, tenor solo, chorus, organ and orchestra, *Du fond de l'abîme*. The text is the French version of the *De profundis*. It is in one continuous movement, everything seeming to grow naturally out of the material heard in the opening pages. Thus the adjacent semitones of the orchestral opening, heard deep in the bass, become part of a design; they are not mere illustration. The prevailing mood is one of passionate supplication, reflecting the spirit of the psalm in being clearly the prayer of an entire people rather than that of an individual. Just as in the Catholic liturgy for the dead, in which, incidentally, this psalm plays an important part, the emphasis is on the whole of mankind's relationship to God, rather than that of the particular person, so here we are conscious of the Jewish people invoking God, and it is this aspect that must have been uppermost in the composer's mind. Continually the choir harks back to the original cry to Jehovah; the faster tempo of some passages inevitably giving way to the slower pulse with which the work began. The listener is held from beginning to end by the extraordinary intensity of the music which is generated by the contrapuntal movement of parts rather than by any form of harmonic progression. The vocal lines are surprisingly simple, generally modal in character, and the harmony, resulting from their interweaving with the orchestra, continually produces unexpected and highly individual results. The scoring is very precise in detail, with a subtle use of orchestral colour; occasional passages look somewhat heavily scored, but the resulting sound is always clear, and the balance carefully calculated.

The Pie Jesu, a setting of the last verse of the sequence Dies Irae from the Mass for the dead, for solo voice, string quartet, harp and organ, written in the last year of the composer's life, is a microcosm of her achievement. To those who have got to know her music, the first few bars carry unmistakable fingerprints. A deep unbroken calm pervades the whole piece. A long melodic line, passing at times from the voice to the strings, is accompanied by a rising and falling chromatic phrase in the organ part, which at moments carries the music to a distant key, but quickly returns to the tonic. Characteristic, too, are the economy and skill with which the material is used; a phrase, for example, sounds at first like something new, but turns out to be a variant of one already heard. Although the music remains consistently quiet and, as it were, outwardly serene, the same rather mysterious intensity that one feels in so much of the composer's work seems to underlie it. It is a strangely haunting piece, not easily dismissed from the mind.

Psalm 24, 'The Earth is the Lord's', is a complete contrast to the works we have been considering. It is an extrovert piece, bright and jubilant, in which open fifths and strongly marked rhythms abound. It is scored for choir, brass (horns, trumpets, trombones and tuba) timpani, harps and organ. The idiom is of a type that has been much exploited in more recent times: one therefore has to think back to the years of the First World War, when it was written, to realise the impact it would undoubtedly have made, but even today its vigour is impressive. In spite of the preponderance of brass instruments there is no feeling of heaviness, the sound remains lively and crisp.

One cannot easily situate Lili Boulanger in the music of this century because though her works, as I have said, are complete in themselves, they cover such a short period and no one can tell in what direction her music would have evolved. Nor are any very obvious influences discernible. It is clear that no one could have written this music without a profound knowledge of the classics. One has only to look at the part-writing to see this. The harmony is French in a curiously indefinable way. Certain technical procedures remind one of Fauré, though in general effect her music is very different from his. The influence of Debussy would have been expected in a young composer writing at this time, but there is little trace of it – perhaps because her mentality was very far removed from his sensuous paganism. She seems, rather, to have found her own idiom, based on the methods of classical composers, but owing little to her immediate forerunners. It is difficult to resist speculating on what would have happened had this greatly talented young woman lived longer. Her bold and independent spirit would surely have led her towards the more advanced styles that we know today, but her strict technical formation and sheer musicality would, one suspects, have prevented her from making too violent a break with the past. One thing is certain: her music would have come always from the heart.

15 Last Week's Broadcast Music [1]

The Listener, 13 February 1969

With Monteverdi as the week's composer, two first performances of English music in the Royal Philharmonic Society's concert, and a lunchtime recital by one of the greatest pianists of today, the BBC offered us a week of unusual scope and interest. The revival of Monteverdi in recent times has revealed a great composer to many to whom he was only a name before. Incomprehensibly neglected for so long, it is only in the last thirty years or so that he has become known to the general musical public. One of the pioneers of this revival was Nadia Boulanger, whose recordings of some of the madrigals were made long before the days of the frequent performances we can now enjoy.[63] In 'This Week's Composer' we were given a wide choice of his music. It included the Mass in four parts sung by the choir of St John's College, Cambridge, under George Guest, *Il combattimento di Tancredi e Clorinda*, motets, madrigals, and a performance of striking intensity of the Magnificat from the *Vespers* of 1651 by the choir of the Carmelite Priory, London, conducted by George Malcolm. A great deal of Monteverdi's music was written for performance in church. One would be unlikely to hear it there today. It is sad that the gulf between such splendid music and the object for which it was written grows wider – as far as the Catholic Church is concerned – as time goes on.

The television programme *Music Now* produced something out of the ordinary in Peter Maxwell Davies's performance with the Pierrot Players of his *L'Homme armé*. This, as he has explained, is a reconstruction of material from a medieval Mass which becomes the basis of a composition in an advanced contemporary idiom. It is a type of music that is not easy to assimilate, but the introduction, delivered with great clarity by the composer, coupled with the sight of the players, brought it alive to listeners who might well have remained somewhat bemused had they encountered it in sound alone.

The Royal Philharmonic Society's concert relayed from the Festival Hall consisted entirely of English music and included the first performance of Thea Musgrave's Clarinet Concerto, specially commissioned by the Society and played with dazzling virtuosity by Gervase de Peyer as soloist with the BBC Symphony Orchestra. This was preceded by Walton's lively *Capriccio burlesco*, played for the first time in this country. The concert, conducted by Colin Davis, ended with Elgar's Second Symphony. It was interesting to hear three succeeding generations of English music thus represented, and one was more struck by the differences of idiom than by any national quality that the composers might have had in common. It is questionable whether nationality in music exists any longer: if one were to hear works by another three composers belonging to the same periods of time as these, but sharing another nationality, there can be little doubt that each would be closer to the foreign composer of the same date than to either of his compatriots. It is certainly difficult to imagine a composer using one of the more advanced techniques in a manner that would reveal his nationality.

---

[63] On HMV in 1937.

Alfred Brendel's superb playing in the Thursday Lunchtime Piano Recital will not be easily forgotten by those who heard it. We have grown used nowadays to technical brilliance; indeed, a technique that would have been astonishing forty years ago is almost a commonplace today. But it is uncommon when allied to deep musical insight. Brendel gives one the feeling of identifying himself with the composer, his technique being only a means to that end. The most striking thing about his playing is perhaps the variety of sound that he can command, as clearly evident in the early Beethoven Sonata in F, op. 10, no. 2, as in Bartók's *Four Dirges* and the Liszt Sonata in B minor. The dry staccatos, infinitely distant pianissimos, liquid scales and arpeggios, were used only to fulfil the composer's directions; it seemed not so much an interpretation as simply a presentation of the music as it was written.

16 Last Week's Broadcast Music [II]

The Listener, 23 October 1969

It was not without some misgivings that I made up my mind to listen to Ronald Stevenson's mammoth Passacaglia.[64] Would I last the course in what the composer himself had described as resembling a sixty-mile cross-country run? In the event, though my attention occasionally wandered, I found the experience rewarding. This work is really a huge set of variations based on a four-note motif. This theme, consisting of the notes D, E flat, C, B, is presented in such a variety of guises that its reappearances never fatigue the ear. The composer uses a freely tonal idiom, and employs a very wide range of pianistic effects. These are incidental; the music itself is always serious and significant. Indeed, I found it sometimes intense and brilliant for too long, and when, in some sections, the cascades of notes endlessly succeeded each other, I was reminded of Disraeli's description of Gladstone as 'inebriated with the exuberance of his own verbosity'. But if Stevenson's facility of invention sometimes ran away with him, he emerged as a composer of considerable talent. The work's immense length (nearly an hour and a half) militates against its chance of frequent performance, and I wonder whether it could not be divided into two or even three sections, complete in themselves, that might be performed separately. However this may be, to compose a work of these proportions that holds together, and to be able to play it with this degree of authority and technical command, is an astonishing achievement.

A broadcast from the Queen Elizabeth Hall on Monday evening included three interesting contemporary works. Humphrey Searle's *The Canticle of the Rose*, expertly written, contained some beautiful and imaginative vocal sound, the voices occasionally being used to make accompanying rhythmical noises. These are more successful with women's voices; emitted by men, they can be disconcertingly reminiscent of the farmyard. I enjoyed Alfred Nieman's *Three Expressions* – most effective pieces that made one want to hear more of this composer's music.[65] Both these works were for unaccompanied choir, the former a setting of a poem by Edith Sitwell, and the latter of words by the composer himself. It was a disadvantage for the listener at home not to have the words, which were difficult to hear. The main work in this part of the programme was Anthony Milner's *Roman Spring*, a choral piece with Latin words and instrumental accompaniment.[66] Here, at least, I recognised, dimly remembered from distant schooldays, Horace's *Diffugere nives* and Catullus's *Vivamus mea Lesbia*, and thus knew, if somewhat vaguely, what two of the poems were about. This was music of real distinction; I was particularly struck by the subtle and evocative use of the orchestra. The vocal writing was

---

[64] Ronald Stevenson (1928–), British composer, pianist and writer with many connections with Scotland, where he has lived since the 1950s. His *Passacaglia on DSCH* (1960–62) uses the German transliteration of the letters in the name of Shostakovich.

[65] Alfred Nieman (1914–97), British composer and pianist.

[66] Anthony Milner (1925–2002), British composer who wrote many vocal works with Roman Catholic connections. Like Berkeley he was appointed a Papal Knight of St Gregory.

restrained but telling in the earlier movements, more forthright in the third, matching thereby the uninhibited mood of the poem.

The choice of Ravel as the week's composer enabled listeners to hear recordings of two of his more rarely performed works: the *Chansons madécasses* and the Mallarmé poems. The former, a setting of native Madagascan poetry translated into French, has always struck me as standing quite apart from the body of Ravel's work. The music's spare lines, the almost total absence of harmony, the sudden bursts of violence contrasting with moments of sultry tenderness, are far removed from the composer's usual style. The only work one could connect with it, and that only technically, is the Sonata for violin and cello written three years before, in 1922, which marks the beginning of Ravel's later manner which culminates in *L'Enfant et les sortilèges*. The *Trois poèmes de Mallarmé* dates from an earlier period. It belongs to the time of the composer's friendship with Stravinsky, and the first of the songs is dedicated to him. It shows the influence of Schoenberg's *Pierrot Lunaire*, and though it certainly shows a tendency to move away from conventional harmony, there is no evidence of any real rejection of tonality such as was Schoenberg's aim, and none at all of any affinity between the two composers. Both works have in this recording the advantage of Janet Baker's splendid voice and interpretative power. In the same programme, I also heard the Septet for harp, flute, clarinet and string quartet, played by members of the Melos Ensemble with Osian Ellis in magnificent form as harpist. Where could one find in the music of today such unashamed delight in sheer pleasure of the ear as in this enchanting piece? Music has in great part lost this element of pleasure and is the poorer for it, but we should soon be due for reaction. Austerity has had a long innings.

17 Charles Burney's Tour[67]

The Listener, 8 March 1970

Charles Burney was one of the outstanding personalities of his time: more remarkable, one might say, as a man than as a musician, though this would not mean that his musicianship as an organist, harpsichordist and composer has ever been in doubt. It is rather that his character, his learning and his infectious enthusiasm impressed themselves more strongly on his contemporaries than his purely musical gifts. His tour of France and Italy in 1770 was undertaken in order to collect material for his *General History of Music*, published a few years later. He was in search of books and manuscripts to add to his collection, and wished to study the condition of music and musicians. He was well equipped for the task: his knowledge, his evident charm of manner, and his gift for establishing easy human relationships bore fruit throughout his long and arduous journey.

It is difficult for us today to realise what it entailed. Having set out from Dover he arrived at Calais 'without any other accident than the very common one of being intolerably ill during the whole passage'. He travelled mainly by coach, occasionally by post-chaise, often in acute discomfort, staying in hostelries infested with fleas and bugs, crossing the Alps on mule-back even part of the way on foot – in perpetual danger from the elements, from robbers and from rascally or incompetent guides. In the face of all this he maintained a degree of good humour, tolerance and tenacity that leaves one amazed. His description of the journey, on his way home, from Lerici to Antibes gives some idea of what had to be endured:

> We had a rapid river to ford twenty times which grew bigger and bigger – such rocks to climb and descend! But all this was nothing compared with the last post where the road was always on the edge of a precipice, with the river above-mentioned, now a roaring torrent below, with such noise and fury as turned one's head and almost stunned one; had it quite done so it would have been for the better; for I neither knew what I did nor what any one of the muleteers or guides said. At every moment I could only hear them cry out 'alla montagna!', which meant to say that road was broken and dangerous. In short, it was so much so that we were obliged frequently to alight and hold by the side of the rock. I got three or four terrible blows on the face and head by boughs of trees I could not see.

Burney visited Paris, Lyons, Turin, Milan, Padua, Siena, Rome and Naples, not to mention the many towns in which he found himself more by necessity than from choice. On arrival in any city, his first undertaking was to make contact with the local musicians, to some of whom he had letters of introduction, and learn from them anything that touched on his purpose. He would then visit any library that might contain material for his history. His insatiable thirst for knowledge went far beyond music: there was no subject, no personality, that failed to arouse

---

[67] Review of Charles Burney, *Music, Men and Manners in France and Italy, 1770*, transcribed and edited by Edmund Poole (London: Folio Society, 1969).

his interest. 'Book-hunting' occupied much of his time. Apart from the countless musicians whose names are hardly known to us today, he met many illustrious personages including Diderot, Rousseau, Voltaire, Padre Martini, Galuppi, Piccini, Farinelli and Mozart – then aged fourteen, and in process of being exhibited all over Europe as a phenomenon. Last, but not least, for he was a man after his own heart, Mr Hamilton (later Sir William), British Minister at the court of Naples.[68] Hamilton was a keen amateur musician, a great collector of works of art, and was, at the time, much preoccupied by the study of volcanic action. Burney, all agog to learn something new, accompanied him on an ascent of Vesuvius.

One has the impression that he was somewhat disappointed by the music he heard in France and Italy: he complains frequently of the poor standard of performance. In Venice, he seems to have been more impressed by the pictures, and his diary abounds in descriptions of Titian, Tintoretto and Veronese. In Naples, his admiration of the performances of street musicians is more wholehearted than what he tells us of music in the churches or in the opera house. He got more musical satisfaction from examining early manuscripts and the scores of sixteenth-century polyphonic composers than from music actually heard. In Rome, where he was again deeply impressed by painting and architecture, he was very well received thanks to the large and influential English colony. Salons were open to him, cardinals unlocked the doors of carefully guarded libraries, he was admitted to organ-lofts, private concerts, and invited to exclusive dinner parties. The journey to Naples was uneventful, though he again encountered the bad weather and dreadful inns to which by this time he had become accustomed.

In recent times our knowledge of Burney has been greatly enhanced by the labours of Dr Percy Scholes, whose monumental work, *The Great Doctor Burney*, has become the standard biography. Scholes also published, in 1959, *An 18th-Century Musical Tour in France and Italy*, which is another version of Burney's journal. The story of the original text is somewhat complicated. Burney published an account of his tour during his lifetime, but it seems that he was persuaded to omit the parts that had no reference to music on the grounds that there were already so many books on the Grand Tour. Later he regretted this, inserted the missing parts in a new version which remained in manuscript. It was this text that Dr Scholes used. Burney, however, added to the confusion by making another version that has also survived in manuscript and is now in the British Museum. Mr Poole tells us that this contains much that does not appear in the other, and that he therefore felt justified in bringing out a further edition. He has added an interesting introduction that sheds fresh light on many aspects of Burney's character.

---

[68] An ancestor of Berkeley's, Lord Fortrose, was a friend of Hamilton and, according to Tony Scotland, made music with the boy Mozart. See Scotland, *Lennox and Freda*, 296–7.

18 Lennox Berkeley Writes about Alan Rawsthorne
The Listener, 30 December 1971

We have all heard of good composers, and even of one or two great ones, who have been ignored during their lifetime, and only recognised at their true value long after their death. There are others who, though they have established a reputation while they are alive, are somehow taken too much for granted: the name is known, but the actual music is not. Alan Rawsthorne, though greatly appreciated by musicians, falls nevertheless into this category: music-lovers speak of him with respect, often with enthusiasm when they have heard one of his works, but seem to know little of his music in general. Considering his impeccable craftsmanship and the individual character of his musical personality, one asks oneself why this should be so. The primary reason is that his works are not enough played, but again one asks why. The answer, I think, lies partly in the nature of the music itself. It requires concentration and a considerable effort on the part of the listener. This may be one of the reasons for its rare appearance in concert programmes. There is an element of austerity in it certainly, but it is never arid or dull, and the intellectual interest with which one can follow the composer's thought is equalled by the sheer pleasure to the ear that his sense of instrumental colour gives. Though the musical idiom he used is basically traditional, a very distinctive personality emerges: as so often happens in all the arts, something truly original occurs when it is not sought after for its own sake. Throughout his life he remained faithful to the musical language he had used at the beginning of his career; his use of it developed and reached a wider scope as he went on, but he preferred to perfect his own style rather than to experiment with more sensational or fashionable trends. This, and the fact that he avoided any easy appeal to the senses, may well be further reasons for the neglect of his music.

The BBC is very rightly taking steps to combat this neglect, and will be broadcasting four Rawsthorne concerts next month. In the first of these, on January 9, we can hear the *Theme and Variations for Two Violins*. Though written early in his career – he was thirty-three at the time – this work seems to me a masterpiece. The vigour and freshness of the themes, the complete command of the medium and the firmness of the linear design – Rawsthorne was a master of counterpoint – combine to produce a work of outstanding beauty. This concert will include the Sonata for Violin and Piano, the Concertante for the same instruments, and the *Suite for Flute, Violin and Harp*.

On January 12 we can hear some of the piano music. This is a medium in which Rawsthorne excelled, though writing at a time when really pianistic composition was not often met with – other than that written by composers who were virtuoso pianists themselves. In the same concert there will be the *Quintet for Piano and Wind* and the *Concerto for Ten Instruments*. This rarely played work is remarkable for the skilful blending of the five wind instruments with the string quintet. Each instrument is given music perfectly suited to its character, yet when combined in harmony they are balanced with the greatest subtlety.

The concert on January 13 includes the First Piano Concerto, one of the composer's better-known and more frequently performed works, and the Third Symphony. The latter is perhaps the finest work of Rawsthorne's later years. It is in classical shape. The first movement is a fine example of the organic growth of a small phrase - always a feature of his music. In a quick tempo, a muttering, scurrying figure establishes an uneasy and rather sinister atmosphere. This permeates the movement and refuses to yield for any length of time to other material. The movement dies away with a deliberate inconclusiveness on a mysterious multiple trill containing all twelve notes of the chromatic scale. There follows, without a break, the *Andantino alla sarabanda*, one of the most beautiful and haunting pieces Rawsthorne ever wrote. The mood is one of intense melancholy and desolation combined with a calm majestic pulse. Entwined around a pedal E (the note that dominates the whole work) a melody slowly unwinds itself: it breaks off for a short interlude, but returns to end the movement. A Scherzo follows, but far from being of the light-hearted type, a rather ghostly atmosphere prevails, and one marvels at the composer's skill in weaving such evanescent material into a shapely whole. The last movement, a robust Allegro, strikingly different from most of the work comes finally to rest on a quiet chord of E major: thus the note around which much turmoil has raged finds at last its fulfilment and resting-place.

The last of the four concerts is on January 14. It contains, together with the Second Violin Concerto, the ballet *Madame Chrysanthème* and the *Symphonic Studies*. This latter work, performed at the Warsaw Festival in 1939, was the first big piece that brought the composer into prominence and revealed his powers of symphonic construction. It foreshadowed much that was to come.

There is in Rawsthorne's music a remarkable balance between the heart and mind, between technique and imagination. Rawsthorne achieved a particularly delicate and individual combination of the two elements. The revision of values that so often comes with the passage of time may well make it apparent that he was a composer of greater stature than has been supposed hitherto. If technical mastery combined with subtlety of feeling and thought are qualities that make music durable, his will live.

19 On Criticism

BBC Radio 3, 7 August 1972

The first and natural reaction of a composer, or indeed of any creative artist, to the critic is to regard him as an enemy. 'What right', he says, 'has Mr X to sit in judgement on my work? Could he do it any better himself? If so, why doesn't he? If not, let him be silent.'

Further reflection, however, will make him realise that there is more to be said than this. He should observe that this first reaction is invariably prompted by adverse criticism. He would be unlikely to have experienced it if he had received a favourable notice. Furthermore, the argument that the critic, because he's not himself a composer or executant, has no right to judge leads to considerable difficulty for it means that only other composers can criticise a composer; that singers and pianists can only be judged by those who themselves can sing and play; and even, if pushed to its logical conclusion, that in order to assess the performance of an orchestra the critic must be able to play all the instruments.

It is in any case doubtful whether it would be advantageous for a musician to be criticised exclusively by his colleagues. For though, in my experience, musicians tend to be tolerant and even appreciative of each other they are often not the best critics, being inevitably affected by the personal predilections that have made them into the composer or the performer that they are and that have led them to evolve an individual style.

A professional critic is not personally involved in quite the same way. It should be easier for him to have a more unbiased attitude. The critic whom the musician may justifiably resent and fear is one who is incompetent, unfit to judge through lack of experience and training such as those described by Pope: 'Some have for wits then poets passed, turned critics next and proved plain fools at last.'

What then are the qualities that good critic should have? Two things, I think, are supremely important. These are knowledge and taste. Knowledge is essential: a true critic should have gone through as thorough a musical training as a composer and have as profound a knowledge of music of the past and present as it is possible to have. This gives him the power of comparing the music he hears with classical examples and of knowing how well the composer has realised what he has set out to do. Taste is something that he must be born with for it is not easily acquired. In a critic, taste is the equivalent of talent in a composer. It is a natural flair and a capacity to recognise quality. A critic, too, should have some practical experience of playing or singing as part of the musical training that must form the basis of his knowledge. He must also be a writer and, considering the difficulty of writing about the most abstract of the arts, a writer of some ability. He must be aware of the essentially subjective character of music itself and yet his critical utterances must be objective or, at least, specific. Description of what he has heard is important too. Many of us feel that we want to be told what the music was like rather than whether the critic liked it. He should also describe it in such a way as to enable us to imagine the kind of sound it made. I have frequently read in the papers an account of a new piece, known to me as being of an extremely advanced type, describing it in terms that suggest a familiar musical idiom and giving no indication that it was, in fact, completely atonal or even further removed from anything the average listener would have considered as music at all. Since the critic in question must have known perfectly well that most of his readers would misunderstand him, his attitude seems to me irresponsible and inconsistent with the functions he's supposed to fulfil.

Needless to say, the critics whom I admire and trust – and I hasten to add that there are such – never do this. I have noticed also that the better the critic the more he's prepared to admit that there are things that he's failed to understand or doesn't appreciate, whereas the inferior critic will always cover this up with a blanket of highbrow jargon.

The critic must also be impartial in the matter of the musical language used. This is difficult today by reason of the bewildering variety of style and idiom. If his chief interest is in the works of the advanced composers he may have difficulty in admitting the validity of a more traditional style. Yet it is surely undeniable that much music of real value and often greater individuality is being written in such a style.

In the past, critics seem to have been too conservative and are made mock of today for their failure to recognise the value of composers now universally admired. It is no doubt because of this that many seem hag-ridden by the fear of not being up to date and hardly dare make any unfavourable comment on avant-garde music. The pressure of fashion is very great but it is something that a critic must at all costs resist.

Another difficulty is to assess a work purely on its merits regardless of by whom it is written. We're all apt to criticise a work by an unknown composer more severely than one written by somebody well known. It is of course right and proper to treat with respect a composer who has established himself, but the critic should remember that whereas a bad notice has little effect on a known composer it can be a devastating discouragement to one who is struggling to achieve recognition. The critic has a grave responsibility here: he must give his true opinion but it can be given in such a way as to help and not hinder the progress of a beginner.

Apart from professional criticism, the reaction of the audience makes itself felt. This can be a form of criticism. In the case of a performer there is without doubt something that emanates from the audience during the actual performance that tells him whether it is with him or not. Executants have told me that the lack of this response in studio broadcasts is very perceptible and a composer listening to the performance of his music in public is aware of whether or not he is communicating with his audience. One remembers instances of hostile audience reaction such as the first performance of *The Rite of Spring* when listeners came to blows between those for and against and elderly gentlemen were seen belabouring each other with umbrellas. Without suggesting that such behaviour is in any way desirable, one can't help contrasting it with the comparatively apathetic reaction of present-day audiences, applauding politely, but without much conviction, whatever is put before them. The incident I've just referred to at least constituted a very crude form of musical criticism.

But to return to the professional critic. If he must be fair to the composer, the composer must be fair to him and recognise that much criticism has to be done in well nigh impossible conditions. The professional music critic often has to make rough notes on a new work while he's listening and then rush panting to the telephone where he dictates his article to his paper. It appears next morning, frequently in an abridged form which makes nonsense of what he had to say. He may have been able and willing to get hold of a score and attend a rehearsal but if not it's unlikely that any reasonable criticism can be made in these conditions. It is the system and not the critic that is to blame for this. The journalistic principle that what happened the day before yesterday is no longer news should not apply to concert notices. The critic of a Sunday paper has, of course, a great advantage here. It is more possible, too, to give a fair criticism of a performance in these circumstances than to assess the value of a new composition. The critic will, of course, have heard the music too often and must have to fight against the feeling of weariness that assails him on having to sit through yet another performance but on the other hand he will be all the more enlivened by one that is really outstanding.

Criticism of performance is perhaps less liable to error than that of music itself but in making it the writer has to bear in mind two quite different things – on the one hand the performer's technical capabilities and on the other his powers of interpretation. In the matter of technique the critic is on fairly safe ground – either the performer's technique is equal to the demands made upon it by the music he plays or it is not. This is hardly a matter of opinion but one of fact. When it comes to interpretation, however, the critic must allow for the possibility of a different conception from his own and if so, except in the case of gross errors of taste, he would be wise to tread warily. A different view of a piece from that generally accepted, if established with authority, should at least be tolerated.

Apart from journalistic criticism there is lamentably little writing about music's deeper aspects compared with what exists in the world of literature and of the other arts. What names can one conjure up to compare with Saint-Beuve, Wordsworth, Coleridge or Hazlitt? In what is perhaps my ignorance, I can think of none among the writers of the past. And in the present I can think of no-one who has done what, for example, Herbert Read did for literature or what Kenneth Clark has done for painting.[69] A few music critics have written books on composers that are not just biographies but works of real scholarship and value. Ernest Newman on Wagner; Alfred Einstein on Mozart; Winton Dean on Handel; and Martin Cooper on Beethoven and on the French composers. But books such as these are rare, while articles and broadcasts are innumerable. These, however, do not constitute a literature. There is perhaps an economic reason for this. A critic who writes an article or delivers a talk is reasonably paid for doing so but gets little reward for the immense labour of writing a book. In the same way in which a composer who gets less for writing music than the critic who writes about him.

In spite of these anomalies real and individual thinking about music is going on, as is proved by the books I have mentioned. Since there is a larger public for music and more interest in it than this country has ever known before, we may hope for the emergence of music criticism of the more creative kind and writers comparable with the great literary critics of the past.

---

[69] Kenneth Clark (1903–83), later Lord Clark, prominent art historian whose half-hour black-and-white film, *Out of Chaos*, had a score by Berkeley. See Scotland, *Lennox and Freda*, 342–3.

20 Berkeley as Song-writer

Prepared statement by Berkeley, written for a recital broadcast 16 November 1973 on BBC Radio 3, introduced by the composer

Meriel Dickinson, mezzo; Peter Dickinson, piano

Five Chinese Songs, op. 78; D'un vanneur de blé aux vents; Tant que mes yeux; Automne; *Five Poems by W. H. Auden*, op. 53

I have never been a prolific songwriter, not because I have anything against the medium, but more because I have great difficulty in finding poems that I could effectively respond to, much as I often like and admire them. This may seem strange when one thinks of the profusion of lyric poetry that exists in English. But the poems that lend themselves to music have so often already been used many times as far as poets of the past are concerned, and those of today present considerable difficulty. Nevertheless I have from time to time come across poems that I felt I could and really wanted to set; and these, spread over nearly fifty years, add up to a fair number. I think many composers feel, as I do, disinclined to set certain texts that they value very highly. Very well-known poetry of the past is perhaps best left alone. One has only to think what a composer has to do to a poem; he has to destroy or at best modify its natural rhythm – he cannot possibly adhere to its actual metre. He then has to translate it into another medium. His only excuse for doing such a thing is that he feels he can recreate its atmosphere and feeling in the language of music. And here he can, if he's a good enough composer, heighten its emotional impact. He may even be able to bring out and stress certain rhymes and assonances that will enhance the actual words, but it remains a risky undertaking on which one hesitates to embark.

There are things, though, that have drawn me to song writing. One of them is the opportunity that the medium gives for melodic music. Another, the fact that music combined with words communicates to the listener more quickly than does music in a more abstract form. I'm old-fashioned enough to want to communicate. And it is perhaps more easily and more immediately done in a song than in other kinds of music, because words, provided you can hear them, help towards establishing the mood of the song.

In writing songs and vocal music generally, I have often been working for a particular artist and have had his or her voice in mind. Thus my *St Teresa Poems* were written for and first performed by Kathleen Ferrier; a later song cycle, *Autumn's Legacy*, for Richard Lewis; the two sets of Ronsard sonnets and *Songs of the Half-Light* for Peter Pears; and the *Chinese Songs* for Meriel Dickinson, who sings them in this recital. In every case, I have found this a stimulant. Thinking in terms of a particular voice is rather like composing for a particular instrument. The character of the voice, its timbre on certain notes, even the manner of articulating the words, can suggest actual music to the composer.

But, to return to the question of choosing words, I've been familiar with French ever since childhood, and though I've never thought it a good language for singing, there is much French poetry that's extremely evocative. In this recital there are three French songs. These may well show some influence of French music. I have long admired French song writers, particularly Fauré and Poulenc. I can't trace any such direct influence in my settings of English poetry. One of the first songs I ever wrote was to a poem by Auden and I was very happy to be able to return to him in the *Five Songs* in this programme.

The *Chinese Songs* you will hear were written two years ago. I was attracted to these verses not only by their poetic quality but also by their brevity and almost epigrammatic style. Much is said in very few words, and this is something that has always appealed to me. I have in music a dislike of over-emphasis and reiteration. My ideal would be to achieve as sparing a use of notes as the Chinese do of words. I hope that in these songs, I have gone some little way towards this.[70]

---

[70] See Dickinson, *The Music of Lennox Berkeley*, 181–3.

21 Maurice Ravel

Adam International Review 404–6 (1978)

Just over a hundred years ago (7 March 1875) Maurice Ravel was born at Ciboure on the Atlantic Coast near Saint-Jean-de-Luz. His mother was from the Basque region of his birth, while his father was of Swiss descent, but the family moved to Paris in his early childhood, and he thus became, by environment and upbringing, a Parisian. For the rest of his life he lived in or near Paris. His father was an engineer, which may well account for an element of almost mechanical precision in his music, while from his mother he inherited no doubt the Spanish flavour that is so often a feature of it. As a character, he was full of contradictions: very reserved and yet gregarious in that he loved to be surrounded by friends, a man of passionate loyalties but of seeming indifference to the larger issues in life, having in some ways a childlike simplicity yet seeking to appear a sophisticated man of the world. He was of very small stature with a head that seemed too big for his body. In everything he was out of the ordinary.

I only knew him in later life when he had shed certain affectations in evidence in younger days, and I find descriptions of him as an elegant dandy, rather unapproachable and given to sarcastic comment, not at all like the kindly middle-aged composer I knew. Unlike many great men, the more successful and famous he became, the less he would allow any trace of self-importance to show itself. I used to meet him sometimes after concerts when he would take me, generally with another student or young composer, to one of the big cafés in the Saint-Lazare district where he would talk with us about the music we'd heard.

It strikes me now, though it didn't then, that he could so easily have spent the evening in better company both socially and intellectually, but I think he was bored by the world he had already conquered, and preferred to be with young musicians however humble. He was apt to prolong the evening by inviting us to accompany him to a night-club. It was in these establishments that one first heard the real virtuoso playing that has characterised good jazz ever since. Ravel loved it, and would remain until the early hours when he would at last walk back to his hotel at a leisurely pace. He suffered from insomnia, and these nocturnal ramblings were I think an excuse not to go to bed. He was not actually living in Paris at this time but at Montfort l'Amaury some thirty miles away. Like everything else about him, his house was unusual. The contradictory element was here expressed in architectural terms. It was built on a hillside, so that when you went in at the front door, you found yourself at the top of the house and had to go down, by means of an outside staircase, to the other rooms. These were all very small, suitably, one felt, and contained Ravel's collection of mechanical toys and ornaments, more remarkable for their ingenuity of design than beauty.

I had a great admiration for his music long before I knew him, when I was still very young. It seemed to me that it could only have been written by someone of exceptionally rarefied mind and heart – an ethereal being, I felt, who must be above the grosser habits of ordinary mortals. So when I actually met him, I was a little disillusioned to find him more down to earth than I had imagined. I was rather shocked when I saw him tucking into a steak or smoking the acrid Caporal Bleu cigarettes which he did continually. I had, of course, formed a mental picture of an absurdly idealised figure which, I'm glad now to think, he didn't resemble at all. Nevertheless the feeling I had did, I think, correspond to a side of his interior life that he would never have allowed one to see. There certainly was with him a barrier that one knew must not be crossed; though he clearly had an affectionate nature, he hated anything too demonstrative and always remained slightly aloof.

The first works of Ravel that I became familiar with were the String Quartet and the *Introduction and Allegro* for flute, clarinet, harp and string quartet – in those far-off days they opened up a new world to me. Hearing the Quartet again recently I was once more moved by its magical charm, though finding its emotional range somewhat limited. The second movement with its jolting rhythm in a mixture of six-eight and three-quarter time I thought as exciting as ever. The *Introduction and Allegro* remains one of the most perfect of Ravel's earlier works, and bears witness to his marvellous ear for instrumental colour. Surely, too, it is as effective a piece of writing for the harp as has ever been contrived. The opening of the piece with its slow succession of major thirds played by the flute and clarinet alone followed by what afterwards becomes the main theme of the Allegro is deeply poetic and full of the Ravelian magic that I found so intoxicating, and still do! The sheer pleasure to the ear, too, rarely encountered in present-day music, is based on a skill in musical construction and instrumentation that many weightier works lack. Ravel was proud of his craftsmanship and would always be happier to receive praise for it than for the music's content. He took the view that the material of a piece of music is something that comes to a composer as a pure gift for which he can't claim merit, whereas the means by which he expresses it is a technique he has worked hard to achieve. Ravel placed capacity for work very high among the qualities a composer should possess. He was certainly right there, but one has to remember that musical ability, in the technical sense, can also be a gift. One thinks of Mozart who clearly was born with a phenomenal ability of this kind in addition to almost every other musical gift one can think of.

Alongside his craftsmanship perhaps Ravel's greatest asset as a composer was his power of creating an atmosphere that was highly individual and immediately recognisable. This was something that he shared with his great contemporary, Debussy. The two composers are sometimes spoken of as having a similar musical language. This is only true speaking very broadly – their idiom was certainly no more alike than was that of Haydn and Mozart. A whole region of harmony much exploited by Debussy – that based on the whole-tone scale – was hardly used by Ravel at all. He became famous early on in his career for his skill in handling the orchestra. His masterpiece in this medium is the ballet *Daphnis et Chloé* well known to English audiences in concert performance. It's curious to think, considering the great success of this work as a concert piece, that it didn't fare so well in the theatre when the Russian Ballet gave the first performance in Paris in 1912. It seems that the dancers had great difficulty in adapting themselves to music of such a symphonic type and scale – moreover, Nijinsky's sensational performance in Debussy's *L'Après-midi d'un faune* on the same evening had made a stronger impression, but one feels there must have been some further reason; perhaps it was, as Ronald Crichton suggests in a recent article, that the music is too self-sufficient, and that Ravel lacked that instinctive feeling for the actual movements of classical ballet that one finds in Tchaikovsky, Stravinsky, and other Russian composers. Be that as it may, *Daphnis* remains one of Ravel's great achievements. Certainly this vast Grecian fresco completely exploded the idea of him as a miniaturist, a *petit maître*, exquisite, but confined to the smaller forms.

An achievement of quite another kind is Ravel's contribution to piano music. It often astonishes people to learn that a musician who wrote outstandingly well for the piano should have played it so badly, but composition and execution are different things. Ravel was not a good pianist, but he understood everything about piano technique, and concentrated upon making his piano music genuinely pianistic in a way that few composers before him, and almost none since, have done. His piano writing is based on the enormous advance in this field made by Liszt. Ravel adapted this kind of technique to his individual style with complete success. This was first apparent in *Jeux d'eau* written as early as 1901. It was followed a few years later by *Miroirs*, and reached its highest point with *Gaspard de la nuit*, written in 1908. These three pieces, *Ondine*, *Le Gibet* and *Scarbo*, have held to this day a unique place in the repertoire of the virtuoso pianist. After this, his only work for piano alone is the suite called *Le Tombeau de Couperin*. In this he adopted a more straightforward style; only the last piece, Toccata, requires a virtuoso technique.

The last work in Ravel's earlier manner is *La Valse*. It is subtitled 'choreographic poem', and was intended for ballet, but is better known as a concert piece. It consists of a succession of charming waltz tunes, all original, but closely following the rhythm and cadences of the Viennese model. Ravel has somehow added another element, very difficult to define. One feels that, without being parodied, the waltz is tinged with irony and pathos; its sumptuous climaxes have a certain emptiness, and the delirium of the ending is nearer despair than gaiety.

From 1920 onward it is clear that Ravel felt the need for a change of style. He wanted to get away from the richly harmonic idiom he had up to then employed. He must have realised that any rejection of tonality would be impossible for him, he therefore contented himself with a more linear, contrapuntal approach to his material. The first work in this new manner is the *Sonata for violin and cello*. With these instruments alone there is little possibility of harmonic writing, which is no doubt why Ravel chose this particular medium. The work is a full-scale sonata in four movements and was the first chamber music work since the Piano Trio of 1914. Needless to say, Ravel overcame the very considerable difficulties of the medium with consummate skill.

Shortly after this came the *Chansons madécasses*, one of the most beautiful and imaginative works of his later period. Scored for voice, flute, cello and piano, it was written in response to a commission from Elizabeth Sprague Coolidge – the well-known American patroness of music at that time. Once again Ravel showed his flair for finding the right text. It is by an eighteenth-century poet, Evariste Parny, who, it seems, lived in the tropics and is thought to have based many of his poems on native material. These songs are similar in style to the Duo Sonata, but they are new in another way, too, for one finds in them an unexpected romanticism. The idea of Ravel as being essentially an anti-romantic is far from true. As has been said, he disliked any too overt demonstration of emotion, but this was in part a reaction to nineteenth-century German romanticism that affected many composers of his generation. There is romantic feeling not far below the surface. Here the first song 'Nahandove' is certainly romantic, not to say erotic: it is as though Ravel, in expressing what a Madagascan native might be expected to feel, was able to cast aside his mask, which he would have had difficulty in doing in other musical circumstances.

Ravel wrote two one-act operas, and it is interesting to note that they represent opposite sides of his personality. *L'Heure espagnole*, written in 1907, shows his sophisticated, somewhat cynical side, whereas in his second opera, *L'Enfant et les sortilèges*, Ravel had the advantage of an immensely talented writer for the libretto. This was Colette[71] who had produced, quite independently, what she originally intended as the scenario of a short ballet. It somehow got turned into an operatic libretto and was shown to Ravel who realised at once that it might have been written for him. It is the story of a naughty child who in a tantrum breaks up his nursery and toys and terrifies the animals of the house and garden. He falls exhausted to the ground, whereupon the arm-chair, the grandfather clock, various other articles of furniture and even the fire, leaping out of the grate, come to life. Together with characters from his picture books and the animals they reproach the little barbarian. When thoroughly frightened he comes to the aid of a wounded squirrel, and the spell is broken. This story gave Ravel endless opportunities, and called forth some of the most brilliant instrumental writing he ever achieved.

It is well known that Ravel's last years were overshadowed by a strange and distressing form of mental illness. It came on gradually, starting with lapses of memory, inability to concentrate, and sometimes causing him to be unable to make certain movements. As it went on he also became unable to write, finding that he couldn't remember how to shape the letters. The curious thing, and perhaps the cruellest part of it, was that he always remained perfectly conscious, understanding what was said to him but often not knowing how to summon the words he needed to reply. As far as I know the exact nature of the disease has never been established.

I hardly met him during all this time as, not unnaturally, he only wanted to be with his closest friends; but I remember seeing him at a concert and being struck by the change in his expression: he seemed to be looking into the distance as though unaware of his immediate surroundings. This condition lasted from two to three years during which time a great friend – the sculptor Léon Leyritz – spent much time travelling with him, this seeming to be the only way of diverting him or of giving him pleasure. Finally an operation was decided on from which at first he seemed to be recovering, later, though, he sank into a coma and died in the early hours of December 28, 1937. He was sixty-two.

It is not easy to point to the qualities in Ravel's music that make him stand out so sharply from the other composers of his generation. One of them is surely the power of evoking atmosphere, already mentioned. Unlike those whose music is entirely abstract, he often takes, as his starting point, sights and sounds of the world

---

[71] Sidonie-Gabrielle Colette (1873–1954), novelist and music-hall artist, author of *Gigi*, used for the Lerner and Lowe musicals.

around us, or the atmosphere of an actual place or country. Thus, for instance, he almost makes us feel the heat of noon where the Madagascan youth waits in voluptuous expectation, or makes us see in the mind's eye the glittering Viennese ballroom of 1850, or the Greek landscape of *Daphnis* in the early dawn. He was not unique though among composers in being able to do this. His true originality lay in his musical language itself, but to describe a composer's idiom, to show how or why his particular arrangement of notes that are available to us all has aesthetic significance is a near impossibility. Music, as has been said, begins where words leave off.

22 Stravinsky: A Centenary Tribute[72]

The Musical Times, June 1982

There can be no doubt that the strongest influence on composers of my generation was that of Stravinsky. That is not surprising when one recalls that he himself had a very thorough technical training before he left Russia from no less a musician than Rimsky-Korsakov. Its effect remained with him throughout his life in spite of the changes in idiom that his music underwent. Both as man and musician he was intensely purposeful. I knew him only slightly when I was a student in Paris, but his younger son, Soulima, was a friend, and through him I got to know the family. This would have been in the early 1930s. Stravinsky's reputation was by then firmly established; already, before World War I, his earlier works – *Firebird*, *Petrushka*, *The Rite of Spring* – had made an enormous impact. Stravinsky himself was then much influenced by Sergei Diagilev, the director of the Ballets Russes. Diagilev was much more than an impresario: he was very much a man of taste, having an understanding of both music and painting that enabled him to awaken the imagination of composers and artists and to draw out of them what he felt was there. When launching a new ballet, he took great pains over selecting the composer, the designer and the choreographer so that they could work productively together. A big man with greying hair and a majestic presence, he had great charm and the gift of inspiring others. Stravinsky had a great admiration for him and always admitted that he owed him much – a situation somewhat made up for by the fact that Diagilev often ran out of money and could not pay him. Luckily there were rich patrons in London who would come to Diaghilev's rescue whenever insolvency seriously threatened.

Stravinsky tells us in his autobiography that soon after World War I he began to long for a return of the melodic element, which he felt was getting lost. 'It seemed to me', he wrote, 'that it was not only timely but urgent to turn once more to the cultivation of this element from a purely musical point of view. That is why I was so much attracted by the idea of writing music in which everything should revolve about the melodic principle'.[73] It was in this frame of mind that he started writing *Apollon musagètes*. I was present at what was, I think, the first performance of that work, and I remember being slightly disappointed.[74] One expected something of the excitement of the earlier music, beside which *Apollon* seemed somewhat tame, but as usual Stravinsky was ahead of his time, for it was not long before the melodic element crept back into music, as – so it seems to me – it is returning in some measure again today. This is a work that I have now come to love and in which I find refreshment and peace. Another work that belongs to the same period is the *Dumbarton Oaks Concerto* – I believe it was this that caused some critics to think it

---

[72] Berkeley wrote *In Memoriam Igor Stravinsky: Canon for String Quartet* in July 1971, published in *Tempo* no. 79 (1971).

[73] Igor Stravinsky, *An Autobiography* (New York, 1962), 136.

[74] The first performance was given on 27 April 1928 at the Library of Congress, Washington DC. Berkeley did not review the Paris premiere.

was so close to classical models that Stravinsky was pulling their legs (Dumbarton Hoax?), but I came to terms with it easily enough. I remember very well, about the same time, hearing a splendid performance of *Les Noces* – surely the most Russian of all Stravinsky's works – and being deeply moved, particularly by the ending.

Stravinsky has sometimes been criticised for the importance he attached to money, and the very large fees he asked when offered a commission. In this connection one should remember that in earlier years he had a hard struggle, having to bring up a family during World War I – a time when he was making no money at all. It was perhaps the feeling of insecurity that this state of affairs induced that later in life made him grasp perhaps too firmly at any pecuniary aid that might be forthcoming. In his last years he was certainly fairly affluent, when appearing as pianist and conductor all over America.

I have often wanted to make a study of Stravinsky's later music, but it would require more time and more discipline than I have been able to muster. It would certainly need time, as it would have to cover the last and most comprehensive change of idiom – the rejection of tonality that is necessary in strict twelve-note music, as taught by Schoenberg, though it can also be used with greater freedom and is so used by many composers today. Stravinsky apparently showed little interest at first, but eventually decided to use an atonal idiom himself. Whether he considered it a passing phase, whether it was just an experiment, or whether he saw it as an ultimate arrival we cannot know.

23 Bid the World Good-Night

From *Bid the World Good-Night: Written Symposium on Old Age and Death*, ed. Ralph Ricketts (London: Search Press, 1981)

I used to wonder, when I was a child, how it was possible that elderly people could be so cheerful in view of their rapidly approaching demise. As many of these were probably only about forty, the phenomenon was less astonishing than I thought, but it has struck me since that many people who really have reached old age display considerable serenity and liveliness of mind, and now that I am myself in this category I find that there are many compensations for advancing years. The fact that one suffers less from the various forms of insecurity or from the violent emotions that beset one in youth is one of them; another the fact that one's individuality is more firmly established and that one no longer cares, or that one cares much less, what other people think of one. There is also the discovery of things that can be enjoyed that one had not taken advantage of earlier. For example, perhaps because of my absorption in music, I had never learned to use my eyes. I now take great pleasure, not only in pictures, but in the visual world in general. I am more aware of the beauty of much that I see around me. Of young people, for instance, and of animals. I have more sympathy with other human beings. This, I feel, is something deeper than the easy-going tolerance that is fashionable today and that springs, as often as not, from a lack of conviction about anything, but I am not claiming it as a virtue. It grows, I think, out of one's experience of life, the realisation that we are all prone to weakness, and that other people's failings are merely different from one's own.

I have just said that in old age one is no longer a prey to violent emotion, but I find that I am very easily moved by all manner of things to which I never gave a thought when I was young. Even in music, I find much more that I like and even love than I did, though this is not true of contemporary music in which I find less. Certainly as old age has approached I have found more that I can enjoy in general through knowing more and having a greater experience of life. This sums up the advantages that I have encountered.

The disadvantages are much more obvious. Even if one is still in reasonably good health, one is aware of ebbing vitality and of tiring much more quickly – I can neither work for as many hours nor walk as far – and it is sad that just when one has become more appreciative and more sure in one's estimate of the relative value of things, one no longer has the energy to take advantage of it. Mental and physical fatigue overtakes one and is not easy to come to terms with. Yeats, in one of his poems, speaks of his soul as 'fastened to a dying animal'.[75] He felt that physical decline was accompanied by increasing mental awareness, and refers often to how much he suffered from opposite states of mind and body. The state of the

---

[75] W. B Yeats, 'Sailing to Byzantium' in *The Tower* (1928). The poet urges the sages 'standing in God's holy fire' to be 'the singing-masters of my soul. / Consume my heart away; sick with desire / And fastened to a dying animal / It knows not what it is; and gather me / Into the artifice of eternity.'

body, of course, becomes of paramount importance in old age for it can make the whole difference to one's desire to go on living.

It seems that many older people living in retirement suffer from boredom and not knowing what to do with themselves, even if perfectly healthy. This is, to me, inconceivable; I am acutely aware of having only a limited future left and little time in which to do so much: books I want to read, places to see and work to do. I think it was only when I reached seventy last year [12 May 1973] that I began to feel this at all strongly and to regret the amount of time I had wasted in my younger days, and the slow pace at which I had developed, musically and otherwise.[76]

A man's attitude to death is of necessity largely determined by whether or not he has any religious belief. Those who believe, as I do, in the Christian doctrine of life after death are bound to feel differently, both from those who believe rather vaguely in some sort of survival, and from those for whom death means extinction. I have been a Roman Catholic for the greater part of my life, and am thereby committed to the Church's teaching. Though deeply conscious of utter failure to live up to what I believe, the fact of believing it has been an immense happiness, and one that in my better moments banishes the fear of death. This does not mean that I do not dread the anguish of parting from those I love or that I do not have doubts and difficulties, but I am convinced that we should be resigned to the fact that our understanding, in this life, is limited, and that disbelief involves quite as many intellectual difficulties as any religion known to me. There is much to be said for the attitude of the recruit Feeble, in King Henry IV: 'I care not,' he says, 'a man can die but once; we owe God a death.'[77] The feeling that death is part of the natural order of things, that it is a debt that must be paid in return for the gift of life is not unreasonable, for we would surely not prefer never to have existed at all. Even those who cannot reconcile themselves to any religious belief may well be able to agree with the many philosophers of the past, and some, no doubt of the present, who believe that the better part of man can live on after death.

---

[76] Although Berkeley was writing in 1974, this article was not published until 1981.

[77] Henry IV, part 2, act 3, scene 2.

– Part IV –
Interviews with Berkeley, 1973–8

Of the four interviews here, two are with me, one (specifically about the Fourth Symphony) is with Michael Oliver, and one is with three men of letters for a poetry magazine. In my own interviews I probably avoided questions to which I knew the answers, so, for example, there was no point in my asking Berkeley what he thought of John Cage or Cornelius Cardew. But the literary men did, and profitably moved the discussion into wider areas than just music. Some repetitions within the interviews have been condensed, but even if Berkeley tells the same story, he may qualify the information from a different angle. Berkeley's first published interview was given to the Canadian composer Murray Schaffer in 1961; it was published in a fascinating collection called *British Composers in Interview* published by Faber & Faber in 1963. I have not included it here because Berkeley dealt with the same issues at greater length in later discussions.

1 With Peter Dickinson, 1973
8 February 1973, 8 Warwick Avenue, London W2

Most of this interview was broadcast on BBC Radio 3 on 10 July 1973 to introduce a Seventieth Birthday Concert from the Cheltenham Festival;[1] some of it appears in *Twenty British Composers: the Feeney Trust Commissions* (J. & W. Chester, 1975). This is a fuller version of our discussion.

PD   What were your earliest musical impressions as a child?

LB   Well, it's rather a curious story. My father was passionately fond of music and had been invalided out of the Navy before I was born.[2] He hadn't been able to learn music as a boy, or hear very much, so he acquired a pianola with all kinds of rolls of classical music – Beethoven Sonatas and arrangements of concertos – which I heard at a very early age on this machine. That was my introduction to music.

PD   Were you a chorister, or anything like that?

LB   I sang in the choir at school, but I was never a chorister.

PD   What about your own playing? When did you start learning the piano?

LB   I started improvising, like a lot of musical children, picking things up by ear and learning to play off my own bat. Then from the age of about eight, I suppose, I was given piano lessons and went on with them throughout my schooldays.

---

[1] See Berkeley's diary, p. 202 below.
[2] Captain Hastings George FitzHardinge Berkeley, RN (1855–1934).

PD Did you practise willingly?

LB Yes, fairly willingly because I was keen to be able to play. But I was slow to learn sight-reading until the moment came when I realised that I couldn't get any further unless I could read.

PD What sort of pieces did you play? Any solos at concerts at Gresham's School, for example?[3]

LB I don't think I ever played solos. I did the usual sort of easier classical music.

PD Did you play chamber music then?

LB I did when I was a student in Paris. I had a friend who was a violinist and we played classical sonatas and things like that, but not in public.

PD But before this you were at Oxford, not studying music but modern languages?

LB Yes, but I was doing some music at the same time. I took organ lessons with W. H. Harris,[4] then organist of New College, and I heard a lot of music during my time at Oxford.

PD What did you play on the organ, because your own organ music came much later?

LB The easier Bach – that sort of thing. [*Laughs*]

PD What sort of music was in the air at Oxford in the frenetic twenties?

LB The modern music then was Stravinsky and, in England, Bliss. In Oxford – always behind the times – Debussy and Ravel were still thought rather modern. [*Laughs*]

PD Wasn't Auden a near contemporary?

LB Yes, I knew him, and Cecil Day Lewis.[5]

PD Were there many people taking composition seriously?

LB Far fewer than now, of course.

PD How important was composition to you then?

LB I think I hadn't yet made up my mind whether I would be able to do music as

---

[3] Berkeley was at Gresham's during the war then went to St George's School, Harpenden, in 1919. There he played in concerts and in March 1921 gained a prize for a piano piece he had composed.

[4] W. H. Harris (1883–1973), later organist at St George's Chapel, Windsor, knighted in 1954.

[5] Berkeley went up to Merton College, Oxford, in 1922 to read French, Old French and Philology at a time when he could not have read music. His lost songs to two poems by W. H. Auden (1907–73) must have been the first settings of the poet; their only known performance was with another poet as singer, C. Day-Lewis (1904–72), and the composer at the piano. For details of this performance, see Dickinson, *The Music of Lennox Berkeley*. However, see also Katherine Bucknell, *W. H. Auden Juvenilia: Poems 1922–1928* (Princeton, 1994), 119, where she corrects my assumption that Berkeley set 'Bank Holiday', and suggests 'Trippers' which was not then published.

a whole-time career or not. It was during my time at Oxford that I decided I must, that this was the one thing I really wanted to do.

PD There's one chromatic progression in the song 'The Thresher', which you wrote at this period.[6] Did you know much Delius?

LB Yes, I did then, and I was very fond of certain things of Delius. He's not been a composer who's worn very well – I don't know quite why. I found I went off him, but there are still some very beautiful moments in his music.

PD What chance did you have to hear your own music?

LB The first orchestral piece I heard performed, an early Symphony for Strings, was conducted by Anthony Bernard with his London Chamber Orchestra.[7] He did a great of French music; I showed him some of my earlier efforts and he took a liking to them. He played my *Introduction and Dance* in London – the first time I ever heard my own instrumental writing. This was before I went to Paris.

PD I don't regard the French influence as something that came in from outside into your music. It seems very natural, and wasn't part of your family French?

LB Yes. Both my parents came from families that had more or less lived abroad and led a very cosmopolitan life – for one reason and another.[8] My father's mother was actually French, so I do have some French blood.

PD What did your course with Nadia Boulanger consist of?

LB I went once a week for private lessons and she put me on to strict counterpoint, and fugue later, because she felt I had no real basic technique. For the first year I was with her I didn't really compose. I did nothing but

[6] 'D'un vanneur de blé' (The Thresher) was performed at the Oxford University Musical Club and Union on 12 March 1925. It became Berkeley's first published composition with Oxford University Press in 1927. *The Complete French Songs*, edited by Roger Nichols, was published by Chester Music in 1992. 'D'un vanneur de blé' is included as the first of *Three (Early) Songs*, but the version that should be used for performance is the later revision. Berkeley visited Delius at Grez-sur-Loing with Gordon Bryan in 1927. See Scotland, *Lennox and Freda*, 144–5.

[7] Anthony Bernard (1891–1963), enterprising conductor and composer who performed Berkeley's lost *Introduction and Dance* at a BBC concert at the Chenil Galleries on 26 March 1926. The *Symphony for String Orchestra*, now lost, was performed by Bernard at the Queen's Hall on 14 December 1931 and mentioned in Berkeley's letter to Boulanger three days later: see p. 51 above. Mary Bernard, the conductor's widow, told me that her husband's scores were lost in the Blitz.

[8] In a diary entry for August 1978 Berkeley explained: 'My parents led a very quiet and outwardly uneventful life. I have realised since that there was a reason for this. It was certainly far from being the case with my grandparents, since they eloped and went to live abroad, my grandmother being married at the time, in order to avoid living together openly in England. ... It was, I think, shortly after their flight from England, that my father and his next brother were born, and a little later my grandmother obtained a divorce. ... I understand now why my father chose to live as unobtrusively as possible – he was very devoted to his mother and anxious that the family situation should not be known and her somewhat unconventional life frowned upon. This, I think, shows great delicacy of feeling on his part and I have always admired him for it.' See Scotland, *Lennox and Freda*.

these strict counterpoint exercises. She thought it better if she didn't see anything of mine, although she had looked at a few compositions when she accepted me as a pupil, but she thought I was so behind with technique that I should concentrate entirely on that. It was a bit arduous, as you can imagine, because these things aren't easy: they are very arid and I hated it. I was almost in despair a good deal of the time, but I stuck to it and I'm glad I did now because I think it does in the end give one a certain facility.

PD   As a teacher, did she rely on making an impact on her students or did she bring out things that were already there?

LB   I think it was a bit of both. She certainly saw what I wanted to do, but, as with all teachers of great personality, one did tend to write the kind of music that she approved of – a bit. You couldn't help it to some extent. But I don't think that's a disadvantage, because any composer who lets himself be swamped by somebody else's personality can't have very much himself. I don't think it does any harm.

PD   Some of the things you said in a recent broadcast talk about Fauré could be applied to your own music.[9] Were you aware of that tradition behind Nadia Boulanger?

LB   She had studied composition with him when he was at the Conservatoire and her teaching took a lot from his. In my turn I think I've passed on to pupils of today something of the same attitude towards the technical basis for composing that comes down from Fauré. It's interesting to think it's gone on into this generation, although the present generation – some of them – don't seem to want to learn anything very much, and certainly not the methods used nearly a hundred years ago! [*Laughs*]

PD   If we look for an ancestor of Fauré we come to Chopin, who is also important to you since you've written a chapter in a book about him and have composed the *Three Mazurkas* in homage.[10]

LB   I've explored Chopin ever since I was a boy. You've got to have a pretty solid technique to embark on most of it, but I can manage enough to play for myself and get the feeling of the piece. I've always loved his music very much, the mazurkas in particular, and that's why I wrote my *Three Mazurkas*, which are definitely based on Chopin. I tried to produce in my own language, as it were, something as close to Chopin as I could because I'd learnt so much.

PD   I sometimes hear Chopin in the glittering passages of your piano writing as well as in your natural melodic style. Does he also account for the strength of your roots in tonality?

LB   Maybe. I've never really thought about that, but there is possibly a connection.

---

[9] See Berkeley's talk on Fauré, p. 112 above.

[10] 'Nocturnes, Berceuse, Barcarolle', in Alan Walker, ed., *Frédéric Chopin: Profiles of the Man and the Musician* (London, 1966).

PD We know very little of the music you were writing during the years with Nadia Boulanger in Paris. Did you have performances then?

LB I wrote a Suite for orchestra that I did manage to get played and it went tolerably well, but I didn't have anything that took on at all in those days.[11] There's a ballet score I wrote for – I can't remember the circumstances now, but I was very grateful for the experience of hearing my music.[12]

PD At the end of this time you must have written the Overture which was performed at the International Society for Contemporary Music in Barcelona in 1936 – and you went to Spain to conduct it.

LB Yes, and – curiously enough – the only other English composer who was represented in that year at Barcelona was Benjamin Britten, and it was there that I met him. Because I'd been living out of England for a long time, I had never met him before. It's important to me because we became very close friends and he had a great influence on me later on. It was in Barcelona that we sat down at cafe tables and wrote down the Spanish folksongs which later became the *Mont Juic Suite*. We did a movement each.[13]

PD How did you feel about the performance of the Overture?

LB It was well played, but I can't really remember it. They played the Berg Violin Concerto and this made such an impression on everybody – it's the most beautiful piece – that it rather cancelled out everything else.

PD When you returned to London, from Paris, did you feel as if you'd come away from the centre, the artistic capital?

LB I did, rather, because London wasn't then what it is now, musically. But it was then that I got together with Ben Britten and I was very interested in his career because he was already a superb technical musician and I could foresee what was coming. Walton had already made a great name for himself, but there wasn't the same sort of interest in contemporary music that has developed since the war.

PD Did you return to opportunities for performance and commissions such as the oratorio *Jonah*?[14]

---

[11] The Suite for Orchestra was given in Paris at the Salle Pleyel on 16 February 1928 and in London at the Proms on 12 September 1929. For details and music examples, see Dickinson, *The Music of Lennox Berkeley*; the Catalogue of Works below shows more Paris performances which were well received.

[12] This is the untitled score dated Paris: May–June 1932. No details of performances have been traced. There are three numbers arranged from it in the *Collected Works for Solo Piano*, ed. Peter Dickinson (Chester 2003).

[13] *Mont Juic: Suite of Catalan Dances*, op. 9: Benjamin Britten, op. 12. For many years Berkeley and Britten had agreed not to divulge who wrote what, but in the 1980s Berkeley told me that he wrote the first two movements and Britten the last two, although they conferred about details. This information was in the first edition (1988) of Dickinson, *The Music of Lennox Berkeley*.

[14] *Jonah*, op. 3, premiered 19 June 1936 in a BBC broadcast; first public performance 7 October 1937 under Berkeley at Leeds Town Hall; first London performance (with organ) 31 March

LB I started it because the story interested me, then I enquired at Leeds and they agreed to perform it. I don't think I was really quite able to speak with my own voice, particularly in such a long work as that.

PD Some of the shorter works from that period – the *Five Short Pieces* for piano, for example – are impeccable miniatures, but some longer works haven't survived?[15]

LB Yes, it was the bigger things I was dissatisfied with.

PD Do you actually destroy rejected scores or keep a bottom drawer?

LB I generally lose them [*Laughs*] sometimes semi-purposely in that I'm not interested in them any more!

PD Like Britten, Rawsthorne and others, you wrote for films at this time.

LB This was a way of hearing my own music in the late 30s when, like all young composers, I found it difficult to get performances. Britten did some films at the same time. The BBC did a lot of feature programmes then – neither films nor plays – illustrating the lives of individuals. I did one on Maupassant.[16]

PD Did you enjoy that kind of working to order?

LB I did, but I don't think I would particularly want to do it now.

PD As the composer of three symphonies at well-spaced intervals, how do you feel about writing a symphony these days?[17]

LB I think any composer can throw his work into a modified symphonic form. The word 'symphony' is no doubt out of fashion now, but I think it's only the word because you make your own form and idiom – any composer would. I see nothing against writing symphonies, even if I can't see anything particularly for it! I think it's just a question of whether you choose to use the word or not. I've left a long time between the three symphonies I've written simply because I'm reluctant to tackle big-scale things, and so I tend to put it off.

PD You seem to prefer lyrical rather than dramatic development.

LB Yes, I do. It tends to make me rather reluctant about what I call the symphonic side of music.

PD Some of the lighter pieces such as the Divertimento illustrate this.[18]

LB That was a BBC commission, actually, during the War. It was written for a chamber orchestra which was abolished almost as soon as I had written the piece, although there are quite a lot of orchestras of that size now.

1990 at St Michaels, Cornhill.

[15] *Five Short Pieces*, op. 4 (1936).

[16] Guy de Maupassant. *A Glutton for Life*, radio feature by Audrey Lucas, produced by Louis MacNeice, broadcast 15 February 1946.

[17] Three symphonies at the time of this interview: no. 1, op. 16 (1942); no. 2, op. 51 (1958); no. 3, op. 74 (1969); and then no. 4, op. 94 (1978).

[18] Divertimento in B flat, op. 18 (1943).

PD I'm curious to know where your very personal kind of bitonality and orchestral colour come from. Milhaud's work, for example, is much cruder, but you knew Poulenc?

LB Yes, I did. There's a very subtle form of harmony in Poulenc, particularly in his songs, which are his most lyrical works. I won't claim that I had been directly influenced by them, but perhaps indirectly. I did just meet Milhaud, and Charles Koechlin, who had quite an influence on young musicians, and a large number of his pupils. I knew Ibert a little, but Poulenc was the one I knew best. Copland was still in Paris when I was there and Henri Sauguet. Also Roussel.[19]

PD Did you get to know much of his music?

LB I've heard it more since. I think there's a great solid mass of music by Roussel that will come into its own some day.

PD His Gallic approach to the symphony must have attracted you because your own routes to sonata or symphony are more French than German.

LB Yes.

PD How does this affect your concertos?

LB They've all been written for definite performers: the Piano Concerto for Colin Horsley, the Two-Piano Concerto for Cyril Smith and Phyllis Sellick.[20]

PD Does this music arise from the players themselves and what they can do?

LB I think so – from the medium and the executant.

PD The music would be different if it had been written for someone else?

LB Slightly, I think. There's also a Flute Concerto for John Francis and a certain amount of chamber music involving players I knew.[21]

PD Are you oppressively aware of tradition when writing a string quartet or trio?

LB A little. There's such a weighty sort of history behind the string quartet and music of the finest quality has been written for it already. That is always rather intimidating.

PD There's a fastidious kind of elegance in your String Trio – could it stem from Ravel?

LB Yes, there's no doubt he was a very great influence on me. When I was a boy, and certainly when I was at Oxford, I was much attracted to Ravel's music. It was that, partly, which made me want to go and study in France. I'd also been given an introduction to him, and I met him first when he came to London to conduct some of his music. It was he who advised me to go to Nadia Boulanger. During my time in Paris I used to see him fairly often. He was very

---

[19] Darius Milhaud (1892–1974); Charles Koechlin (1867–1950); Jacques Ibert (1890–1962); Henri Sauguet (1901–89); Albert Roussel (1869–1937).

[20] Piano Concerto, op. 29 (1947–8); Concerto for Two Pianos, op. 30 (1948).

[21] Flute Concerto, op. 36 (1952).

kind, after we'd met in London, and took an interest in what I was doing. I remember going to see him at Montford l'Amaury where he lived just outside Paris. I've never ceased to love Ravel's music and to find something that's very close to me – something in his music that helped me to find myself in mine.

PD Ravel rather than Debussy, whom we now see as more revolutionary?

LB I think it's true that Debussy is more important. He has a wider scope than Ravel, who was closer to me personally.

PD I can see that, because of the clear tonal harmony which is a framework for Ravel's music but not for Debussy. What was Ravel like as a person?

LB He's regarded as an enigmatic personality, and he remained so even when one knew him. He was easy to talk to – rather bright and gay, a thoroughly entertaining and lively personality – but one always felt that one would have great difficulty in getting nearer the man himself, so-to-speak underneath this. And I think, when you know his music, you realise there's a sort of shyness, something he desired to keep hidden under an elegant exterior. This was very true of the man himself. He disliked any too intimate probing into what he felt about music. In other words, I think he didn't like to lay his soul bare. He preferred you to admire his skill and technique than to say something had moved you. That approach was characteristic of his attitude. I think it all sprang from a sort of modesty and shyness about his deeper feelings.

PD What has it felt like to change from being a young avant-garde composer performed at the International Society for Contemporary Music to being an elder statesman?

LB Very bewildering, I think, because I don't suppose such a violent change can ever before have taken place so quickly as what has happened in my lifetime. The only thing a composer of my generation can do – unless he is moved to switch to some entirely different medium, as some older composers have done – is to go on being himself. I don't think I could write completely non-tonal music. It wouldn't be true for me, and I think I have managed to develop my own idiom a little. It's much better for me to go on doing that. One has moments of feeling that one's been left behind, one's completely on the shelf and all this kind of thing, which naturally one would feel when the more up-to-date music of today is so utterly different.

PD When did you first become aware of this?

LB My first awareness of a radical change in the language of music was when the serial technique began to be widely used. All that has happened since really arises out of the overthrow of tonality, as preached by Schoenberg over fifty years ago. Only it didn't become a current musical language until twenty years ago. Although I've used, as other tonal composers have, certain aspects of serial technique, I couldn't use it as my ordinary idiom in the 1950s. I felt I must develop my own way of feeling harmonically and melodically.

PD What sort of public did you imagine you were writing for in the 1950s, say at the time of the grand opera *Nelson*?

LB I don't think I thought about it in quite those terms. One thinks about the public a bit more now when there seems to be such a divorce between the general public and the avant-garde, because there's a bigger gulf between them and the general public than ever before.

PD Don't you think this must have been a feature of earlier times?

LB I think it must, and yet it somehow didn't seem quite so violent.

2 With C. B. Cox, Alan Young and Michael Schmidt, 1974

An interview published as 'Talking with Lennox Berkeley' in *Poetry Nation* no. 2 (1974), reprinted by courtesy of Carcanet Press Ltd. C. B. Cox was an academic, writer and editor, finally John Edward Taylor Professor of English Literature at Manchester University; Alan Young was Head of the Department of Arts Education at Didsbury School of Education, Manchester University; and Michael Schmidt is the poet, novelist, critic and Professor of English in the University of Glasgow; he founded and directs Carcanet Press, based in Manchester. The three interviewers, whose contributions are not differentiated, began by asking questions about Berkeley's early musical experiences.

LB   I didn't go to concerts very much when I was a child. It was only when I went to Oxford as an undergraduate that I began to take an interest in live music. It was at Oxford that I began to compose, without knowing quite what I was doing, or how to set about it. I did write music there, especially songs, but even then I hadn't learnt anything about how to write music; that came later.

Q   Do you remember any of those early works?

LB   I set one or two French poems, and I remember that one of the first English poems which I set was by Auden whom I knew well at Oxford. He was a bit younger than me, and I think my last year there was his first. The song was performed at a sort of private concert by Cecil Day Lewis who had a very nice light baritone voice. That was another lifelong friendship that started at Oxford.

Q   It was at Oxford, then, that you decided you wanted to be a musician?

LB   Yes. I knew Dr Ley, who was then organist of Christ Church, and later became responsible for music at Eton.[22] He used to let me go up in the organ loft at Christ Church. I heard him play a lot of Bach, and this was one of my earliest experiences of live music. After that I used to go to all the chamber music concerts in the Holywell Music Room at Oxford during those years.

Q   Music was obsessive even then?

LB   So much so that I didn't really attend to what I was supposed to be learning. It was during this time that I realised music was what I really had to do.

Q   Did you come into contact with much modern music at Oxford?

LB   Yes, a little, though much of it wouldn't be thought of as modern now. I remember the Debussy and Ravel quartets at the Holywell music room; I was particularly attracted by French music, which was one of the things that made me decide to go to Paris to study afterwards. ... Ravel looked at all my earliest efforts and suggested that I should go to Nadia Boulanger. She looked at some of those early things and she said she would take me as a pupil. So off I went to Paris in 1926. ... She has the enormously strong personality that

---

[22] Dr Henry Ley (1887–1962), organist of Christ Church Cathedral, Oxford (1909–26).

everybody says she has, and this made me work in a way that I can't imagine anybody else making me do. It was impossible to bring to her anything that one hadn't sweated over.

Q You worked very long hours?

LB I found them long, yes. Of course, as well as Nadia herself, the French are very strict about matters of discipline, technique, and so on. I think now that although it was somewhat painful at the time, it was a tremendous asset to have this rather severe training.

Q Do you feel that the French were strict to excess, even after their studentship period?

LB I think that they do tend to be so. Certainly they were at that time. For instance, with executants, with young pianists and violinists, they make them learn the whole of music, including counterpoint and so on, as well as the techniques of performance.

Q Did this apply to those French composers you had most admired?

LB To nearly all of them, yes. They'd all been through the same strict training. A composer like Debussy would never have been able to compose within an idiom that was then completely new and strange, and to do it so successfully, if he hadn't had this technical background, the sort of training which won him the Prix de Rome as a young man.

Q Are you saying that musical innovation means a close relationship with tradition?

LB Yes. I think that innovation can be made to work if it is rooted in tradition, though I'm not saying that all innovators need the same tradition.

Q But don't you think that excessive training in any given tradition could restrict a composer's scope? Take a French composer you admire, Poulenc, for example.

LB I don't think Poulenc ever went through the strictest academic teaching, and, of course, it's perfectly true that so much of his music is instinctive, isn't it? I love a lot of his music, particularly the songs, which I think are his best things. There is an element of hit or miss, however, in some of his work, depending on whether he was really on his best form or not when he wrote it. But that sounds like a judgement on another composer, which is something I don't like to make.

Q What would you say were the major influences on you of this French experience, apart from the disciplined training we've been talking about?

LB I think hearing a lot of music by the established composers of that time, including some Russians, such as Prokofiev and Stravinsky; they'd been through a different kind of academic training, of course, though it was still a fairly strict discipline.

Q Does any of the music which you wrote at that time still survive?

LB There are one or two songs which I wrote early on that I still like. But though I wrote a good deal of music I've scrapped most of it. The first things that I own to, so to speak, weren't written until the late 1930s.[23] The whole period in France was a sort of formative period.

Q Were you developing a conscious theory as a composer?

LB Not really. I think everything I did was part of a natural eclecticism, moving towards what I wanted to do myself.

Q When did you return to England?

LB I didn't come back permanently until 1936.

Q What did you think about the English musical scene at that time?

LB I found it more restricted, more limited to fewer composers than I'd known in France.

Q Who were the dominant English figures then?

LB Well, Vaughan Williams, William Walton, and Constant Lambert, I suppose. Lambert didn't leave as much as one would have hoped, but he was a remarkable musician. The works of Arnold Bax and Arthur Bliss were being played. There were some interesting things, certainly.

Q Was it difficult for you to move into this sort of scene?

LB I didn't really try to. Not because I didn't think it any good – because obviously there was a lot of talent here – but I think I didn't find any composer in England with whom I had any real affinity.

Q Until you met Benjamin Britten?

LB That's right. He was the first English composer with whom I felt any special affinity. I met him at Barcelona in 1936 and I saw a good deal of him when I came back to England. He's ten years younger than I am, but he's had a big influence on me and on my work.

Q You wrote the *Mont Juic Suite* together. Was that in any sense a political response to Spain in the 1930s?

LB We wrote the dance suite when we got home, but I don't think it had any direct political bearing. Mont Juic was the name of the park in Barcelona where we heard the tunes. We heard later that it was also the name of the prison in Barcelona.

Q If not in *Mont Juic*, did the political issues of the 1930s have no relevance to music?

LB I think they did. Ben felt very strongly about the Spanish Civil War, though any influence on his music and mine was indirect, I believe. I do think that events or political attitudes can produce feelings that might cause one to write music.

Q Like Britten's *War Requiem*?

---

[23] However, there are now several early works in circulation and on CD.

LB Yes, that's a good example of what I mean. I think Britten has been affected very much in this way – more than I have, certainly. Some composers and artists in other media connect their art with actual events more directly than others do.

Q If you set words to music, your choice of words could carry a political or moral content? The music would reflect the content of the words, wouldn't it?

LB Yes. It's rather difficult to show that any music was directly inspired by a particular type of influence, though it's clear, say, that Beethoven was strongly affected by political happenings.

Q Some English composers, like the Marxist Alan Bush have claimed a political relevance for music?[24]

LB Yes. Bush has remained faithful to his political creed, but, of course, this has manifested itself chiefly in political operas.

Q What about British composers who align themselves with the would-be-radicals in poetry and the other arts, composers like Cornelius Cardew? Does this kind of radicalism in the arts relate to radical politics?

LB I don't think it follows. Radical alterations in the language of any art aren't necessarily produced by political radicals. Some so-called revolutionary composers, in the political sense, are very traditional musicians.

Q An artist who works for a popular revolutionary cause would have to work inside a very popular musical medium, wouldn't he?

LB Not always. There's the instance of Mozart's *Figaro*, which was, in a sense, a politically radical opera. Beaumarchais's play was designed to make some fun of the aristocracy, and it's obvious that Mozart agreed with those critical views. But it's also true that his music didn't appeal to the general public in his day, not so much as that of Cimarosa did, for example.

Q But Mozart was always able to convey the other side of any moral debate, especially in the operas?

LB Yes. He obviously sympathises with all his characters whenever they can deserve sympathy.

Q And he's like Shakespeare in this, isn't he, in his ability to sympathise at all levels, to show compassionate understanding for all sides, almost to the extent that sometimes there is no other side?

LB Yes – which is why Mozart's music was infinitely richer than that of his eighteenth-century contemporaries. They often produced music which was nearer to what people expected. As he grew older – though he never grew very old – Mozart's music developed apart from this common expectancy.

Q When you came back to England finally, did you have a different sense of the Englishness of music here?

---

[24] Alan Bush (1900–95).

LB   Yes, although not all English composers belonged to it. Alan Rawsthorne didn't attach himself to any particular English tradition, for instance.[25]

Q   But aren't you talking now of a recent, rather local, English tradition, which includes Elgar, Vaughan Williams and such composers?

LB   Well, if we're thinking of a longer tradition, going back to the Elizabethans, we have something quite different. Someone like Michael Tippett has been influenced a good deal by Elizabethan madrigal and song.

Q   But, as a song-writer, aren't you part of that wider sense of Englishness?

LB   Well, yes, a bit, certainly.[26]

Q   You talked earlier of your eclecticism. Isn't it a curious thing about your music that your critics trace so many influences in your work, especially French ones? The 1920s style of Poulenc found in the 1940s style of Berkeley is supposed to demonstrate, once more, the existence of a time-lag between the Continent and here.

LB   It's difficult for me to say, because I'm not conscious of these influences. I don't think that any of my music is very much like the 1920s music of Poulenc, quite honestly. As I've said, I do feel more affinity with his later music, especially the songs. I don't think this time-lag idea is true. I don't claim that my music is at all up-to-date, so there's a time-lag there, if you like, but not in the sense that I hark back to Poulenc and the 1920s.

Q   To suggest that music has to be up to date suggests that there is inevitable progress in the arts, doesn't it? This time-lag idea assumes the same thing?

LB   The whole question of being up-to-date is a very difficult one, because if we think of the music of the past, the music of even a hundred years ago, it's not necessarily the avant-garde composers of their day who were the best. I don't think we consider very much the actual date when something good was written. Whether it was thirty years behind the times in the nineteenth century doesn't really trouble one very much today, does it? In any case, I never really consider it. I think simply of writing the kind of music that's right for me.

Q   Do you think that twentieth-century music has tended to become too aridly intellectual?

LB   Well, yes. A good deal of it has suppressed the human element, I feel. I'm not sure that the gradual disappearance of subjective feeling hasn't been anti-musical. Music based only on mathematical calculation seems to me to be a different kind of activity, different from music, I mean.

Q   Couldn't this be seen as part of your eclecticism? That you tend to work inside

---

[25] See Berkeley's article on Rawsthorne, p. 138 above.

[26] Stephen Banfield suggests: 'One might even argue that Berkeley's acceptance and furtherance of a fundamentally traditional song-maker's craft places him and not Britten most directly in the post-war line of succession of English song'. *Sensibility and English Song* (Cambridge, 1985), 389.

music, distrusting extraneous factors, political or theoretical? And couldn't that be construed as a sort of music-for-music's-sake viewpoint?

LB I've never been sure quite what that means. Certainly, I regard music as an act of communication, but I don't think about an audience very much when I'm composing. I just think of how to present the musical ideas that come to me in the best way that I can. Music is a language or medium which one explores. I don't think the composer should be consciously delivering a message.

Q Were you ever influenced at all by such developments as serialism?

LB I believe that serial technique is interesting to all composers because it did provide a different way of musical construction. It can be used in ways different from those intended by Schoenberg and his followers sixty years ago. If I've understood this rightly, his object was to abolish tonality which had had its day. But I don't think anybody since the 1950s, when the serial system came into common use, has used it so very strictly. It's now employed in a tonal manner, recognising the wider scope of the whole chromatic scale, but employing tonal centres in way that would have been anathema to the early dodecaphonic composers. In the end, I believe, tonality is something you can't get away from entirely.

Q Why do you think this is?

LB Because the harmonic series seems both to be a mathematical truth and also to have emotional relationships within it for human beings. It's something nobody's ever satisfactorily explained.

Q When did you first become a teacher?

LB Immediately after the war. The Royal Academy of Music appointed a few composers with the idea of helping young composers. They thought that it would be a good thing to help pupils with actual composition rather than with technical learning of harmony and so on.

Q Did Nadia Boulanger's teaching serve as a model?

LB More or less. In her attitude to composition she was very good indeed. She encouraged the right things – individuality and boldness – and she showed great insight into our musical intentions.

Q Can we return to your own compositions? You have rarely gone in for very large-scale works – *Nelson* was the only grand opera, in 1954. Is this apparent preference for the small scale a personal thing, or do you believe that large-scale works of art are not possible now?

LB It does seem to be the case that in poetry the large-scale work has gone out – nobody writes epics nowadays. But I'm not sure about painting. There are certainly some large canvases, though that's only physical largeness, which isn't the same thing at all. I choose to work on a small scale because I prefer to do so. I've always liked song and other short forms. Not that I would mind trying to write another full-length opera. I've had more experience of the stage since I wrote *Nelson*. I feel that I learnt something from the three one-act operas, and I'd be better equipped to do a full-length opera now. But it would take such an immense time.

Q You've written some longer choral pieces for the Roman Catholic Church?

LB Yes, I've done two masses, but they're liturgical masses rather than concert masses. One's an ordinary four-part work with organ, and I also wrote a five-part unaccompanied mass.[27]

Q Do you think there's such a thing as a distinctly religious style in your work?

LB Not really, though it does depend on whether I'm writing for a liturgical purpose – a work to be performed in church - or for a concert platform. I think in writing liturgical music perhaps one does modify one's style a bit – a more contemplative, less extrovert approach, maybe.[28]

Q You feel less need to express your own subjective feelings in liturgical music?

LB Yes, exactly. And I think to that extent I have rather modified the things I've done for church performance. But I've also done things on religious words that are designed for the concert occasion, like the St Teresa songs, and one or two other things.

Q What is the relationship between words and music; doesn't something disappear in a poem set to music?

LB I've thought about this a lot, because I like setting words, and I do feel that when a composer sets a poem he has in a way to destroy one side of that poem in order to recreate it in another form. I think that this is legitimate if he is able to reproduce the atmosphere of the poem very strongly, so that the poem is, as it were, rewritten in another language, translated, remade.

Q Doesn't this mean that the greatest poetry is more difficult to set to music?

LB Oh, exactly, because I think one hesitates much more to interfere with it. I know that some of the Schubert songs were by Goethe but some of his most beautiful songs are to words which, though certainly not trivial, were not great poetry.

Q How do you get ideas? Do they come simply as music, or in some other way?

LB I generally find that musical ideas only really come to me when I am working, when I'm sitting there thinking about an actual piece. It isn't so much having ideas, because if you're a composer you must have ideas, otherwise you couldn't create at all. But it's having the right idea at the right moment that's so difficult, the feeling that you must go on with that particular piece. Very often one knows in theory, so to speak, what the idea must be, only the right notes to express it just won't come. That's really what I mean by the right idea, finding the right notes for that particular moment.

Q Has your work ever been influenced by contemporary popular music?

---

[27] *Missa Brevis*, for SATB and organ, op. 57; *Mass*, for SSATB, op. 64.
[28] Compare this with Malcolm Williamson, p. 253 below.

LB   Pop in the usual sense seems to me a very threadbare form of music. The harmony's abysmal, mostly, and melodically it has very little to offer either. I think perhaps the Beatles have been the only ones who had some genuine talent of a musical kind. I've been interested in jazz, which seems to me something much more important. A good many of the developments in contemporary music have been related to jazz – the improvisatory side of it, for instance, and jazz sometimes has quite interesting rhythms and harmonies too.

Q   How far do you approve of aleatory music?

LB   Well, it varies a good deal. Lutosławski uses aleatory methods within fairly strictly controlled limits, and I think they sometimes work. But he's a very fine composer, in any case. I must confess that I'm old-fashioned enough to prefer his earlier, more traditional pieces, which were marvellously constructed.

Q   What about extreme examples, like Cage's *4'33"*?[29]

LB   Quite honestly, it doesn't mean anything at all to me.

Q   Do you think that English culture has really missed out on the sort of explosion in the arts which occurred on the continent around the time of World War I? It's been said of your music and it's said quite often nowadays of our art in general, that we've failed to develop in radical ways?

LB   Yes, I've heard all that. But I think we've got as good, if not better, composers in this country as in any other, really. No, I won't say better, because that sounds very chauvinistic, but they're certainly as good, I honestly think.

Q   Is there a distinctive English quality in English music? Aren't modesty and a distrust of grandiloquence qualities common to English composition even in modern times?

LB   I suppose that's true. There's a distinctive sort of English nostalgia which you find in Vaughan Williams sometimes, and in Elgar's *Introduction and Allegro*, that's quite unique. But I'd have thought that French composers such as Ravel and Fauré had the quality of modesty, though it was combined with a particular kind of French charm.

Q   Finally, what are you working on now?

LB   I'm doing another piece for string orchestra, commissioned by the Arts Council for the Westminster Cathedral String Orchestra which is conducted by Colin Mawby and I'm trying to do a work for chamber orchestra and guitar which Julian Bream has asked me to do.[30] This is a difficult combination, because the volume of sound from the guitar is so tiny compared with even a chamber orchestra.

Q   You've written for guitar before?

LB   Yes. I've a Sonatina which was written for Julian too, and he's played that a

---

[29] John Cage (1912–90), *4'33"* (1952), the notorious 'silent' piece.

[30] Suite for string orchestra, op. 87: Guitar Concerto, op. 88.

great number of times. Also a set of variations for guitar.[31] But there's little music for guitar with orchestra. And, yes, Peter Pears has asked me to write some new songs with harp accompaniment for him and Ossian Ellis.[32]

Q Are there some modern poets you admire and would like to try to set to music?

LB Well, I admire many modern poets, Dylan Thomas, for example, though I like him for the sound of the words rather than the meaning, about which I'm not always very clear. I've set poems by E. E. Cummings, who is very individual but difficult.[33] Everybody seems to be setting him nowadays, don't they? Auden, of course. But I've not found any really contemporary poets I'd like to set. Perhaps I don't know them well enough yet.

---

[31] Sonatina for guitar, op. 51/2; *Theme and Variations* for guitar, op. 77; but Berkeley had forgotten he had written *Quatre pièces* for Segovia in about 1927 (this came to light only in 2001).

[32] *Five Herrick Poems*, op. 89 (1973), for high voice and harp.

[33] In 1972 Berkeley set one poem by Cummings. This was 'i carry your heart with me' from *95 Poems* (1958) and he dedicated this song to the counter-tenor Tay Cheng Jim. I had suggested Cummings for the song cycle commissioned for Meriel Dickinson and gave him a book, but he chose Chinese poems instead for *Five Chinese Songs*, op. 78 (1971).

3 With Peter Dickinson, 1978

An interview to mark Berkeley's seventy-fifth birthday published in *The Musical Times*, May 1978. These are answers to written questions.

PD   Fifteen years ago, on your sixtieth birthday, I ended a *Musical Times* article by saying that twentieth-century English music would be seriously incomplete without your work. That view has been confirmed for me by getting to know your earlier music better and by the new works you've written since then. So I think it's very satisfying to find that some of your larger pieces are now recorded: the Concerto for Two Pianos and Orchestra, as well as the symphonies – the first three anyway – and the Concerto for one piano and orchestra. Do you feel that this is your most important public music, or would you equally like to see the operas and larger choral works on record and more widely performed?

LB   I don't really attach more importance to works of longer duration or using larger forces than to small pieces, though I think it's necessary for a professional composer to be able to cope with them. They certainly make more impression on the public, and involve a much bigger effort en the composer's part, so it's gratifying that I am now being offered recordings of them.

PD   Have there been any surprises in the way that your music has been received over the last fifty years? In other words, would you have expected your career to have turned out as it has done, after you decided to work exclusively in music and study with Nadia Boulanger?

LB   I think I should say that I hoped for a successful career in music rather than that I expected it, but for a long time my music was very little performed; then certain works, including some quite early ones, began to be played more frequently, and now the Serenade for Strings, the Divertimento and the St Teresa Songs seem to be in the repertoire and appear fairly regularly in programmes. The Auden songs too are now beginning to be more widely known.

PD   At the time of your seventieth birthday I was aware of some new directions in your work of the later 1960s. For example, the cogent Third Symphony, and *Windsor Variations*, and the extension of this more-or-less atonal style into chamber works like the Duo for cello and piano and the *Five Chinese Songs*. But you have continued to write tonal pieces as well, such as the Canzonetta of the *Sinfonia concertante* for oboe and orchestra. Are you able to make a distinction between your dissonant and less dissonant manners? Is this anything new in your later music, or have you felt consistently about it from your earliest pieces?

LB   My music has always been fundamentally tonal, though it is true that I felt the need to explore more dissonant harmony round about the period you mention, and still use it, though I think I have managed to incorporate it in my usual style in some of my later music. I'm not sure that I'm always successful in this aim. When the feeling I want to convey in a particular piece seems to demand it, I use traditional harmony (the Canzonetta which you mention is a case in point) at the risk of being accused of eclecticism by the critics. I don't think this need destroy unity of style because I believe that traditional harmony can be used in an individual manner; whether I've been successful in this is not for me to say.

PD What is your attitude to harmony? Are you more interested in certain kinds of chords: for example, bitonal ones, or versions of the dominant thirteenth?

LB My attitude to harmony is that it should always be the result of the horizontal movement of parts and not thought of as an alignment of individual chords – this gives point to harmony and enables one to employ chords like the dominant thirteenth (yes, I admit it without shame) which otherwise sound too sugary. The same is true of a tendency in the opposite direction, i.e. dissonant harmony – if that expression is not a contradiction in terms. In other words, I want music to be above all contrapuntal – if it is good counterpoint the harmony will take care of itself.

PD But do you think that you now hear in the same way as you did when writing the earlier pieces, from the 1940s, which show such an acute ear for detail and sonority?

LB No, I've not found my way of hearing has altered.

PD What will the Fourth Symphony be like? Can we expect something as terse as the Third, with its division of the twelve notes into two groups of six?

LB My Fourth Symphony is, I think, a good deal less terse than the Third – if I didn't dislike the word I would say that it is more romantic. I don't think I've used any material derived from the twelve-note scale in it. I've not done this purposely – the work has just turned out like this. I don't feel I can say much more until I've heard it.

PD When you have heard your own music, perhaps many times, do you feel able to judge it? I'm wondering if you have any critical interest in comparing, say, the First and Fourth Symphonies, or the First and Third Quartets, both separated by some thirty years.

LB I think one can only judge one's own music after a considerable lapse of time – it being almost impossible to look at it objectively at first.

PD But do you feel, for example, that what you had to say was better expressed at one period in chamber music, in another in songs, or orchestral music?

LB I don't think the music I write now is in itself more suitable for the orchestra than for chamber ensembles, but I think I am able to write more effectively for orchestra than I could in earlier years.

PD Why did you write three operas within about three years in the mid-1950s and not return to the medium until the late 1960s?

LB I wrote *Nelson* because I thought the subject suitable for operatic treatment, and because I'd been much influenced by Ben's operas. It was at that time that I met Paul Dehn, and we planned to do a light one-act together – this of course was *A Dinner Engagement*. I think *Ruth*, which followed soon after, was commissioned by the Aldeburgh Festival – it was certainly first performed by the English Opera Group. After these three I got commissions for other things and it was not until the late 1960s that I was free to try my hand at opera again. I had long wanted to do another opera with Paul, and it was he who suggested the episode from the Odyssey which became *Castaway*. It was not originally a commission, we just wrote it because we wanted to. Paul was an excellent classical scholar, and knew the original Greek well. We got the offer to have it put on at Aldeburgh when it was already written.

PD John Tavener said, in a seventieth birthday tribute to you in *The Listener*, that he felt your finest music was on religious themes. Obviously he instanced the St Teresa of Avila songs, and I think the later Donne setting of 'Batter my Heart' – a telling choral setting so different from Britten's one for solo voice and piano. But do you feel that your sacred music, much of it too difficult to be used regularly for the liturgy, is at the core of your inspiration? What is the relation between sacred and profane in your music?

LB I make no distinction between music written to a liturgical text and any other – except that in the former there is an element derived from plainsong and the sixteenth-century music associated with such texts. Being a Catholic has meant that I feel at home with the Roman liturgy (though it has now largely disappeared to the great discomfort of many Roman Catholics). I felt attracted to these texts because I believed what they were about.

PD Since 1936, when you first met Britten, until his death in 1976, you followed each work with interest, each one as it came out. In the later 1930s you both dedicated works to each other, and even wrote *Mont Juic* together as a collaboration. Have you felt at all intimidated by the fact that, for a time, you were working on similar lines? Now that Britten's work is concluded, can you say what he meant to you as a composer?

LB I was one of Ben's earliest admirers. As a young man his musical gifts were really amazing – it was not only the invention of music but an instinctive comprehension of how to organise it that struck me. He was already a fine craftsman in his early twenties. He had a strong influence on me, though ten years younger – but I was a late developer. When I felt that I could speak with my own voice as it were, I found it necessary to detach myself from his influence, but this in no way diminished my admiration for his music.

PD It's interesting to compare your lighter music with Britten's, which is quite different, but you both clearly admired some of the same sources, such as Mozart. I'm thinking of your Divertimento, the Piano Concerto, the two-piano Polka and much later the *Palm Court Waltz*. The sparkling wit of these mostly earlier pieces is less obvious later on. Do you feel this? Have your tastes changed over a period of fifty years?

LB There's undoubtedly a spontaneous element that most creative artists have at the beginning of their careers that tends to diminish with age. This may have happened to me, but I don't feel that I have changed much, and my love of the composers I most admire certainly has remained.

PD So you would say that your tastes haven't changed much over some fifty years?

LB I can't think of changes of taste within myself.

PD Would you mind being remembered as the composer of the lighter works? Which of these do you prefer?

LB I'm content to let this work itself out. Only too pleased if I'm remembered at all!

PD Assuming your present good health, can you imagine a situation where you wouldn't want to go on composing?

LB I don't think I could stop composing – the urge is still too strong; besides, there's nothing else I can do!

4. With Michael Oliver, 1978

Interview about the Fourth Symphony for 'Music Weekly', BBC Radio 3, 28 May 1978

Michael Oliver (1937–2002) was an exceptionally fluent and well-informed broadcaster. He presented 'Music Weekly' on BBC Radio 3 (1975–90) and 'Kaleidoscope' on BBC Radio 4 (1974–87). He wrote for various periodicals and published biographies of Stravinsky and Britten.

MEO Sir Lennox Berkeley's First Symphony is obviously not music of grand gestures or extravagant colour. Words like 'civilised', 'elegant', 'unassertive' are often applied to his work. But it would be wrong to assume that those adjectives add up to a noun like 'miniaturist' or 'water-colourist'. The First Symphony shows remarkable variety of invention, a closeness of argument, and meticulous economy. Berkeley may never write a ninety-minute symphony with a choral finale, but to take on a new symphony with this degree of tight discipline is a major, even a rather daunting job.

LB It is a big task and I feel slightly alarmed and despondent about starting on it. Once I've got into it, I'm driven on somehow by a kind of urge – it's a bad thing if one isn't because it means one's got to construct artificially instead of the thing taking hold of you as you write, so to speak.

MEO I've spoken to one or two composers of symphonies who seem to be spurred on by one symphony to write another – a sense of unfinished business where, having written one symphony, they now know what to do in the next. Did you feel that way?

LB Yes, a little. In my Third Symphony, in one fifteen-minute movement, I felt that I'd acquired a somewhat more forcible way of writing that I was able to put to the test. When the RPO commissioned the Fourth Symphony I was anxious to do it because it's a splendid thing if an orchestra commissions a contemporary composer. That was one reason but I was also keen to see if I could do it on a bigger scale. This one has three movements: I hope I've managed to use this slightly more expansive manner.

MEO I know it's always difficult to answer this kind of question, but when you knew you were going to write the Fourth Symphony what was the first step? Do you sit waiting for ideas?

LB Up to a point, but what I always find is that ideas tend not to come if I just sit waiting for them. I generally have to put down almost anything that comes into my head; I fiddle about with the notes; and very often, like that, something catches fire. I think that most composers find that it is in searching for ideas that something comes alive.

MEO Does that happen in an orderly way? Does an idea gradually grow and then you're able to identify the second subject of the third movement?

LB I don't think you can pinpoint it as accurately as that. When you've found some sort of material it's often susceptible of growth. I believe it's a partly subconscious thing. Composers have often found in the past that musicologists have uncovered all kinds of things about the inter-relation between parts of a work that the composer had never thought of. Musical ideas grow that way.

MEO The knowledge that you're writing a symphony must bend your mind to symphonic ideas?

LB Yes, that may cause the right kind of idea to crop up as you think about it.

MEO In the Third Symphony you said you'd found a harder musical language, and I think that everybody who heard it agreed. Which came first – the idea that you needed to develop this sort of language or the fact that you were embarking on another symphony?

LB It was because I wanted to get a bit more strength and directness into my music. After I came back to England after my training in France I wrote some fairly modest things at first and I was rather too often put down as a miniaturist with a certain French charm. It took a little time to break out of that. I felt the need to enlarge.

MEO Was the casting of the Third Symphony as a three-section single movement almost an act of caution? Were you not sure the new language would sustain a greater length?

LB That entered into it, now I come to think of it. A thing on a smaller scale is, of course, easier. To embark on something on a big scale is much more challenging.

MEO Another feature of the Third Symphony was the way that it largely avoided repetition: ideas continually grow throughout the work. Have you taken that up in the Fourth?

LB Yes. I think every composer feels that it's impossible to repeat note-for-note the way the eighteenth-century composers did. Somehow it makes things move at much too slow a pace for the way we feel and think today. I think it's instinctive. The musical language reached a point at which exact repetition doesn't seem to be suitable.

MEO But some sort of repetition is surely at the heart of most of the classical forms that one would use to define a symphony?

LB Yes, but I think the modified form of repetition is essential because otherwise your material goes for nothing. You've got to exploit it, which does mean going over the same notes again but making them sound different.

MEO In the new symphony do you use sonata or rondo forms?

LB Yes, very loosely. In the first movement there's a first theme and two subsidiary themes – not so tightly organised as in classical music, but the same principle is there. The second movement is a theme and variations. I like variation form and have used it a great deal. In this slow movement there are five variations;

three are slow and there are two quick ones in the middle. It's very easy to be boring in a slow movement [*Laughs*] and that's what frightened me off writing a full-length slow movement, so variation form came in useful.

MEO Did you encounter what has been called the finale problem? First movements are fine; middle movements are all right; but finales are terrible!

LB I agree entirely. [*Laughs*] I think that's why I adopt a slightly lighter tone.

MEO With the last movement of the Fourth Symphony I get the impression that only when it was safely down on paper could you stand back and discover what form you'd cast it in.

LB It's more like a rondo where the ABACA comes back to the opening motif of rising thirds mainly. It does follow the classical pattern more or less.

MEO Is there any degree of thematic reference between movements?

LB Not really: certainly not intentionally.

MEO You'll leave that to the analysts?

LB Yes, exactly.

MEO Does the work change as you're writing it?

LB It always does a bit, I think. Obviously you have to make a plan but you also have to allow for things that happen to come into it. You find some part of a theme or motif lends itself to development which you may not have foreseen. Things can happen by accident. I've found sometimes that I've copied something out wrong – a transposition perhaps – and it's given me a different slant on what I was trying to do. So one does take advantage of mistakes as well as chance happenings.

MEO How do you feel about a new work in the period between sending it off to the copyist and the first performance? Do you hope that people are going to like it?

LB Yes, I think so. One's glad to be rid of it in some ways but at the same time one has moments of panic that it's not going to sound right. On the whole, with more experience, you're not likely to have any seriously unpleasant surprises in the sense that something simply doesn't come off on the orchestra, as happened sometimes in my early efforts.

MEO When the work has been performed, are you able to stand back from it in some detachment? I remember once that you said to me, about your Second Symphony: 'Yes, some people like that piece but I'm not crazy about it myself.'

LB I do find I like some things I've written more than others.

– Part V –
Extracts from Berkeley's Diaries, 1966–82

INTRODUCTION

Berkeley wrote his diaries with some reluctance. He obviously found he was short of time for composition, and more than once in these extracts wonders whether it was worth while to keep this kind of record. It certainly was, for the light it throws on Berkeley's life in his final years. We read of his visits with Lady Berkeley to Monaco and elsewhere, his connections with the Royal Family and Prime Minister Edward Heath, and follow Berkeley's travels round Britain to attend or take part in performances of his music. Most of these occasions are recorded in appreciative terms. He was increasingly cherished by performers as he became an elder statesman of British music.

Another aspect of the diaries is that they reveal Berkeley as a devotee of opera, which he attended regularly and of which he was an experienced and well-informed critic. He was struggling with a new grand opera when the diaries peter out in the early 1980s. It was to have been called *Faldon Park*, with a libretto by Winton Dean, a close friend and eminent Handel scholar. Sadly it was at about this time that Berkeley became severely handicapped by the onset of Alzheimer's disease, so he was denied the chance of competing with his admired Verdi, who wrote *Otello* and *Falstaff* in his late seventies.

Berkeley is much more frank in these diaries than in any published commentary and more outspoken than he was normally in general conversation. He honestly says what he feels, which makes the diaries especially refreshing.

Footnotes have been provided to explain the context

5 November 1966

We left for Geneva where I am one of the adjudicators for Queen Marie José's Composition Prize, spending a few days in Paris on the way.[1] We went to Roland-Manuel's funeral. ... he combined a brilliant mind with goodness and charm.[2]

We both enjoyed Geneva which we both knew from the previous year when I had been on the jury for the piano prize. It is an attractive town, the lake and the rushing waters of the Rhine, the wide and open streets, all this is agreeable; it's strange that it should have been the home of Calvinism – the most detestable of the many perversions of Christianity.

Queen Marie is very charming, she has a shy and gentle manner and is passionately fond of music. She gave a dinner for the members of the jury on our last evening – it included (the jury, I mean, not the dinner) Capdevielle, Dutilleux and

---

[1] Queen Marie José of Belgium (1906–2001). The prize she initiated was based in Switzerland.
[2] Alexis Roland-Manuel (1891–1966), French composer and musicologist who wrote early studies of Ravel.

Marescotti.³ Capdevielle told me how when he was a student at the Conservatoire he sent in, as an end of term composition, a setting of that institution's regulations. The prank was so little to the taste of the authorities that they threw him out, but Ravel and Florent Schmitt were much amused and befriended him.

We returned to Paris by train. The weather was cold and misty but the leaves had stayed late on the trees and turned to a deep golden colour. I thought of the Apollinaire poem I set a few years ago ...⁴

I finished *Castaway* at the end of the month.⁵

December 1966

This month we shall have been married for twenty years. I feel that I've been so immensely lucky, and I know that to have lived with someone so good, so sweet and so generous has made me into a different person.

Concert at the Festival Hall to hear Rostropovitch. I met him at dinner after the concert; he has enormous vitality and animation, and one quickly understands what it is that makes him such a great performer. It was difficult for me to communicate with him as he speaks only Russian and German, and I haven't got even what Marion Harewood⁶ calls 'Aldeburgh Deutsch', but he's so overflowing with friendliness, so warm and human, that language hardly seems to matter.

Ben [Britten]. What I feel and have always felt is that of all the outstanding composers of today, he is the most purely musical. I love much of his music in the same way that I love Mozart; I don't mean 'as much as' but in the same way. He has extraordinary musical ability, but there is much human feeling in his music as well, which is perhaps what accounts for his popularity as a composer. He's got things the right way round – technique for him is only a means of communication, and yet his craftsmanship is equal to that of anyone living today. I owe him a great deal; in the days when I spent a lot of time with him – nearly thirty years ago now – we talked endlessly about music, and he somehow unlocked a door for me that previously I'd been unable to open. It amuses me, now that he's universally known and that honours are showered upon him, to think that I used to have to try and persuade people that he was a great musician only to be told that he was but another clever young man – brilliant, but lacking anything really substantial. The Serenade, the Nocturne, *Albert Herring* and the *Turn of the Screw* are the works I like best, and parts of *A Midsummer Night's Dream*. The *War Requiem* has pages of great beauty, but seems to me to have less individuality than some of his music.

---

³ Pierre Capdevielle (1906–69); Henri Dutilleux (1916–); André-Francois Marescotti (1902–95).

⁴ *Automne*, op. 60/3 (1963), for medium voice and piano.

⁵ *Castaway*, op. 68 (1966), one-act opera with libretto by Paul Dehn.

⁶ The Countess of Harewood, later Marion Thorpe, pianist and daughter of Austrian music publisher Erwin Stein.

23 October 1967

Performance of *Signs in the Dark* at Stroud.[7] Considering that it was really an amateur effort, it was not bad at all. I feel on the whole happy about the music, particularly the last movement. I felt that Laurie genuinely liked it. ...

24 January 1968

John Tavener's *The Whale* at Queen Elizabeth Hall.[8] It's very effective and makes a strong impact. His sound imagination is truly remarkable. I found it somewhat too full of tricks – for instance, the reading from the encyclopaedia was boring and added nothing. A pity, as John doesn't need gimmicks, but there remains something of the very gifted amateur in his music. I blame myself for this; a severer teacher would have forced him to acquire an ordinary technique which would enable him to write anything to order – a professional composer should have this. That is why I wanted to send him to Nadia [Boulanger]. I liked very much Henze's *Apollo and Hyacinthus* given in the same concert.[9] No lack of technique here! From what I've read about it, I don't know that I should like his later music so much, but this had a marvellous poise and lyrical feeling.

6 February 1968

Michael Howard's choir, Cantoris in Ecclesia, at the Queen Elizabeth Hall. I thought it the best small choir I had heard for a long time: they sang with great intensity and warmth. The Byrd motets are really great music – particularly the wonderful *Ne Isacaris*. They also sang Francis Poulenc's *Motet pour un temps de penitence* which I thought among his best music. How happy he would have been to have heard this performance. *The Times* critic said the work was let down by occasional touches of facile sentiment, but how grateful one is these days for sentiment of any kind; it is at least a relief from the showy gimmickry of the avant-garde. ...

I've got on faster with the *Magnificat* than I expected. Michael has been a great help in copying out my piano reduction and his enthusiasm has been a great encouragement.[10]

---

[7] *Signs in the Dark*, op. 69 (1967), for SATB and strings, to poems by Laurie Lee (1914–97).

[8] Sir John Tavener (1944–). This premiere performance of *The Whale* was given by the London Sinfonietta under David Atherton, who recorded the work for the Beatles Apple label in 1970.

[9] Hans Werner Henze (1926–), *Apollo et Hyacinthus* (1948–9).

[10] *Magnificat*, op. 71 (1968), SATB, orchestra and organ. See also Berkeley's article, p. 127 above.

1 May 1968

We left London for Monaco via Dover–Calais and the Blue Train. I've been making this journey off and on since my childhood – every feature of the landscape from Calais to Paris is familiar, even the very featurelessness of the Pas de Calais, the sand dunes round Étaples where the British war graves are, then the streams, poplars and willows as one approaches Amiens and further on the forest of Chantilly and the bridge where one looks down on the tops of trees.

5 May 1968, Monte Carlo

The jury this year are all old friends: Nadia [Boulanger], Georges [Auric], Boudeville, [Vagn] Holmboe, [Conrad] Beck and [Pietro] Montani. The entries are much the same too, with little in between hopelessly dull or incompetently written traditional style music and the more arid type of ultra-modern. ...

Yesterday we were taken out to dinner and when we got back we found the casino invaded by coach-loads of Germans. On being told that they were only there for half an hour, Georges said: 'so long as they don't stay for four years!'

Very difficult to reach any decision for the prize, but we finally chose a very well-written but rather academic piece which turned out to be by Apostel.[11] This caused some amusement as Apostel had been a member of the jury the previous year and we'd all found him difficult to get on with – he was querulous, fussy and didactic. But it showed the value of anonymity; had we known who the composer was, we would inevitably have been prejudiced in some degree against the work.

16 May 1968

I've just read Julien Green's *Chaque homme dans sa nuit*.[12] I felt that the fact that he is now almost totally taken up with religion has rather narrowed his range, but he writes as beautifully as ever and his compassion for humanity remains as strong. ...

25 May 1968

I went to lunch at Buckingham Palace. There were about eight of us guests, all men. It was much more informal than I had expected; we were given drinks in the dining room and told not to put them down when the Queen came in, but just to stand in a sort of semi-circle so that she could more easily speak to each of us in turn. She was very relaxed and easy to talk to, charming and intelligent in everything she said. I had the good fortune to sit next to Paul Scofield[13] at lunch which made

---

[11] Hans Eric Apostel (1901–72), Austrian composer, pupil of Schoenberg and Berg.

[12] Julien Green (1900–98), American writer mainly resident in France who wrote mostly in French. *Chaque homme dans sa nuit* (1960).

[13] Paul Scofield (1922–2008), English actor for stage and screen.

things easy – he's extremely nice and very modest. I didn't know anyone else except Maurice Bowra who sat on one side of the Queen and seemed to be doing all the talking.[14] I thought what an ordeal this sort of thing would have been in the days of Queen Victoria and how vastly things have changed.

31 May 1968

First performance of my Oboe Quartet.[15] I've never had anything of mine played better. It's a first class ensemble and Janet [Craxton], of course, is an outstanding musician.

Went to Glyndebourne ... and saw *Eugene Onegin* – what a delightful opera, it has long been one of my favourites. The letter song is touching and effective, but as an operatic composer Tchaikovsky lacks the fire of Verdi – the duel scene, for example, is surely rather feeble. Very good décor and production.

16 June 1968

Falstaff at Covent Garden. Musically, it was first class. Geraint Evans as Falstaff and John Shaw as Ford were superb. The women – Minton, Ligabna, Robertson and Resnik, very good too. The production, by Zeffirelli, I thought bad – continually getting in the way of the music rather than supporting it. In *Falstaff*, Verdi (wicked old man) makes mock of everything, including himself (there is surely self-parody at moments – 'e il viso tuo' for example, and 'per lei sprecei tesai') but he doesn't need the assistance of the producer. The long held high A flat in the Nanetta–Fenton duet is very moving and I always have to hide a few tears at this point. It's not as great a work as *Otello*, but of its kind another masterpiece.

After many years I heard *Peter Grimes* again, at Sadler's Wells. I thought of the day when Ben played me the first act (it must have been in 1944) in a flat he then had over a grocer's shop in Marylebone High Street.[16] Though greatly excited, I was not astonished, because I knew already that he was capable of something like this and was expecting it. What I didn't know was that success would come so quickly. Hearing it now, twenty-three years after its first performance (which I heard) it remains a great achievement. He has gone further now in that his music has become more individual, and yet he has hardly surpassed what is best in *Grimes*, for instance the wonderful and moving passage just before the storm – 'What harbour can embrace ...' which to me ranks with the greatest operatic moments.

---

[14] Sir Maurice Bowra (1898–1971), classical scholar and Oxford don.

[15] Oboe Quartet, op. 70 (1967).

[16] 45a St John's Wood High Street, London NW8, was Britten's and Pears' London address from February 1943 until 1946.

8 July 1968

My *Magnificat* at St Paul's Cathedral, City of London Festival. The performance was very unsatisfactory. To begin with the abominable acoustics of the building eliminate any sort of clarity; the choirs (St Paul's, Westminster Abbey and Westminster Cathedral) were not used to singing with orchestra; and we had insufficient rehearsal. In addition to all this, for the first time in my life, I got very little support from the orchestra (LSO) and never felt that it was really backing me up. The leader seemed bored and indifferent, and gave me no help. Composers are often amateurish and not wholly competent conductors, but for this very reason the orchestra often makes a double effort, and I've always previously had maximum support. ...

16 August 1968

Freda and I spent most of the day in Oxford. Having been born and brought up there (apart from my four years at Merton) I've always taken Oxford for granted; because too familiar, it never made much impact. Seeing it again as a visitor, I was amazed by its beauty and architectural richness, so much so that I hardly noticed the crowds and traffic in my eagerness to look at what I now saw with fresh eyes. I realise now that I had very little visual sense in my young days, perhaps owing to my obsession with music. It was only later that I learned to see as far as pictures and architecture were concerned...

19 August 1968

Went to Berkeley Castle. I came away feeling no regrets and thankful that I didn't have to live there. The building itself has a rather beautiful colour in certain lights, but otherwise is remarkable only for its antiquity. It is a gloomy place, and its chief claim to fame is that it was the scene of one of the most horrible murders in history.[17]

25 August 1968

Conducted *Signs in the Dark* at the Prom.

I was thinking about Francis [Poulenc]. He was not a great composer, but some of his songs have a unique charm – 'La grenouillière', for example; the nostalgic charm of the poem is more than reproduced – it's enormously heightened. The harmony is conventional if analysed chord by chord, but not one phrase could be by any other composer, and the last-minute return to the tonic shows the kind of skill that only the ear can command.

---

[17] Edward II (1284–1327) reigned from 1307 but was deposed in favour of his wife Queen Isabella. He was an incompetent and indulgent monarch and, although there is some uncertainty about his exact fate, he was supposed to have been murdered at Berkeley Castle.

4 November 1968

I went with Yehudi [Menuhin] to see his school at Stoke d'Abernon.[18] It's an answer to the problem of what to do with musically gifted children, but this sort of thing should be done by the state as in Russia. Here, I gather, parents pay if they can but I suspect that Yehudi pays for some himself.

December

I finished the organ pieces in the autumn and have now begun my Third Symphony for Cheltenham next year.[19]

17 January 1969

I went to Birmingham for a recital and talk in the series got up by Peter Dickinson.[20] He and his sister Meriel did my Auden and Greek Songs – she has become a fine singer and they gave a very good performance – I thought they both felt and understood the music. Renna Manduell played my Preludes, also very well. I got through the rest of it not too badly with Peter's support. I gave two more question and answer talks to students next morning – I manage these better now but have no gift for public speaking.

4 February 1969

Went to the Festival Hall for an LSO concert. André Previn, their new conductor, has a lively springy beat to which the orchestra responds well. They played Richard Bennett's new Symphony.[21] I always like his music very much when I hear it, the sound is invariably attractive, and the construction and craftsmanship perfect, and yet somehow I never find that I carry much away me or that I've been much moved. After this Previn gave what I thought the best performance of *La Valse* that I've heard. I can never quite explain why I like this piece so much. I think it must be its bitter-sweet quality, its moments of sentiment and charm, tinged with irony, which contrast with the more robust passages equally characteristic of the Viennese waltz – what Roland-Manuel called 'ses élans de volupté et sa pompe éclatante'. I suppose it's only a light piece, but nowhere, except in *Daphnis et Chloé*, has Ravel's subtle ear for harmony or the virtuosity of his scoring been more evident.

---

[18] The Yehudi Menuhin School, a specialist music school founded by Menuhin in 1963.
[19] Symphony no. 3, op. 74 (1969).
[20] At the Midland Institute in collaboration with the Extramural Department of Birmingham University.
[21] Sir Richard Rodney Bennett (1936–), Symphony no. 2.

April 1969

I finished the Symphony at the last minute – completing the full score on the morning we left for Monaco. Jury the same as last year except that we had [Marcel] Mihalovici instead of Holmboe ...

June 1969

I began the *Windsor Variations*.

9 July 1969

My Third Symphony at Cheltenham. It was well received even, on the whole, by the critics. Well played, too, by Jean Martinon, but I felt that he didn't quite understand what I wanted, particularly in the last section which he took too fast, losing much of the detail and harmony.[22] I longed to conduct it myself but this doesn't always give good results either, owing to my lack of experience and authority.

4 August 1969

Adrian Boult conducted my *Magnificat* at the Proms. Much better performance than last year at St Paul's: the Albert Hall is much improved acoustically.

19 September 1969

Yehudi conducted my *Windsor Variations* (first performance) in St George's Chapel.[23] He did it well, though there were one or two places where the balance was not quite right – perhaps my fault. The chapel is beautiful, somewhat like King's Chapel, with fan vaulting. Quite good for sound if a shade over-resonant. ...

26 September 1969

Les Troyens at Covent Garden. It was very well done, excellently produced and sung.
There are striking and sometimes beautiful moments, but I simply cannot rate Berlioz as highly as some people do today. I'm always worried by the poverty of his harmony. The best thing is his scoring, always imaginative and effective; it must have been electrifying in 1863. ... A few days later I went to *Un ballo in maschera* and felt much more at home. It's not one of the great operas perhaps but full of melody and warmth. ...

---

[22] Jean Martinon (1910–76), conductor of the Orchestre National de France (1968–73). See John Manduell's account of this occasion at Cheltenham, p. 246 below.

[23] *Windsor Variations*, op. 75 (1969), for chamber orchestra.

6 November 1969

To Oxford for a Subscription Concert at which Rubbra and I both played. There was also a work by Wellesz.[24] I played my Auden songs with Ameril Gunson, a young singer with a good voice ... and my duet sonata with Edmund.[25] Very warm and appreciative audience. ...

I've never been able to make anything of electronic music, but I listened today to a piece by Stockhausen for basset horn and electronic tape which, to my surprise, I found had a certain beauty of sound. It was very quiet, and the electronic sound had a vague murmuring background to the basset horn's interjections (very well played by Alan Hacker). I couldn't detect any shape to the piece and it seemed only to use a small part of music – that of sound colour, but it made an impression on me none the less. ...[26]

7 December 1969

Pelléas at Covent Garden on the whole the best performance I've heard. It was conducted by Boulez who brought out the many subtleties of the score while keeping a firm control of everything. I thought George Shirley the best Pelléas I've seen, he looked young enough, which is rare and sang the difficult part admirably. Donald McIntyre a very good Golaud, and Söderström I thought perfect as Mélisande. She looked lovely and had exactly the right vocal quality. ...

January 1970

After the long struggle to choose four composers for the Radcliffe Award, it was a reward to hear their string quartets – all of a high standard. The four were [Elizabeth] Maconchy, [Sebastian] Forbes, [Peter] Sculthorpe and [Robert] Sherlaw Johnson. I have for some time much admired Betty Maconchy and consider her one of the best living English composers – sadly underrated and far too little known. I was impressed by Sebastian Forbes' work – it's real music and he shows astonishing technical competence for one so young. ...

---

[24] Egon Wellesz (1885–1974), Austrian composer and musicologist, pupil of Schoenberg. Wellesz settled in England in 1938 and taught at Oxford where he was a Fellow of Lincoln College.

[25] Sonatina for piano duet, op. 39 (1954).

[26] Karlheinz Stockhausen (1925–2007). *Solo* for melody instrument and electronic tape, op. 19 (1965–6). Stockhausen's note says: 'the soloist's playing is picked up in part by microphone(s) during the performance, The recorded parts are superimposed in greater or lesser degrees of density (and possibly transformed) and at a varying interval of time are mixed with the soloist's playing through two-channel loudspeakers'.

16 April 1970

Richard Bennett's new opera *Victory* at Covent Garden. Beautifully written technically and the sound always imaginative, but it never moved me, and I came away thinking that skill is not enough, though wishing I had as much of it.

20 April 1970

We flew to Nice for the meeting of the jury. We decided unanimously to give the prize to a Polish composer – Krzysztof Meyer[27] – for a rather weird opera in the avant-garde manner, but having individuality and musicianship.

Nadia has become nearly blind and can't read anything at all: she therefore can't really take part in our deliberations. She is immensely courageous and as full of vitality as ever.

13 May 1970, Ischia

We went to see the Waltons this evening.[28] The house is not beautiful in itself but well designed and supremely comfortable, the garden lovely, entirely made by Susana. William took us up to his work room, and I felt envious of the ideal conditions in which he can compose, so different from mine – and yet I thought I might easily do nothing in such perfect surroundings, having been accustomed to struggle against the noise and interruptions of family life, I might well be unable to concentrate in such complete calm.

3–4 June 1970

I went to Birmingham to conduct two performances of *A Dinner Engagement* at the Music School. Singers and orchestra almost entirely students and very good, particularly the singers. The orchestra was not able to cope with the more difficult passages – nor was I, but it came over remarkably well. … Paul's brilliant and amusing libretto does much to keep the piece alive – the music too, I feel, is still good of its kind. …

---

[27] Krzysztof Meyer (1943–), Polish composer, pianist and writer, Boulanger pupil – his comic opera *Cyberiada* (1970).

[28] La Mortella, Forio, Ischia.

5 June 1970

We went to Oxford for my honorary degree. Nothing could have pleased me more and we had a delightful time. ... I was very happy to renew my connection, hitherto so utterly undistinguished, with Oxford. On Sunday morning we heard my *Missa brevis*[29] very well sung at Christ Church. It was sung in Latin with the rest of the service in the beautiful English of the Prayer Book – a contrast to what one hears in the Catholic Church today!

31 July 1970, Houghton Hall, Norfolk

The house is magnificent and must surely be one of the finest in England that is still lived in by the family. ... We went with Sybil Cholmondeley[30] and her daughter to one of the King's Lynn Festival concerts – a chamber orchestra conducted by Ben – Mozart and his own *Les Illuminations*. On the Sunday we were taken to lunch with the Queen Mother at Sandringham. On sitting down to lunch (I was next to her) she said with a merry twinkle in her eye: 'You've come from the most beautiful house in Norfolk to the ugliest!' It's true that Sandringham looks rather like an institute – it's built of very unattractive brick and having been added on to at various times, is rather shapeless. After lunch Ben and Peter gave a recital – Purcell, Schubert, Debussy and folk-song arrangements. Peter in good form – he has a wonderful performing gift, everything is alive and meaningful, supremely musical too, though it's not a great voice. Ben, as always, accompanied perfectly.

September 1970

I went to Nic Maw's opera *The Rising of the Moon* at Glyndebourne ... and thought it was one of the few successful modern operas I've seen.[31] There was much real beauty in the music, and good singing parts throughout. His scoring is rather too elaborate for the theatre, I think, but most imaginative. Above all he is more concerned with real music than most of the younger composers and one comes away having been made to feel something. It is individual music too – not like anything else today.

November 1970

I started my piece for King's Lynn last month. It is for chamber orchestra and solo cello – not a concerto – I don't yet know what to call it. Also two songs on Chinese poems in Arthur Waley's translation. I plan to do two or three more if I can find the right poems.

---

[29] *Missa brevis*, op. 57 (1960) for SATB and organ.

[30] Sybil Sassoon Cholmondeley, Marchioness of Cholmondeley (1894–1989) lived at Houghton Hall, Norfolk.

[31] Nicholas Maw (1935–2009). See his interview, p. 248 below.

27 November 1970, Dartington Hall, Devon

First performance of my Third String Quartet.[32] The Dartington Quartet played well; it was thoroughly competent and professional – a little lacking in anything more, I thought, and this feeling was confirmed in the Mozart (K465) which bordered on the perfunctory. It's a pity they can't get a bit deeper into the music as they have the necessary technique. My piece was particularly well received ...

8 December 1970

The Knot Garden at Covent Garden.[33] I wish I really knew why I disliked it. It's good music, dramatic and compelling, but I find the whole atmosphere unsympathetic. The opera is clearly about the problem of reconciling the inner life of the characters with their inter-relationships, but they approach it is a spirit of hysterical megalomania which robs one of any sympathy with them, and the last act, meant, one supposes, to provide a solution, fails to do so. I felt uneasy, too, about the music itself, though brimming with ideas, there is a lack of clarity in the sound that I found distressing. For example, the jazz ensemble (blues, boogie-woogie) at the end of the first act could have been enchanting, but was so overlaid with notes that one heard nothing distinctly. It was to me a great disappointment, as I've always admired Michael's music, and liked both the *Midsummer Marriage* and *King Priam*. I feel I ought to go again, but can't bring myself to do so – there is something about it that is the opposite of what I believe in both musically and philosophically. I've read nearly the whole of it in the piano score but can't get any nearer liking it. It was very well sung – Josephine Barstow very impressive as Denise and Jill Gomez excellent, and the décor very ingenious and pretty. ...

I've done more work on the Chinese poems, and had the luck to hit on one ('The Riverside Village') that I felt could have been made for me – I've seldom had so much pleasure in writing anything than this small song of twenty-two bars. ... I feel happy, too, about 'Dreaming of a Dead Lady'. It's very difficult to find a poem that will form a contrast to the mood of nostalgia and melancholy that pervades most of these. ...

6 January 1971

I recorded my Third Symphony with the LPO, very exciting for me, and I think in the end, in spite of my amateurish conducting, we got a good result.[34] I felt happy with the orchestra – they were helpful and really took trouble to get things right. There was some beautiful playing. I was glad of the opportunity to record something recent as all my recorded music is twenty years old and more.

---

[32] String Quartet no. 3, op. 76 (1970).
[33] Sir Michael Tippett (1905–98).
[34] Symphony no. 3, LPO/Berkeley, Lyrita SRCS 94.

18 January 1971

I finished the *Chinese Songs*. Peter Dickinson came and seemed delighted with them. He is to perform them with Meriel in March.[35]

I've gone back to the piece for King's Lynn and am much absorbed in it.

19 January 1971

Pierre Bernac's lecture on Francis Poulenc was excellent.[36] I think he has never got over Francis' death – he spoke of him with touching affection, and described some of his best music very well, without disguising the fact that there is a good deal that is not of the best quality. He showed too how sheer high spirits and charm go a long way to make up for the things he obviously lacked.

I've so often been asked who is my favourite composer and never been able to answer, feeling that I liked so much by so many, equally; but the older I get the more I feel that it is Mozart I most love. I felt this strongly at a performance of *Figaro* last year, and yesterday, listening to the D minor Piano Concerto [K466], I was in a kind of ecstasy throughout. I can't feel that about his early music, but the great works of his later period have about them an infallibility, a rightness in the choice and placing of every note that seems superhuman in its perfection and beauty. I often think there was an element of luck, or perhaps it was some divine dispensation, that caused the very great creative artists to be born at exactly the right time – when the language they inherited was ready for them to bring to perfection. This is true of Mozart, just as it surely is of Shakespeare; Mozart started by using the musical language as he found it, but deepened and enlarged it to a degree that made it entirely his own. He is a composer's greatest joy, but also his despair. ...

4 February 1971

I went to Adrian Boult's rehearsal of my Divertimento.[37] He's not exactly an inspiring conductor, but extremely efficient, and gets from the orchestra, with his unostentatious manner, far more than many can achieve with violent gestures. I was impressed by his remarkable control of the baton and by his sensitive ear for balance.

---

[35] The only problem was with the end of the third song. Berkeley had a melisma on 'surging' that lasted five bars. We persuaded him to break it after three bars and repeat the word 'surging'.

[36] Pierre Bernac (1899–1979), French baritone who gave many recitals with Poulenc.

[37] Divertimento in B flat, op. 18 (1943).

7 February 1971

Honegger's *Jeanne d'Arc au bucher* at the Albert Hall. I was rather disappointed; although there are good things, it's too cut up into illustrative sections so that it sounds like incidental music rather than a real work. Curiously enough Honegger's idiom which sounded so ultra-modern in the 1920s now seems outdated. He somehow failed to develop, as he got older, and lost the freshness he had in his early works. ...

22–3 March 1971

First performance of my *Chinese Songs* and first London performance of my Third String Quartet.[38] Meriel and Peter Dickinson doing the former (very well) and the Alberni Quartet the latter – this was better than at Dartington, and I think they will play it very well. Good notices.

2 April 1971

Yehudi recorded my Violin Concerto with Adrian and the Menuhin Festival Orchestra.[39] I felt I had never heard it properly before as we never had enough rehearsal time when I did it with Yehudi at Bath and King's Lynn and because of the sketchy performance I'd written it off as a failure. Now I think it's a much better piece than I had imagined.

3 May 1971

Left by air for Monte Carlo ... the great thing for me was to meet Julien Green whom I've admired for so long, and who was on this year's literary jury. On being introduced to him I was at first overcome with shyness and emotion and couldn't think of anything to say, while he, as is well known, is very reserved so our first conversation was halting. Later we managed to talk and approach each other more successfully. It appears that he is about to become a member of the Academy, and I was very happy to find that he is held in great esteem among the more literary people for his beautiful French prose and for his deep understanding of humanity. ...

---

[38] *Five Chinese Songs*, op. 78 (1971).

[39] HMV ASD 2759; on CD in EMI British Composers CDMS 66121-2. See Dickinson, *The Music of Lennox Berkeley*, 164–6.

June 2

Humphrey Searle's *Hamlet* at Covent Garden. It's well-written music – good in its way, and the orchestra always effective and aptly illustrating the drama, but the wonderful poetry seems to meet with no response in the music – splendid lines going for nothing. Humphrey set himself an impossible task: what composer could match such a masterpiece? If a foreign composer was to set a translation he might get away with it, though even then one feels he would need to be another Verdi. ...

3 June 1971

I went to hear Tippett's *Vision of St Augustine*. It's a fine work and I got a lot from it, though, as always with him, the texture is thick and the sound confused. He has a great power of big-scale construction which I envy, and there are moments of real spiritual insight. He conducted the whole concert, and obtained a very good performance of Elgar's *Introduction and Allegro* for strings, which I so much admire.

22 June 1971

Richard Buckle's Gala. In spite of all the misgivings one had, it went quite well owing to the good dancing. ... I conducted my Waltz which went fairly well and I think struck the right note – people seemed to like it, and I'd enjoyed writing it.[40]

29 June 1971

I finished the score of the *Dialogue for cello and orchestra* and having changed the ending had to rewrite the last pages of the piano reduction to send to Maurice [Gendron]...

11 July 1971

Peter Grimes at Covent Garden. Once again I was captivated by the skill and sheer musicality with which it's done. The big choruses are very powerful and wonderfully constructed. Jon Vickers sang Grimes – vocally very accomplished, but musically not so good: in many passages he dragged out his high notes to the detriment of the melodic line. Norman Bailey very good as Balstrode, as was Forbes Robinson as Swallow. Heather Harper (Ellen) sang beautifully but I felt didn't give any strong feeling of the character. Colin Davis conducted, I thought, very well.

---

[40] Richard Buckle (1916–2001), ballet critic who wrote biographies of Nijinsky and Diaghilev. *Diana and Actaeon Waltz (Palm Court Waltz)*, op. 81/2 (1971), also for piano duet.

30 July 1971

To King's Lynn. Final rehearsal of my *Dialogue*. Maurice Gendron was very difficult, having got a quite wrong idea of the tempo of the last movement (much too fast). He kept rushing ahead, and wouldn't keep with Ray [Leppard] who was none the less very patient and tactful. In the end it went quite well. Maurice has a beautiful tone and always accurate intonation; as soon as he decided to collaborate, all was well, although he seemed uncomfortable in the passage (last movement) which has changes of time (3/8 – 4/8 – 6/8). Odd that anyone could find this sort of thing difficult today. ...

September 1971

I finished the piece for double bass and piano.[41] Rodney Slatford seems delighted with it. It's rather light, so at least will make a good contrast to the Maconchy and Lutyens pieces written for him recently which are very good but distinctly gloomy.

25 September 1971

Götterdämmerung at Covent Garden. I hadn't been to a Wagner opera for years. Having been (musically) brought up at a time when anti-Wagner opinions prevailed, particularly in France, I'd never really got to know him, and was amazed at how much of it I liked and admired. In spite of its length I was never bored. The orchestral writing is marvellous in its resource and effectiveness, and must have been something quite new when it was written, as must have been the rich and voluptuous harmony. The big climaxes are built up with unerring skill and sense of timing. It's not music I could ever love as I do Verdi, but that Wagner was a great master is undeniable. ...

1 November 1971

I got to the end of the *Duo for cello and piano* after the usual struggles.[42] It was difficult to get the form right as I didn't want to follow any traditional pattern. Great difficulty, too, in finding the actual notes and timing of the ending, but I think I've got this right. The shape I finally arrived at is Moderato – meno vivo – Tempo primo (condensed recapitulation) – Presto con fuoco (material related to the opening but given a much more urgent character) ...

---

[41] *Introduction and Allegro*, op. 80 (1971). Rodney Slatford gave the first performance with Clifford Lee at the Purcell Room on 14 January 1971. Recorded by Leon Bosch and Sung-Suk Kang on *The British Double Bass*, Meridian CDE 84550.

[42] *Duo for Cello and Piano*, op. 81/1 (1971), recorded by Julian Lloyd Webber and John McCabe, Oiseau-Lyre DSLO 18.

I've been reading Julien Green and Mauriac novels. Green is more poetic, his style perhaps more elegant. His novels take place in a world of fantasy, but one feels that he has compassion for the many odious characters he invents. This he shares with Mauriac who, however, is much closer to reality, and whose characters one can more easily believe in. Both are great writers: I wonder whether we have at the present time novelists who can equal them. ...

29 November 1971

Rawsthorne Memorial Concert. It confirmed my admiration for him.[43] Though I didn't like everything, it's always very well carried out – always meaningful and effective. The *Theme and Variations for two violins* is, I think, a masterpiece. The Wigmore Hall was full and I've never seen so many composers at a concert – William (Walton), Malcolm Williamson, Humphrey [Searle], Betty Maconchy, Liz Lutyens, Alan Bush, Richard (Stoker) and quite few others. ...

On revising my copy of the Duo I've found a lot of things wrong, and have been rewriting it. The first section was too short, and after the first meno vivo, needed to be returned to, in tempo, though not with the same material; then comes (now) a slower meno vivo, followed by a short reprise (modified) of the opening, and then the final presto. I finished it at the end of the month.

29 November 1971

Rodney Slatford played my double bass piece at the Academy. He gives a very entertaining talk about the instrument and plays well – quite a turn in fact. I can't think that the double bass is a very satisfactory solo instrument. Apart from the harmonics, some of which make a very good sound, the low notes, which are those that other instruments don't have, are indistinct and buzzy.

19 December 1971

The LPO played my Third Symphony at the Festival Hall. I think it's one of my better things and I enjoyed hearing it. John Pritchard conducted a rather perfunctory performance – I think and hope the record is very much better than this. Two good notices – by William Mann (to my great astonishment)[44] and Ronald Crighton.

---

[43] See Berkeley on Rawsthorne, p. 138 above.

[44] William Mann pointed out that the composer received an ovation from a sold-out Festival Hall. The LPO and Pritchard 'had a good deal more to say for Berkeley's Third Symphony than some of us gathered' at the premiere. 'The performance supported the eloquence and poetic stature of the work': *The Times* 20 December 1971.

9 January 1972

On Friday I had to talk about my musical background and training at the British Institute of Recorded Sound. Not being good at this, I kept going for a time and then asked for questions which luckily were forthcoming and, helped by some live performances (Sonatina and *Theme and Variations* for piano duet and *Duo* for cello and piano) it passed off reasonably well. Peter Dickinson, who played with me, was a great support. In listening to my own music alongside younger contemporaries I am rather painfully aware of the gulf that separates music that is based on tonality and music that repudiates it, and yet I think that where a genuinely individual voice is heard, the separation ceases to matter. ... The curious thing is that a lot of the new music is very conventional, and it's difficult to distinguish one composer, or even one piece, from another. If this really is so, not much of it is likely to survive, because what we value in the music of the past is surely its individual character – not the date at which it was written or whether the composer was an innovator or one more traditionally inclined.

11 February 1972

ECO concert at Queen Elizabeth Hall. My *Dialogue* very well played by [Thomas] Igloi and the orchestra under Ray Leppard.[45] I was sandwiched between Rawsthorne and Richard Bennett, both such expert composers that I felt my piece was a little tentative – however it went down well with the audience.

21 March 1972

It's often the easy things in music that are so difficult. I mean things that are technically easy. An instance of this that I always remember was a rehearsal of the Fauré Requiem conducted by Nadia. In the 'In paradisum', the organ has to play [the repetitive figure] quite slowly. This was not played exactly enough for her and she made the player do it several times alone before she was satisfied. The incident had a comic side to it as the organist, unknown to Nadia, was Simon Preston who is considered the most brilliant virtuoso in the country!

April 1972

I finished the *Four Piano Studies*.[46] I don't feel very pleased with them musically – they are too derivative, but at least they are good piano music and should be effective as such. I began the motets and nearly finished the first – 'Eripe me'. It's a text that I've always found very moving in the Good Friday liturgy. If I can put even half of what it makes me feel into the music, I shall be happy. ...

---

[45] *Dialogue*, op. 79 (1970), for cello and chamber orchestra. Raymond Leppard (1927–), conductor and musicologist. Thomas Igloi (1947–76), Hungarian-born cellist who made his London debut in 1969.

[46] *Four Piano Studies*, op. 82 (1972).

16 April 1972, Monaco

Igor Markevitch, whom I knew so well in Paris when he was about nineteen and I was twenty-seven, is now conductor of the Monte Carlo orchestra. I've hardly seen him since, and though I was never really fond of him, I was strangely moved at meeting him again after all these years. He has immense charm and something that fascinates and even subjugates one. I was greatly impressed by the performance he obtained of the Tchaikovsky *Pathétique Symphony* – one of the best I've heard. This great romantic masterpiece was wonderfully controlled in a way that allowed the music to speak for itself; his interpretation showed perfect taste without underplaying any of its warmth and passion. ...

26 May 1972

To *Il ritorno d'Ulysse* at Glyndebourne. ... Much of the music is Monteverdi at his best and it was extremely well sung in a production by Peter Hall. Ray's realisation very good – if he does put in bits of his own it's always with good reason and the style is so well imitated that they are, to me, indistinguishable from the rest.[47] Anyway, the present day mania for authenticity is a very boring preoccupation and one which the composers themselves would not have understood at all. Janet Baker admirable as always.

8 June 1972

To Aldeburgh. I conducted my *Ronsard Sonnets* with Peter as soloist, in a rather strange concert of English and Danish music. Of the other works played, I liked Thea Musgrave's *Night Music* and Holmboe's Ballad – a witty and subtle piece though hardly representative. ... I sat with Ben during part of the concert. I find him rather lacking in warmth and real friendliness – his character seems somehow changed. I suppose it's difficult to remain the same if one has had such immense success – he was perfectly civil but nothing more.

18 June 1972

To Glyndebourne to see *Seraglio* – very well done and delightful music though it's a long way below the later operatic masterpieces and I find little of what I so deeply love in them. ... We were intrigued when told that the Prime Minister was to be a fellow guest.[48] He turned out to be most agreeable, easy to talk to, and keen about the music ... he was not at all pompous – at moments he looked a little (understandably) preoccupied, but not unduly so. ...

---

[47] Leppard's realisations of Monteverdi and Cavalli were found controversial by the purists.
[48] Edward Heath (1916–2005), Conservative Prime Minister, 1970–74.

9 July 1972

As a result of our meeting with Mr Heath we were invited to Chequers for a recital by Clifford Curzon and supper. It's an old and very fine brick house in a lovely and typical Buckinghamshire valley. ... Clifford was in splendid form and played the Schubert B flat posthumous sonata with all his usual warmth combined with perfect control. The PM seemed radiantly happy and was a most attentive host – he is clearly able to relax in spite of the formidable problems he has to struggle with daily. ...

Great difficulty in getting started on anything for the BBC (Proms 1973) ...[49]

8 August 1972

I went to Cambridge to hear the St John's College Choir rehearse my *Three Latin Motets*. I was pleased with their singing – very accurate intonation, and a good full-toned sound from the boys. The artificial hooting that used to be such a characteristic of Anglican choirs seems to have gone – due, I think, largely to what George Malcolm did at Westminster Cathedral and the influence his performances have had. ...

I decide to do an oboe concerto for Janet [Craxton] for next year's Proms. ... I have ideas about making it quite different from the classical concerto and have already started it.

21 September 1972

Recording of the *Ronsard Sonnets* in the Maltings with Peter.[50] Very good orchestra (London Sinfonietta) who were helpful throughout. I think I managed reasonably well, but I wish I had more freedom and authority as a conductor. The first movement with its continual changes of time and the 5/8 bars that are sometimes 2+3 and at others 3+2 make it difficult. ...

18–25 October 1972

Signs in the Dark at Manchester – it was well sung, a little rough but with that extra vigour and enthusiasm that north-country choirs always have. I was glad to hear it again: I like the last movement the best. They are lovely poems.

---

[49] Berkeley wrote a brief introduction to every Prom concert; these appeared in the *Radio Times*.

[50] *Four Ronsard Sonnets*, Set 2, op. 62 (1963), recorded by Peter Pears and the London Sinfonietta under the composer on Decca Headline HEAD 3.

9 November 1972

To the Royal College of Music to hear performances of my Sextet[51] played first by two ensembles of students and later by professionals including Hugh Bean, Jack Brymer and Alan Civil. Splendid performance ... came to the conclusion that it was better than I'd thought.

29 October 1972

To the ballet at Covent Garden – *Firebird*, *Prelude à l'après-midi* and *Dances at a Gathering* – the last two choreographed by Jerome Robbins. I always find his choreography individual and moving – the *Dances* are to music by Chopin excellently played on the piano by the Ballet's principal pianist – Anthony Twiner. ... I thought the dancing almost perfect throughout, and deeply poetic, not so much trying to interpret the music as to create an equivalent atmosphere by movement. The choreography is extraordinarily unfussy (I can't think of another word) – the dancers often come in walking and just stand still for a time before beginning to dance, so it seems as though they just invented what they have to do on the spot. I've never forgotten the wonderful ballet by Robbins called *Moves*, which I saw some years ago, without any music at all. ...

21 November 1972

I am urged to concentrate on my diary since no composers, except Berlioz, have kept diaries. I reply that I only do it to record certain things I want to remember, but that at the same time, having no talent as a writer (unlike Berlioz), it's a great effort to go on with it.

10 December 1972

At last I've got to the end of the second movement of the oboe piece and am feeling faintly more hopeful.

I much enjoyed Quentin Bell's biography of Virginia Woolf but felt her to be an unsympathetic character. I didn't in fact feel much drawn to any of the Bloomsbury Group who all make such a feature of intellectual superiority. I don't find this among intellectual people today. Perhaps they felt this attitude was necessary in order to attack the philistinism of the upper class of those days which was, I suppose, more pronounced than it is today. ...

---

[51] Sextet, op. 47 (1953), for clarinet, horn and string quartet.

28 December 1973

Reading Robert Craft's *Stravinsky*.[52] Everything about Stravinsky is interesting to me and Craft writes well, if a little pedantically at times. There's too much about the author rather than about the subject of the book – long descriptions of travel, not uninteresting. Craft has good observations and sensibility, but it's not his reactions one wants to know about in a book about Stravinsky. On the other hand he's clearly fascinated by Stravinsky and devoted to him. He should have written two separate books. ... The account of Stravinsky's last illness and death is moving. Craft is clearly extremely intelligent, but rather prone to exhibit his intellectual acumen on the slightest pretext. All the same I feel grateful to him for telling one so much about the most interesting and universally admired composer of our time. It made me look back to the evening, so many years ago, when I was taken to dinner by Soulima at the Stravinsky flat, where the family was living in the Rue St Honoré, but I was so awestruck at finding myself in the company of the great man (I was still a student) that I remember little of what was said – I do remember though that he was kind (even making me play something I had written) very good-mannered and elegant. This must have been about 1930.

20 January 1973

Lutosławski's concert. It confirmed my opinion that he's the best and most deeply musical composer of the advanced type. I liked best the *Funeral Music* composed when he was still writing more tonally-centred music, but I also much admired *Preludes and Fugues*, though one hearing is not sufficient to take it all in.[53] In this, and in the other later pieces, the constant aleatoric passages tended to be too similar in effect, though he handles this technique far better than do most composers. In everything there were moments of great excitement and significance.

20 January 1973

Julian Bream came to play me my *Theme and Variations*[54] ... we went to his recital the next day at the Queen Elizabeth Hall. He's without any doubt a great musician who adds to his purely musical talent and fabulous technique a superb sense of performance. His playing of my piece was as nearly perfect as I could imagine, and this indeed was true of the whole recital. I was very glad to hear him play Turina's *Fandanguillo* – a piece I know well and am very fond of. The hall was packed. Immense success with the public.

---

[52] Robert Craft, *Stravinsky: the Chronicle of a Friendship, 1948–1971* (New York, 1972).

[53] Witold Lutosławski (1913–94); *Funeral Music* for strings (1954–8); *Preludes and Fugues* (1970–72).

[54] *Theme and Variations*, op. 77 (1970), for guitar.

17 February 1973

I finished the sketch of the *Sinfonia concertante* but still have most of the scoring to do. I must at the same time start the piece for string orchestra for Cheltenham. ... Meriel and Peter recorded some of my songs. They do them very well and I am delighted.[55]

22 February 1973

I went to the Festival Hall to hear Bartók's Concerto for Orchestra and *Bluebeard's Castle* – LPO conducted by Solti. Excellent performances – both works masterly and beautiful. *Bluebeard* must be one of the very few works that can compare in importance with late Debussy, and Ravel of the same period. The Concerto is a masterpiece of orchestral writing, though rather episodic and perhaps lacking the depth of the best movements in the string quartets. Like so many before him, Bartók was under-valued in his lifetime, but stands out today as one of the great composers.

28 February 1973

Recording of my *Latin Motets*[56] with Colin Mawby and his choir. ... I have to confess to being pleased with them – particularly the first ('Eripe me') into which I think I've been able to put much of the feeling I have for the Latin liturgy, nowadays so shamefully cast aside.

March 1973

I work every day at the string piece for Cheltenham. All my usual difficulties about the actual musical language persist (is it really valid or something too firmly rooted in the past to have any present-day relevance?) and yet, when I hear my music performed, I feel it has a certain individuality that justifies it. ... I listened to the BBC recording of part of *Nelson* recently and thought it better than I had supposed, but I had chosen the best parts, and there's a lot that I would want to re-write if it were ever put on again.[57]

---

[55] *Chinese Songs*, 'D'un vanneur de blé', 'Tant que mes yeux' and 'Automne'. Argo ZRG 788, the *Chinese Songs* now on Heritage HTGCD 240.

[56] *Three Latin Motets*, op. 83/1 (1972), Meridian CDE 84216.

[57] There was a complete recording of *Nelson* put out by BBC Radio 3 on 23 October 1983 and repeated on 18 May 1988. There was a fine cast, including David Johnson (Nelson), Eiddwen Harrhy (Lady Hamilton), Brian Rayner Cook (Sir William Hamilton), Elizabeth Bainbridge (Mrs Cadogan), Mary Thomas (Madame Serafin), Margaret Kingsley (Lady Nelson), Richard Angas (Hardy), Eric Shilling (Admiral Lord Minto), Richard Jackson (naval surgeon), Francis Egerton (wounded man) with the BBC Singers/Simon Jolly and the BBC Symphony Orchestra/Elgar Howarth. Presentation by Peter Dickinson; producer: Clive Bennett.

Cheltenham

The Festival made a special feature of my music. Never before have I received so much attention. It began with an outstanding performance of my Third Symphony by the BBC Symphony Orchestra under John Pritchard. This really got off the ground and was the best performance I've heard. John P's rather leisurely manner in rehearsal had given me no idea of how good the actual performance was to be. The next day there was a luncheon in my honour. ... William Glock made a most touching and delightful speech to which my reply was, I fear, sadly inadequate.[58] In the evening there was the first performance of *Antiphon* by the St Martin's in the Fields Orchestra conducted by Neville Marriner. This again was an excellent performance. I wish I'd been able to make the piece a bit longer – I felt it rather lacked weight, though I like a good deal of it.

10 July 1973

Birthday Concert in the Pittville Pump Room – Sextet, *Autumn's Legacy* and the Horn Trio, all excellently played, mainly by young musicians.

11 July 1973

Rehearsal and performance of my *Windsor Variations* with Charles Groves and the ECO. Very careful rehearsal and good performance. To hear all these things in a week was a new experience – I don't quite know what I think, it's so difficult to judge one's own efforts except that I thought a reasonably good degree of craftsmanship seemed to prevail; it's impossible for me to say anything about the actual quality or significance of the music. ...

3 August 1973

My *Sinfonia concertante* and Third Symphony at the Proms, both conducted by Ray [Leppard]. Janet [Craxton] played perfectly in the Sinfonia. ... I was pleased with the Symphony, and though I enjoyed the Sinfonia, I need to hear it again to be sure about it.[59]

---

[58] On 13 June 1973 Sir Arthur Bliss, President of the Cheltenham Festival, wrote to Berkeley: ' Much looking forward to Cheltenham, and presiding at the lunch for Freda and yourself. I am afraid I shall have to call on you for a short speech in reply to Glock's. I know you hate this, but as a matter of fact you do it excellently.'

[59] On 15 August 1973 Raymond Leppard wrote to Berkeley: 'I did enormously enjoy working on the new piece and the Third Symphony – both splendid in their different ways – and look forward to doing them again soon. What a player Janet is – I was full of admiration for the way she made the Concertante blossom.'

22 August 1973

I conducted *Voices of the Night* at Hereford (Three Choirs Festival).[60] I think it was a satisfactory performance and felt happy about the piece which does what I meant it to do, and seemed to come off well, though I can't judge as well if taking part in the performance as I can if merely listening. ...

26 August 1973

Very good performance of my *Missa brevis*, I thought the best I'd heard, at the Brompton Oratory. It's not a concert piece, and sounds much better when sung liturgically.[61]

22 October 1973

I conducted *Antiphon*[62] at the Queen Elizabeth Hall with the Fine Art Orchestra – very good players – we had to do it on little rehearsal and this kept them on their toes. They certainly back me up splendidly.

2 November 1973

... Stravinsky's *Apollon musagète* – surely one of his best works, the scoring for string orchestra is quite wonderful, subtle and immensely effective. I remember seeing one of the first performances by the Diaghilev ballet in Paris and being rather disappointed. I think I was expecting something like *Les Noces* – Stravinsky's neo-classic idiom being then quite new and rather disconcerting, though I can't think now how I can fail to have appreciated it – but it strikes me now very differently from the way it did in 1928.

7 November 1973

Hearing Ben's setting of Thomas Hardy's poem 'Before life and after', I've been thinking about Hardy's philosophy in general.[63] It clearly sprang from his intense compassion for human suffering, which led him to believe that it was impossible to suppose that a God of love rules the world. In the poem he imagines a time 'before the birth of consciousness when all went well' when 'if something ceased, no tongue bewailed, if something winced and waned, no heart was wrung' and that the only hope was to return to a state of nescience. This is surely a philosophy of

---

[60] *Voices of the Night*, op. 86 (1973), dedicated to Charlotte Bonham-Carter.

[61] *Missa brevis*, op. 57 (1960), for SATB and organ.

[62] *Antiphon*, op. 85, dedicated to Sir John Manduell, premiered on 7 July 1973 at the Cheltenham Festival by The Academy of St Martin in the Fields under Neville Marriner. Berkeley conducted the first London performance.

[63] The final song in *Winter Words: Lyrics and Ballads of Thomas Hardy*, op. 52 (1953).

utter despair – life without feeling would reduce mankind to a sort of vegetable existence, no suffering but no joy, nor art, no poetry or music, and even no Thomas Hardy. And yet one understands him well enough; even if the necessity for human suffering is admitted, what about the world of animals? They can gain nothing but they are destined to prey on each other with hideous results – it is difficult to understand how the God of Christianity can have permitted, still less ordained, their condition. I have never come across a satisfactory explanation of this. Hardy however is only concerned with human suffering but he rather overstates his argument – heaping disaster upon disaster in the case of certain individuals, quite beyond the bounds of probability. Did he really believe that the world was ruled by an evil and cruel God or President of the Immortals as he calls him in *Tess of the D'Urbevilles*?

1 December 1973

Composers' Guild[64] lunch. ... I was presented with the Guild's Composer of the Year award. To mark the occasion I had previously been asked to choose a present, and thus acquired the full score of *Albert Herring* which I delight in reading.

Much celebration of Ben's 60th birthday culminating in last Sunday's Third Programme being entirely his music. It would have been better spread over the week than concentrated in a single day. However I heard the whole of *Death in Venice* and liked it better than the first time (in Aldeburgh). Needless to say there are many sections of great beauty, but I still feel it to lack the spontaneous quality so abundant in his earlier music. Perhaps I've simply not caught up with his later idiom, and yet I was much moved by the part near the end when he uses the text of Plato's *Phaedrus*.

11 January 1974

To Covent Garden for *A Midsummer Night's Dream* – excellent performance – one of Ben's best works, I think – everything superbly realised in the music. The yokels' performance in the last act even better and funnier than in the play – but there's much more than that. I love the whole passage of Lysander's mistaken declaration to Helena, always leading up to the same chord in a different key and the amazing simplicity of the final chorus (in F sharp major) 'Now until the break of day'. Very good cast – particularly James Bowman as Oberon. ...

---

[64] The Composers' Guild, founded in 1944 with Vaughan Williams as first president, was the leading organisation for British composers at that time. In 1958 it started a journal, *Composer*, and set up the British Music Information Centre in 1967.

1 February 1974

I started my piece for guitar and chamber orchestra not without misgivings on account of the difficulty of combining a solo instrument that has such a small volume of sound with other instruments. ...

13–14 March 1974

Recording at Walthamstow of my Two-Piano Concerto and First Symphony by the LPO under Norman Del Mar.[65] The two Canadian pianists [Garth Beckett and Boyd McDonald] were very good, Norman a most efficient and capable conductor and I thought the whole thing a real success. I still like the Concerto after all this time. ... I really enjoyed hearing it again.

15 April 1974

I find it very difficult to go on with this diary, though I'm glad to have a record of musical experiences. ... I find it rather boring. Also it's impossible to write about so many things that really matter to me without writing at much greater length, which I have no time to do.

The Concerto for Guitar[66] is the most difficult thing I've ever attempted; the fact that it can't sustain the sound, as with all plucked instruments, and that the normal compass is low, make it very difficult to combine with any but the lightest accompaniment. ...

18 April 1974

Castaway and *A Dinner Engagement* broadcast as a double bill ... with the BBC Northern Orchestra conducted by Meredith Davies. I was glad to hear a real professional cast in *A Dinner Engagement*. *Castaway* was good too, though I've yet to hear an Odysseus who can really suggest the character with any subtlety. Here the Demodocus (Anthony Rolf-Johnson) was excellent and Wendy Eathorne a very good Nausicae. It remains the work I prefer, I think, to any I've written – it was a great joy to hear it again.

1–3 May 1974

Worked with Julian Bream on the Guitar Concerto, at last finished. I learn a lot about performance with him. He has a wonderful sense of what will come off best, and great determination in finding it.

---

[65] Lyrita RCS 94; on CD SRCD 249. See interview with Norman Del Mar, p. 230 below.

[66] Berkeley initially described it as Concertino.

17–24 May 1974

Julian Bream came again to work with me on the Concerto. His suggestions have enormously improved it. The cadenza near the end of the third movement he has practically written himself, as I hoped he would, using what I had written merely as a guide to what I felt would be suitable. Osian Ellis came to go through the *Herrick Songs* and though most of my harp writing seems all right, he made some excellent suggestions which I adopted at once.[67]

7–10 June 1974

The Aldeburgh Festival. Went to a rehearsal of Thea Musgrave's opera.[68] ... Bill Alwyn's song-cycle *Mirages*, a very well-written work but there is something about its atmosphere that I disliked – I felt he was too much preoccupied with its emotional impact and not enough on the musical quality. This, I think, is a wrong approach – intensity should grow out of the music, not be applied to it. ... Peter and Osian did my *Herrick Songs* with much warmth and feeling. (I wasn't satisfied with the last one, which I have since rewritten.)

15 June 1974

We had known about my knighthood for the last month but it was only announced today. Having found four bottles of champagne, left over from some previous festivity, in the cellar, we asked a few neighbours and friends in to celebrate. The following day and during the week an avalanche of letters and telegrams arrived – there were about two hundred – many of them so touching and heart-warming that we felt it had given almost more pleasure to friends than to us. Nevertheless I was much pleased by this official recognition.[69]

4 July 1974

My Guitar Concerto (City of London Festival) at St Bartholomew's Church. I was rather nervous about how well the guitar would be heard, though I knew Julian would bring it off. In the end it came off better than I had dared hope – Julian played superbly, and I had very good press notices. ...

---

[67] *Five Herrick Poems*, op. 89 (1973), for high voice and harp. Recorded by James Gilchrist and Alison Nicholls on Chandos 10528.

[68] *The Voice of Ariadne* (after Henry James), English Opera Group, Snape Maltings, 11 June 1974.

[69] On 28 June 1974 Britten wrote: 'Congratulations on the knighthood. It will please your many many fans, I know.' When Berkeley was awarded the CBE Britten was more fulsome and wrote on 2 January 1957: 'How very glad I was to hear of the great honour – it is so <u>very very</u> much deserved and, in these days, all the more wonderful that it has been recognised. You have written such lovely music for so long without always the acclamation we've wanted for you, that we are all rejoicing now. I'm sure you'll go on from strength to strength.'

26 July 1974

To a National Trust concert with the Edinburgh Quartet. ... I was glad to hear the Ravel again, which I so greatly loved in earlier days, and to find that I still loved it, though I now think the first two movements better than the other two. There is something slightly limited in the music's emotional range, but it has real beauty, perfect craftsmanship, and great individuality – its magic and pathos still move me as they did forty years ago. On hearing it again, I liked particularly the second movement: the cross-rhythm of the 3/4 – 6/8 is brilliantly effective and exciting, and was particularly well played.

I received my knighthood on the 21st ... I, together with my fellow recipients, was ushered into a drawing room where we remained, rather like sheep in a pen (it was cordoned off) and were rehearsed in how we should advance, kneel, shake hands, bow and retire. ... I carried out the drill more or less successfully. The Queen was very charming and spoke to each of us informally. She asked me whether I was working and I said: 'Yes' – not strictly true, as I was having a period of rest and only contemplating what I next had to write. ... What impressed me was the way in which the Queen knew who we all were, speaking to each about what he did without any prompting. This must entail a lot of work and memorising. ...[70]

28 October 1974

I listened to the broadcast of Henze's opera *The Bassarids*[71] ... It's a powerful and dramatic work and, whether one likes or dislikes it, there can be no doubt that he is a composer of immense talent. The music is fundamentally tonal in the sense that tonal centres are strongly felt, though he has evolved a musical language of great freedom. The orchestral writing is very imaginative, and there are real singing parts both for chorus and soloists. Everything comes off and there are passages of real beauty.

6 November 1974

I think I made a mistake in deciding to write my *Quintet for Piano and Wind* for the same instruments as Mozart's great masterpiece; I keep reading his which induces despair, and a feeling of the futility of attempting the same thing.

12 November 1974

It was an exciting experience rehearsing the RPO and conducting the performance of my Third Symphony at the Festival Hall, but only because of the friendly attitude of the orchestra who made allowances for my incapacity as a conductor. ... I found

---

[70] Berkeley attended two further receptions and two lunches at Buckingham Palace between 1976 and 1983.

[71] *The Bassarids* (1966), libretto by Auden, ENO revival with the composer conducting.

the 5/8 passage horribly difficult to keep steady; it's ironical that many professional conductors confine themselves to classical music that the orchestra knows by heart anyway, whereas the wretched composer-conductor has to face difficulties of this kind continually. I suppose one shouldn't attempt it, though some composers have been or are good at it – Ben, for example. Mahler was a professional conductor, as was Wagner in his young days, but they, in any case, were great musicians. On the other hand, Ravel was a bad conductor, and some good composers are quite incapable.

December 1974

Speaking in public has always frightened me, but having to do it three times in the last week, I've become a little more confident. Last week I spoke at the PRS, the Composers' Guild lunch and at the opening of the Music Department at Keele University. ...

28 December 1974

Julian Bream and I spent a long time revising the Guitar Concerto; apart from his virtuosity as a performer he has great musical insight, and I always enjoy working with him. ...

15 January 1975

Arnold Cooke's Fourth Symphony at the Philharmonic concert.[72] It is an enjoyable, very well-written piece, somewhat lacking in individuality, but his craftsmanship and effective scoring made it well worthy of performance. There is room for good music in a tonal idiom; Peter Heyworth's prejudiced and insolent remarks on it in the *Observer* struck me as unworthy of a critic of his standing. Shostakovich's 15th Symphony which concluded the concert is a most stimulating and imaginative work – almost too idiosyncratic in fact – but providing the very qualities that Arnold's Symphony lacked.

March 1976

I finished the Piano and Wind Quintet at the end of the month.[73] It took me the best part of six months which is slow going. I'd originally intended three movements – 1) Andante – allegro – andante 2) Scherzo 3) Theme and variations – but the Scherzo goes so fast that I felt something more was needed before the

---

[72] Arnold Cooke (1906–2005), pupil of Hindemith.
[73] Quintet, op. 90 (1975), commissioned by the Chamber Music Society of Lincoln Center, New York. Recorded with Colin Horsley on Meridian E 77017.

Theme and variations, so I added a short intermezzo leading into the last movement. I think it now makes a reasonable shape.

21 April 1975, Monte Carlo

I can't bring myself to go to Mass in France; the Latin has been even more completely done away with than in England and with it every trace of the former spirit of Catholicism. A letter to *The Times* ... implied that catholics who are kept away from Mass on account of this are catholics for the wrong reason. There may be some truth in this. I myself may have become a catholic because I loved the liturgy. ... I believe it was never the intention of the Second Vatican Council that the Latin liturgy should be abolished – this is something that has been thrust upon us by the bishops and the clergy, though how a priest, for whom the traditional words must be especially sacred, can be willing even to get rid of them passes my comprehension.

2 May 1975

I listened yesterday, more or less by accident, to the second set of Chopin Studies on the radio; although I've known and loved them all my life, I was quite bowled over by their beauty and perfection. Somehow I now seem able to listen to music differently – with the best music, I notice more that is beautiful, and it moves me more. I have to admit though that music of indifferent quality bores me more than it used to in about the same proportion.

24 May 1975

I've started the piece for the BBC Singers, having found some verses by Spenser that suited what was needed.

6 June 1975

To the Aldeburgh Festival, where the Gabrieli String Quartet played an early work of Ben's, written at the age of eighteen, already technically accomplished but quite lacking the individuality of his later music.[74] Ben was in his box for the first part of the concert, looking very frail and much aged by his illness. ... Later, I went to speak to him ... he was very charming and seemed to have acquired a new serenity, perhaps because of the suffering and frustration he has had to go through. I was much moved by meeting him after so long a time.

---

[74] String Quartet in D major (1931).

26 June 1975

My formal election at the AGM as President of the PRS. I still find it difficult to understand how I, who never utter at directors' meetings, can have been chosen to succeed Arthur [Bliss] ...

27 June 1975

Death in Venice at Covent Garden. A new production which is, I think, an improvement on the original one. To my great disappointment, I can't really get to like the music and find long stretches of it boring, though skilfully contrived. It simply doesn't move me. The only place in which I really begin to feel something was right at the end. In general I thought the second act better than the first, which is far too long, but there is a lack of melody which is all the more disconcerting in that Ben has shown in his earlier music that he can combine melodic material with a perfectly valid and individual style.

19 July 1975

My *Radio Times* job (writing a few sentences on each of the Proms) took up a lot of time during this month and proved difficult. I think some were successful, others rather feeble ... when I had something I wanted to say, it was an opportunity to say it, but it was a challenge to keep it up.

24 August 1975

Recording of my Piano Concerto at Walthamstow Town Hall.[75] David Wilde was the soloist and I thought him really first class. His playing is deeply musical, going much further than virtuosity, though his technique allowed him to be completely relaxed so that he only had to think about the music. It was in the technically easiest parts that his musicianship showed up the most – beautiful cantabile tone and variety of tone-colour. ...

4 September 1975

Voices of the Night at the Proms. Adrian Boult conducted and I was very pleased with the performance. There was some very good individual playing (BBC SO). The only thing lacking was the sort of unified playing that can only happen when the various groups know what the others are doing ... impossible on one rehearsal.

---

[75] Lyrita SRCS 94, on CD as SRCD 250: New Philharmonia Orchestra under Nicholas Braithwaite.

20 October 1975

The BBC Singers gave the first performance of *The Hill of the Graces*.[76] They did it very well – their intonation is wonderfully accurate and they are good sight-readers. I like the piece and enjoyed writing it. They gave my *Latin Motets* in the same concert at St John's, Smith Square.

December 1975

I've given most of my time [following a visit as President of the PRS to Australia, including Hong Kong and Bali] to revising and partially rewriting my Second Symphony, having never been satisfied with it. I rewrote the Scherzo movement first (before we went away) and since have been working on the first movement. I think it's greatly improved in the new version. I've treated the themes in a way which is much more natural to me.

24 January 1976

We flew to New York. It was a great excitement to find ourselves here, and I was astonished to find New York a much more beautiful and impressive place than I'd expected. The famous skyscrapers grouped together look very fine. First rehearsal of my Quintet – though it still needs a good deal of work, the players are excellent, particularly Leonard Arner (oboe), Gervaise de Peyer (clarinet) and John Browning (piano). I like the piece and think it has a certain toughness that was lacking in much of my earlier music.

1 February 1976

Second performance of the Quintet – even better than the first, it was marvellous playing. At John Browning's party after the concert I talked to the players at some length – they seemed truly delighted with the piece and as pleased as I was with them. I also met Sam Barber[77] whom I last saw in London some thirty years ago!

2 February 1976

A real blizzard in New York brought things to a standstill. … finally got to Princeton where I visited the University and had a long talk with Peter Westergaard[78] who is at present in charge of the Music Department. I was pleased to find that he wholeheartedly agreed with the view that students should go through traditional

---

[76] *The Hill of the Graces*, op. 91/2 (Edmund Spenser), SATB unaccompanied.

[77] Samuel Barber (1910–81), one of the most widely performed American composers of the mid-twentieth century.

[78] Peter Westergaard (1931–), American composer and theorist.

training in counterpoint and fugue before embarking on electronic or whatever. Later I spoke to one of the lecturers who told me that the majority of the students write music entirely by mathematical calculation: moreover they sincerely think that the classical composers did so too – though how they can believe this of Mozart and Beethoven passes one's comprehension. I said I thought that Boulez had done a lot of harm by the nonsense he taught and wrote in his earlier days.

14 February 1976

Dinner with Virgil [Thomson].[79] He lives in the celebrated Chelsea Hotel which has long been the haunt of artists and bohemians of various sorts. His apartment there reflects his personality to perfection – books stacked all over the place, music, some beautiful and most original pictures, all showing taste for what is good but also somewhat bizarre. He has great character, but it's curious that he's never made much impact as a composer. Maybe his critical faculty is stronger than his creative gift. I like him very much.

17 March 1976

James Galway came to see me. He wants me to orchestrate the Poulenc Flute Sonata; up to now I've rather stalled on this as I know I shall find it very difficult, but I finally agreed to do it in due course as he's such a brilliant performer.

7 April 1976

Court Dinner of the Musicians Company. As Master it fell to me to provide musical entertainment. I got two Academy students – Patricia Calman and Stephen Salkeld (violin and piano) who turned out to be absolutely first class. They played the Franck Sonata and my *Elegy and Toccata*.[80] ... Franck is surely underrated nowadays – the Violin Sonata is his masterpiece and comparable with the Brahms sonatas.

2 July 1976

To Glyndebourne to see *Capriccio*. It was an excellent performance with Söderström in the principal role, but I can't get to like Strauss any better, the music to me is so lacking in form, and I dislike the particular type of sentimentality in which it abounds. The last act seemed interminable. I quite see that Strauss is a master of his style whose technique no musician could fail to admire, but I still can't like it.

---

[79] Virgil Thomson (1896–1989), American composer, pupil of Boulanger, resident in Paris before becoming chief music critic on the *New York Herald Tribune* (1940–54).

[80] *Elegy and Toccata*, op. 33/2–3 (1950).

20 July 1976

The new Henze opera at Covent Garden [*We Come to the River*]. I found it musically disappointing, it seemed more preoccupied with its political message and more like incidental music to a play. For a composer of his great talent it had little to offer – I may have been influenced by my dislike of communist ideology, but had the music been of real beauty and significance it would have swept away other considerations.

3–4 August 1976

My Second Symphony, written originally twenty years ago and which I've spent much of the last year rewriting, was recorded for Lyrita by the LPO [under Nicholas Braithwaite].[81] I think I managed to improve it greatly. ... the third movement was unchanged. I didn't find there was any great difference of style or idiom between what I wrote in 1957 and today, but I think I do it better now. Certainly the scoring is more effective.

The task of orchestrating Poulenc's Flute Sonata ... proves as difficult as I had feared. ... The difficulty is the entirely pianistic nature of the accompaniment, extremely difficult to translate into orchestral terms. ... Another difficulty is that Francis, though there are things I love in his music, has passages that are strangely clumsy and that I long to rewrite, but of course I can't add or subtract anything and I should only spoil the whole thing if I tried to put in too much of myself. I have to think all the time of how he would have wanted it to sound.

27 August 1976

I listened to Richard Bennett's *Zodiak* (Prom) on the radio and greatly enjoyed it. It's beautifully written music, very spare – never a note more than needed, and full of lively and significant orchestral sound. I long to study the score. It has the controlled freedom that only real craftsmanship can achieve.

9 September 1976

I've been reading from a piano score Verdi's *Macbeth*. Like all his earlier operas, it's very uneven in musical quality, but it has great moments. The middle section of the chorus (after Duncan's murder) has extraordinary grandeur and power; its climax is really tremendous and irresistible in the way it sweeps back, after some unexpected modulation, to the key of D flat like an incoming tide. Another wonderful passage is Lady Macbeth's 'Ai trapassati' – only eight bars, but of a dark and gloomy splendour that is unforgettable. ...

---

[81] Symphony no. 2, op. 51 (1958), Lyrita SRCD 249; later recorded by the BBC National Orchestra of Wales under Richard Hickox, Chandos 10167.

1 July 1976

… I've started work on the [Fourth] Symphony for the RPO but have had a long period of difficulty in arriving at the kind of ideas I want to use, and felt I was drying up altogether. However, I still have a very great urge to compose and hope that I'm emerging. I wish I could do more away from the piano. … I have, however, felt better about it since Stravinsky was incapable of writing a bar of music without the piano!

19 October 1976

To Keele University. I gave a kind of tutorial to two students and we had a concert of Copland's music – he was there, and it was a great pleasure to be with him. I liked the music too: his Violin Sonata is a very good piece which I much enjoyed. He spoke after the concert and his direct manner and absolute truthfulness in answering questions was a delight to hear – he was amusing as well.[82]

6 November 1976

I discussed the libretto [for *Faldon Park*] with Winton [Dean] in some detail. I think it is a possible one for me and now that George Harewood[83] has said he would put it on, I've been thinking about it seriously.

12 November 1976

To *Troilus* at Covent Garden. … It was nice to see William [Walton] on this grand occasion. He has aged a lot recently and clearly found it all rather overwhelming, but I think was happy, for it was a splendid performance and he received a well deserved ovation at the end. … It is a full-blooded romantic piece and the orchestral writing is masterly, but one doesn't come away with any lasting impression. It seems to go through the motion of passion, romance and excitement, but I didn't find that they moved me. However, I found much to admire in his power of invention and technical know-how.

19 November 1976

To *Così* at Covent Garden. It is a masterpiece and I was (once again) deeply moved by the many parts of it that remain with me always. It was an excellent performance – Kiri te Kanawa was an almost perfect Fiordiligi. With Ryland Davies, Thomas Allen, Josephine Veasey and Richard Van Allan, all first class … Steuart Bedford conducted well.

---

[82] Copland's interviews on this occasion are published in *Copland Connotations*, ed. Peter Dickinson (Woodbridge, 2002), with further material in *Tempo* 57 (April 2003), 11–15.

[83] The 7th Earl of Harewood (1923–2011), Managing Director of English National Opera.

1 December 1976

Nicholas Kynaston played the first performance of my *Fantasia for Organ*, commissioned by the Organ Club, at the Festival Hall.[84] I am pleased with the piece, but I feel I shall never really like the organ – the sound is so often lacking in clarity – so blurred and indefinite. Only in quiet passages is it pleasing to my ear.

4 December 1976

First performance in this country of my *Quintet for Piano and Wind* by members of the Melos Ensemble ... In some ways I liked the performance better than the New York one – for example, though John Browning has a very fine technique, Howard Shelley's performance was much more sensitive ...

Ben, after a worsening of his heart condition, died on December 4. It seems that he was wonderfully serene, showing great courage and patience during his last weeks. It's consoling to know that there is general agreement that he was the greatest musician this country has produced in recent times. Unfortunately I saw very little of him in the last few years, but I remember so well the happy and exciting times we had together when I first knew him. Exciting because I had never come across such wonderful all-round musical gifts and realised what he was capable of when he was still largely unknown and by those who did know him regarded as brilliant but superficial. I knew he was much more, and though much impressed was not surprised when, on his return from America, he played me the first act of *Peter Grimes*. He remained essentially a tonal composer but was able to bring such freshness to his use of tonality that it sounded new and original.

10 March 1977

Memorial (or rather Thanksgiving, as they are now called) Service for Ben at Westminster Abbey. It was very well organised; Peter read the story of Abraham and Isaac admirably; and the music was well performed, though the service was too long – the Schubert (slow movement of the string quartet) was rather lost in such a big building, lovely as it is. Purcell's 'Hear my prayer' was magnificent.

I'm rather against Memorial Services; one of the advantages of being a catholic is that one can ask for a simple requiem mass in Latin with the plainsong, and that the emphasis is on asking for God's mercy rather than having panegyrics, well meant but less suitable. I always think of Francis Poulenc who asked to have just such a service, and not to have any of his own music sung, but added that he would like the bells rung 'pour emporter mon âme'.[85]

---

[84] Fantasia for organ, op. 92 (1976), recorded by Jennifer Bate, Hyperion A66061 (1982).

[85] Ironically, Berkeley was commemorated in an elaborate Memorial Requiem Mass celebrated on 20 March 1990 by the Archbishop of Westminster, at Westminster Cathedral, broadcast on BBC Radio 3. See the memorial address by Sir John Manduell on p. 281 below.

3 May 1977

Flew to Nice for the annual composition prize. A very poor entry and no prize awarded. ... We were joined on the jury by Henri Dutilleux whom we all liked very much. He is a much respected figure in French music and I felt ashamed that he is so little known in this country. I've asked him to send some scores. It is a scandal that European composers outside the avant-garde are so little played. ...

1 June 1977

The Lord Mayor's Banquet at the Mansion House. The principal speaker was A. L. Rowse[86] whom – without knowing him – I have always disliked on account of his almost unbearable conceit and the way in which he assumes, for instance in his writings on Shakespeare, that his opinions, often based on mere conjecture, are incontrovertible fact. On this occasion he delivered a virulent attack on the establishment in this country – that is to say on the government, the universities, the public schools etc. One has to admit that a good deal of what he said was true, and that his speech was clever, but one felt his object was to annoy his host and most of his (admittedly conventional) fellow guests. In the end, I felt a sort of grudging admiration for his courage. He was sitting opposite me, and on sitting down after his speech glared at me for some time, and then, very slowly, he winked. I laughed, not knowing what to make of it, but I think he may have meant me not to take all that he had said too seriously, while hoping that others would.

30 June 1977

At a dinner for Virgil Thomson, with whom we'd dined in New York. Virgil is a stimulating talker and can be relied upon, if conversation seems to flag, to make some provocative remark that will get it going – he has unrivalled knowledge of the musical world both European and American. If he doesn't know the answer to something, he will invent one much more amusing and get away with it. I enjoyed being with him again.

20 July 1977

To Chichester for Janet Baker's recital in the cathedral at which she gave the first performance of my three De la Mare songs.[87] They were well sung and seem to have greatly impressed Andrew Porter who wrote the most favourable notice I've ever had, but I felt she didn't bring quite the intensity to them that she can command.

---

[86] A. L. Rowse (1903–97), historian and Shakespeare scholar.

[87] *Another Spring*, op. 91/3, for medium voice and piano.

26 July 1977

Michael Tippett's *The Ice Break* at Covent Garden. One can't have much more than an impression of a new opera on one hearing, but I was musically disappointed at finding so little I could enjoy – in fact, for me, so little real music. It is a genuinely dramatic entertainment, and one cannot but admire the imaginative power of a composer who can think it up, writing the libretto as well as the music, but apart from musical considerations, the characters were all symbols – the angry young man, the popular leader etc. – who never emerged as individuals, except possibly the black girl, nor did they become part of a musical design. I wished I had been able to like it more as I admire so much of Michael's music.

1 August 1977

Peter Pears wants to do my first set of *Ronsard Sonnets* (for two tenors and piano) written for him twenty years ago. I have never had them published since then, when he performed them with Hughes Cuènod, the reason being that I was not entirely satisfied with them. How right I was: I now find the piano part badly written and many clumsy things in the vocal parts too. So I am rewriting them for him to do at the next Aldeburgh festival. ...[88]

25 October 1977

... I've been reading James Lees-Milne's diary *Prophesying Peace*. He describes the 1944 air-raids very well and takes one back to the extraordinary lives we had in London at that time – interesting and rather salutary reading for young people today who can have little idea of what it was like, and almost nostalgic for those who experienced it because, although it was far from pleasant, the danger and excitement made one forget smaller worries. One remembers too the joy of finding oneself still alive after the heavier raids, particularly if one had to be out in the streets on air-raid wardens' duty to get people into shelters or the underground, occasionally lying down with one's face in the gutter when the whistle of a descending bomb seemed directly overhead.

4 November 1977

To Oxford for the performances of the John Radcliffe Trust prize. I was one of the judges and for the occasion had to come to terms with some fairly advanced music. My co-judges were Betty Maconchy and Susan Bradshaw. We found ourselves in immediate agreement in giving the first prize to Nigel Osborne.[89] ...

---

[88] The original version is at the Britten-Pears Library, the revision at the British Library.

[89] Nigel Osborne (1948–), Reid Professor at Edinburgh University.

10 November 1977

To Essie Craxton's funeral at Hampstead.[90] ... sang at the end, in full-throated unison, 'The Day though gavest, Lord, is ended' which was my favourite hymn when I was a schoolboy.[91] I remember being reprimanded for liking it and told it was too mellifluous ... but I still liked it and it was moving to hear it sung so well. ...

23 November 1977

The Booker Prize dinner. ... Philip Larkin made an excellent speech. He is a good deal older than I had imagined – tall, dark, spectacled, and going rather bald, he looked more like a family doctor than a writer. He talked to me after dinner very pleasantly.[92]

5 December 1977

The War Requiem at Westminster Cathedral. Hearing it again after many years, I found it very moving, and a near masterpiece in that its best moments are splendidly achieved, but it has weaker passages here and there – for instance the recitative 'It seemed that out of battle I escaped' which I found too long and somewhat lacking in musical interest. But there is much more that I greatly admire – the dark and solemn opening, the orchestral brilliance of the 'Dies Irae', the long crescendo of the 'Libera me' with its really terrific climax at the entry of the organ on a chord of G minor, the lovely 'In paradium' and the final 'Requiescat in pace'. The technical skill with which the whole work is accomplished is beyond praise. The performance was on the whole good – Peter [Pears] sang most movingly and John Shirley Quirk and Felicity Lott were excellent. ...

21 December 1977

Finished at last the sketch of the Fourth Symphony but quite a lot of work remains to be done. ...

1978

Complete failure to keep this diary during the first months of this year. ...

---

[90] Widow of pianist and teacher Harold Craxton (1885–1971), mother of oboist Janet Craxton.

[91] *St Clement* by Rev. C. C. Scholefield (1830–1904), *Hymns Ancient and Modern*, Standard Edition, 477.

[92] Larkin's own flippant account of this meeting comes from a letter to Barbara Pym on 14 December 1977: 'A little man came up to me late on and said "I'm Lennox Berkeley", and I nearly said "I loved all those dances you arranged", and then I remembered that was Busby Berkeley, and this chap was some sort of Kapellmeister'.

16 June 1978

My career as a composer having been somewhat unobtrusive, I've been amazed at the amount of attention I've received on reaching my seventy-fifth birthday, particularly by the concert given by the Park Lane Group[93] in the Queen Elizabeth Hall on the day itself [12 May] with the *Antiphon* for strings, the *Dialogue for Cello and Orchestra* and the *Stabat Mater*. ... I was particularly pleased to hear the *Stabat Mater* resuscitated after so many years; it seemed to make a deep impression on the audience.[94] Two days later at another concert in the Wigmore Hall we had three of my French songs (Meriel and Peter [Dickinson]), piano duets and two-piano pieces (Susan Bradshaw and Richard Bennett) and a Passacaglia specially written by Michael [Berkeley] for the occasion. ... I was very much touched by the friendly almost cosy atmosphere of the whole concert and shall always remember it.

August 1978

I've had great difficulty in finding time to complete the piece for Jimmy Galway since both Cheltenham and the Carl Flesch competition have intervened since I began it. ... but I have managed to write the third movement in two weeks ... which is quite a record for me. I wanted it to be light and gay (the most difficult kind of music to write today) but I think it is right.[95] ...

18 August 1978

My Symphony no. 4 at the Proms. Good performance with the RPO under Charles Groves. Before it I was invited to speak to a small gathering. Robert Ponsonby, to whom I had said that I was hardly capable of it (I hate explaining – the music itself should be sufficient) came to my rescue ... and led me on to answering questions and all went reasonably well.[96]

I have been reading Frances Partridge's *A Pacifist's War* – her wartime diaries. She writes well but, Lord (as Pepys would say), how depressing the rationalist philosophy is. How can one function in life in the belief that human reason is sufficient, when there is so much that it is quite unable to explain? Unbelief raises as many difficulties as belief. However this may be, Frances reveals herself as a deeply human and sympathetic person as, of course, we already knew.

---

[93] The Park Lane Group, concert-promoting agency founded by John Woolf in 1956, with an outstanding record for identifying and presenting young artists.

[94] Rescored for orchestra by Michael Berkeley, op. 28a.

[95] Sonata for Flute and Piano, op. 97 (1978), recorded, along with the Flute Concerto, by Galway and Philip Moll on RCA Red Seal RS 9011 (1983).

[96] Robert Ponsonby (1926–), Controller of Music, BBC, 1972–85.

28 August 1978

Very good performance of my *Antiphon* conducted by Donald Hunt (organist of Worcester and chief conductor of this year's Three Choirs Festival) – he also conducted my *Magnificat* in a concert with *Voices of the Night*, which I conducted. I also heard my *Fantasia for Organ* very well played in Pershore Abbey.

2 September 1978

Mahler's huge Eighth Symphony in what seemed to me an extremely good performance, but I fear I shall never like Mahler really whole-heartedly. Though I admire his obvious musicianship and his warmth and breadth of feeling, there is something about the quality of his music and his love of the grandiose that is to me unsympathetic. Curiously enough, I was the only composer represented in this concert which began with my motet *Judica me*.[97] Whether this was in order to provide the greatest possible contrast or because there would only be time for a very short piece, I don't know – a mixture of both, I expect.

7 September 1978

To Oslo by air. Our visit was sponsored by the British Council in order that I should attend the concert at which the RPO were playing my Fourth Symphony and also that I should meet some Norwegian composers. The RPO were doing a Scandinavian tour but were conducted on this occasion by Per Dreier who did my piece very well. ...

9 October 1978

To Manchester, where the Royal Northern College had organised a series of concerts of my chamber music to mark my 75th birthday. I was much touched by the student performances which showed some very promising playing. Ray Leppard gave a lively performance of my Fourth Symphony. ...

12 December 1978

To the Festival Hall. Andrew Davis conducted a fine performance of *The Rite of Spring*. ... It remains one of the most exciting works ever written but one can understand the dismay of the audience who heard it in 1913. How unlike what people imagine Stravinsky was as a man. I remember his good manners, his elegance – he was small but very well dressed – and his courtesy to whoever he was with, though he held very definite opinions about everything and could be

---

[97] *Judica me*, op. 96/1 (1978), for SSATBB.

devastatingly critical of what he didn't like. I wonder how he will be rated in a hundred or even fifty years' time. That he was pre-eminent in his younger days is beyond discussion – *The Firebird, Petrushka* and *The Rite of Spring* are universally acknowledged masterpieces, and some of the works of his neo-classical period such as the *Symphony of Psalms*, the *Duo Concertant*, the Two-Piano Sonata and *Apollon Musagète*, are outstanding, but what of the late works in serial technique? I find it impossible to love them as I do his earlier music – I suppose through my inability to come to terms with atonality.

15 December 1978

Jimmy Galway gave a brilliant performance of my Flute Concerto at the Festival Hall.[98]

Christmas Day

Throughout the last two months of the year, I have been working on *Una and the Lion* – a cantata for soprano, recorder, viola da gamba and harpsichord.[99] I have enjoyed writing it but have found the ensemble difficult to manage, partly because of my lack of experience in writing for old instruments. Carl Dolmetsch, for whom it is written, will no doubt help about this in rehearsal. …

1979

Complete failure to keep up this diary in the early part of the year. …

1 June 1979

The Verdi Requiem at Westminster Cathedral. I have loved it ever since I can remember my first hearing, and was much moved to hear it in a place that has played such a big part in my life. It was a good performance conducted by Richard Hickox who seems to be the best of our young conductors. …[100]

---

[98] Concerto for Flute, op. 36 (1952), which he recorded on RCA Red Seal RS 9011 (1983). Recorded by Emily Beynon with the BBC National Orchestra of Wales under Bramwell Tovey on Chandos 10718 (2012).

[99] *Una and the Lion* (op. 98), cantata concertante for soprano, recorder, viola da gamba and harpsichord, commissioned by Carl Dolmetsch. Recorded on *The Rose Tree – Music in Memory of Basil Deane,* Prima Facie PFCD005.

[100] Richard Hickox (1948–2008). Indeed he was, and his tragic premature death deprived Berkeley's music of its most sympathetic British conductor since the composer's death. See The Berkeley Edition, the fine series of Chandos recordings.

18 June 1979

... I decided some time ago that I would set Winton Dean's libretto provided that I could make considerable changes in it – for instance, I like plenty of opportunities for duets, trios and even larger ensembles but here there are really too many; also I think it lacks points of dramatic tension. ... George Harewood has offered me a commission to write the opera and is prepared to put it on at the Coliseum ... but to begin something on this scale at the age of seventy-six is rather daunting – shall I live to complete it?

6 July 1979

Cheltenham Festival. Very good performance of my Fourth Symphony by the Hallé with Charles Groves. We had Maxwell Davies' opera *The Martyrdom of St Magnus*. Max Davies is technically a more than competent composer ... but I find he lacks warmth, and that I'm unable to get on his wavelength. The other opera was familiar ground – Ben's *Turn of the Screw*. If not a total success, the performance was a good attempt. Nobody will ever sing the part of Quint with the subtlety and magic that Peter brought to it, but the boy was good, the governess (Felicity Lott) good also, though not having quite the intensity of Jennifer Vyvyan. ... I've long thought that this is Ben's masterpiece – it seems to me the most perfect of his operas. This time I was struck by the wonderful timing of the ending – I think only a composer knows how difficult it is to achieve this.

29 October 1979

... We heard of Nadia's death – not unexpected ... she was desperately ill.

It is difficult to describe her or to account for the extraordinary influence she exercised on all who came into contact with her, particularly on her pupils, beyond saying that in her a brilliant intelligence and musical understanding was allied to goodness and warmth of heart. She had no particular method in her teaching other than insisting on a disciplinary training in academic counterpoint and fugue and general acquiring of an accurate ear. To this task she was utterly dedicated. She distrusted systems, and had no use for serialism at the time I was with her. She had a deep love of the great masters of the past and of the music of Stravinsky, though how she reconciled this latter admiration with his own conversion to serial technique in his later works, I have never understood. Indeed there were many things about which I was unable to agree with her, but these are of no matter in comparison with the enormous debt I shall always owe her and the love and admiration I shall always feel.

7 November 1979

To Paris for the concert of my chamber music given by the British Council at the Embassy. It was a great joy and the most encouraging thing that has happened for some time. The programme consisted of the Viola and Piano Sonata, the String Trio, the Oboe and Piano Sonatina and the Oboe Quartet.[101] I was particularly glad that the last two works were included as they are nearer my present-day language.

1980

I've made some progress with *Faldon Park*, but I'm well aware that it's a gamble to start a full-length opera at my age. However, I had a real longing to try, and so far it has gone rather well, though the work entailed is enormous. Having got about halfway through the first act, I've begun the full score as I can get on with scoring when the right idea in actual composition fails me …[102]

9 February 1980

Once more *Otello* at Covent Garden. … This was the best performance of the many I have heard. Placido Domingo was certainly the best Otello – a splendid voice and much power and variety in his acting. He has a very sympathetic stage personality. Margaret Price, though having a somewhat unromantic appearance, sang Desdemona with great accomplishment. A good Iago too (Silvano) – in fact the whole thing was one of the best performances I have ever seen at Covent Garden.

16 February 1980

I've recently heard twice Ben's *A Midsummer Night's Dream* and studied the full score – a wonderful use of a small orchestra. It is inevitable that in opera one loses a lot of the words, and when the librettist is Shakespeare, it is a serious disadvantage. However, the music itself makes up for this very largely for it captures the spirit of the text continually. For instance, the scene, early on, between Lysander and Hermia, where a free-ranging melodic line passing from voice to orchestra and vice-versa, beginning at 'How now, my love? Why is your cheek so pale?'; or Oberon's magical 'I know a bank'; or (much later on) the quarrel between the two girls; or the infinitely poetic ending of the second act – all convey the meaning and atmosphere of the text admirably.

---

[101] Sonata for Viola and Piano, op. 22 (1945); String Trio, op. 44 (1953); Sonatina for Oboe and Piano, op. 61 (1962); Oboe Quartet, op. 70 (1967).

[102] Berkeley was beginning to suffer from Alzheimer's and never got much beyond Act 1. However, a tenor aria, 'You married couples are all the same', was sung by Edward Byles at an 85th birthday concert given at St Mary's, Paddington Green, on 22 May 1988.

In the intervals of work on the opera I wrote the motet *Ubi caritas et amor* for the Benedictine celebrations of St Benedict's birth, in Westminster Cathedral, and a Magnificat and Nunc Dimittis for John Birch to be performed at Chichester.[103]

August 1980

It was only about now that I realised that a film about my life was being planned.[104] Flattering as the idea might be, I felt rather dubious about it; a composer's life is bound to be somewhat uneventful as he has to spend so much time constructing his music, scoring it, copying etc, that he has little time for anything else. Not only this, but music is very difficult to talk about, and not many composers are gifted writers – the great exception being Berlioz, who, to me, was a better writer than composer.

15 January 1982

My failure to keep this diary going last year was mainly due to the opera that I've been struggling with – and still am. I've never attempted anything on this scale before. ...

I have to confess that I've not been able to bring myself to go to the play *Amadeus*[105] because it seems that the author portrays Mozart as a loutish young man given to much scatological language; from the very little that one knows about him, this is totally unlike the impression he gave in public. It is true that in his letters to his sister he was wont to recall childish jokes that were far from being in good taste, but there is never any suggestion that his public behaviour was anything but exemplary. I merely have such a great respect and love for him that I cannot bear to see him brought down by lesser men to their own level. ...

---

[103] *Ubi caritas et amor*, op. 96/2 (1980), for SSATB. *Magnificat and Nunc dimittis*, op. 99 (1980), for SATB and organ.

[104] The film 'Composers' about Lennox and Michael Berkeley in the ATV Network 'Contrast' series, produced by Jim Berrow, was transmitted on 14 May 1981.

[105] Play by Peter Schaffer (1979), film released in 1984.

– Part VI –

Interviews with Performers, Composers, Family and Friends, 1990–91

1 PERFORMERS

Julian Bream

At BBC Broadcasting House, London, 28 January 1991
(edited by Julian Bream, 1 March 2011)

Julian Bream has been widely acknowledged as one of the greatest masters of the guitar and the lute. He was born in London in 1933, studied at the Royal College of Music, where the guitar was not then taught, and made his London debut in 1950. His international career developed from 1954. He had a crucial role inspiring and working with some of the leading composers – including Lennox Berkeley. He was made a CBE in 1985.

PD How did you first come across Lennox Berkeley?

JB I knew a little bit about his music when I was a boy. The first time I met him was in 1957 when he was about to write the Guitar Sonatina, which was a BBC commission for me to play. So I went to see him to discuss the instrument, show him how it worked and how best to write for it. I was delighted that he took the commission, because of all the composers, which the exception of Britten, he had the musical style and the clarity of texture in his music that would suit the guitar. He then went on to write the lovely Sonatina which I played for many years – I must have done over 200 performances and I went on to record it for RCA in 1960.[1] It's a beautiful piece, wonderfully written for the instrument and the obvious Latin connotations of the guitar did not in any way obscure his own musical personality.

PD Had you heard any of his music before that meeting about the commission?

JB I think I'd heard the Serenade for Strings and the *Four Poems of St Teresa of Avila*. Both intensely lyrical pieces so I more than welcomed the commission.

PD Did he know much about the guitar?[2]

JB He didn't, but he had a very good ear for what it could do. When writing for the instrument it's not just knowing where the fingers go but arriving at

---

[1] Sonatina for Guitar, op. 52/1, premiered by Bream on 9 March 1958 at Morley College, London. Now on CD in *Twentieth-Century Guitar I*, Julian Bream Edition, vol. 12. RCA Victor 09026–61595–2. See Peter Dickinson's corrected edition of the score, with the assistance of Bream (Chester Music 2011).

[2] In fact Berkeley had written *Quatre pièces pour la guitare* for Segovia at some time in the later 1920s. Published in The Andrés Segovia Archive, general editor Angelo Gilardino (Berben Edizioni Musicali, 2002).

PD   musical ideas that sound characteristic on the instrument. In the Sonatina all the ideas emanated from the guitar but are very Lennox too.

PD   What does that imply?

JB   Lennox could be very vague, and at times you wondered just how he sat down and wrote music! Whether he would find the appropriate pencil and manuscript paper – things of that nature. On the other hand, underneath there was an element of toughness. But he was so well mannered and gracious that you were rarely aware of it. In his music you hear that strong stoical quality. He was very considerate, and underneath I believe there was a very serious religious quality in his thinking. He was a fascinating man, old-fashioned, who belonged to another period where artists could lead civilised lives and could take an interest in other things beside their own passionate pursuit of music. He was a well-read man, interested in literature and poetry.

PD   Did you get any sense of the religious side of his life?

JB   I didn't know how important it was to him as a composer. It was something instinctive about him. I suppose it was connected with the fact that he took particular care to send his sons to Choir School at Westminster Cathedral. That was indicative of his inner spirit.

PD   How did he compare with Britten when you played his pieces?

JB   I never found that he was especially tough in criticism of one's performance. His manner was too urbane, too kindly, whereas Britten would let you know not by saying much but just by looking at you! Lennox did care how his music was performed but also understood the problems of playing instruments and actual performance.

PD   Do you remember anything about him composing?

JB   I was once staying with some friends in the country many years ago and Lennox and Freda were there too. Lennox was in the middle of writing something and he went off from time to time. We saw him at the slightly open door of the room where he was composing, sitting at the piano with a pencil in his mouth playing some extraordinarily dissonant chords and muttering under his breath: 'Not nasty enough! Not nasty enough!' [*Laughs*] It says something, because there was nothing really nasty in his character.

PD   If we were describing his music to somebody who didn't know it, could we say what his music is about?

JB   It's difficult to answer that question, because that's why we have music. [*Laughs*] He composed music that was, in a sense, old-fashioned, and yet he didn't mind. In his best works there's an intense lyricism. It is interesting that his tunes are not readily accessible. For the average music-lover he hasn't written a big tune, as Ben did or – a perfect example – the slow movement of the Rodrigo Guitar Concerto. I think that's a pity, because if he'd written one indelible tune his music would be identified and played more often.

PD Is it because his music isn't played enough that people don't know it?

JB I don't think he'd be a popular composer like Stravinsky, Bartók or Britten. I think that as the history of music unfolds there will be periods when his music is revived. Interest will ebb and flow. That does happen to certain composers and I think Lennox will be one.

PD Do you think his personal life and his late very happy marriage affected his work?

JB I hadn't thought of that at all. Some people are rosy both sides! I think Ben admired Lennox. I never heard him praise any composer, except Shostakovitch latterly, but I remember him saying about the Guitar Sonatina: 'You know, Julian, that is *almost* a very good piece.' So in Ben's book it must have been rather good!

PD That tells us about Britten too! Did he say anything else about Lennox?

JB I think that Ben was a little bit irritated by Lennox's music at times. I also think he admired it. He felt that compositionally, in terms of form, there were some weaknesses. I don't know enough about musical composition to ascertain whether Britten had a point, but there is sometimes in Lennox's music a slight waywardness which I think is also part of its charm. It happens along the way but is not music that has been construed.

PD What Britten might have found irritating is that Lennox hero-worshipped him and became somewhat influenced by his music. It was all rather near home?

JB I don't really think that was the case, but there was something. One has to admit that Lennox was in many ways – certainly harmonically – a more sumptuous composer. His style was less bony – his music had a mellifluous quality rarely found in Ben's music. Ben may have thought that he was, in a sense, just going over the top.

PD With Lennox there's the French influence of Fauré and Ravel?

JB Yes, but Lennox was his own man. Ben knew that Lennox admired him, but Lennox also went his own way. Personally I don't find a great deal of Britten's influence in his music.

PD Did you see any of the operas?

JB Yes, *A Dinner Engagement*, but I wouldn't have thought opera was Lennox's real forte. I like the chamber music, and of course the *Stabat mater* is a wonderful piece.

PD So is the Guitar Concerto, thanks to you. How did it start?

JB It was commissioned by the City of London Festival run by Ian Hunter, who said: 'I'd like you to play a concerto but wouldn't it be fun to commission a new piece?' So I mentioned Lennox, asked him, and he said he'd like to do it. It's a fine concerto and I was amazed how well he scored it. Guitar concertos are tricky things and amongst other things you've got to have a translucent

PD   orchestration. I love the opening and the end of the first movement. The slow movement has a wonderful tune where the notes are in just the right part of the instrument – in the tenor register, a lovely sonority.

PD   Does it work in the concert hall as opposed to a recording?

JB   I think it does but I must confess that over the last twenty years whenever I have played a concerto, which is rather rare, I do use a tiny bit of discreet amplification. The sonorities of the guitar must be relaxed and you mustn't feel you're forcing the sound. Even more important, the orchestra needs to be able to play because when you play with a guitar acoustically, without any help from a microphone, the string players tend to sit on the edge of their seats and use half a centimetre of bow. That is not the way to make music.

PD   The Berkeley must have reached a lot of people because it's on the other side of your LP of the Rodrigo concerto?[3]

JB   That was one of the reasons why I included it – so that people became aware of Lennox's music. You've got to have something on the other side anyway!

PD   There are some differences between what's in the score and what you play, especially at the end of the last movement.

JB   Where some composers might have written an *ossia*, I don't think Lennox would have done. It could have been published in an original version and then, as with all these pieces, they undergo a transformation because some of the guitar writing may be too difficult or inappropriate for the musical character that it conveys. Or that it just needs some small adjustment. I wouldn't put it past Lennox that he forgot to write in things that we'd come to an agreement about! I also think he may have had second thoughts about it – that he may have preferred his original idea. That explains a part of his character. There was the stoic side of Lennox who decided he wasn't going to have his arm twisted by Julian, but he would agree while I was there! There could be a certain duality in his character.

PD   You worked with both Britten and Tippett. Why isn't Lennox as well known?

JB   I don't think it's to do with his music, but his personality. Britten always had an eye for doing things appropriately and finding meaningful ways to do them. The *War Requiem* is a case in point – the rebuilding of Coventry Cathedral, the War and they needed a piece. Ben was very clever how he brought things together, but I don't think Lennox would ever think like that. He would have been too other-worldly. Tippett had very good public relations – a Tippett newsletter would arrive regularly from his publisher. A Lennox newsletter might have got a few more performances. It's all to do with promotion finally, but he was not a man who had to face continually the commercial practicalities of a composer's life. He composed because he wanted to rather than because he had to – at least that's how I feel. He was very passionate about his work, and when things were not going well he was very upset – it was a desperate time. He was not aggressively ambitious – quite the contrary.

---

[3] Original LP RCA Red Seal ARL 1 1181 (1975): CD RCA GK 81181.

Unlike other composers who feel they've got something important to say and want to find the means of conveying it as practically as possible, he just wanted to write music.

PD Mozart was his god.

JB I never knew that – but he's god for quite a lot of people!

PD Of the Frenchmen he admired Ravel and Poulenc.

JB And Fauré – in many ways their music is rather similar. Intense lyricism in common but Fauré's harmony was more adroit. Lennox's harmony could sometimes give you a feeling that maybe there are several ways a chord could be achieved – with different notes sometimes. The harmony is heard but could be modified. Academics may say it's a slightly weak aspect of his music but I think his harmonic colouration gives his music quite a lot of character.

PD A human quality?

JB Yes, it's the tenacious and the vulnerable. The vulnerable quality in Lennox was touching so one entered into his orbit in a friendly and even protective way. He wouldn't have known how to promote himself. Happily Freda did, and without her I don't know what would have happened.

PD What was it like going to their house?

JB I often went to Warwick Avenue and thought how beautiful the whole place was. It had a certain air of aristocratic ambience. He composed in a room which had lovely proportions and after working we went into the drawing room with its interesting pictures, fine wallpaper, and strong pink gins! It was always a pleasant social occasion: his children were around, quite lively, and it was fun. It was a real artist's home, with lovely things and a spontaneous spirit: it was always a joy to go there.

Norman Del Mar

At Witchings, Hadley Common, Hertfordshire, 21 December 1990

Norman Del Mar (1919–94) was one of the leading British conductors of his generation. He was born in London and studied horn and composition at the Royal College of Music. He made his professional debut as a conductor in the Richard Strauss Festival in 1947. From 1948 to 1956 he was principal conductor of the English Opera Group, then held a variety of appointments for the BBC and with orchestras in Sweden and Denmark. He wrote a three-volume study of Strauss and several books about the orchestra and conducting. He was awarded the CBE in 1975.

PD   When did you first become aware of Berkeley as a composer?

NDM   He did music for a film called *The First Gentleman* conducted by Beecham.[4] I was with him at the time; he picked me out of the orchestra; promised me some concerts and I became his right-hand man – a very nice thing to be. When he was doing this film we picked up Lennox and the three of us went in the car together. I remember a vignette when he told me he was pleased that Tommy thought well enough of him – but the whole thing was new to me from the point of view of film music and Lennox.

PD   It must have been fairly awe-inspiring for Berkeley to have his film music conducted by Beecham at that time?

NDM   Tommy didn't do films anyway, so it was a curious exercise. He wasn't particularly *routiné* in the business of fitting films to the screen, but it was fun and Tommy was in a good humour all the time, which was a help.

PD   Do you remember anything he said about Berkeley's music?

NDM   He wouldn't because he always avoided saying anything serious about the music he conducted. If anybody asked him serious questions he would always come up with a quip. I remember he once did one of Delius's *Dance Rhapsodies* and some fool of a journalist said: 'Sir Thomas, would you tell me which of the two *Dance Rhapsodies* you prefer.' He said: 'I don't know that I care for either of them!' It was a perfect answer, knowing that he did them all the time and loved them both! Absolutely typical.

PD   That was a curious entry into Berkeley – as a film composer, since he didn't do many and didn't make his reputation that way.

NDM   The first music of Lennox's that I conducted was with an amateur orchestra in Croydon when I put on the First Symphony.[5] I don't remember how it

---

[4] *The First Gentleman*, Columbia feature film adapted from the play by Norman Ginsbury, directed by Alberto de Almeida Cavalcanti. Music with the Royal Philharmonic Orchestra, conducted by Thomas Beecham: film on general release 31 May 1948.

[5] Symphony no. 1, op. 16, premiered on 8 July 1943 at the Royal Albert Hall, with the London Philharmonic Orchestra under Berkeley. Del Mar first conducted it on 19 November 1949.

came about. I did the Symphony in 1949 and my first performance of the Divertimento, which I did so much, was in 1951.[6]

PD   So you've a long perspective on the First Symphony right from then to making the first recording.[7]

NDM   The anxiety one has about composers is that the music one first learned to love from around that period is what one thinks of as the best. One can apply that to Ben – the Serenade, *Les Illuminations* and *Peter Grimes* – or to Michael Tippett – the Double Concerto and the *Midsummer Marriage* – where one thinks back to those earlier works and it's probably an injustice but one ends up loving those works more than the later ones. For me the best of Berkeley – alas – always remains the First Symphony, Divertimento, Serenade for Strings and the Sinfonietta, which is a short piece that can be rehearsed easily and quickly and it works a treat. It attracts an audience at once, like an English Poulenc in a way.

PD   If it is so attractive why is Berkeley not performed more regularly now?

NDM   Why are things not played? Will an audience be turned away by a name? Will any contemporary composer be thought to be an audience dropper? Those earlier works are so immediately appealing – there seems no reason on earth why they aren't permanently in the repertoire. The Divertimento seems to me to be totally successful. I don't know that I would say that of any of his other works – I hope this isn't heresy! There does seem to be an uncertainty in his writing. In the copyist's handwritten scores of the Divertimento some figures appear in different ways, and in the parts a third way. Every conductor coming to any of Lennox's works, I find, has to make up his mind all along the line as to exactly what he's going to play and what he's going to tell the orchestra is right or wrong.

PD   Is it a bit like Delius with Beecham?

NDM   I think it's more so. With Delius the notes are more solid – he always knew exactly what the harmonies must be. Delius didn't phrase or balance – Tommy did it to perfection and he got the sense of the ebb and flow in a way that Delius never set down on paper. Apart from misprints, the notes are always there. But with Lennox there were sometimes real doubts. In the style he used, which became increasingly dissonant later, one doesn't really know which note he did want. I had the odd experience at a social occasion when we discussed a performance I was going to give – perhaps the *Windsor Variations* – and I remember I brought the score, we sat at the piano, and I played it to him both ways.[8] He couldn't make up his mind and it didn't

---

[6] Divertimento in B flat, op. 18, premiered 1 October 1943 with the BBC Orchestra under Clarence Raybould. Del Mar first conducted it on 12 July 1951 with the Philharmonia in Colchester.

[7] With the London Philharmonic Orchestra on Lyrita SRCS 80 (1975): on CD Lyrita SRCD 249 (2007).

[8] *The Windsor Variations*, op. 75, premiered 18 September 1969 at St George's Chapel, Windsor, by the Menuhin Festival Orchestra under Yehudi Menuhin.

seem to make too much difference to him. This is not an attack, because there's a famous story about Brahms who brought his Fourth Symphony to Meiningen when Strauss was the assistant to von Bülow. They were uncertain about a note, so they went to Brahms, who scratched his head and said: 'Try it both ways!' So that's a feature of composers who detach themselves from their works afterwards and don't mind too much what notes are actually played!

PD   Is it anything to do with Lennox's temperament? He was so vague.

NDM That's certainly true and I suppose Delius was too – a contrast to somebody like Mahler who cared so dreadfully about absolutely every note. Lennox was vague and a bit withdrawn: once he'd written it down it didn't necessarily mean it was right for ever. All his scores are full of slight changes, or something that's been put down wrong, or the slurs don't correspond with the time before.

PD   Was he too much of a gentleman to read his proofs?

NDM I wonder, from looking at those scores and parts, whether there were any proofs. Publishers are notorious, although he's been lucky to have had a very loyal publisher all his life.[9] Before the score of the Divertimento was printed, the handwritten scores and parts were unbelievably full of errors. For example, on the first page of the score of the Divertimento one doesn't know whether the woodwind entries should be played by one player each or in pairs. I play it in pairs because I think that's what he wanted and what sounds right. [*Laughs*] But if you're going to try and produce a corrected edition I think you're in for a very hard time! You'll probably end up with what they call a *Revisionsbericht* in which you'll have to come clean and say there's no way of knowing which it is.

PD   You compared him with Poulenc. Is there a real connection?

NDM Patently. He was with Nadia Boulanger and part of the Boulangerie. The post-Stravinsky group of Les Six produced a kind of witty music – some more serious but quite a lot tongue-in-cheek. I think he had that light element which very little English music has in the same way. He's a very valuable part of our heritage.

PD   But the First Symphony, written in the war years, is not simply a light piece.

NDM The slow movement is serious – unexpectedly, so that when you get to the sudden dramatic middle section it takes one aback. But I wouldn't agree about the rest of it. It's all lightweight, although I don't use that word in a derogatory sense. Skilfully moulded in the orchestration with only a few instruments at a time and the way in which he's organised links between strings and wind in a kind of open orchestration is more typical of the Parisian school – and very attractive.

---

[9] J. & W. Chester Ltd, now part of Music Sales.

PD The first movement with its minor third motif and the switches to different kinds of music –

NDM – that's right –

PD – is a big Berkeley compared with the miniatures?

NDM Yes, but it's unmistakably the same style and the same man, whereas in some of the later pieces this is not necessarily so. Sometimes it gets thicker and the harmonies more abstruse. Then you don't know which is the right note. I've had this experience even with Ben. I once had to check whether it was the right note or not – he looked at me with a rueful grin and said he wasn't sure he could remember! Of all composers I thought he would have known every note.

PD How would you compare Lennox and Ben as composers?

NDM Their styles are not the same. The only thing that's rather curious is that when they collaborated on *Mont Juic* they were careful not to say who had done what, and it is absolutely impossible to tell.[10]

PD Lennox hero-worshipped Ben from first meeting him in 1936. Did he live under his shadow?

NDM I wouldn't have said so. However much he worshipped Ben – we were all fond of him – I don't connect the two in the actual creative work. I can't see the connection at all. I think of Lennox developing in his own way from the Boulangerie despite Ben.

PD They wrote for some of the same performers.

NDM Yes. Lennox wrote the *Stabat mater*, one of his most successful pieces, for the English Opera Group orchestra and voices – Ben's combination. One connects the two in that sense, but there is no moment in the *Stabat mater* when I would say: 'That sounds just like Ben.' No – it sounds just like Lennox.

PD Lennox went on into opera. …

NDM That was under Ben's influence. He wrote *A Dinner Engagement* for the English Opera Group. I didn't do that – I think I was already away from Ben by the time that came up.[11] I'm very sorry I didn't conduct any of Lennox's operas apart from the Suite from *Nelson*. This means there's a side of Lennox I don't know.

PD What are the problems for a conductor in the longer movements in the orchestral pieces?

---

[10] Berkeley told me in the 1980s that he wrote the first two movements and Britten the last two. See Dickinson, *The Music of Lennox Berkeley*, p. 35.

[11] From time to time Britten dispensed with the services of musicians and administrators, usually rather abruptly, and Del Mar did not appear at Aldeburgh after 1957. *A Dinner Engagement*, op. 45, was premiered on 17 June 1954 at Aldeburgh with the English Opera Group under Vilem Tausky.

NDM That's one of the hardest questions to answer. I do these things instinctively. I don't think the problems with Lennox's work are any different to anybody else's – you have to get the concept of how the whole thing adds up. There are contrasted sections juxtaposed and you have to sense how they add up even though the parts are so different. But, as in the third movement of the First Symphony, I didn't think I should under-stress the severe jolts.

PD What about the concertos?

NDM I conducted the Violin Concerto with chamber orchestra – with Manoug Parikian and later with Menuhin, for whom it was written.[12] There's a curious thing – before the last movement there's a little horn duet followed by a cadenza. Yehudi forgot all about the interlude with the horns and we never played it! [*Laughs*] I looked at the horns and we shrugged our shoulders![13]

PD Was Berkeley's style suited to concertos?

NDM I can't think why not. I did *Dialogue* for cello and chamber orchestra.[14] The only thing that worries me about some of those works was that there was an element of improvisation about the continuity. It didn't seem to me that he'd got the logic sorted out.

PD Lennox admired Delius early on.

NDM The harmonies are very different. Delius is sensuous; Lennox more astringent. I would never have thought of that! [*Laughs*]

PD You did the recording of the Concerto for Two Pianos.[15]

NDM The link between the variations in the second movement is wider than I would have expected. I had to cope with a feeling of discontinuity – more disconcerting than in the symphonic works.

PD There's a kind of style-modulation between the sections.[16]

NDM That's exactly it!

PD Does it matter?

---

[12] Concerto for Violin and Chamber Orchestra, op. 59, premiered on 1 June 1961 at the Bath Festival, with Yehudi Menuhin and the Festival Chamber Orchestra under Berkeley.

[13] Del Mar is referring to the Lento introduction to the third movement for two horns and two oboes. The recording was made by Menuhin with the Menuhin Festival Orchestra under Adrian Boult. HMV ASD 2759: EMI British Composers CDMS 66121–2.

[14] *Dialogue* for cello and chamber orchestra, op. 79, premiered 30 July 1971 at the King's Lynn Festival by Maurice Gendron with the English Chamber Orchestra under Raymond Leppard.

[15] On the same Lyrita LP as the First Symphony – SRCS 80 (1975): on CD Lyrita SRCD 250 (2007).

[16] See Peter Dickinson, 'Style-Modulation as a Compositional Technique' (Goldsmiths University of London, 1996), or 'Style Modulation: an Approach to Stylistic Pluralism', *Musical Times* 130 (April 1989), 208–11. What Del Mar calls 'the link between the variations' is no wider than in Britten's *Variations on a Theme of Frank Bridge* (1937).

NDM Perhaps not – if there is a problem there one shouldn't necessarily try and smooth it.

PD These days it's fashionable – look at Schnittke?[17]

NDM I personally don't believe in this, I'm afraid. I can't help feeling he's playing the fool with it. It doesn't seem to have any real style at all.

PD The contrast of styles in Berkeley is very slight compared to Charles Ives.[18]

NDM Berkeley was a serious composer; Ives was an experimenter; and I'm doubtful of the validity of Schnittke at all [*Laughs*] – three quite different elements!

PD Is there a kind of restraint about Berkeley that will always make it difficult for him to reach an international audience?

NDM If you're going to present English music to a Continental audience I wouldn't start with Berkeley, but I have played both the Divertimento and the First Symphony in Sweden – and it went down a bomb! I presented the Nocturne[19] in Sweden and Denmark – a splendid piece which is hardly ever played – but I wouldn't take the *Windsor Variations*.

---

[17] Alfred Schnittke (1934–98), Russian composer many of whose most influential works juxtapose violent stylistic contrasts.

[18] Charles Ives (1874–1954), pioneering American composer also involved in style-modulation whose disorganised manuscripts have created probably the most complex editorial problems in musical history.

[19] Nocturne, op. 25, premiered 28 August 1946 at the Royal Albert Hall by the BBC Symphony Orchestra under Adrian Boult.

Colin Horsley

At BBC Broadcasting House, 30 November 1990

Colin Horsley was one of the leading British pianists of his generation. He was born in New Zealand in 1920. In 1936 he came to England, where he studied at the Royal College of Music with Herbert Fryer. He made his Proms debut in 1943, was awarded the OBE in 1963, and has taught at the Royal Northern College in Manchester and the Royal College in London. His advocacy of Berkeley's piano music in concertos, chamber music and solos has been outstanding.

CH   I did my first broadcast for the BBC in January 1942 and met Lennox shortly afterwards through Val Drewry, a great admirer of Lennox's music.[20] He ran chamber music for the BBC where Lennox was in charge of orchestral programmes.

I think poor Lennox was dying to get on with his own compositions. He built very good orchestral programmes but I was told that under the desk he was really trying to do some composition, keeping his own music going. But the BBC commissioned short pieces from various composers to fill in between programmes and to keep the wavelength secure from enemy interference. These were the Preludes, and he had just finished them when the war ended. I wasn't aware of much piano music then although I was introduced to the *Four Concert Studies* a little later.

I didn't come across the *Six Preludes* until about 1948, when I was making my first recordings for HMV. I was given two double-sided 78s to make – one was Prokofiev's Third Sonata and the other was the Prelude in E minor by Rachmaninov, with lots of fast octaves, and the Szymanowsky Etude in B flat minor. I thought I'd played well and David Bricknell, the producer, was very pleased and said: 'Have you got anything else to play for us?' I said: 'Well actually I have *Six Preludes* by Lennox Berkeley in my case. Would you be interested in them?' He didn't know Lennox Berkeley, so I produced them, played them and they recorded them. They were a best-seller and sold much better than the other two 78s.[21] So that was really the start for me. I didn't give the first performance of the Preludes because another pianist had played them at the Wigmore: I think he played the first two, then felt ill and walked off the platform. Lennox, who was in the audience, had to leave his seat and finish the rest. As a pianist Lennox was not exactly refined, although capable, and that was the end of the Preludes for the moment.

PD   What a fascinating story. What was Lennox like then?

CH   Of course he was a gentleman and I mean that in a very nice way. He was kind, charming, bright and a nice person to be with and to play to. I was never nervous playing to him. But, being so kind, he rather held back on

---

[20] *Six Preludes*, op. 23, are dedicated to Drewry, who wrote 'Lennox Berkeley – Some Recent Compositions', *Chesterian* 26 (October 1951), 1–4.

[21] HMV C 3940 (78 rpm): Lyrita REAM 2109 (2 CDs).

criticising. I played the *Six Preludes* from the same copy for years and made another recording for Lyrita. When I came to record them for Meridian much later I bought another copy for the engineer.[22] I found that on the last page of the sixth Prelude where I had been playing a bottom A flat and a B flat in the new copy it was an octave B flat. Lennox had altered it without telling me. [*Laughs*] I corrected it for the last recording. He wouldn't say specifically at times whether I was playing a right or wrong note, so there are some moments in the Lyrita recording of the *Concert Studies*. I also recorded the first *Concert Study* in Australia with the *Three Mazurkas* and there are one or two notes in those where Lennox later had different ideas.

PD He was famously vague. Did it apply to the notes too?

CH I think he was vague but delighted to have his music played, and I suppose that once he'd written it he was thinking of the next piece. We also recorded the Horn Trio, which I commissioned because I very much enjoyed playing the Brahms with Dennis Brain. We gave the first performance at the Victoria and Albert Museum, and the next day recorded it.[23] The recording had been in the bag several weeks when Lennox telephoned and said: 'Do you think HMV could change two bars for me? I've rewritten two bars in the slow movement.' I explained that we'd have to leave it as it was, but the printed copy is different.

PD Did Lennox give you any indications about style in the piano music?

CH Basically he liked things played in a classical way because the Piano Concerto was influenced by Mozart and French music too. He couldn't bear anyone to pull things about. I remember him saying that Ravel couldn't either. But listening to my own recording of the *Three Mazurkas*, written in homage to Chopin, I realised there could have been more freedom – as in a Chopin mazurka with the ornamentation, arabesques and so on.

PD In your recording of the Piano Sonata there's quite a lot of freedom in the two outside movements in terms of rubato and changes of tempo. Lennox presumably went along with that?

CH I think he did [*Laughs*] but he wouldn't have said so if he didn't! I think he was quite pleased.

PD What about your connection with the Piano Concerto, one of his finest works?

CH Val Drewry and I got together and decided to commission a concerto from Lennox. It's really a chamber concerto with Mozart at the back of his mind. I remember him saying that K503 in C was one of his favourites: the unisons were so beautiful and in Lennox's slow movement you have them. I think it's charming, elegant – all his music is elegant – and quite a lot of spirit and

---

[22] Meridian E77017.

[23] Horn Trio, op. 44, premiered 28 March 1954 at the Victoria and Albert Museum by Dennis Brain, Manoug Parikian and Horsley. HMV CLP 1029; HMV HQM 1007 etc.: on CD EMI Classics 5 85138 2.

fun in the last movement. There's a very good cadenza in the first movement. In my heyday as a young man a lot of pianists were not very good and that type of writing didn't benefit from the shallow-sounding pianos. Although Lennox has lots of harmony much of his writing is contrapuntal and you can't put the pedal down and get a big mush as you can with Rachmaninov, which sets up vibrations and improves a poor piano. So I had that to contend with in some places.

PD   Are you saying that the Concerto – surely a masterpiece – didn't have enough appeal for performers?

CH   I think it's delightful, but all music is ahead of its time from the audience's point of view. You have barriers to break down when you play any piece but twenty-five years later it seems easy to understand.

PD   But it's played less now than when you were performing it.

CH   I think pianists are awfully lazy not to play these works. You can't play Lennox's work without two rehearsals. The other day I played a Mozart and a Beethoven concerto on one rehearsal on the day. I couldn't have risked Lennox's concerto.

PD   What about the ISCM Festival performance at Palermo in 1949?

CH   That was in a marvellous opera house – just as beautiful as Covent Garden – and all the aristocrats on the island came. Lennox wasn't there. I stayed at the Villa Igiea, a wonderful hotel, and the people were delightful. I had a rather old Steinway without much quality. We had the Rome Radio Symphony Orchestra; rehearsals in Rome first; and it was very well received. But on the day Constant Lambert, who had been ill, appeared to be the worse for wear: he was no use whatsoever on the platform, which annoyed the orchestra very much indeed. Although we played, we had no driving force apart from the piano. It wasn't easy to play to that audience. In 1949 taste in Palermo was probably about 1899! [*Laughs*]

PD   But what did Lambert think of the piece?

CH   He thought it was a delightful work and was all for it. I played the piece on many other occasions with famous conductors. Charles Groves, at Bournemouth; Barbirolli, in Manchester; Goossens in Australia, where it went down very well; and Basil Cameron, who conducted the first performance.[24] I played it under Lennox at the Festival Hall when I put on the concert myself with the London Philharmonic under Anatole Fistoulari, playing the third Rachmaninov in the first half and then Lennox conducted his concerto in the second half. It was a joy to play with Lennox, very comfortable, and I was not on tenterhooks as you can be with an indifferent conductor.

---

[24] Piano Concerto, op. 29, premiered 31 August 1948 at the Royal Albert Hall with the London Symphony Orchestra. The performance at the 23rd Festival of the International Society for Contemporary Music was on 26 April 1949.

PD   This is fascinating because some people have said his beat was difficult to follow.

CH   There was no problem with his beat and the orchestra were delighted.

PD   Did Berkeley's Piano Concerto feel like avant-garde music then?

CH   Quite a bit of it did.

PD   But he had a gift for melody.

CH   He wrote charming melodies – the second subject of the first movement, and the slow movement has a beautiful melody. But I did find in those days that people had to hear it a second time, which is true of any new music.

PD   Lennox himself has referred to that – so does it make his music elusive?

CH   Not at all, except for some of the later music. But the Preludes have a direct appeal. Because I often followed the Preludes with a Stravinsky etude, he wrote me the Scherzo for my 1950 tour of Australia and New Zealand. So I played the *Six Preludes* and the Scherzo everywhere. He wrote it because he thought I had a good fast wrist technique. I must have done about ninety performances of the Preludes.

PD   After the Piano Concerto you commissioned another work which is practically unknown – the Concerto for Piano and Double String Orchestra (1958).

CH   Again we commissioned it from Lennox. I think we'd thought about piano and double strings because of the *Tallis Fantasia* of Vaughan Williams. The Royal Philharmonic Society was delighted to have the premiere at the Festival Hall. The first two movements were produced very easily and then we had only about ten days to go to the concert when Lennox found he was having trouble with the last movement. I received it page by page from him – a desperate situation – and just at that time there were the first instances of Asian flu. Gina Bachauer got it, so I was roped in to play the third Rachmaninov at the Festival Hall about a week before I was due to play Lennox's Concerto. The Rachmaninov went fine, but a few days later I went down with Asian flu myself. For three or four days I couldn't eat, felt ghastly, and that was the day I had to play Lennox's Concerto with the César Franck *Variations symphoniques* and the BBC SO under Rudolph Schwartz. The manager of the BBC orchestra said he'd announce that I'd got out of my bed to go and play. But he didn't make any announcement at all; everything seemed dim to me; and it wasn't the best performance in the world. A week later we played it for a broadcast from Maida Vale which went well.[25]

PD   Did you get the score in time?

CH   Only just!

---

[25] Concerto for Piano and Double String Orchestra, op. 46, premiered 11 February 1959 at the Royal Festival Hall with the BBC Symphony Orchestra under the composer, broadcast performance under Rudolph Schwarz, transmitted 14 February 1959. It has been neglected ever since.

PD How would you rate the piece compared with the Piano Concerto?

CH I think it's more advanced from a compositional point of view and a fascinating work.

PD Nobody else took it up?

CH No, because it wasn't well reviewed at the Festival Hall because I was under the weather.

PD This was the period of Berkeley's greatest celebrity. Did you go to *Nelson*?

CH Yes. You know he had to change the ending? The producer wanted a more rousing finish and I think that spoilt it.

PD Emma Hamilton's final aria was added?

CH Yes. I also saw *Ruth* which I enjoyed very much. Thinking about all Lennox's music, the piano works show him as a miniaturist of great finesse and they're very pianistic. I wouldn't say Lennox is a colossal large-scale oil-painting kind of composer but he was a genius as a refined miniaturist. Immediately after I played the Piano Concerto, the Two-Piano Concerto – a very good work – was commissioned and other soloists followed, such as John Francis with the Flute Concerto.[26] We were all playing Lennox Berkeley.

PD Do you see any connections between Lennox and Britten?

CH Quite honestly I really don't think Lennox's music was influenced by Britten, because Lennox had so much of his own personality. Lennox's music is Lennox. The exquisite *Stabat mater* is the essence of Lennox.

PD Something to do with his religious beliefs?

CH That plays a part as well as the church music he was used to hearing. And, through his ancestry, there's a strong Gallic flavour both in his music and in Lennox himself. So we have elegance, beautiful phrases as well as subtle, pungent harmony.

PD What did you think of Lennox's music as it became more dissonant in the later 1960s?

CH I did play the Quintet for wind and piano and recorded it for Meridian.[27] When I first tried it I thought: 'My God, this is a tough nut!' But within a few days I realised that it was easy to enjoy and appreciate as a development in his work.

PD Did you miss the beautiful harmonies of the Piano Concerto, Piano Sonata and works of that period?

CH Not really – it was fascinating in its own right.

---

[26] Flute Concerto, op. 36, premiered 29 July 1953 at the Royal Albert Hall by Francis with the BBC SO under Malcolm Sargent.

[27] Quintet for Piano and Wind, op. 90, commissioned by the Chamber Music Society of Lincoln Center and premiered 30 January 1976 at Alice Tully Hall; British premiere 4 December 1976 at the Wigmore Hall by the Melos Ensemble; Horsley's recording is on Meridian E 77017.

PD   I'm still left wondering why some of the finest piano music by any British composer is so neglected.

CH   I think Lennox had a large hand. I have found that people with small hands find the stretches difficult. The *Five Short Pieces* are easier. Also his music is exposed in clear textures.

PD   From a technical point of view, the *Four Concert Studies*, for example, have fingering patterns that change rapidly, unlike Prokofiev or Scriabin studies. Does that make them difficult?

CH   Quite well-known pianists who have played the Preludes have said to me: 'They're much more tricky than I thought!' You can get caught out not concentrating. They're all so clear that any mistakes are obvious.

PD   It's the third Prelude that's a problem.

CH   Yes.

PD   Those fingering problems are even more striking in the *Four Concert Studies*. But am I making too much of it?

CH   I think you are. The earlier *Concert Studies* are delightful – the first rather jazzy; the second one like a slow winter scene; the third one, with those patterns you've mentioned, is a winner as an encore; and the last one is a double-note study.

PD   The last two are hard to play?

CH   I think the first takes a lot of playing. I used that one with the *Three Mazurkas* on tour in Australia, and recorded them that way for HMV Australia, because they wanted me to record from the programmes I was playing. It meant that I couldn't repeat that first étude on my Lyrita LP. People have often wondered why, thinking I couldn't play it! [*Laughs*]

PD   I can't imagine anybody would think that! [*Laughs*] Are there other chamber works you played?

CH   Max Rostal introduced me to the Sonatina for violin and piano – we played together for over twenty-one years – and I think it's a masterpiece. Again there's a vital first movement; a wintry slow movement; and the delightful variations with the uneven rhythm in the third movement – very typical.

PD   You've played the two Rawsthorne concertos and other British music. How does Berkeley compare with other composers?

CH   I think Lennox had a genuine harmonic structure of his own – his seconds, fourths, sevenths and ninths all gelled naturally, whereas a lot of other people added dissonance for its own sake – to be modern. With Lennox you could memorise easily, because it would go up by a second or a third, but with some others it was hit or miss and more risky.

PD   Was Berkeley the most modern music you've ever performed?

CH   When I played Stravinsky's *Duo Concertant* for violin and piano I thought:

'My God, the man's a hoax!' [*Laughs*] until I realised there were so many contrapuntal lines that my brain couldn't take them in first of all.

Looking back, after many years, I don't think Lennox's music was devastatingly modern – except for some people with the larger pieces at a first hearing – which made me realise that with anything worth knowing you have to study to appreciate.

Lennox's music also depends on the performance. I remember hearing the *Stabat mater* with indifferent singers years ago – intonation was a problem – and it didn't find any winners at all. More recently at Lennox's Memorial Concert I thought it was super – the essence of his music.

2 COMPOSERS

John Manduell

At BBC Broadcasting House, 27 November 1990

Sir John Manduell was born in Johannesburg in 1928 and studied at Strasbourg, Jesus College, Cambridge, and with Berkeley at the Royal Academy of Music. He joined the BBC in 1956, co-ordinated the new Music Programme from 1964 to 1968, and then became first Director of Music at the University of Lancaster. From 1971 to 1996 he was Principal of the Royal Northern College of Music, Manchester, establishing its international reputation. He ran the Cheltenham Festival 1969–94, a period which included Berkeley's presidency. He was knighted in 1989.

PD   Do you remember how you first came across Lennox Berkeley's music?

JM   I can remember it distantly and yet with enormous affection: it was when I was at school at Haileybury. Colin Horsley, a New Zealander who hadn't been in this country very long, came down to play along with Alan Loveday. He must have played the piano Preludes because I remember the first one very clearly.

PD   What led to your studying with him?

JM   I came to him quite late: I'd been to Cambridge then won a scholarship to the Royal Academy. Initially I studied with William Alwyn, for whom I also have affectionate memories. I was so drawn to Lennox's music and somehow instinctively felt I was drawn to him, although I'd met him very briefly. I felt, as a student, that I wanted to be learning from this very remarkable man.

PD   What was it about this music that seemed important to you at that age?

JM   It was the economy, the cleanness. Before that I'd been guided by one or two people who wrote music that was very English in a big frame and wasn't necessarily highly poetic like Lennox's. His French influences have often been spoken about, and perhaps I had them too because I'd done a diploma at Strasbourg and was very much into French poetry, as he was. I think there was an instinctive groping on my part towards a tutor who would be sensitive to those elements.

PD   Not just the roast beef of Old England?

JM   Not at all – that was the absolute thing to get away from! Away from the rigidity of the English bar-line.

PD   Do you remember your first lesson?

JM   Oh, vividly. I was enormously shy and he struck me as being shy. It was at his house in Warwick Avenue and I remember going up the rather overgrown path, knocking at the door, waiting and waiting, almost certain I'd gone to the wrong house. Then the door opened and I was ushered in.

PD Then what happened?

JM I always remember the wallpaper in the study – dark maroon with a musical motif, lyres and things in gold. We were both hesitant to start – I was waiting to be told and he was waiting to hear because his way of teaching was relaxed in a very gentle way. He was quite clear what he felt he had to help his pupils to acquire. Quite a lot of that derived from his studies with Nadia Boulanger and the way she had instilled all sorts of technical disciplines. He was hesitant about prescribing – never did, really. He might say: 'Why don't you try your hand at a string trio? In a funny way it's much more difficult than a string quartet – but don't write too many double-stoppings for the viola.' That sort of teaching was lovely, but you had to pick it up that one time and make sure you remembered. When you left you might sit down by the canal and write 'not too many double-stoppings for the viola' before you forgot. Or he'd say: 'Do you really want to use a tremolo?' It was a gentle sort of enquiry which really meant: 'I think some kind of figuration would be better here.'

PD What else happened in the lesson?

JM Quite often he would respond if one asked to spend some time on a work of his – sometimes a work in hand. When he was working on the Sextet and the Concertino, where he'd hit on the device of having two duets, he would advise one about what sort of basis you were going to build a movement on – not structure or form but foundation.[28] I learnt a lot from hearing him generously and frankly talking about the problems he was confronted with in a work in progress.

PD This was his operatic period.

JM When I first went to him, I suppose *Nelson* must have been just about finished awaiting production at Sadler's Wells. I've always felt that we must keep alive Lennox's work in the four operas. I'm absolutely convinced about that. We went to *Nelson*, and I remember there was a lot of talk about Nelson's first entry being unobtrusively up-stage – why had the producer decided not to make a hero of the central figure at the outset? I mentioned this to Lennox afterwards and he seemed puzzled, as if it didn't matter and was a curious question.

PD It seems typical of Lennox's reserve that his hero should emerge almost unnoticed?

JM Yes. I don't think – to offer a criticism with all the affection in the world – he had natural instincts in the theatre. He did have a wonderful capacity for characterisation. If you're in a field in the Old Testament setting of *Ruth*, in a kitchen for *A Dinner Engagement*, or the open spaces of *Nelson*, it was the characterisation that mattered. I think he looked to his librettist for essential

---

[28] Sextet, op. 47, premiered 11 July 1955 at Cheltenham College by the Melos Ensemble; Concertino, op. 49, for recorder, violin, cello and harpsichord, commissioned by Carl Dolmetsch, premiered 24 January 1956 in a BBC broadcast. The two central movements are duets.

elements – might not have changed the text very much. He would rely on a producer who could put the characters he'd drawn so sensitively into the right context.

PD   Which is the most typical of the operas?

JM   I would say the pastoral *Ruth*. I think there are elements in *Ruth* that are so totally Lennox – very beautiful. I think he wrestled a bit with the heroic. *A Dinner Engagement* is probably the one with the most consistently exquisite quality, but there's something very distinctive about *Ruth* – I think the Reaper's Chorus is one of the finest tunes he ever wrote.

PD   He hasn't been as successful with opera as Britten and Tippett, and I wonder why?

JM   He writes most beautifully for the voice – songs with piano, with orchestra and opera – handling it with sensitivity and cunning. The problem is not how he used the voice but with theatre, or how he didn't let theatre use him. Britten had a wonderful instinct for the theatre. He couldn't move into a theatre without feeling it but when Lennox walked in he probably wouldn't look around and feel himself within that proscenium arch and about to be dealing with grease-paint, dust and a performance. But I'm speculating.

PD   Do you think that what foreigners call the English reserve places a distance between him and his audience?

JM   By disposition he was tremendously gentle, infinitely kind and sensitive to others. There was nothing theatrical in his character. He was always concerned about other people. Those are things that don't immediately flourish in the artificial atmosphere of lights, footlights and the rest of it. When you move beyond this you reach those personal spiritual qualities – respect for the person and sanctity of thought. Not particularly theatrical elements.

PD   His aristocratic background implies a tradition where it was not done to be too good at something, to try too hard or to be too artistic. Is there some of that in Lennox's reserve?

JM   Possibly. It's interesting to imagine his first reactions to Paris after Oxford. It must have been a shock but very quickly excitement in the whole atmosphere and the stimulus of working with Boulanger. That was where the new Lennox emerged.

PD   And then the connection with Britten is a landmark in the history of British music?

JM   I often wish that they'd remained somewhat closer in professional terms following the collaboration in *Mont Juic*. Obviously Ben asked Lennox to write a number of pieces for Aldeburgh – and distinguished works resulted. The whole difference lay in that there was nothing entrepreneurial about Lennox – the idea of organising anything was beyond him. Ben's respect for Lennox's music is well chronicled, but he went in different directions and at a different speed. But that relationship had a tremendous bearing on the sort of music Lennox was writing up to and into the war. But when we come to some of the most passionate music he ever wrote, such as the *Four Poems of St Teresa of Avila*, he was writing for Freda and the new richness that had come into his life. She is a remarkable person. She understood Lennox in an extraordinary way; was a wonderful mother; and she helped him all sorts of ways. Publicly she was a great partner and it was an enormously happy partnership. All this came into the music.

PD It's a wonderful period – do you feel that the best of Berkeley is in the 40s and 50s?

JM Up to a point, but I believe he wrote great music afterwards – I mean great. The Third Symphony as late as 1969 is one of the most tightly wrought and powerful pieces he ever wrote. I remember vividly talking to Jean Martinon, the chief conductor of the French Radio Orchestra, who conducted the first performance at Cheltenham.[29] He was talking in terms similar to the remarks Strauss made about Elgar: 'Mais c'est formidable: c'est un grand compositeur!' As a conductor he was immensely excited by this work. So, 40s and 50s yes, but 60s and 70s too.

PD What was he like as President of the Cheltenham Festival?

JM He was a marvellous President who just wished to be there and was friendly to everybody. He seemed to take to the town and the Festival as they took to him and Freda with affection. He preferred not to have to make speeches, but he came to at least two events a day for the six years when he was President!

PD He was able to be a kind of moral force without having to be assertive. That was his genius?

JM In all his contexts, such as the Performing Right Society, he was seen as a humaniser in a fairly dry process. But he worked hard, and when he was at Cheltenham he would compose from 8.30 in morning before nipping into his car and beetling off to the morning concert. He was an adventurous driver, which was one side of him – you couldn't call it aggression – where there was that bit of assertion!

PD Later on there were some quite tough pieces – the *Windsor Variations*, the Partita and the Third Quartet. They aren't a soft ride?[30]

JM I'm glad you mention the *Windsor Variations* because one is always telling conductors they don't have to do the Divertimento or the Serenade. There is *Antiphon*, one of the finest of the late works, and there's a hard core to the *Windsor Variations*. It's true of some of the smaller works too, such as the earlier Horn Trio.

---

[29] Jean Martinon (1910–76), French conductor and composer. Symphony no. 3, op. 74, was premiered at Cheltenham on 9 July 1969.

[30] *Windsor Variations*, op. 75, premiered 18 September 1969 at St George's Chapel, Windsor by the Menuhin Festival Orchestra under Yehudi Menuhin.

PD Does it ever worry you that he recapitulates his themes, even in a piece like the Cello Concerto, in varied form? Having got a good tune, he alters it slightly. The same thing happens in the Piano Concerto, with the bluesy second subject of the first movement. Did he ever discuss that sort of thing?

JM He had a great way of encouraging you as a student to make subtle shifts in a melodic outline or a rhythmic pattern. He would say that there was always a way of repeating something slightly differently. He often said that. One of the great strengths of his music is the way he ends his pieces. I always felt he never had any real difficulty about finishing a work convincingly – a lot of composers do – but he may occasionally have had difficulty about continuing a work in mid stream. There are moments in the operas when we're waiting for something and not enough is happening. But you can apply that criticism to any number of operas, including those by the greatest operatic composers.

PD Who were Lennox's gods amongst composers?

JM He had a tremendous admiration for Fauré. There were times when we were looking at something and he would pull out a piece from the shelves and say: 'That's how he did that.' Also Ravel and Poulenc – those three Frenchmen in particular, and Ben, of course. In one or two of our earlier lessons we were looking at Palestrina masses quite rigorously. And he loved Mozart.

PD Do you see much influence of his music on British composers of the next generation?

JM Not as much as I'd like to see, in the sense that I wish they'd look at what Lennox didn't put into his scores – rather as you can do with Debussy. What has he left out and why? This is how we can guide young composers now – selectivity and restraint. His instinctive judgement was so good and so sensitive. He was never afraid to be entirely personal and he never sought any sophisticated complication in his music. I think that's a lesson younger composers could learn today.

Nicholas Maw

At BBC Broadcasting House, London, 18 October 1990

Nicholas Maw (1935–2009) was one of the leading British composers of his generation. He was born at Grantham, Lincolnshire, and studied with Berkeley when he was at the Royal Academy of Music (1955–8). After that he went to Paris to work with Nadia Boulanger and Max Deutsch. Major landmarks in his career are *Scenes and Arias* (1962); the 90-minute orchestral *Odyssey* (1987); and the opera *Sophie's Choice* (2002). From 1984 he spent most of his time in the United States but continued to maintain a high profile on both sides of the Atlantic.

NM   I heard a performance of the *Six Preludes* by Paul Hamburger[31] when I was at Wennington School, a boarding school at Wetherby in Yorkshire. He used to come and give recitals with his wife Esther Solomon and he played solo pieces as well. I think I heard some more of Lennox on the radio but I was charmed by the Preludes, which influenced my schoolboy efforts to write music myself.

PD   What was it about those pieces that attracted you?

NM   It was their Gallic elegance and a certain harmonic astringency of a tonally-based kind. Also their extreme clarity, a kind of stringiness and a very clear definition of function – there's an accompaniment and a melody. They were pieces making a statement, a meaningful way of writing music, saying something which came as a real experience. It was so beautifully done, almost like Japanese calligraphy, that it enters into the blood-steam, gets into your consciousness easily.

PD   Was it his special gift for melody?

NM   Yes: that had meaning for me because the whole question of trying to write melody is something I've addressed myself all the way through my own music.

PD   Can you bridge the gap between hearing the *Six Preludes* and when you went to Lennox as a teacher? Why did you study with him?

NM   He seemed at the time the most interesting person for me to study with at the Royal Academy. I didn't then know much about Howard Ferguson[32] although I later came to admire him and his music very much. It was the attraction of Lennox's name and the music I knew. I had a dim perception – because I was a raw provincial at the time – that he would be able to tell me something which would be useful to me. It was to do with making music, putting it together in the clearest possible way, saying what you have to say then stopping. Subsequently I turned away from the kind of interests he had and the kind of music he wrote. But I always think of what he taught me in

---

[31] Paul Hamburger (1920–2004), British pianist and writer born in Vienna.

[32] Howard Ferguson (1908–99), composer and musicologist.

those early years as very useful. In my smaller works, such as choral pieces and things for children, I can still see the influence of Lennox.

PD   I'm aware of the Berkeley tradition even in your *Odyssey*.

NM   How interesting. I wouldn't have seen it in that piece, but that doesn't make your observation any less valid. What other people see in it seems to me to be just as interesting as what the composer himself sees in it! He's merely the composer – he happens to have written it! What's important here – I'm talking about small-scale things – is this question of melody and harmony and the clarity with which it's done, trying to draw a melody which is well structured, balanced in itself and is clearly rooted in some kind of harmonic field. That aspect of Lennox's music still seems to me to be important. The melodic elements don't just float around in a kind of stellar gas: they are truly rooted in a soil of both harmony and texture within the piece.

PD   It's functional harmony?

NM   Indeed it is. You can't get more functional than directing a melody.

PD   Many people have heard Britten and Tippett in your music but the reason they don't hear Berkeley is that they don't know his music. Why isn't he as well known?

NM   There are several reasons. Britten was a phenomenon with extraordinary gifts that he was able to realise in a spectacularly evident fashion. The major works in his œuvre are operas. Anyone who can write successful operas is going to have a very high profile. The appreciation of Tippett has come much later in his life. His originality of language is something people have had to chew on for some time in order to digest it. It has taken much longer and contains riches that are not entirely evident at a first hearing, particularly in the 1940s and 50s, when his work often produced mystification if not consternation. I don't think there was anything in Lennox's work which would ever have done that. Also there is something about the English temperament which is miniaturist – I'm not suggesting he belongs to that but there is in his work great restraint of language. One side of the English tradition is very much the opposite – Vaughan Williams, whose Sixth Symphony I heard again last night. I was struck again by how full-blooded and ruddy-cheeked this music is. This side of English art is very forward in what it's presenting to the perceiver. I don't think Lennox's work is like that at all. Some of it is on a large scale but not what I would describe as grand. Do you see my point?

PD   I'm not sure I do. The Third Symphony packs quite a punch, and the Piano Concerto and Two-Piano Concerto are both large-scale pieces with melodic appeal. Could they be popular if played more?

NM   It's always difficult to say whether somebody could be popular or not. There have been some extraordinary surprises in the past. It might have something to do with fluency, although we know that Lennox agonised about his music and worked extremely hard at it. He didn't write quickly but has a large output. There are many elements in Lennox's music which sound remarkably natural and spontaneous but in the larger pieces you can sometimes hear the formal wheels grinding. It's the opposition of those two things. Sometimes his formal schemes are a little too academic – they evidently fall into traditional patterns where he could have been more adventurous.

PD But in recapitulations he usually doesn't repeat his themes the same way, so there's a continuous invention which, with a good tune, almost goes against him?

NM Yes – that does happen and that's the best of him. With this kind of natural artefact, heard and put straight down on paper, it's difficult for any composer to make that happen all through the piece without the intellectual exercise invading the process, especially when these elements are so transparent.

PD Do you see a debt to Mozart?

NM He did revere Mozart above all – he had some of the same kind of ability in spontaneous regeneration of material throughout the piece, as in the Horn Trio and the String Trio.

PD What function has the orchestra in Lennox's music?

NM That's another side of his musical character. I admire his orchestration – that certainly has a French quality, with Ravel as an influence as well as Roussel. At his best you feel the material – that particular oboe or flute solo – is being invented on that instrument at the time. A very admirable quality.

PD Talking about the English temperament, does the man fit the music?

NM I think it does. He was an extraordinarily charming and kind person. His dislikes were expressed with irony in a low key, which I always found one of the most attractive qualities about him. He was also extremely encouraging and capable of genuinely appreciating things which were very far removed from his own work, because he felt he couldn't do it and admired somebody who could. I found him an almost wholly admirable human being. To draw an analogy between him and the work in those terms is rather more difficult. There are works I hold in high affection and others I don't. I very much like the Auden cycle containing 'O lurcher-loving collier',[33] the *Ronsard Sonnets* for tenor, the St Teresa poems, and the opera *Ruth*. I never saw *Nelson*.

PD In terms of Lennox's personality we've left something out. Do you think his religious beliefs are central to his life and work?

NM Yes, I do. I didn't know him all that well, particularly in later years, but I think his Catholicism informed his whole life in a meaningful way. In this he seems to have an affinity with a most unlikely character such as Bruckner. There is a sense in which his work is an offering up to the deity. I don't want to say that in too pompous a way, because Lennox was the opposite of pompous, but he was, in a humble way, doing what he could do as well as he could do it in the eyes of God.

---

[33] The second song of *Five Poems* (W. H. Auden), op. 53, commissioned by Alice Esty and premiered by her 26 March 1959 at Carnegie Recital Hall, New York.

PD I quite agree. Lennox studied with Boulanger: so did you. Was he a perfect Boulanger student?

NM He remained faithful to her for all his life – much more than I did, I'm rather ashamed to say. I don't think I know what a perfect Boulanger student is. Even that generation of eminent American composers she taught were very different animals. His work and personality were informed by a strong Gallic strain in his temperament.

   I always remember that early photograph of him together with Ravel, when he came to Oxford to get a DMus [1928; see plate 4]. There's the slim young Lennox looking at a score with Ravel by his side. That summed up how much this whole French connection meant to Lennox right from the beginning of his life.

PD Do you feel his music is French? Has it put people off here?

NM There is a strong French strain in the music which is not allied to a figure like Poulenc but more to Roussel.[34] I agree that there are surprising tough qualities in the music – the Third Symphony is a good example. It's absolutely not salon music, although there are pieces in a light-hearted manner. I think there's a tendency in this country to think of all French music as salon music [*Laughs*], which couldn't be more unjust!

PD Britten once told him to do what he wanted regardless of what Boulanger would think.

NM That's a typical Ben remark. I suppose there was a feeling in the early part of his career that she was looking over his shoulder and perhaps directing his pen.

PD Did he need someone to look up to – first her and then Ben?

NM I think he probably did. His humility was extraordinary: he never ceased to talk to you about what he admired – in other people's work. I found it difficult to get him to talk about his own music. I had to badger him to show me things he was doing – that's not surprising – but even to go through what he'd done before.

   One thing I always remember was a time when Nadia came over to conduct a concert. I had deliberately divorced myself from the Nadia camp because one had to be either right in it or right out. I found the people surrounding her very stifling. Lennox insisted that I accompany him to the concert, where she accompanied Menuhin playing the Stravinsky Violin Concerto, a somewhat fractured performance, and then came her party piece, the Fauré Requiem. Afterwards everybody had to queue up backstage and see her. Lennox made me go; there was a tremendous affectionate greeting from him to her and *vice versa*; and then he suddenly turned round and said: 'Of course you remember Nicholas, don't you?' There was a terrible silence, which seemed to last half an hour but must have been three seconds, and she stretched out her arms towards me and said: 'I forgive you everything!'

[34] Albert Roussel (1869–1937) wrote four symphonies, ballets and opera.

[*Laughs*] Lennox had intuited that I was no longer a member of the Boulanger family and he wanted me to be.

As a teacher he had the most wonderful way of encouraging you in your own imaginative enterprises which I liked very much. He never said you should do something in a certain way. He'd say: 'I should try this', and never suggested pieces to write but asked you what you were doing. He sometimes said he thought you might have bitten off more than you could chew.

PD Richard Bennett has said that Lennox was too kind to be a good teacher.

NM I have wondered about this – he was so considerate to everybody, no matter who they were. It might have been good for someone to have some martinet who said: 'I insist you do this but when you leave me you can do what you like.' It's difficult to know because that might have been disastrous. It could have been something I couldn't have handled, that my temperament wouldn't have been able to deal with at all. On the whole I'm grateful for how Lennox did it.

PD He had the instinct to know that David Bedford should be sent to Luigi Nono and not to struggle with him himself![35]

NM He did have some most unlikely pupils like Brian Ferneyhough. One wonders what they said to each other but I'm sure Lennox was just as kind and considerate as to those who were closer to him.

PD We agree that everybody loved him and he had nothing whatever to do with the whole promotional mechanism.

NM Nothing at all. He left that entirely to other people and he was always grateful when it happened. Another thing was that he never told me when pieces of his were going to be played, even prestigious performances.

PD It's hard to imagine Lennox surviving as a composer without Freda's support.

NM It was wonderful to go into the household with three young boys. Freda understood the centre of the man in a beautiful way and what he was trying to do. His work was offered up, as we've said, in a humble way to whoever would take it.

---

[35] David Bedford (1937–2011), versatile composer with a wide range of activities ranging from popular music to music in education. Luigi Nono (1924–90), prominent Italian figure in the European avant-garde.

Malcolm Williamson

At Rooksnest House, Old Stevenage, Hertfordshire, 22 February 1991

Malcolm Williamson (1931–2003) was born in Sidney and studied at the NSW State Conservatory with Eugene Goossens. After moving to London in 1953 he worked with Elisabeth Lutyens and Erwin Stein; gained the influential support of Sir Adrian Boult; and was recognised as one of the leading composers of his generation. Williamson's prolific output, drawing on a wide range of musical styles, benefited from his virtuosity as pianist and organist. He was appointed Master of the Queen's Music in 1975 and awarded the CBE in the following year.

PD   When did you first become aware of Lennox Berkeley's music?

MW   I'm an Australian and after the war we had a little knowledge of Vaughan Williams, and obviously Elgar, Delius, Bax and so on, through my teacher Sir Eugene Goossens.[36] Lennox Berkeley's music exploded on us. I learnt the piano pieces and the songs and thought this was an absolutely new voice. French culture meant a great deal to us but we had thought of English music as what Lizzie Lutyens used to call 'cow-patch' Cotswolds music.[37] To discover what the English had in Lennox Berkeley was a revelation. There was a cleanness and a classicism. I think people are wrong in saying it came from Nadia Boulanger. I believe that Lennox himself was responsible. He had a clear clean-cut mind. I'm sick to death of hearing him associated with Britten, because it was a much more profound mind. There was spirituality there right from the beginning.

We in Australia picked that up and when I came to England in 1950, and I became a Catholic, I suppose it gave me a deeper contact with Lennox. I first set eyes on him on 21 November – the eve of St Cecilia's Day – in 1953. It was a bizarre occasion of the Catholic Musicians' Guild. If I dare say it, they were more Catholic than musical! We had Rubbra, Egon Wellesz and Lennox. There was mass in the morning then a terrible lunch and we had to listen to speeches afterwards. Rubbra – a wonderful composer – said he came to the Catholic church through devious and macabre paths. Lennox got up and said he came to the church through even more macabre paths – nobody knew where to quite put their faces! He was looking at me, a young composer who had only just come out of the egg, and it was almost like seeing God come out of heaven! Just to set eyes on the greatest composer since the English renaissance of Vaughan Williams and so on. I was rather frightened of him – looking back, I can't think why because he was the least frightening of people. What was most frightening about him was this modesty. Every time you said you loved his 'Ode du premier jour de Mai', or something like that, he

---

[36] Eugene Goossens (1893–1962), British composer and conductor, member of a distinguished line of musicians, who worked in the USA and Australia.

[37] Elisabeth Lutyens (1906–83), pioneering British serial composer who also wrote for films.

would say: 'Of course, that's just an early work.'[38] He never acknowledged a compliment but none the less I thought he was a great master.

Richard Rodney Bennett and I were both working with Elisabeth Lutyens and we were coming back from her house one evening when Richard said: 'Who is the greatest composer in England?' I said: 'There can be no two ways about it – Lennox Berkeley.' He said: 'I'm so pleased to hear you say that because I'm going to have lessons from him.' Richard had a scholarship to the Academy. Some time later I asked him what he thought of his lessons. He said that Lennox was a guide, a mentor, not really a teacher at all, since he wasn't strict enough: he just pushed you in the right direction. Lennox certainly pushed him in the right direction. He put into his music a lyricism that wasn't there before. He was also a very hard taskmaster but it was all said in half-voice. I don't think anybody realised quite how serious and tough Lennox was. I'd always loved the music but sometimes I felt that it sounded soft but underneath that softness – quoting from Schumann – it was guns covered with roses.[39] It was very hard.

Moving to the end of Lennox's life, that Fourth Symphony is the most amazing piece. It sounds genial, pliable, but is structurally sound – the same applies to all the symphonies. Also the supposedly light music. Criticism is levelled against Lennox for being too middle-of-the-road. But it wasn't until my Violin Concerto was coupled with Lennox's and I listened to it over and over again that I realised how very steely it was.[40]

PD What pieces made that initial impact in Australia?

MW The piano Preludes in the first place; the early songs such as 'Night covers up the rigid land' – it's better than Auden's poem;[41] the first String Quartet and the chamber works that followed it. He had the veneration of Goossens and we thought that here is something entirely outside our orbit. Subsequently came the Serenade for Strings, the Divertimento, the Sinfonietta – works that sounded like a soufflé. But if you want to make a soufflé you have to have a very good recipe!

The greatest composition teacher in Australia, Margaret Sutherland, used to use the piano Preludes as teaching pieces.[42]

PD What is it that's so special about them?

MW When I asked Colin Horsley what made the first of the Preludes work so

---

[38] *Ode du premier jour de mai*, op. 14/2, premiered 20 February 1945 at Fyvie Hall, London, by Sophie Wyss and the composer.

[39] In the *Neue zeitschrift für musik*, 1841, Schumann said: 'Chopin's works are guns buried in flowers.'

[40] Yehudi Menuhin and the Menuhin Festival Orchestra under Boult. HMV ASD 2759; EMI British Composers CDMS 6612-2.

[41] 'Night covers up the rigid land', op. 14/2, dedicated to Britten.

[42] Margaret Sutherland (1897–1984), composer and pianist who studied with Bax and supported other Australian composers.

well he said he thought of murmuring flutes – and I realised suddenly what Lennox meant.

In my Mass, written after Lennox's death, I used the last Prelude.[43] It's one of the subtlest pieces of composition this century. Why is it that with so few notes Lennox has managed to say so much?

PD   It's his own personality too.

MW   But it's also technique. There are lots of composers but very few *total* composers, and Lennox was a total composer. This comes through in the symphonies and the concertos for one and two pianos, and in the gigantic – I'm talking about conception – Piano Sonata written for Clifford Curzon.[44] It's a faultless stupefying masterpiece. There's not a bad note in it – what more can I say than that?

PD   What was it like when you went to see Lennox for the first time?

MW   Terrifying because he was so modest – and he wanted to talk about *The Turn of the Screw*. I didn't. I have to tell you that Ben Britten has never been my composer. I was working in Boosey & Hawkes for Erwin Stein, for whom the world began and ended with Britten. He said about Lennox: 'It is a pity he is not such a good composer but he is a nice man.' I disagreed.

The English Opera Group had a season at Sadler's Wells and I was earning practically no money. An inveterate smoker, I had just enough money for a week's supply of cigarettes. I was waiting in the freezing cold – couldn't afford gloves – for the bus to take me to Sadlers Wells and thought that nothing on earth would persuade me to see *The Turn of the Screw* again, but nothing will prevent me from going to see *Nelson* for the second time – and I'd bought my ticket. As I was getting my bus fare out it all dropped down and the entire pack of cigarettes. I then had no cigarettes for a whole week. I got to Sadler's Wells and what do think was on? *The Turn of the Screw*!

PD   What did you show Lennox?

MW   I took him work in progress, and he was gentle and precise. I don't care whether his ancestry was Scottish or French, but he had the precision they both have. There's a relationship between them. Lennox was able to see to the heart of things. I took him my first two piano sonatas. I think enough time has passed for me to say the truth about Elisabeth Lutyens. Liz had no sense of form; Erwin Stein, who also taught me, had no sense of sound; Lennox had both. And he never took a penny from me. The Berkeleys were kindness itself. It was all very well to have Stein and Lutyens, but the person who could see the whole piece – sound, shape and tidiness – was Lennox.

---

[43]   *Mass of St Etheldreda on Themes of Lennox Berkeley* (1990) for SATB and organ.

[44]   Piano Sonata, op. 20, premiered 22 July 1946 at the Wigmore Hall, London, by Clifford Curzon.

PD   Does *Nelson* stand out?[45]

MW   Certainly. I shall never forget Nancy Evans as Lady Nelson in that wonderful scene looking out over Regent's Park – she told me many times how much that meant to her – and the closing scene with the death of Nelson. It's a most beautifully constructed opera.

PD   Britten helped Lennox in various ways, encouraged him by putting on the operas in Aldeburgh and so on.

MW   Britten was a very successful careerist. To get grants you had to have some other composers. Lennox was obsessed with music – not careerism. He was such a gentle person.
     I'm quite proud of the fact that I was one of the judges of the Guinness competition that gave Michael a prize [1977]. It was the best work submitted. At that stage Lennox would not pass any of his son's music. We were sitting in the garden one wonderful sunny afternoon and he said: 'What Michael has to learn is that he must take a tiny germ of music and develop it and not just imagine one enormous panorama.' I can still hear Freda saying: 'Lennox, Lennox, don't you dare say that!'

PD   What was Freda's role?

MW   Was there ever a happier marriage? She was never afraid to be critical, but there were other people who supported Lennox, like his publisher Sheila MacCrindle.[46] I was President of the Royal Philharmonic Orchestra and, although I'm no conductor, I had to conduct a concert. It was very nice of them – they wanted the President to conduct. I insisted on their putting in Lennox's *Serenade for Strings*. I'd told Lennox some time earlier and his reply? 'Of course, it's only an early work.'

PD   This self-denigrating modesty is quite an obstacle?

MW   He was like that but music was what interested him.

PD   Was it anything to do with his religious faith? How did that affect his life and work?

MW   It was terribly important. I can remember that at Aldeburgh Lennox and I went to Mass together. To him Latin was a great comfort, the language of holiness through tradition – as it is to me. His faith was a natural way of life to him – as it is to Freda. Long before his actual conversion in 1929 he was interested. Michael said to me once: 'The one thing that will make Daddy furious is if anybody makes mock of religion.'

PD   Are the religious pieces therefore some of his finest?

MW   Every work Lennox ever wrote is religious. Never mind the subject or anything else – like Palestrina he was a religious composer. He could

---

[45] *Nelson*, op. 41, premiered 12 September 1954 at Sadler's Wells, following a concert reading at the Wigmore Hall which, according to Basil Douglas – see his interview below – Britten helped to arrange.

[46] See Hugh Wood, 'Sheila MacCrindle: Business as Usual' [obituary], *Guardian*, 24 July 1993.

conceive of life only in religious terms – like Poulenc, but he was a better composer. His faith was unshakeable – it wasn't a struggle.

PD People have said his conversion was something to do with Nadia Boulanger.

MW Fiddlesticks! It wouldn't have mattered if she'd been a Mohammedan!

PD Lennox actually said he liked Britten's music better than his own. Isn't that crippling?

MW I suppose it is but it's exactly the sort of thing he would have said. I have a letter written after the first performance of my *Hammarskjöld Portrait*, which arrived the next morning.[47] He'd followed the score with Desmond Shawe-Taylor at home and wrote the letter praising me to the skies, saying he wished he could write a piece of music as good as mine. I don't wish to praise myself or the piece, but it was Lennox in character. It was simply typical of Lennox to draw attention away from himself. This was part of his asceticism. At that meeting of the Catholic Musicians Guild Egon Wellesz got up and said that Stravinsky's *Symphony of Psalms* was not genuinely Byzantine.[48] Lennox came up quite violently and said: 'Possibly not, but it's a masterpiece!'

In church music Lennox admired what might be called the George Malcolm sound, heard at Westminster Cathedral and on the Continent.[49] It's what the Sistine Chapel should sound like but doesn't! In a good performance of 'The Lord is my Shepherd'[50] or the masses you really need to hear that sharp, almost nasal sound rather than the Anglican hoot. That's how his counterpoint should sound – and he knew his counterpoint.

PD He did all those strict counterpoint exercises with Boulanger and it came out in his own music.

MW Certainly. It's important to say that we are the legatees of Lennox Berkeley – in counterpoint and chastity of line and structure. Like a good butcher he's cut away the fat and kept the lean meat.

PD Do you think of Lennox in terms of Mozart?

MW He had the classicism of Mozart and the spirit of adventure. He was not a Beethovenian. I didn't realise until later that he had a terrible reaction to Bax, Vaughan Williams and Elgar. He found them impure, and his whole Gallic spirit rebelled against them. It was Lennox, not Britten, who cleaned up British music. His legacy will go on longer than we think – even though he perpetually denigrated himself. It's easy to write a piece with lots of notes but difficult to write one with few notes. But to make sure that they are all the right notes – this Lennox Berkeley did.

[47] *Hammarskjöld Portrait*, for soprano and string orchestra, 1974.
[48] Egon Wellesz (1885–1974), Viennese composer and musicologist who settled in Oxford in 1939. Leading authority on Byzantine music.
[49] George Malcolm (1917–97), British keyboard player and conductor, master of the music at Westminster Cathedral from 1947–59.
[50] 'The Lord is my Shepherd', op. 91, no. 1 (1975), now a widely performed anthem for treble solo, SATB and organ. See plate 19 for a facsimile page from the autograph score,.

3 FAMILY

Freda Berkeley

At 12 Hereford Mansions, London W2, 28 January 1991

Lady Berkeley, née Bernstein, was born in London in 1923. Both her parents had died by the time she was four and a half, and so she grew up with maternal grandparents, foster-parents in a country parsonage and boarding school. In 1941 she qualified at Miss Kerr-Sander's Secretarial College and got a job with the BBC as secretary to Lord Kingsale in the Monitoring Service near Evesham. Through the BBC she moved to Caversham and then London, where she met Lennox Berkeley in 1944.[51]

PD   When did you first become aware of Lennox?

FB   The Music Department was at 35 Marylebone High Street in 1944, and I went as a secretary to the Music Programmes Organiser – Ronald Biggs. Not the Great Train Robber – the other one! I was in the canteen and a colleague said to me: 'There's Lennox Berkeley' – and he was going up to get some food or drink. That was the first time I was aware of him. Subsequently his secretary went to America and I was asked to take on Lennox as well as Ronald Biggs and Basil Douglas. Lennox was then building the programmes for the BBC Symphony Orchestra, a wartime job. That was how it was – we were all together.

PD   And you took on more than the secretarial part of the job?

FB   Yes, but that wasn't until 1946, when we were married in December.

PD   What was Lennox like in an institutional post?

FB   He'd come wandering in most mornings, rather later than he should have done, and couldn't wait to get away in the evening and back to his own work. He was composing in his own time and, had he not been colour-blind, would have gone into the navy. He was in the Home Guard, did fire-watching on Broadcasting House, and was an Air Raid Warden. He happened to be in the Reform Club when the Carlton next door was bombed. He helped to get the books out of the library.

PD   Did you have any musical training yourself?

FB   No, not at all. I learnt the piano, never practised, and at school I was always thought to be tone-deaf. Lennox always thought I ought to have been trained to be a singer but I don't know how that would have worked out.

PD   Do you remember what music meant the most to him when you first met him.

FB   It was the time of the first performance of *Peter Grimes* – he had a great

---

[51] For full biographical details of Freda Berkeley, see Scotland, *Lennox and Freda*.

admiration for Britten. Mozart he always loved and the French composers Fauré, Poulenc and Ravel, needless to say, who sent him to Nadia Boulanger. Debussy too.

PD Did he say much about his time in Paris?

FB Yes, he talked a lot. There was an old friend, John Greenidge, who'd shared a flat with him in Paris. We saw him a lot, and he was Michael's other godfather.[52]

PD Was Paris a sort of growing-up phase?

FB I don't know about that. He'd already been to Merton College, adored Oxford and had made a lot of friends there. It was a different phase when he lived in Montmartre, became a Catholic and was very influenced by Nadia.

PD What did his religion mean to Lennox?

FB An enormous amount. He took his Catholicism very seriously indeed and went to Mass every Sunday. I've recently found two Catholic prayer books given to him in 1924 and 1926 which show he was considering Catholicism as early as that, which I didn't know.

PD Do you think his conversion had anything to do with Nadia Boulanger?

FB It was certainly to do with Nadia: she was a very devout Catholic. When we were in Monaco with her she'd go off to Mass every Sunday.

PD What was she like?

FB She was always Mademoiselle until her last years, when Lennox allowed himself to call her Nadia. He was devoted to her, respected her enormously and was always bowled over by any performance she gave of the Fauré Requiem.

PD Was she a kind of mother-figure?

FB Not really. He was devoted to his own mother, whom he looked after when she was an invalid in the last years of her life. Nadia was very much the professor to him. There was a great bond between them, with religion playing a major part binding them together.

PD It's difficult to give an idea of what Lennox was like to people who haven't met him.

FB He was a very private person. When we were first married we went to concerts, to dinner with friends and so on.

PD I always think of you both in terms of a house – 8 Warwick Avenue in Little Venice.

FB After we were married in December 1946 we moved to Warwick Avenue in June the following year. It was a very long span in that house.

PD I always think of it as an environment that reflected your life with Lennox.

---

[52] With Benjamin Britten.

FB I think that's true. When I first saw it I said we couldn't possibly live there because we'd never have enough furniture to fill it. But it became so cluttered that it was an appalling job clearing it when I eventually left after he died.

PD Had you any idea what it was going to be like being married to a composer?

FB None at all – I never thought I'd marry a composer! In fact it was wonderful because he was such a marvellous person. He was so wrapped up in his own work and yet tremendously protective of me and the family. I think I was dead lucky.

PD Did it ever worry you that he was rather impractical?

FB Not at all. In fact I think I rather liked it. That's how I felt a composer should be.

PD Many people have said how lucky Lennox was but did you feel you had a hand in his career?

FB Only marginally, I think. Sometimes, if he wanted something to set, I found possible poems for him, which he sometimes used, sometimes didn't. Apart from that I was just a background for him.

PD I think you're being far too modest but what were his routines like?

FB They were very rigid. He always composed in the morning; in the afternoon he taught pupils either at the Academy or privately; and then went out for a walk. After tea he'd start again and work till dinner. Very often he'd get up at 6.00 or 6.30, go down to his study, and work before breakfast. He was tremendously hard-working.

PD When he was working you'd hear the piano?

FB Absolutely: he couldn't compose without a piano. He always envied Ben who could. When we were travelling Lennox would make little notes to refer to – but he needed the piano.

PD The connection between Lennox and Ben is a fascinating subject that will be discussed well into the future.

FB Undoubtedly.

PD What did he say about the music and the man?

FB He was devoted to Ben and had an enormous admiration for him. He said that Ben was a genius, and for that reason alone it would have been impossible for him to have gone on sharing a house with him. It gave Lennox rather an inferiority complex about his own work.

PD He felt he owed him a great deal?

FB I think he felt he'd learnt a lot from Ben.

PD Did you get any impression of what Ben thought about Lennox's music?

FB   There's a card from Ben saying Lennox's *Missa brevis* was marvellous, and he'd like to hear it done by the Westminster Cathedral Choir.[53]

PD   Ben supported Lennox by putting things on at Aldeburgh.[54]

FB   Absolutely. He was very loyal, and he and Peter Pears commissioned things.

PD   What was it like when Lennox was having a piece performed?

FB   He was very nervous beforehand, got in an awful state, and was tremendously relieved when it was over.

PD   Do you remember the premiere of *Nelson*?

FB   That was thrilling and he was very excited about it. It's only sad that it didn't have a better production or libretto. There was some wonderful music in it; Lennox realised that; and he was disappointed that it didn't go on. It was well received at the time but there were faults with it.

PD   Stephen Banfield, in *The Musical Times*, once said that nobody has given any thought to the fact that Lennox might have been identifying with Nelson in the opera.[55]

FB   I certainly don't think that! He'd always admired Nelson as a character. He'd read Carola Oman's book – a wonderful picture of the period too – and, of course, his father was a naval officer. He'd have liked to have gone into the navy himself – but the navy might have suffered! [*Laughs*]

PD   How did being colour-blind affect Lennox's life?

FB   He was only red–green colour-blind. He couldn't see a field of poppies because the red would merge into green, or apples on a tree, or holly-berries. I don't think it affected his life apart from being turned down for the Navy because of it. He did drive but knew what was happening from the way the lights were placed.

PD   Was his colour-blindness the reason he was more attached to literature than painting?

FB   I don't think that's true. He loved pictures, but when we went to exhibitions together he enjoyed looking at things from the point of view of patterns.

PD   Did Lennox mind the interruption of having pupils?

FB   I think he always had a great sympathy for young people and felt that older composers should help younger ones. He said he learnt a lot from his pupils. He did BBC auditions for a time and wasn't much in sympathy with that use of his time. Meetings he didn't enjoy, but teaching at home, where all his Academy pupils came, gave him a lot of pleasure.

---

[53] *Missa Brevis*, op. 57, premiered 12 March 1960 at Westminster Cathedral by the Westminster Cathedral Choir under Francis Cameron.

[54] In Britten's lifetime there were twenty-four performances, including repeats, of works by Berkeley at Aldeburgh Festivals. This compares with twenty-two by Tippet and twenty-seven by Frank Bridge, which included several short songs.

[55] Stephen Banfield, 'The Cultivated Ear', *Musical Times* 132 (January 1991), 709.

PD He wrote for a marvellous collection of performers.

FB Dennis Brain, Janet Craxton, Yehudi Menuhin, James Galway and more – they all became marvellous friends. A great supporter was Colin Horsley, who pioneered his piano music.

PD Were you aware of Lennox's music being more fashionable at some times rather than others?

FB Yes, indeed. I think it was inevitable. When we were first married the Serenade and Divertimento were played a great deal; then he wrote the St Teresa songs, which made a big impact on people; and his music was much to the fore then. When the atonal music came in he wanted to try it.

PD You prefer the old tunes?

FB Yes, I do! The one-act operas have wonderful tunes – *A Dinner Engagement* and I wish *Ruth* could be done more often. I don't necessarily think of it as an opera: I think Lennox didn't either.

PD How did Lennox respond to criticism?

FB He never rushed to look at criticism of his own works, but he took it seriously. If he read an unfavourable review of something he'd always say that he thought the critic had a point and he'd go to the piano and look at that particular part again.

PD Julian Bream said that Lennox probably didn't read his proofs, but he thought you did.

FB Absolutely untrue! [*Laughs*] He did read the proofs, if not always very carefully.

PD What would Lennox have been like if he'd become the Earl of Berkeley?

FB He always felt that he'd been lucky not to have been the Earl of Berkeley. He could never then have made his own life as a composer in the musical world. He would have had to run the estate; then there's the Berkeley hunt – Lennox could never have taken that on. I think he honestly felt it was good that things worked out the way they did.

PD He did hold public responsibility as President of the Performing Right Society and other roles.

FB I think at times he found that exhausting but it was a good cause he wanted to support.

PD Did Lennox ever say much about meeting Stravinsky?

FB He talked about him in the Paris days, admired him enormously, but his son Soulima was more of a friend.

PD What are your favourite pieces?

FB The piano music and songs, especially the French ones.

PD If we had to choose one composer who meant the most to Lennox who would it be?

FB   Mozart undoubtedly. He liked the Verdi operas too.

PD   What was his attitude to conducting his own music?

FB   He didn't really enjoy it. He wanted to have a go but wasn't a good conductor – he hadn't enough authority. He enjoyed the thought of it more than actually doing it.

PD   All the same, the recordings he conducted came out quite well. But was his attitude to playing the piano in public the same?

FB   Yes, he'd always say he wasn't a pianist. In the *Six Preludes* he'd play four and say the other two were too difficult for him. He played the piano for the recording of the Violin and Piano Sonatina with Frederick Grinke, but somebody else in the studio took over and played a bit that Lennox couldn't manage.[56]

PD   What was his sense of humour?

FB   It was wonderful – that was one of the best things of our marriage. We used to laugh so much. I always knew when Lennox had seen the funny side of things and even if we were at a function I would see him trying to hide a smile. But when we were in New York things that seemed funny at the time were not in retrospect, because the memory lapses foretold the beginning of the Alzheimer's.

PD   But he was very vague before that.

FB   When people ask me when his Alzheimer's started, it's almost impossible to say because he was so vague. He even said that whereas some composers burnt their manuscripts others lost them – like him! [*Laughs*] I'm sure there are things still to come to light.

PD   How French was Lennox?

FB   Very. Whenever we went to France people always thought he was French because he spoke so perfectly. He always had a great sympathy with French writers and composers: he loved Paris. I remember when he took me there for the first time just after the war – he was excited at the idea of showing it to me.

PD   He went back to Paris even after the war had started.

FB   He had a flat in Montmartre with a friend living there who was killed in the war.[57] I have great regrets about that because after the war was over he heard that there were things of his in store, but he didn't want to know about it. Quite a lot must have been lost then. Had I known more about things I'd have done something about it myself. He said he'd brought all his papers and manuscripts with him, but, knowing Lennox, I don't know.

PD   Was Lennox at all political or patriotic?

---

[56] Rubbra–Berkeley–Reizenstein, Frederick Grinke (violin), composers (piano), Dutton Epoch CDLX 7232.

[57] 1 Cité Chaptal, Paris IX, shared with the Corsican N. José Raffalli (1899–*c.* 1941).

FB I wouldn't say so – certainly not political.

PD In the letters he was very much behind the war effort.

FB He was very keen to do something and was far from being a pacifist.

PD When he was working, were there any difficulties?

FB Yes, if he got stuck he'd get very depressed. Usually he'd go out for a walk, thinking about it, pacing around. A sort of gloom descended on the household and then, when he'd got the idea, one heard him getting very excited on the ivories! One knew he'd found the solution. He never inflicted any of that on me. I knew him so well that I sensed what was happening and we'd talk about it.

PD He never grumbled at you!

FB Not really: I think he was very tolerant. [*Laughs*]

PD It's rare to find composers who don't take it out on the people they live with!

FB I know, especially when the children were little and in and out of his study. He had a wonderfully even personality, but if anything infuriated him he could get really angry.

PD What sort of things?

FB He got very worked up about the loss of Latin in the Mass, wrote letters to *The Times* and *The Tablet* about it, and he set the Latin text.

PD The *Missa Brevis* can be done in Latin or in English.

FB Rather under protest, I think.

PD I think I've played down the religious works in my studies of Lennox's music. Do you feel they're the most important?

FB Possibly, yes. He chose to write anthems for the church – they were tremendously important to him.

PD That was very evident in the Memorial Requiem Mass at Westminster Cathedral.[58]

FB I wish he could have heard that – I expect he did.

---

[58] Memorial Requiem Mass for Lennox Randal Francis Berkeley 1893–1989, at Westminster Cathedral, 20 March 1990.

Michael Berkeley

At BBC Broadcasting House, London, 27 November 1990

Michael Berkeley, born in London in 1948, is the eldest son of Lennox Berkeley and a godson of Benjamin Britten. He was a chorister at Westminster Cathedral, attended the Royal Academy of Music, and was affected profoundly by his studies with Richard Rodney Bennett. Alongside a substantial catalogue of prominently commissioned works, including four operas, Michael Berkeley has maintained a parallel career as broadcaster in radio and TV, notably with the long-running *Private Passions* on BBC Radio 3.

PD   What are your earliest memories of your father as a composer?

MB   Every morning he would be in his study working on his piano, and any interruption of this process was viewed with some dismay. He seldom got angry, just rather wretched after a while! [*Laughs*] Then my mother would be summoned to deal with us. Music was always there in the way that he would sing us to sleep and he would show us things on the piano. Music was such a central part of my life that I can't say that I was suddenly aware of him being a composer.

PD   Do you remember what he played or sang in those early days?

MB   Whenever he was in the middle of composing something he would hum certain phrases rather self-consciously. He would seldom sing his own music, but if you caught him unawares, having a drink or reading the paper, you might suddenly see an expression come over his face and he'd start humming a tune – usually his music. If he was singing you to sleep it might be Verdi or Mozart, from a concert he'd been to, and if he was stuck in the morning he'd study their scores – and Britten – to see how they'd done it.

PD   What pieces did you get to know first?

MB   The first music that interested me was what he wrote for Westminster Cathedral. When I was a chorister at the age of about eight I was able to think about it as something he had actually written. I remember *Nelson* going on and being very excited about it. Because it was a new opera in London there was quite a lot of attention in the papers. I remember even then that there were problems over the libretto, which caused him a certain consternation.

PD   1954 was an extraordinary year, with the launch of *A Dinner Engagement* as well.

MB   I don't think there was ever a period like that again. He was riding the crest of a wave. As I got older he seemed to become less fashionable in some ways. Although he was always enormously respected, the premieres were greeted with less excitement. But he was always at peace with his own gifts. We live in an age where the quiet personality is unfashionable – a big splash is much more important. I used to get slightly frustrated with his music as a student because I wanted it to do something more sensational. But now, with the benefit of age and a small amount of wisdom, I have come to see that he was very much his own man. You've said he was like Fauré and he's compared himself to Fauré in some ways. I think that to achieve that sort of position, that technique and consistent quality of invention, is no small thing. He was very happy with that. He didn't feel he was going to be a Britten or the more flamboyant side of a Walton or a Tippett. He knew he had something to offer and something to say. It takes time for us to see and value those qualities.

For me there are certain works which will always stand the test of time. Little masterpieces of their sort but not on the grand scale which perhaps knocks you out and makes you rethink your life and philosophy as some composers do. It's not that sort of gift. He knew that and he never cared what people wrote about him. A lot of people say they don't read critics, and you know they do. But he really didn't, and I could never understand it. That was a side of his character that I found slightly frustrating – I wanted him to be more frail, more human. He could live in his own world and get on with his own music. I sometimes felt that he wasn't very up on what was happening in the world around him. Some composers, like Britten and Tippett, felt the need to express that; others less so.

From his Boulanger days, but also in his character, he was a craftsman. He loved writing music because of the craft. That's not to say he was a cerebral composer – he was very emotional and hated music that he thought was purely cerebral. He always understood fundamentally the importance of having the technique in order to get the ideas onto the page. That's one of the things he always taught me and his students. Of course, the most important thing is having something to say, but if you haven't got a means of getting it onto the page it's not much use.

PD   Which works have these special qualities?

MB   When I went to the Royal Academy I was able to conduct one or two pieces. I did the *Four Poems of St Teresa of Avila*. The slow movement 'Let mine eyes see Thee, sweet Jesus of Nazareth' brings tears to my eyes every time I hear it – a perfect piece of music. The Serenade and the Divertimento are wonderfully crafted. There are broader canvasses that work – the Third Symphony is very powerful because it's muscular and taut. At that time I was working a little bit with him and I can remember trying to tempt him to push out even further. I suggested the side-drum rim-shot on the last chord! [*Laughs*] Luckily he was his own man; there was a wry smile on his face; but he did like talking to me about his music.

He wasn't a very good teacher for me – it's difficult for a father to teach a son anyway – because he wasn't a disciplinarian. He was good for people who went to him already with a certain technique, getting them to be themselves. I needed the whip and you couldn't associate him with that. I then went to Richard Rodney Bennett, who'd studied with him. He said: 'Lennox would never be able to give you what I'm going to give you', which was six of the best, technically. [*Laughs*]

PD You talked about his unworldly quality. Isn't that part of his religious faith?

MB I think they went hand in hand. 'Let mine eyes see Thee' brought from him some of the strongest emotions. The sacred went straight to his heart and the music came back out again. When he was dealing with secular passion there's a slight politeness, a niceness. Even in the humour: it's almost dated. The pieces that move me deeply are either abstract instrumental compositions or settings of poets he particularly admired. The *Stabat mater* is another good example.

PD Do you remember him as a conductor?

MB He was not a wonderful conductor. He was a good enough musician to do it technically, and it was interesting for people to have these performances just to see how it should go. He was neither strict enough in the Stravinskian sense, with a tight little beat which would drive the orchestra on, or flamboyant enough to make large gestures. The music he recorded was all right, but no more than that. There are pieces that could benefit from new recordings, such as *Mont Juic*, which he wrote with Britten. It is interesting from the point of view of tempi but I can see places which could be made to tell even more strongly with more emotional elasticity.

PD The connection with Britten must be one of the most fascinating relationships in British music.

MB Britten was a fundamental part of my childhood and upbringing. He ran through my musical life like one of the two rails of a railway, because my father was so involved with him both personally and musically, although by the time I was growing up they saw less of each other, but they kept in touch. My father kept musically on top of everything that Ben did. He couldn't wait for a new score to come through the post – such was his admiration. I think he felt he'd learnt a lot from him, and there were always things in the scores that he could learn from even later in life. I remember him pointing things out to me and just being in awe of the simplicity, the economy of means. The way, with just a few notes, Britten could summon something up and it would be absolutely right.

There was a period when he felt they'd grown slightly apart when Britten became surrounded by a clique and didn't keep up so much with his old friends. I think that happens with important people. It never deeply worried him, and they continued to correspond.

PD It's extraordinary that he said he liked Britten's music better than his own and thought it was better. This kind of humility is almost an inferiority complex?

MB He was realistic. I don't think he actually felt inferior – I disagree about that – he felt there were things he could say that were totally his. I never got the feeling of inferiority. It was quite simply open admiration – this is a wonderful composer, a bigger talent than mine. There are pieces my father wrote that he felt were better than some of Ben's pieces – and they are.

Nobody has a complete hit list all the way through. They both wrote some duff pieces.

I came to see what my father knew from the beginning. Ben was almost like Mozart in his abilities; he was the most all-round musician I've ever met; but he was much more single-minded than my father. He was more ruthless too, and got what he wanted. He could be very difficult when things weren't going right. My father was more polite, less ruthless. Nevertheless he knew what he had and worked within that.

PD Was some of his reserve to do with his aristocratic background?

MB Some aristocrats are ruthless about getting what they want, but there was a gentility about him, a kindness, which perhaps stopped him from ever being shocking in his music. He wouldn't savage you like a composer who has perhaps had to dig in the dirt. He'd had an existence that had been reasonably pleasant and civilised, which is different from scraping your way up the side of a very slippery barrel, like composers from a less fortunate background. It's hard to generalise, because there are composers who've come from privileged backgrounds, like Lord Berners. It can be more difficult for them starting with something which is not a driving passion so it doesn't come from the root of your soul with such ferocity.

My father was totally uninterested in publicity, which could be irritating for his publishers when he couldn't see the point of it. Usually it would work because he was so endearing that people loved him. This kind of unworldly modesty did have its comic side. Once when we were at a party after a concert I saw my father talking at length to a member of the royal family. My mother and I got slightly nervous and wondered what on earth they could be talking about, especially since the royal in question was not noted for an interest in music, especially contemporary music. When my father eventually came over to us he said: 'I've been having such a nice chat – who was she?' It was Princess Margaret! He did love the ladies and would make an effort for a pretty girl.

PD Did he ever get angry when you were growing up?

MB When his temper broke he could. I remember one occasion at our cottage in Norfolk where my father used to work in the old laundry room, separate from the cottage. My brother and I had one of these rockets that you filled with water and then pumped air in – you got incredible pressure – and then you'd let it off. Julian and I decided we'd play a trick on my father and we let the rocket off at the door where he was sitting at the piano. It made an enormous bang. He came out absolutely livid – it had given him a terrible fright. I managed to climb up onto the roof of the garage but he caught Julian, who did get a couple of belts for it. So my father could lose his temper and certain things would make him irascible. He was quite tight if he was worried about money and things like that, but generous to other artists and in wanting to help people.

PD What about his influence on the next generation of composers?

MB I think the influence may be more now (1990) than it would have been ten years ago. Composers are looking back to scores where there is a natural and finely crafted use of tonality. I know the Divertimento gets used as a lesson in orchestration. I remember him showing me Mozart pieces where a bassoon or a horn would have a held note to hold the harmony together, or how certain doublings would work. I can see that in the Divertimento – that tradition is being passed on.

PD Was Boulanger too domineering?

MB The combination of her dominance and his gentleness meant that he had to surface from that more than Copland did. He always felt it was the right thing for him at the time. I'm astonished that for a year or so he wasn't allowed to write a note of his own music but had to do counterpoint and nothing else. He felt it paid off.

PD Do you think his concertos are among his best works?

MB He wrote them for particular artists and, as with Britten, it paid dividends. One thinks of Colin Horsley – the piano writing is so good – Janet Craxton, Yehudi Menuhin, and James Galway. He got to know these people and singers too. I think there are certain genres where his contribution was very important. There haven't been many composers of great piano music in this country, and I think his piano output, despite the fact that Ben was a better pianist, is more important.

The guitar repertoire is a great contribution too: the collaboration with Julian Bream was enormously profitable. He was always very amused when Julian would turn up and say: 'Well, better get the old box out then.' [*Laughs*] He loved Julian, who was very good at showing him how to realise his ideas on the guitar. My father was always strong enough not to let Julian have his head and rewrite things when he made suggestions. It's quite wrong to think of that gentleness as meaning he wasn't firm and didn't know what he wanted. He did know what he wanted and got cross when people got it wrong. There are various recordings of the Teresa of Avila songs where 'Let mine eyes see Thee' is taken too slowly and too romantically. He hated that.

Denis Brain inspired the Horn Trio – composers throughout the ages have responded to particular artists. He loved the human voice – writing for certain singers and particularly using certain poets was important to him.

If he had one regret in his life I would say that it was that he'd never written a really great opera. He would love to have done that – he adored the Mozart, Verdi and Britten operas. Although his achievements in that area are considerable he never really found the right libretto. That ruthlessness we discussed earlier is the key to this. Ben had an extraordinary knack in finding the right libretto and getting what he wanted from it. My father's keenness to write opera meant that he sometimes allowed himself to be swayed into using a libretto that wasn't right. It meant that, apart from *A Dinner Engagement*, those pieces are flawed.

The choice of dramatic subjects is also revealing. One of the powerful things about Britten is that the subject matter grows out of personal turmoil – the corruption of innocence and Britten having to deal with his own sexuality. My father wasn't the sort of composer who ever confronted that in his music. Therefore it has an élan, a style, but it doesn't signpost you into those areas of enormous turbulence, which we find attractive at the moment. That's an area that I find myself more naturally drawn to. I look for subjects that dig deep into one's soul, where one has things to say that you cannot avoid saying. I remember him being worried about this aspect of my work – music involved with political commentary or a message. He would never have wanted to do that and wasn't happy about me doing it.

PD There's a wonderful radiance about the works he wrote after meeting your mother.

MB Perhaps his tragedy is that he was rather too happy for too long? If there'd been more inner turmoil then the music would have torn us apart more. That's what people seem to need: it's curious. That happiness in those pieces is very infectious. It's interesting that the music from the period when he was living with Britten and they clearly had an important relationship, followed by a time when his sexuality changed, is not reflected in music of great angst. It seems to have been a quite natural transformation. That's one of the aspects of his work that I've found slightly perplexing. The music is the work of an impeccable jeweller, a craftsman – he didn't like baring his soul. It's a different way of working. He was quite private, had an elegance and didn't like too demonstrative a show of emotion. You shouldn't wear your heart on your sleeve too openly.

PD Like Mozart, it's a classical attribute?

MB The standards and traditions which he espoused were very much classical. But there is that naughty Frenchness that he enjoyed – Poulenc and the orchestration of Debussy and Ravel. It's a marriage of French classicism.

PD He was never as unbuttoned as Poulenc?

MB One comes back to that slight self-control, keeping things within a certain confine.

PD The English reserve?

MB There was an element of that. It's the quality that I both admire and occasionally find frustrating.

4 FRIENDS

Basil Douglas

At 8 St George's Terrace, London NW1, 28 November 1990

Basil Douglas (1914–92) was born in Edinburgh. He read classics at Magdalen College, Oxford, where he was President of the Music Society, and then studied singing at the Royal College of Music. His health made a performing career impossible, so he worked for the BBC until 1950, when he left to run Britten's English Opera Group for seven formative years. Finally he ran his own concert agency, Basil Douglas Ltd.

BD   I first met Lennox before the war and remember him as being a very charming and rather insecure person. His oratorio *Jonah* was rather different from the music he had been writing before and nobody was very happy about it. It was an important moment for him but I don't think it got a good press. I was in the BBC Music Department and heard the premiere in a broadcast. It was a pity that the performers didn't like it, and I'm not sure it was the best performance it could have been.[59]

PD   What did people think was wrong with *Jonah*?

BD   One had always associated Lennox's music with a warm, rather sensitive approach to words. This seemed to be a deliberate attempt to alienate himself from that kind of reputation. Whether this was the influence of Nadia Boulanger, you would know better than I.

PD   It was a serious piece that he wrote in memory of his parents. He wasn't just trying to alienate people.

BD   No, but he was under Nadia's influence at that time. He was an impressionable person. [*Laughs*]

PD   What did you mean about him being insecure?

BD   I don't think he was secure about his private life and was having domestic trouble. I think that affected his music too.

PD   Lennox went from one person to another.

BD   Exactly, until the traumatic time when he fell in love with my secretary. [*Laughs*]

PD   Do you remember Peter Fraser during the war? Not a very happy relationship?

BD   No, I don't think so. Lennox could have been happy, but I don't think Peter Fraser helped very much.

---

[59] *Jonah*, op. 3, oratorio for tenor and baritone, SATB, boys' voices and orchestra. Premiere in a BBC broadcast under Clarence Raybould, on 19 June 1936; first public performance, conducted by the composer, at Leeds Town Hall on 7 October 1937; first London performance, with organ, under Jonathan Rennert, at St Michael's Church, Cornhill on 31 March 1990.

PD   What about the relationship between Lennox and Britten?

BD   There was a great sympathy between them. Lennox enormously admired Ben's music, and Ben was ready to help Lennox as far as he could. I think that was immensely useful to Lennox. So he did have one or two lucky breaks in his life!

PD   Do you remember Lennox saying that he liked Ben's music better than his own?

BD   I think that's very characteristic of him. When he was asked to write an opera for the English Opera Group his one idea was to be as like *The Rape of Lucretia* or *Albert Herring* as possible.

PD   Is that really true?

BD   One has to remember that he was asked to write his operas by Ben for a certain ensemble, and therefore it was natural that Lennox would want to do it as well as possible, and, in his view, it couldn't have been done better than by Ben. It all followed. I don't think he was influenced for ever by Ben, but at that time it was important.

PD   What was the set-up in the BBC where you and Lennox worked and he met Freda?

BD   During the war I was trotting around the regions, but I returned to London making programmes for the BBC Symphony Orchestra and for recitals. I worked with Adrian Boult. Then it was decided that more specialisation was important and Lennox was brought in primarily to do orchestral programmes. I was pleasantly surprised at the efficiency with which he made these programmes. His knowledge was tremendous and he learnt how one had to choose the pieces to suit the orchestration. You couldn't have an enormous piece then nothing more for the big orchestra in the rest of the programme. He and Adrian Boult got on extremely well. Lennox's tastes were very catholic at that time. If he got a chance to put in some French music that was underrated and neglected he would take it. Some music got featured more because of Lennox being there.

PD   What was he passionate about then?

BD   I don't think the thick Mahler–Bruckner–Schoenberg Viennese school interested him much, but it didn't stop him from putting it in if he thought it was what was required. His sympathies were with clearer writing.

PD   Freda worked for you?

BD   She was my secretary for quite some time. It was very nice that Lennox kept popping in, ostensibly to be consulted about my programmes. [*Laughs*] We would talk about his programmes, and Freda would sit there smiling sweetly, and I had no idea that there was anything closer happening. The first thing I knew that there was anything serious was a notice in *The Times* saying that they were engaged! [*Laughs*] Everybody was highly surprised but very delighted!

Interviews with Performers, Composers, Family and Friends

PD It's been a wonderful partnership.

BD Oh, remarkable. Freda has been very supportive and given him enormous confidence – so different from when I first met him.

PD Did it get difficult at the BBC when he put his own music forward?

BD There was a rule that all music had to go through the Music Advisory Panel. We never quite knew who the grey-suited figures were, but we got the impression that they were against certain kinds of music and anything that was associated with Ben. He was very much off at that time. Lennox's music did suffer from that connection.

PD Are there any pieces that stand out?

BD *A Dinner Engagement* will always come to mind because I was devoted to that piece and we spent a lot of time getting it on the stage. In subsequent years I remember the piano concertos.

PD Were you connected with Aldeburgh?

BD I was quite involved, mainly through Peter Pears, and contributed a programme to the first Festival in 1948. I got to know them after they came back from America when they had difficulties in getting work – I was able to give them broadcasts, which I don't think Head Office was greatly pleased about. I got it through all the same. [*Laughs*]

PD Because they were conscientious objectors?

BD Yes, they weren't quite right.

PD Do you remember actual performances of Lennox's music?

BD Yes. I remember Phyllis Sellick doing the Piano Concerto: she and Cyril Smith doing the Two-Piano Concerto.

PD Another two-piano duo Ethel Bartlett and Rae Robertson did the early Polka.

BD Yes, that was very jolly.

PD But he soon became regarded as a kind of avant-garde composer?

BD As soon as he started writing *Jonah* he was! [*Laughs*] Before that he was regarded as a charming sort-of salon composer. After *Jonah* he came under suspicion from the establishment.

PD When did he change from being a modernist?

BD I think it was after he got married. Freda got him writing his own music.

PD Was the religious side important?

BD It was – in the same way that religious music was to Poulenc, who felt guilty and wrote religious music to make amends! [*Laughs*]

There was an occasion when Poulenc came to Aldeburgh to play his own concerto and Milhaud's *La Création du monde*. Curiously, he couldn't play

PD   Did Lennox play anything?

BD   Only for me – we used to do little song evenings together. He liked the way I sang French songs so we had quite a lot of evenings in his house – he was a very good accompanist. He particularly liked Fauré – we did most of the songs – and the easier songs of Debussy. We did some of his own songs as well: 'Tant que mes yeux', 'How love came in' and so on.[60]

PD   Lennox admired Mozart.

BD   I think he was a god – and so was Schubert. The later German composers were not particularly sympathetic to him. Certainly not when it got to the Second Viennese School.

PD   But Lennox did take on something of Schoenberg's technique. Did you find his music becoming more difficult from the later sixties?

BD   Yes I do, but he was trying something new all the time. He explored quite a bit.

PD   Did you go to *Nelson*?

BD   I worked quite hard for *Nelson* because, in the English Opera Group, we thought Sadler's Wells were dragging their feet in a rather disgraceful way. With Ben's help I arranged a concert performance in the Wigmore Hall. I made all the arrangements and booked the artists. That was full and very successful. Sadler's Wells were impressed. I wrote to Norman Tucker[61] and suggested that they should take *Nelson* more seriously as it had aroused a great deal of interest. I got a very rude letter back. [*Laughs*] But the next season *Nelson* was put on. Whether there was any connection I don't know, but it created a climate for the piece, which helped a lot.

PD   Did you see *Ruth* not long after?

BD   I did. We were a bit anxious about it because there seemed to be a lack of theatre and structure in the piece. But there were passages of great beauty that were just enough to make a success, but not, I think, a lasting one. *A Dinner Engagement* had always been successful and it was part of the Group's policy to commission works from other composers. I knew Paul Dehn, a good poet, who wrote a first-rate libretto.[62] I saw *Castaway* but I don't think it was a success – certainly not theatrically.

PD   Was *Nelson* successful in the theatre?

BD   Not very, but it proved it was worth putting on and it encouraged a lot of

---

[60] 'Tant que mes yeux', op. 14/6, premiered 20 February 1945 at the Fyvie Hall, London, by Sophie Wyss and the composer. 'How love came in' (1935), recorded by Pears and Britten in 1955, Decca LW 5241: Eclipse ECS 545.

[61] Norman Tucker (1910–78), director of Sadler's Wells 1947–66.

[62] Paul Dehn (1901–65), British writer for films, including *Murder on the Orient Express* (1974), librettist for *A Dinner Engagement* and *Castaway* as well as Walton's *The Bear*.

composers to write operas. It wasn't a success financially, and I doubt if it's regarded as one of his best works.

PD Was Lennox too restrained to deal with a heroic figure like Nelson?

BD I think he found it difficult to write a full-blooded love duet, for example.

PD Why did everybody love him so much?

BD He was a very lovable person who had no sense of grandeur or of his own achievements. He was a very modest person, likeable and very good fun. His giggling was infectious – sometimes at the expense of the powers that be.

PD Do you remember Lennox as a conductor?

BD I watched him conduct, and wondered how they could follow his beat. [*Laughs*] But he managed to convey what he wanted without a good beat.

PD Lennox never got a conductor for his music the way Tippett had Colin Davis.[63]

BD Tippett was better at publicising his own work. Lennox would never push his pieces at all, and his publishers weren't very effective either. Tippett had a bigger sense of what composing is about than Lennox did, but for many reasons I prefer Lennox. I've admired Tippett from the Double Concerto and *Boyhood's End*, but I've never loved it as I have Lennox's music. It seemed that I was listening to him – very much his personality.

PD Is that a handicap for people who didn't know what Lennox was like?

BD Yes – but they can read a biography to get a better idea! [*Laughs*]

---

[63] This changed with the outstanding recordings and live performances under Richard Hickox (1948–2008).

Desmond Shawe-Taylor

At 15 Furlong Road, London N7, 28 November 1990

Desmond Shawe-Taylor (1907–95) was music critic of the *New Statesman*, 1945–53; chief music critic of the *Sunday Times*, 1958–83; and he wrote regularly for other journals, pioneering the study of recording. He was ahead of his time in championing Berg's *Lulu* in 1937 and drew attention to Janáček's operas in the 1950s, long before they were widely known. He played truant from school in order to go to recitals by Yvette Guilbert. Over his long critical career he showed an especially sensitive response to Berkeley's new works as they emerged.

DST   I think we must have met at Oxford in the late twenties because I knew Sybil Jackson, his godmother, who lived in Boars Hill.[64] She was active in Oxford musical circles and began to talk about Lennox. I don't remember any performances of his music there but I occasionally heard things in London during the thirties. I didn't get to know him well until towards the end of the thirties; I remember his association with Benjamin Britten, and Edward Sackville-West[65] was a mutual friend.

PD   What was he like then?

DST   He was very similar in attitude and manner right through his life until illness struck him down at the end. A quiet, modest unassuming manner; very polite and inclined to listen to what anybody else said. That was a feature of his character right from the beginning.
   The first pieces I heard were the Serenade and the Divertimento.

PD   What about the connection between Berkeley and Britten?

DST   I knew Lennox before I met Ben, whom I didn't know well until he came back from America. Lennox was one of the most modest men I've ever met with gifts as definite as that. He would be inclined to minimise his own part in anything, but I think Britten had absorbed something from that particular spare delicacy of Lennox's style and approach to music. They were naturally related in tastes, and although Lennox had a stronger French influence through Nadia Boulanger – which Britten lacked – I think there was a close sympathy about their outlook on music. They enriched each other.

PD   Does Lennox suffer from the comparison?

DST   I think that modest as he was – to a fault – he must have been aware of his less brilliant musical personality. He made no bones about openly admiring Ben's music, his facility and all-round musicality – he would belittle his own status. Not as a way of making one want to contradict him, but quite genuinely. He knew he didn't have this direct on-the-spot quality that Britten had. It was

---

[64] Sybil Deane Jackson (1877–1976).

[65] Edward Sackville-West, 5th Baron Sackville (1901–65), music critic, biographer and novelist.

rather like somebody admiringly watching another footballer who can get up the side of the field faster than he could ever hope to.

PD Did that affect his music or was it like his straightforward admiration for Fauré?

DST I think it is, if you can compare something so distant in time and nationality as Fauré and Britten. In a curious way Lennox remained his own man and wasn't influenced by who he'd lately encountered, even if it was somebody like Britten. I don't think his music fell into a pre-Britten and post-Britten era.

PD From your vantage point of knowing and reviewing the music for so many years which is the best period?

DST I've always liked the chamber music and the concertos, which brought out the best in him – more than the four symphonies and more even than the vocal works, although the *Stabat mater* and the choral works are good. I think the Horn Trio is one of the most beautiful and natural pieces I know in that vein, peculiarly happy in the writing for all three instruments. Oddly, he was quite a decent pianist without any pretensions whatsoever yet he wrote frightfully well for the piano. The sets of Piano Studies are real virtuoso pieces but enjoyable and the kind of thing normally written by somebody who is a considerable pianist himself. That spilt over into the concertos – the Two-Piano Concerto is one of his best works. In the second movement the variation form, which attracted him, brought out the best in him. I remember saying to him: 'I love your variations but I don't altogether feel happy when you sit down at the end of each and we have to start again. I wish there was some method of linking.'[66] He listened but I don't think he changed! [*Laughs*]

PD Do his variations stem from Bach or Stravinsky?

DST Stravinsky was a strong influence. Lennox had a civilised taste in musical background – Fauré as we all know was a strong influence, not common among English composers.

PD But Stravinsky?

DST I do think that's important but I suppose that everybody who passed through Nadia Boulanger's hands – unless they were rebels – was bound to have a special relationship with Stravinsky. There's no doubt that Lennox did. I felt he was a quiet ultra-civilised English relation of Stravinsky who had his wild side – musically if not personally. Lennox was never a very wild composer. Some people would have thought he was just too safe. But it suited him – what he did he knew he could do, rather than trying for things beyond his grasp. Not the wilder reaches of Stravinsky. He was reluctant to use much percussion. I remember once complaining about some modern scores that had a battery of percussion going all the time and Lennox said: 'I do agree – I find it quite an effort to use any percussion at all!' [*Laughs*]

[66] Norman Del Mar makes the same point, but Berkeley was right not to change anything.

PD He was adventurous in some ways. In the 1950s, following Britten, he went into opera. What do you think of his operas?

DST He has beautiful incidental things, but I don't think it drew out the best of him and none of his librettos quite hits the mark. *Nelson*, the most ambitious, is flawed as a libretto, even though it went through various modifications. Perhaps the subject was a bit on the strong side for both librettist and composer. The rest are more-or-less playful or religious – not mainstream.

PD *Ruth* was close to his heart because of the religious subject?

DST I like *Ruth* very much when I hear it, but I don't think of it as an opera, more a scenic cantata.

PD How important is the religious side to Lennox?

DST I tread warily in the matter myself, being irreligious by nature. But it obviously meant a great deal to him, which I respected. The *Stabat mater* is outstanding among the religious works, and there are smaller works for Westminster Cathedral, for which his formal yet quiet style was suited.

PD That's the context of *Ruth* too.

DST Yes. It's a sacred drama and strongly pastoral. That's the vein he naturally fell into. You may say that all English composers are only too glad to become pastoral at the drop of a hat, but I think it was natural to him.

PD How far is he English and what stems from his French ancestry and training?

DST I think that too much can be made of the French influence. Boulanger was a tremendous influence, as she was with all those Americans who passed through her hands. As with Copland, it didn't stop them from being American when they got back home, and I don't think it stopped Lennox from being thoroughly English. The French influence gave a polish, style and ease to what he had to say rather than taking over the subject matter.

PD Do you think Boulanger was a bully? Copland was subservient and Britten urged Lennox to forget what she'd think about his music.

DST Ben never came across quite such a forceful personality. He admired Bridge but was probably not in awe the way some of Boulanger's pupils were. I met her with Lennox quite late and she was very proud of him.

PD How has Berkeley fitted in with fashion since World War II?

DST That's not what he did. I think he was extraordinarily free from fashionable influences. He found a style that suited him; it took him longer than many composers; then he gave music, as Strauss said, 'as a cow gives milk' – and quite a lot of it too. [*Laughs*]

PD He was like Tippett as a late starter rather than Britten.

DST He hadn't got that maverick vein of Tippett who was prepared to take on anything, however wild. Lennox filled a niche in the musical world extremely well.

PD How consistent was his output?

DST I think an admirable kind of consistency began to show itself, also great productivity, which surprised people. His music maintained a high general level.

PD What did you think of his involvement with aspects of twelve-note technique in the 1960s?

DST I think it did no harm – if no special good.

PD Works like the Third Symphony and the Guitar Concerto owed their harmonic language to it. Was this natural?

DST I think not, but I remember him saying to me: 'I don't think I could become a real twelve-note composer because I don't feel, after eleven notes have been sounded, any particular pull towards the twelfth.' I understand that well – he had to remember which the twelfth note was and put it in! [*Laughs*]

PD He might forget because he was so vague?

DST You've analysed his works, but I should think it was quite likely there are a few slips. [*Laughs*]

PD He was a forgetful person though?

DST He became forgetful – perhaps he always was.

PD Do you remember him in public roles?

DST At Cheltenham he was a popular and admired President but I should have thought he threw his weight around remarkably little! As a figurehead he was absolutely un-pompous and everybody respected him. He worked very hard and successfully as President of the PRS.

PD Do you remember when Lennox met Freda?

DST It was when they were both at the BBC; soon was a very great success; and became one of the happiest marriages I know. The family was a great source of happiness to him as well.

PD It must have been a surprise to some of his friends that he married?

DST Yes – he had other tastes, not the same. But in that quiet way of his he was very adaptable.

PD Do you remember his last boyfriend, Peter Fraser?[67]

DST Oddly enough I believe I introduced them – that was a source of happiness and then anxiety.

PD What do you think the future holds for the best works? [There was nothing on CD except piano music in 1990.]

---

[67] Peter Fraser (1920–76), who shared a flat with Berkeley 1944–6. Berkeley dedicated Nocturne, op. 25, to him, an anguished piece premiered 28 August 1946 at the Royal Albert Hall by the BBC Symphony Orchestra under Adrian Boult. For details of this relationship, see Scotland, *Lennox and Freda*.

DST It won't just die away. There were ups and downs in his lifetime. In the last two decades of his life performances multiplied. I'd expect similar returns in the future. His writing is thoroughly effective and he's got an ability to present things in the most compelling way – not at all stuffy or old-fashioned.

PD Is his melodic gift important?

DST I think it was very real: lovely tunes seem to surface spontaneously as in the Flute Sonatina.[68]

---

[68] Winton Dean recalls: 'Several of us were discussing the twelve-note system, of which Lennox was fairly critical after trying it (as he did with almost everything) when he suddenly produced a seraphic smile and declared, "But I *can* write tunes!"' Letter to Peter Dickinson, 20 June 2012.

– *Part VII* –

Memorial Address by Sir John Manduell

The Memorial Requiem Mass for Lennox Randal Francis Berkeley (1903–1989) took place at Westminster Cathedral on Tuesday 20 March 1990 and was broadcast on BBC Radio 3. Before the service radio listeners heard a recording of Berkeley's Duo for cello and piano, op. 81/1 (Julian Lloyd Webber and John McCabe, Oiseau-Lyre DSLO 7100) and Fr Cormack Rigby was responsible for presentation throughout. The music in Westminster Cathedral opened with Bach's 'Herzlich tut mich verlangen' and then the second of Berkeley's *Three Pieces* for organ, op. 72/1. The celebrant was His Eminence Cardinal George Basil Hume, OSB, Archbishop of Westminster. The address was given by Bishop Gordon Wheeler; there were readings by Tony Scotland and this tribute by Sir John Manduell CBE. The music consisted of Berkeley's *Mass for Five Voices*, op. 64; *Ubi caritas*, op. 96/2; Michael Berkeley's *Qui me dignatus est*; Lennox Berkeley's 'O that I once past changing were' (Festival Anthem, op. 21/2) and Toccata (*Three Pieces*, op. 72/1) with James O'Donnell, Master of the Music, and Iain Simcock, organ.

I am conscious that I shall be speaking for many people in this cathedral today when I say that to have known Lennox is to have enjoyed the precious privilege of receiving and sharing the friendship of a man who possessed many rare qualities in wonderfully rich profusion. To endeavour on this memorable occasion to describe adequately those qualities as they emerged in Lennox the man, or as they may have been reflected in Lennox the composer, is to embark on a task to which it is near impossible to do justice and for which it is a great honour to have been asked by Freda to undertake.

While Lennox was known to all for his kindness and gentleness, and for those qualities of quiet restraint and tender courtesy which so endeared him to all who met him, he was also, as a composer, inevitably confronted with private challenges of considerable complexity. It is, perhaps, one of the many significant measures of Lennox's achievements as an artist that his music in its final form emerges with such natural assurance and seeming inevitability. It is, of course, scarcely possible within a few short minutes to pay adequate or just tribute to Lennox's achievements as a composer. Thankfully our great blessing is that no factor of human mortality can take from us the hundred and more works which, in their rich diversity, collectively represent his life's work.

That diversity is perhaps typically exemplified in Lennox's four operas, which offer – through the heroic in *Nelson,* the comic in *A Dinner Engagement,* the pastoral in *Ruth,* and the classical in *Castaway* – a range to satisfy any opera enthusiast. Richly complementary are the four symphonies. No less satisfying is the refreshing variety of Lennox's chamber music. No British composer has written more sensitively for the human voice, or has left us songs more beautifully moulded.

No British composer has written more distinctively for the piano. Of such richness and diversity is Lennox's bequest to us and to posterity. It is, moreover, all cast in a style and language unmistakeably his, with characteristics which we instantly identify as his and his alone. Above all, perhaps, his great natural gifts as a melodist.

If Lennox's supreme achievement must incontestably lie in the wonderful way he has, as a composer, enriched not just our lives but the very art he served, we should not overlook the many ways in which he served and benefited his fellows in his lifetime. He rendered generous and distinguished public service to many important organisations, as their representatives among this morning's congregation will readily testify. He gave selflessly of his kindness and wisdom to guide and support undertakings to which he felt drawn. In particular, organisations concerned with the well-being of his fellow composers. Among these were the Performing Right Society and the Cheltenham Festival, both of which he served with distinction as President, while he also maintained a close interest in many other important organisations, such as the Composers' Guild of Great Britain. He was honoured by many societies and academic institutions and we rejoice that his gifts and generosity were recognised in his lifetime by church and state alike.

Just as Lennox gave generously of himself to public organisations, so did he also in more private capacities, such as teaching. For over twenty years he lent distinction to the Royal Academy of Music as Professor of Composition. In this capacity he would, with infinite sensitivity and tolerance, endeavour to pass to those who came to study with him something of what he had long learned and absorbed, almost from the days when, as a young man, he enjoyed Ravel's kindness and interest and certainly from the time of his concentrated studies with Nadia Boulanger in Paris.

One's step, as a student approaching his house in Warwick Avenue, may sometimes have been somewhat anxious, but it also had a spring of eager anticipation deriving from an awareness of the strength of this tradition and linked to consciousness of the generosity of the man who was so patiently concerning himself with one's endeavours.

That Lennox and his wonderful close family should have been so beloved of many was inevitable. Who could not respond to somebody of whom it was always true to say, as Bulwer Lytton did of King Arthur, that 'in him kindness, like light, speaks in the air it gilds'. Lennox's gentleness was a byword, although he would never, with that playful sense of humour he possessed, have entertained any aspirations of saintliness. Nor, indeed would he have denied that he could on occasion offer a little impromptu stimulus to indolent road-users when he was at the wheel of his car. His may possibly, in Browning's words, have been 'the great mind that knows the power of gentleness' – but perhaps not quite always.

We have this morning come together come to show our love for Lennox through this Requiem Mass. As we have listened again to his music, and that of his son Michael, we will all have felt closer to him and to Freda and all his family. Let us with them, and all who loved Lennox, rejoice that he lived a long and fruitful life.

Catalogue of Works

This list of works has been brought up to date from the one in *The Music of Lennox Berkeley* (2003). Recently discovered items are now included and there are more dates of first performances. Some works were never given opus numbers. The publisher is Chester Music unless otherwise stated. However, incidental music, film scores, radio scares and arrangements (apart from Berkeley's orchestration of Poulenc's Flute Sonata) are all unpublished. The abbreviations for instrumentation etc. are those used in *New Grove*.

DRAMATIC

Opera

Nelson, op. 41, 1949–54 (3 acts, Alan Pryce-Jones), soloists, Sadler's Wells Chorus and Orchestra/Vilem Tausky, London, Sadler's Wells, 22 September 1954

A Dinner Engagement, op. 45, 1954 (1 act, Paul Dehn), soloists, English Opera Group Chamber Orchestra/Vilem Tausky, Aldeburgh, Jubilee Hall, 17 June 1954

Ruth, op. 50, 1955–6 (3 scenes, Eric Crozier), English Opera Group Chorus and Orchestra/Charles Mackerras, London, Scala Theatre, 2 October 1956

Castaway, op. 68, 1966 (1 act, Paul Dehn), soloists, English Opera Group Chorus and Orchestra/Meredith Davies, Aldeburgh, Jubilee Hall, 3 June 1967

Faldon Park, incomplete, op. 100 (Winton Dean), 1979–83

Ballet

Ballet (untitled, unpubd), 1932 (see *Three Dances*, arr Dickinson, pf)

The Judgement of Paris, 1938, The Vic-Wells Orchestra/Constant Lambert, London, Sadler's Wells, 10 May 1938 [Boosey & Hawkes]

Incidental music

Puppet Play and Farce: *The Seven Ages of Man/The Station Master* (Montague Slater), vc, cl, vn/dulcitone, pf, 1938, London, Mercury Theatre, 22 June 1938

The Tempest (Shakespeare), BBC Singers, National Symphony Chamber Orchestra, Stratford, Shakespeare Memorial Theatre, 20 April 1946 (See voice and orchestra)

Jig-Saw, 1948, and *Venus Anadyomene*, 1945, 2 pf, perc, in revue *Oranges and Lemons*, London, Globe Theatre, 29 January 1949

Tiger at the Gates, (Giradoux, trans. C. Fry), London, Apollo Theatre, 4 October 1955

A Winter's Tale, Wind Band/Brian Priestman, Stratford, Shakespeare Memorial Theatre, 30 August 1960

Film scores
[dates are months of review]

Sword of the Spirit, December 1942

Out of Chaos, January 1944, London Symphony Orchestra

Hotel Reserve, June 1944, BBC Northern Orchestra/Muir Mathieson

The First Gentleman, April 1948, Royal Philharmonic Orchestra/Thomas Beecham

Youth in Britain, April 1958

Radio scores

Westminster Abbey (Louis MacNeice), 1941, section of BBC Northern Orchestra, London, BBC, 7 September 1941

Yesterday and Today (Phillipa Stewart Craig), 1943, Wireless Singers/Father J. B. McElligott, Evesham, BBC, 19 April 1942

A Glutton for Life (Audrey Lucas), *c.* 1946, ad hoc orch/Walter Goehr, London, BBC, 15 February 1946

The Wall of Troy (Homer/Patric Dickinson), 1946, ad hoc orch/Lennox Berkeley, London, BBC, 21 November 1946

Iphigenia in Taurus (Goethe), *c.* 1954, Welbeck Orchestra/Lennox Berkeley, London, BBC, 3 October 1954

The Seraphina (George Barker), 1956, Sinfonia of London/Lennox Berkeley, London, BBC, 4 October 1956

Look Back to Lyttletoun (Caryl Brahms), 1957, English Opera Group Orchestra, Ambrosian Singers/Norman del Mar, London, BBC, 8 July 1957

Orchestra

Suite, 1927, Straram Orchestra/Walter Straram, Paris, 12 September 1929 [Novello]

Overture, op. 8, 1934, BBC Symphony Orchestra/Lennox Berkeley, London, 1 October 1935

Mont Juic, op. 9, suite of Catalan dances, 1937, collab. Benjamin Britten (op. 12), BBC Orchestra/Joseph Lewis, London, BBC, 8 January 1938 [Boosey & Hawkes]

Symphony no. 1, op. 16, 1940, London, Philharmonic Orchestra/Lennox Berkeley, London, 8 July 1943

Divertimento in B flat, op. 18, 1943, BBC Orchestra/Clarence Raybould, Bedford, 1 October 1943

Nocturne, op. 25, 1946, BBC Symphony Orchestra/Adrian Boult, London, 28 August 1946

Overture, 1947, London Chamber Orchestra/Anthony Bernard, Canterbury, 27 June 1947

Sinfonietta, op. 34, 1950, London Chamber Orchestra/Anthony Bernard, London, 1 December 1950

Suite, 1953, BBC Symphony Orchestra/Malcolm Sargent, London, BBC, 6 June 1953

Suite from *Nelson*, op. 42, 1955, Cheltenham, Hallé Orchestra/John Barbirolli, 29 July 1955

Interlude from *Nelson*, c. 1955

Symphony no. 2, op. 51, 1958, City of Birmingham Symphony Orchestra/Andrzej Panufnik, Birmingham, 24 February 1959; rev. for recording, 1976

Overture, 1959, BBC Concert Orchestra/Vilem Tausky, London, 4 July 1959

Suite from *A Winter's Tale*, op. 54, 1960, BBC Symphony Orchestra/Rudolf Schwarz, Norwich, 27 May 1961

Partita, op. 66, chmr orch, 1965, Frensham Heights School Orchestra/Edward Rice, Farnham, 17 May 1965

Symphony no. 3 in One Movement, op. 74, 1969, L'Orchestre national de l'office de radiodiffusion télévision Française/Jean Martinon, Cheltenham, 3 August 1969

Windsor Variations, op. 75, chmr orch, 1969, Menuhin Festival Orchestra/Yehudi Menuhin, Windsor, 18 September 1969

Diana and Actaeon Waltz (see *Palm Court Waltz*, pf duet), op.81/2. 1971, Welsh Philharmonia Orchestra/Lennox Berkeley, London, 22 June 1971

Voices of the Night, op. 86, 1973, City of Birmingham Symphony Orchestra/Lennox Berkeley, Hereford, 22 August 1973

Symphony no. 4, op. 94, 1978, Royal Philharmonic Orchestra/Charles Groves, London, 30 May 1978

Orchestrations

Sarawak National Anthem, orch/military band, 1941, BBC Scottish Military Band, London, BBC, 23 September 1941

Ballet: *La Fête étrange* (Gabriel Fauré), 1947, Sadler's Wells Ballet Orchestra/Constant Lambert (?), London, Sadler's Wells Theatre, 25 March 1947

Air and recitative from *Ruth* (George Tolhurst), soloists, First Orchestra and Chorus of the Royal Academy of Music/Anthony Lewis, London, 6 March 1973

Flute Sonata (Francis Poulenc), op. 93/2, 1976, James Galway, Royal Philharmonic Orchestra/Charles Dutoit, London, 24 March 1977

String Orchestra

Serenade, op. 12, 1939, Boyd Neel Orchestra/Boyd Neel, London, 30 January 1940

Variation on an Elizabethan Theme – Sellinger's Round (no. 3 of collaboration), 1953, Aldeburgh Festival Orchestra/Benjamin Britten, Aldeburgh, 20 June 1953

Antiphon, op. 85, 1973, Academy of St Martin's in the Fields/Neville Marriner, Cheltenham, 7 July 1973

Suite, op. 87, 1974, Westminster Cathedral String Orchestra/Colin Mawby, London, 1 June 1974

Elegy, op. 33/2b, 1978, arr. of *Elegy*, op. 33/2a, St John's Smith Square Orchestra/John Lubbock, London, 26 April 1978

Solo instrument(s) and orchestra

Introduction and Allegro, op. 11, 2 pf, orch, 1938, Lennox Berkeley, William Glock, London Symphony Orchestra/Henry Wood, London, 6 September 1940

Concerto for Cello, 1939, Moray Welsh, Hallé Orchestra/James Loughran, Cheltenham, 17 July 1983

Concerto for Piano, op. 29, 1947, Colin Horsley, London Symphony Orchestra/Basil Cameron, London, 31 August 1948

Concerto for Two Pianos, op. 30, 1948, Phyllis Sellick, Cyril Smith, London Symphony Orchestra/Malcolm Sargent, London, 13 December 1948

Concerto for Flute, op. 36, 1952, John Francis, BBC Symphony Orchestra/Malcolm Sargent, London, 29 July 1953

Concerto for Piano and Double String Orchestra, op. 46, 1958, Colin Horsley, BBC Symphony Orchestra/Lennox Berkeley, London, 11 February 1959

Five Pieces for Violin and Orchestra, op. 56, 1961, Frederick Grinke, BBC Symphony Orchestra/Lennox Berkeley, London, 31 July 1962

Concerto for Violin and Chamber Orchestra, op. 59, 1961, Yehudi Menuhin, Festival Chamber Orchestra/Lennox Berkeley, Bath, 1 June 1961

Dialogue for Cello and Chamber Orchestra, op. 79, 1970, Maurice Gendron, English Chamber Orchestra/ Raymond Leppard, King's Lynn, 30 July 1971

Sinfonia concertante, op. 84, ob, orch, 1973, Janet Craxton, BBC Northern Symphony Orchestra/Raymond Leppard, London, 3 August 1973

Concerto for Guitar, op. 88, 1974, Julian Bream, English Chamber Orchestra/ Andrew Davis, 4 July 1974

CHORAL

Choir with orchestra

Ode (Pindar), SATB, tpt, str, 1932

Jonah, op. 3, oratorio, T, B, Tr, SATB, orch, 1934–6, Joan Cross, Jan van der Gucht, William Parsons, BBC Chorus and Orchestra/Clarence Raybould, BBC Broadcasting House, London, 19 June 1936

Deux poèmes de Pindare, SATB, orch, c. 1935, Oriana Madrigal Society Choir and A Capella Singers, London Symphony Orchestra/Nadia Boulanger, London, 24 November 1936

Domini est terra, op. 10 (Psalm 23), SATB, orch, 1937, London Select Choir, BBC Orchestra/Arnold Fulton, London, 17 June 1938

Colonus' Praise, op. 31 (W. B. Yeats), SATB, orch, 1948, BBC Choral Society, BBC Symphony Orchestra/Leslie Woodgate, 13 September 1949

Variations on a Hymn by Orlando Gibbons, op. 35 (I. Watts) T, SATB, str, org, 1951, Peter Pears, Ralph Downes, Aldeburgh Festival Choir and Orchestra/Lennox Berkeley, 21 June 1952

Batter my Heart, Three Person'd God, op. 60/1 (J. Donne), S, SATB, ob, hn, vcs, dbs, org, 1962, Riverside Church Choir of New York/Richard Weagley

Signs in the Dark, op. 69 (L. Lee), SATB, str, 1967, The Festival Choir and Orchestra/Eric Saunders, Stroud, 22 October 1967

Magnificat, op. 71, SATB, orch, org, 1968, choirs of St Paul's Cathedral, Westminster Abbey and Westminster Cathedral, London Symphony Orchestra/Lennox Berkeley, London, 8 July 1968

Choir with organ

Lord, When the Sense of Thy Sweet Grace, op. 21/1 (R. Crashaw), SATB, org, 1944

A Festival Anthem, op. 21/2 (G. Herbert/H. Vaughan), SATB, org, 1945, Northampton Parish Church Choir, Charles Barker/Lennox Berkeley, Northampton, 21 September 1945

Look up Sweet Babe, op. 43/2 (R. Crashaw), Tr, SATB, org, 1954, Westminster Abbey Choir/William McKie, London, December 1954

Salve Regina, op. 48/1, vv, org, 1955

Sweet was the Song, op. 43/3 (W. Ballet), SATB, org, c. 1957

Thou hast made me, op. 55/1 (J. Donne), SATB, org, 1960, combined choirs/John Dykes Bower, London, 22 November 1960

Missa brevis, op. 57, SATB, org, 1960, Westminster Cathedral Choir/Francis Cameron, London, 12 March 1960 (also English text)

Hail Holy Queen, vv, org, 1970

Adeste fideles, arr. Tr, SATB, org/pf, c. 1964

Hymn for Shakespeare's Birthday, op. 83/2 (C. Day Lewis), SATB, org, 1972, Exsultate Singers/Garrett O'Brien, London, 23 April 1972

The Lord is my Shepherd, op. 91/1, Tr, SATB, org, 1975, Choir of Chichester Cathedral, Ian Fox/John Birch, Chichester, 14 June 1975

Magnificat and Nunc dimittis, op. 99, SATB, org, 1980, choirs of Chichester, Salisbury and Winchester Cathedrals/John Birch, Chichester, 26 July 1980

Unaccompanied choir

The Midnight Murk (Sagittarius = Olga Katzin Miller), SATB, 1942, BBC Singers/Trevor Harvey, Bedford, BBC, 20 June 1942

Legacie (J. Donne), SSATBB, unpubd

There was neither Grass nor Corn (F. Cornford), SATB, 1944, BBC Singers/Leslie Woodgate, Bedford, BBC, 5 December 1944

Ask me no more, op. 37/1 (T. Carew), TTBB, c. 1952

Spring at this Hour, op. 37/2 (P. Dehn), SSATBB, 1953 (no. 5 of *A Garland for the Queen*), Cambridge University Madrigal Society and the Golden Age Singers/Boris Ord, London, 1 June 1953

Crux fidelis, op. 43/1, T, SATB, 1955, Peter Pears, Purcell Singers/Imogen Holst, London, 6 March 1955

Justorum animae, op. 60/2, SATB, 1963

Mass for Five Voices, op. 64, SSATB, 1964, Westminster Cathedral Choir/Colin Mawby, London

Three Songs for Four Male Voices, op. 67/1 (R. Herrick/R. Bridges), TTBB, 1965, the Schubertians/Carl Zytowski, Santa Barbara, 15 March 1966

The Windhover, op. 72/2 (G. M. Hopkins), SATB, 1968, BBC Northern Singers/Stephen Wilkinson, Stonyhurst, 13 December 1971 [*Musical Times*, November 1968, Novello]

A Grace, SATB, 1971, Linden Singers, London, 8 July 1971

Three Latin Motets, op. 83/1, SSATB, 1972, Choir of St John's College, Cambridge/George Guest, St Asaph, 28 April 1972

The Hill of the Graces, op. 91/2 (E. Spenser), SSAATTBB, 1975, BBC Singers/John Poole, London, 20 October 1975

Judica me, op. 96/1, SSATBB, 1978, Festival Chorus/Donald Hunt, Worcester, 2 September 1978

Ubi caritas et amor, op. 96/2, SSATB, 1980, Westminster Cathedral Choir, London, 11 July 1980

In Wintertime, op. 103 (B. Askwith), SATB, 1983, Choir of King's College/Stephen Cleobury, Cambridge, 24 December 1983

Other works

La Poulette grise, 2 children's chs, tpt, 2 pf, *c.* 1935

Hymn tunes: 'Christ is the World's Redeemer' (St Columba), 1963, local choirs, Britannia Band of Derry/Lennox Berkeley, Gartan, Co. Donegal, 2 June 1963 [Novello]

'Hail Gladdening Light', *c.* 1963, unpubd

'Hear'st Thou, my Soul' (R. Crashaw), 1967, *Cambridge Hymnal*, no. 40; 'I Sing of a Maiden' (15th cent.), 1967, *Cambridge Hymnal*, no. 152; 'Lord, By Whose Breath' (A. Young), 1967, *Cambridge Hymnal*, no. 61

SOLO VOCAL
Songs with orchestra

Where the Bee sucks, S/T, 2 fl, ob, 2 cl, bn, 2 hn, tr, 3 tbn, timp, str, 1946 (see incidental music to *The Tempest*) unpbd

Four Poems of St Teresa of Avila, op. 27 (trans. A. Symons), A, str, 1947, Kathleen Ferrier, Goldsbrough String Orchestra/Arnold Goldsbrough, London, BBC, 4 April 1948

Stabat mater, op. 28, solo SSATBB, fl, ob, cl, bn, hn, hp, perc, str qt, 1947 (orch. M. Berkeley, op. 28a, 1978), English Opera Group/Lennox Berkeley, Zurich, 19 August 1947

Four Ronsard Sonnets, Set 2, op. 62, T, orch, 1963, Peter Pears, BBC Symphony Orchestra/Lennox Berkeley, London, 9 August 1963; arr. chmr orch

Songs with one voice and piano

Three Early Songs (J. du Bellay/13th cent. anon./C. d'Orléans), 1: *D'un vanneur de blé aux vents* (1st version) 2: *Pastourelle* 3: *Rondeau*, S/T, pf, 1924–5; *D'un vanneur de blé aux vents/ The Thresher* (J. du Bellay, trans. M. D. Calvocoressi), Mez/Bar, pf, 1927 (revised version) [OUP/Chester] 1: C. Day Lewis, Lennox Berkeley, Oxford, 12 March 1925; 2: Oxford, 16 June 1924

Tombeaux (J. Cocteau), S/T, pf, 1926, Charles Sautelet, Lennox Berkeley, Paris, 1 June 1927

Trois Poèmes de Vildrac (C. Vildrac), Mez/Bar, pf, 1929

How Love Came In (R. Herrick), S/T, pf, *c.* 1935 [Boosey & Hawkes]

Night Covers up the Rigid Land, op. 14/2 (W. H. Auden), S/T, pf, 1937 [Boosey & Hawkes]

Lay your Sleeping Head, my Love, op. 14/2 (W. H. Auden), S/T, pf, *c.* 1937

The Beacon Barn, op. 14/2 (P. O'Malley), Mez/Bar, pf, 1938

Eleven-fifty, op. 14/2 (P. O'Malley), Bar, pf, 1938

Bells of Cordoba, op. 14/2 (F. Garcia Lorca, trans. S. Richardson), S/T, pf, 1938

Ode du premier jour de mai, op. 14/2 (J. Passerat), Mez/Bar, pf, 1940

Tant que mes yeux/A Memory, op. 14/2 (L. Labé/trans. M. D. Calvocoressi), S/T, pf, 1940, Sophie Wyss, Lennox Berkeley, London, 20 February 1945 [OUP/Chester]

Five Housman Songs, op. 14/3 (A. E. Housman), S/T, pf, 1940

The Ecstatic (C. Day Lewis), S/T, pf, 1943

Lullaby (W. B. Yeats), S/T, pf, 1943, unpubd

Five Songs, op. 26 (W. de la Mare), Mez/Bar, pf, 1946, Pierre Bernac, Francis Poulenc, London, 9 February 1947

The Low Lands of Holland (anon., ed. J. Hayward), arr. Mez/Bar, pf, 1947, Sophie Wyss, Lennox Berkeley, London, BBC Broadcasting House, 12 July 1947

Three Greek Songs, op. 38 (Sappho/Antipater/Plato, trans. F. A. Wright), Mez/Bar, pf, 1951, Iris Kells, John Gardner, London, 15 March 1951

Four Ronsard Sonnets, Set 1, op. 40 (P. de Ronsard), 2 T, pf, c. 1952, Peter Pears, Hugues Cuénod, George Malcolm, London, 8 March 1953; rev. 1977, Peter Pears, Ian Partridge, Steuart Bedford, Snape, 14 June 1978

Five Poems, op. 53 (W. H. Auden), S/T, pf, 1958, Alice Esty, New York, 26 March 1959

So sweet Love seemed (R. Bridges), Mez/Bar, pf, c. 1959, Meriel and Peter Dickinson, Manchester, 30 October 1975

Autumn's Legacy, op. 58 (T. L. Beddoes, L. Durrell, A. Tennyson, G. M. Hopkins, W. H. Davies, H. Coleridge), S/T, pf, 1962, Richard Lewis, Geoffrey Parsons, Cheltenham, 6 July 1962

Automne, op. 60/3 (G. Apollinaire), Mez/Bar, pf, 1963, Alice Esty, New York, 13 January 1964

Counting the Beats, op. 60/4 (R. Graves), S/T, pf, 1963, Gerald English, John Constable, London, 16 July 1963; rev. 1971 [Thames]

Five Chinese Songs, op. 78 (trans. A. Waley/R. Kotewell/N. L. Smith), Mez, pf, 1971, Meriel and Peter Dickinson, London, 22 March 1971

i carry your heart with me (e. e. cummings), Mez, pf, 1972

Another Spring, op. 93/1 (W. de la Mare), Mez/Bar, pf, 1977, Janet Baker, Geoffrey Pratley, Chichester Cathedral, 20 July 1977

Four Score Years and Ten (V. Ellis), v, pf, 1977, unpubd

Sonnet, op. 102 (Louise Labé), S/T, pf, 1982, Janet Watson, London, 26 June 1990

Other songs

Songs of the Half-Light, op. 65 (W. de la Mare), S/T, gui, 1964, Peter Pears, Julian Bream, Aldeburgh, 22 June 1965

Five Herrick Poems, op. 89 (R. Herrick), S/T, hp, 1973, Peter Pears, Ossian Ellis, Snape, 19 June 1974

Una and the Lion, op. 98 (E. Spenser), S, sop/tr rec, gamba, hpd, 1979, Elizabeth Harwood, Jeanne and Marguerite Dolmetsch, Joseph Saxby, London, 22 March 1979

CHAMBER AND INSTRUMENTAL

Three to eight instruments

Prelude – Intermezzo (blues) – Finale, fl, vn, va, pf, 1927, Aeolian Players, Gordon Bryan, October 1927, London

Serenade, fl, ob, vn, va, vc, *c.* 1929, unpubd

Piece, fl, cl, bn, 1929

Suite, fl/pic, ob, vn, va, vc, *c.* 1930, unpubd

Polka, op. 5/1, 2 pf, tpt, cym, tambour de Basque, triangle, *c.* 1934, arr.

Trio, fl, ob, pf, 1935, Sylvan Trio, 1935

String Quartet no. 1, op. 6, 1935, Pro Arte String Quartet, London, November 1935 [Boosey & Hawkes]

String Quartet no. 2, op. 15, 1940, Stratton Quartet, London, 5 June 1941

String Trio, op. 19, 1943, Frederick Grinke, Watson Forbes, James Phillips, London, 7 August 1944

Trio, op. 44, hn, vn, pf, 1953, Dennis Brain, Manoug Parikian, Colin Horsley, London, 28 March 1954

Sextet, op. 47, cl, hn, str qt, 1955, Melos Ensemble, Cheltenham, 11 July 1955

Concertino, op. 49, rec/fl, vn, vc, hpd/pf, 1955, Carl Dolmetsch, Jean Pougnet, Arnold Ashby, Joseph Saxby, London, BBC, 24 January 1956

Diversions: Four Pieces for Eight Instruments, op. 63, ob, d, bn, hn, pf, vn, va, vc, 1964, Delphos Ensemble, Cheltenham, 13 July 1964

Oboe Quartet, op. 70, ob, vn, va, vc, 1967, London Oboe Quartet, London, 22 May 1968

String Quartet no. 3, op. 76, 1970, Dartington String Quartet, Dartington, 28 November 1970

In Memoriam Igor Stravinsky, str qt, 1971, John Tunnell, Peter Carter, Brian Hawkins, Charles Tunnell, London, BBC, 8 April 1972 [*Tempo* 97, 1971, Boosey & Hawkes]

Canon, str tr, 1971 (contrib. to *Greetings to Sir Arthur Bliss*)

Fanfare for the Royal Academy of Music Banquet, 7 tpt, timp, 1972, Trumpeters of the Band of the Royal Marines/Paul Neville, London, 14 July 1972

Quintet, op. 90, ob, cl, hn, bn, pf, 1975, Members of the Chamber Music Society of Lincoln Centre, New York, 30 January 1976

Two instruments

Minuet, 2 rec, *c*. 1924

Petite Suite, ob, vc, 1927, London 1928

Sonatine, cl, pf, 1928, unpubd

Suite, ob, vc, *c*. 1930, Paris, 31 May 1930

Sonata no. 1, vn, pf, 1931, Yvonne Astruc, Madeleine Grovlez, Paris, 4 May 1932

Sonata no. 2, op. 1, vn, pf, 1932/33, Orrea Pernel, Kathleen Long, London 6 June 1933

Sonatina, op. 13, rec/fl, pf, 1939, Carl Dolmetsch, Christopher Wood, London, 18 November 1939 [Schott]

Sonatina, op. 17, vn, pf, 1942, Max Rostal, Lennox Berkeley, London, 25 September 1944

Sonata in D minor, op. 22, va, pf, 1945, Watson Forbes, Denise Lassimonne, London, 3 May 1946 (also original finale, unpubd)

Elegy and Toccata, op. 33/2–3, vn, pf, 1950, Frederick Grinke, Ernest Lush, London, BBC, 27 September 1950

Allegro, 2 tr rec, 1955; arr. 2 ob, 1981 [Boosey & Hawkes]

Andantino, op. 21/2A, vc, pf, 1955, arr. A *Festival Anthem*, op. 21/2, 1945

Sonatina, op. 61, ob, pf, 1962, Janet Craxton, Alan Richardson, London, 19 November 1962

Introduction and Allegro, op. 80, db, pf, 1971, Rodney Slatford, Clifford Lee, London, 14 January 1971 [Yorke]

Duo, op. 81/1, vc, pf, 1971, Elizabeth Wilson, Kathleen Sturrock, London, 11 January 1972

Canzonetta, ob, pf, 1973, arr. Sinfonia Concertante op. 84

Sonata, op. 97, fl, pf, 1978, James Galway, Phillip Moll, Edinburgh, 30 August 1978

One instrument

Quatre pièces, gui, *c*. 1928 [Bèrben]

Three Pieces, cl, 1939

Introduction and Allegro, op. 24, vn, 1946, Ivry Gitlis, London, 19 June 1947

Theme and Variations, op. 33/1, vn, 1950, Frederick Grinke, Zurich, 8 September 1950

Sonatina, op. 52/1, gui, 1957, Julian Bream, London, 9 March 1958

Three Pieces (for Stephan Deak), va, *c*. 1965, unpbd

Nocturne, op. 67/2, hp, 1967 [Stainer & Bell]

Theme and Variations, op. 77, gui, 1970, Angelo Gilardino, Tronzano-Vercelli, Italy, 19 December 1971 [Bèrben/Chester]

KEYBOARD

Piano solo

March, pf, 1924

Mr Pilkington's Toye, hpd/pf, 1925

Toccata, 1925, J. F. Waterhouse, Oxford, 6 March 1926

For Vere, pf, 1927

Piano Pieces, 1927, Jan Smeterlin, London, 1929

Three Dances: Les Amoureux, Andante (Blues), Java, arr. Dickinson, from Ballet (untitled), 1932

Polka, op. 5/1a, 1934, arr. Polka op. 5, 2 pf

Three Pieces, op. 2, 1935 [Augener/Stainer & Bell]

Three Impromptus, op. 7, 1935 [Boosey & Hawkes]

Five Short Pieces, op. 4, 1936

Four Concert Studies, op. 14/1, 1940 [Schott]

Paysage, 1944, Lennox Berkeley, London, 20 February 1945

Sonata for Piano, op. 20, 1945, Clifford Curzon, London, 22 July 1946

Six Preludes, op. 23, 1945

Three Mazurkas (Hommage à Chopin), op. 32/1, 1949, Colin Horsley, London, BBC, 23 March 1950

Scherzo, op. 32/2, 1949, Colin Horsley, Sydney, Australia, 18 May 1950

Concert Study in E flat, op. 48/2, 1955, Colin Horsley, London, BBC, 20 January 1955

Improvisation on a Theme of Manuel de Falla, op. 55/2, 1960

Four Piano Studies, op. 82, 1972, Margaret Bruce, London, 9 December 1975

Prelude and Capriccio, op. 95, 1978, Roger Woodward, Cardiff, 24 February 1978

Mazurka, op. 101/2, 1982 (contrib. to Homage to Haydn), John McCabe, London, BBC, 18 March 1982

Piano four hands

Sonatina, op. 39, 1954, Michael Lindsay, Sybil Jones, Stoke on Trent, 8 July 1954

Theme and Variations, op. 73, 1968, Annie Alt, Gerald Stofsky, Stroud, 20 October 1971

Palm Court Waltz, op. 81/2a, arr. from *Diana and Actaeon Waltz*, 1971

Two pianos

Polka, Nocturne and Capriccio, op. 5, 1934–8, Ethel Bartlett, Rae Robertson, London, 4 February 1938

Sonatina, op. 52/2, 1959, Ashley Clarke, Nini Straneo, Rome, 26 May 1959

Bagatelle, op. 101/1, 1981, Margaret Bruce, Jennifer Bowring, London, 1 May 1983

Organ

Impromptu, 1941

Three Pieces, op. 72/1, 1966–8, Simon Preston, Cheltenham, 5 July 1968

Fantasia, op. 92, 1976, Nicholas Kynaston, London, 1 December 1976

Andantino, op. 21/2a, org, arr. J. Bate, 1981, from *A Festival Anthem*, op. 21/2, 1945

Other

Suite for Harpsichord, 1930

Prelude and Fugue, op. 55/3, clvd, 1960

LOST WORKS

La belle dame sans merci (J. Keats), v, pf, Oxford, 16 June 1924

Two songs: *Sonette de Ronsard* and *Les Dimanches* (anon.) v, pf, Oxford, 4 December 1924

Two Dances, pf duet, Oxford, 12 March 1925

Four Pieces for Organ, 1925

Four Pieces for Flute, Oboe and Piano, 1925

Two Songs (W. H. Auden), v, pf, C. Day Lewis, Lennox Berkeley, Oxford, 1926

Introduction & Dance, chmr orch, London Chamber Orchestra/Anthony Bernard, London, 26 April 1926

Four Pieces, chmr orch, 1926

Sinfonietta, chmr orch, 1926

Concertino, chmr orch, London Chamber Orchestra/Anthony Bernard, London, 6 April 1927

Sonatina, vn, 1927, Jane Isnard, Paris, 26 February 1929

Two Pieces for String Quartet, Paris, 2 May 1930

Symphony, str orch, London Chamber Orchestra/Anthony Bernard, 14 December 1931

Three Poems by Mary Webb, v, pf, 1938

Bibliography

WRITINGS BY LENNOX BERKELEY
Chronological list

Regular reports 'Music in Paris' in the *Monthly Musical Record*: June 1929, 174; August 1929, 242; December 1929, 370; May 1930, 143; August 1930, 242; January 1931, 4; March 1931, 82; May 1931, 146; July 1931, 210; December 1931, 360; February 1932, 37; March-April 1932, 63; June 1932, 112; September 1932, 159; December 1932, 365; March-April 1932, 63; June 1933, 112; December 1933, 231; June 1934, 110–11

'Britten and his String Quartet', *Listener*, 27 May 1943, 641

Letter, in N. Demuth, *Maurice Ravel* (London, 1947), 177

'Open Forum: Variations on a Theme – Tonal or Atonal?', *Music Today* [Journal of the ISCM] 1 (1949), 145

'The Composer looks at the Opera', *Philharmonic Post* 5, March/April 1950, 12–13

'Britten's Spring Symphony', *Music & Letters* 31/3 (July 1950), 216–19

'Poulenc's Piano Concerto', programme note, BBC Symphony Orchestra, 8 November 1950, 11–12

'The Light Music', in *Benjamin Britten: a Commentary on his Works from a Group of Specialists*, ed. D. Mitchell and H. Keller (London, 1952), 278–94

'Composers' Forum' (Nelson), *London Music*, November 1954, 23–4

'Composers' Forum' (Ruth), *London Music*, October 1956, 20–21

Special Correspondent, 'Mr. Lennox Berkeley on the Composer's Need to hear his own Works', *The Times*, 12 April 1959

Review of A. Robertson, *More than Music*, *Tablet*, 9 December 1961, 1178

'The Sound of Words', *The Times*, 28 June 1962, 15

'Concert-going in 1963', *Sunday Times*, 30 December 1962, 28

'Francis Poulenc' [obituary], *Musical Times* 104 (March 1963), 205

'Britten's Characters', *About the House* 1, no. 5 (1963), 14

'Boulanger the Dedicated', *Piano Teacher* 8, no. 2 (1965), 6–7

'Nocturnes, Berceuse, Barcarolle', in *Frédéric Chopin: Profiles of the Man and Musician*, ed. A. Walker (London, 1966), 170–86

'Truth in Music', *Times Literary Supplement*, 3 March 1966, 158

'Berkeley Describes his Setting of the Magnificat', *Listener*, 4 July 1968, 25

'Lilli Boulanger', *Listener*, 21 November 1968, 692

'Last Week's Broadcast Music', *Listener*, 13 February 1969, 218

'Last Week's Broadcast Music', *Listener*, 23 February 1969, 579

'Charles Burney's Tour', *Listener*, 5 March 1970, 321

'Lennox Berkeley writes about Alan Rawsthorne', *Listener*, 30 December 1971, 913

'Alan Rawsthorne – 1', *Composer* 42 (Winter 1971–2), 5–7

'A Composer Speaks – 2', *Composer* 43 (Spring 1972), 17–19

'Walton – Yesterday', *Performing Right* 57 (May 1972), 18–19

Tribute to A. Robertson, in *Dear Alec – a Tribute for his 80th Birthday from his Friends Known and Unknown* (Worcester, 1972), 11

'Views from Mont Juic', *Tempo* 106 (September 1973), 6–7

Comments on each Prom in *Radio Times*, 19–25 July to 20–26 September 1975

'Foreword', in P. Bernac, *Francis Poulenc, the Man and his Songs* (London, 1977), 11–12

'A Composer Looks Back', in *250 Years of the Three Choirs Festival*, ed. B. Still (Gloucestershire, 1977), 45

'Maurice Ravel', *Adam International Review* 404–6 (1978), 13–17

Introduction, in C. Headington, *Britten*, (London, 1981)

Remarks in *Bid the World Good-Night*, ed. R. Ricketts (London, 1981), 19–21

'Igor Stravinsky: a Centenary Tribute', *Musical Times* 123 (June 1982), 395

Tribute in B. Monsaingeon, *Mademoiselle: Conversations with Nadia Boulanger*, trans. R. Marsack (Manchester, 1985), 120

Tribute in *Michael Tippett – a Celebration*, ed. G. Lewis (Tunbridge Wells, 1985), 21

SELECTED WRITINGS ABOUT LENNOX BERKELEY
Chronological list

G. Bryan, 'The Younger English Composers – Lennox Berkeley', *Monthly Musical Record* 59 (June 1929), 161–2

A. Frank, 'Jonah', *Listener*, 10 June 1936, 1134

M. D. Calvocoressi, 'Oratorio in Modern Idiom', *Radio Times*, 12 June 1936

B. Falk, *The Berkeleys of Berkeley Square and some of their Kinsfolk* (London, 1944)

D. Brook, *Composers' Gallery* (London, 1946), 20–22

E. Lockspeiser, 'The Music of Lennox Berkeley', *Listener*, 10 July 1947, 76

R. Hull, 'The Music of Lennox Berkeley', *Chesterian* 23 (January 1948), 61–4

M. Flothius, *Modern British Composers* (Stockholm, 1949), 31–5

R. Hull, 'The Style of Lennox Berkeley', *Chesterian* 24 (April 1950), 84–7

A. Frank, 'Contemporary Portraits: Lennox Berkeley', *The Music Teacher*, September 1950, 395 & 404.

H. F. Redlich, 'Lennox Berkeley', *Music-Survey* 3 (1951), 245–9

V. Drewry, 'Lennox Berkeley – some recent compositions', *Chesterian* 26 (October 1951), 1–4

N. Demuth, *Musical Trends in the 20th Century* (Liverpool, 1952), 322–3

C. Le Fleming, 'The Shorter Works of Lennox Berkeley: an Appreciation', *Chesterian* 27 (April 1953), 98–104

A. Frank, *Modern British Composers* (London, 1953), 64–8

I. Holst, 'Lennox Berkeley's Stabat Mater', *Chesterian* 28 (April 1954), 115–18

P. Dehn, 'A Dinner Engagement', *Opera* 5 (June 1954), 335–8

W. Mellers, 'The Music of Lennox Berkeley', *Listener*, 24 June 1954, 1113

A. Pryce-Jones, 'Some Notes on the Text of *Nelson*', *Opera* 5, October 1954, 595–8

W. Dean, 'Lennox Berkeley's Orchestral Music', *Listener*, 7 April 1955, 637

C. Mason, 'The Progress of Lennox Berkeley', *Listener*, 27 September 1956, 485

C. Headington, 'The Instrumental Music of Lennox Berkeley', *Chesterian* 32 (Winter 1958), 82–5

M. Cooper, 'Lennox Berkeley and his new Symphony', *Listener*, 19 February 1959, 351

H. Costley-White, *Mary Cole, Countess of Berkeley* (London, 1961)

M. Schafer, *British Composers in Interview* (London, 1963), 83–91

P. Dickinson, 'Berkeley on the Keyboard', *Music and Musicians*, April 1963, 10–11, 58

P. Dickinson, 'The Music of Lennox Berkeley', *Musical Times* 104 (May 1963), 327–30

M. Cooper, 'Lennox Berkeley', *Listener*, 9 May 1963, 805

P. Dickinson, 'Lennox Berkeley', *Music and Musicians*, August 1965, 20–23, 54 (reprinted as 'Senior British Composers 2: Lennox Berkeley', *Composer*, Summer 1970, 3–9, 11)

F. S. Howes, *The English Musical Renaissance* (London, 1966), 274–7

P. Dehn, 'New Operas for Aldeburgh – *The Bear* and *Castaway*', *About the House* 2/6 (1967), 35–7

P. Dickinson, 'Berkeley's Music Today', *Musical Times* 109 (November 1968), 1013–14

M. Berkeley, 'Lennox Berkeley's Third Symphony', *Listener*, 3 July 1969, 25

D. Shawe-Taylor, 'Berkeley's Achievement', *Sunday Times*, 16 January 1972, 30

J. Tavener, 'Lennox Berkeley at 70', *Listener*, 10 May 1973, 625

D. Shawe-Taylor, 'Lennox Berkeley: Success at 70', *Sunday Times*, 6 May 1973, 37

A. Wood, 'Lennox Berkeley, 70, hits the high point of his career', *Oxford Mail*, 3 August 1973, 12

A. Porter, 'Berkeley', *Financial Times*, 4 August 1973

P. Dickinson, 'Interview with Sir Lennox Berkeley', in *Twenty British Composers: the Feeney Commissions* (London, 1975), 23–9

P. Sudlow, 'Lennox Berkeley at 75', *Music and Musicians*, May 1978, 27

D. Shawe-Taylor, 'Berkeley – Homage to a Craftsman', *Sunday Times*, 21 May 1978, 39

S. Mundy, 'Lennox Berkeley at Seventy-Five', *Classical Music Weekly*, 27 May 1978, 14

P. Dickinson, 'Berkeley at 75 talks to Peter Dickinson', *Musical Times* 119 (May 1978), 409–11

D. Mitchell with J. Evans, *Benjamin Britten: Pictures from a Life, 1913–1976* (London, 1978)

E. Hughes and T. Day, *Sir Lennox Berkeley*, Discographies of British Composers 1 (London, 1979)

P. Dickinson, 'Berkeley, Lennox', *New Grove Dictionary of Music and Musicians*, ed. S. Sadie (London, 1980), vol. 2, 560–63

A. Blyth, 'Sir Lennox Berkeley', in *Remembering Britten* (London, 1981), 43–6

E. Levi, 'Music by Lennox Berkeley – 1: Chamber Music' (followed by tributes), *WH-News* 1 (1983), 2–10

D. Shawe-Taylor, 'The Master of Melody', *Sunday Times*, 15 May 1983, 43

P. Dickinson, 'Peter Dickinson salutes the Composer on his Eightieth Birthday', *3: The Radio 3 Magazine*, June 1983, 4–6

W. Dean, 'Heroic Stature', *Listener*, 20 October 1983, 32

W. Hussey, *Patron of Art: the Revival of a Great Tradition among Modern Artists* (London, 1985), 94–6

R. H. Hansen, 'The Songs of Lennox Berkeley' (DMA diss., North Texas State University, 1987)

J. Redding, 'A Descriptive List of the Musical Manuscripts of Sir Lennox Berkeley' (MSc (Library Science) diss., University of North Carolina at Chapel Hill, 1988)

P. Dickinson, *The Music of Lennox Berkeley* (London, 1988)

—— 'Sir Lennox Berkeley' [obituary], *Independent*, 27 December 1989

—— 'Sir Lennox Berkeley as Teacher: an Appreciation', *Guardian*, 28 December 1989

H. Cole, 'Obituary: Sir Lennox Berkeley. 'Music with a French Accent', *Guardian*, 27 December 1989

R. Nicholls, 'Sir Lennox Berkeley' [obituary], *Independent*, 27 December 1989

Unsigned, 'Sir Lennox Berkeley', *Daily Telegraph*, 27 December 1989

Unsigned, 'Sir Lennox Berkeley: Composer of Restrained and Courteous Virtues', *The Times*, 27 December 1989

M. Williamson, 'Sir Lennox Berkeley', *Independent*, 29 December 1989

D. Shawe-Taylor, 'A Man at Peace with Melody', *Sunday Times*, 31 December 1989

H. Hansen, 'Lennox Berkeley: his Influence and his Songs', *NATS Journal* 46 (March/April 1990), 4–11, 50

M. Williamson, 'Sir Lennox Berkeley (1903–1989)', *Musical Times* 131 (April 1990), 197–9

—— 'Genius out of Tune with the Voice of Britain', *Independent*, 4 April 1990

M. J. White, 'The Persuasive Voice of Lennox Berkeley', *Sunday Independent*, 8 April 1990

P. Dickinson, 'An Unobtrusive Man: Sir Lennox Berkeley's Wide-Ranging Achievement', *Listener*, 14 June 1990, 44–5

S. R. Craggs, *Lennox Berkeley: a Source Book* (Aldershot, 2000)

P. Dickinson and J. Redding, 'Berkeley, Lennox', *New Grove Dictionary of Music and Musicians*, 2nd edn, ed. S. Sadie and J. Tyrrell (London, 2001), vol. 3, 359–63

L. Hardy, *The British Piano Sonata, 1870–1945* (Woodbridge, 2001)

M. Berkeley, 'We lived in a secret, intoxicating world: Michael Berkeley recalls the special bond he had with his father', *Guardian*, 10 February 2003

R. Nicholls, Lennox Berkeley', *BBC Music Magazine*, June 2003, 50–53

P. Dickinson, *The Music of Lennox Berkeley* (revised and enlarged; Woodbridge, 2003)

P. Dickinson, 'Britten, his Mentor and some Colleagues', in *New Aldeburgh Anthology*, ed. A. Banks and J. Reekie (Woodbridge, 2009), 136–9

T. Scotland, *Lennox and Freda* (Norwich, 2010)

Douglas Stevens, 'Lennox Berkeley: a Critical Study of his Music' (PhD diss., University of Bristol, 2011)

SELECTED GENERAL WORKS

Acton, H., *Memoirs of an Aesthete* (London, 1970)

Annan, N. *Our Age: the Generation that Made Post-War Britain* (London, 1990)

Auden, W. H., *Juvenilia, 1922–28*, ed. K. Bucknell (Princeton, 1994)

Banfield, S., *Sensibility and English Song*, 2 vols. (Cambridge, 1985)

Banks, P., ed., *The Making of Peter Grimes* (Woodbridge, 1996)

Bliss, A., *As I Remember* (London, 1970)

—— *Bliss on Music: Selected Writings on Music, 1920–75*, ed. G. Roscoe (Oxford, 1991)

Briggs, A., *The BBC: the First Fifty Years* (Oxford, 1985)

Brindle, R. S., *Serial Composition* (London, 1966)

Britten, B., *Letters from a Life: Selected Letters and Diaries of Benjamin Britten, 1913–1976: Volume One, 1923–1939*, ed. D. Mitchell and P. Reed (London, 1991); *Volume Two, 1939–1945*, ed. D. Mitchell and P. Reed (London, 1991); *Volume Three, 1946–1951*, ed. D. Mitchell, P. Reed and M. Cooke (London, 2004); *Volume Four, 1952–1957*, ed. D. Mitchell, P. Reed and M. Cooke (Woodbridge, 2008); *Volume Five, 1958–1965*, ed. P. Reed, M. Cooke (Woodbridge, 2010)

Britten, B., *My Brother Benjamin* (Bourne End, 1986)

Brooks, J., 'Nadia Boulanger and the Salon of the Princesse de Polignac', *Journal of the American Musicological Society* 46 (1993), 415–68

Carpenter, H., *W. H. Auden: a Biography* (London, 1981)

—— *The Brideshead Generation: Evelyn Waugh and his Friends* (London, 1989)

—— *Benjamin Britten: a Biography* (London, 1992)

—— *The Envy of the World: Fifty Years of the BBC Third Programme and Radio 3* (London, 1996)

Clarke, M., *The Sadler's Wells Ballet* (London, 1955)

Cocteau, J., *The Difficulty of Being*, trans. E. Sprigge (London, 1966)

Cohen, H., *A Bundle of Time: the Memoirs of Harriet Cohen* (London, 1969)

Copland, A., and V. Perlis, *Copland, Volume I: 1900–1942* (London, 1984)

—— *Copland since 1943* (London, 1989)

Craft, R., *Chronicle of a Friendship, 1948–1971* (New York, 1972)

Day Lewis, C., *The Buried Day* (London, 1960)

Deane, B., *Albert Roussel* (London, 1961).

Demuth, N., *Albert Roussel* (London, 1947).

Dickinson, P., *Lord Berners: Composer, Writer, Painter* (Woodbridge, 2008)

——, ed., *Copland Connotations: Studies and Interviews* (Woodbridge, 2002)

Duncan, R., *Working with Britten* (Bideford, 1981)

Evans, J., P. Reed, P. Wilson, eds., *A Britten Source Book* (Aldeburgh, 1987)

Foreman, L., *From Parry to Britten: British Music in Letters, 1900–1945* (London, 1987)

Fuller, J., *W. H. Auden: A Commentary* (London, 1998)

Garnham, M., *As I Saw It: Basil Douglas, Benjamin Britten and the English Opera Group* (London, 1998)

Glock, W., *Notes in Advance* (Oxford, 1991)

Grogan, C., ed, *Imogen Holst: a Life in Music* (rev. edn; Woodbridge, 2010)

Harding, J., *The Ox on the Roof: Scenes from Musical Life in Paris in the Twenties* (London, 1972)

Headington, C., *Britten* (London, 1981)

—— *Peter Pears: a Biography* (London, 1992)

Junge, E., *Anthony Bernard: a Life in Music* (Tunbridge Wells, 1992)

Kahan, S., *Music's Modern Muse: a Life of Winaretta Singer, Princesse de Polignac* (Rochester, NY, 2003)

Kavanagh, J., *Secret Muses: the Life of Frederick Ashton* (London, 1996)

Kendall, A., *The Tender Tyrant: Nadia Boulanger – a Life Devoted to Music* (London, 1976)

Kennedy, M., *Portrait of Walton* (Oxford, 1989)

—— *Britten* (London, 1993)

Kildea, P., ed., *Selling Britten: Music and the Marketplace* (Oxford, 2002)

—— *Britten on Music* (Oxford, 2003)

Koechlin, C., *Gabriel Fauré*, trans. L. Orry (London, 1945)

Lambert, C., *Music Ho!: a Study of Music in Decline* (London, 1934)

Lees-Milne, J., *Diaries* (London, 1970–98)

Lockspeiser, E., *Debussy: his Life and Mind* (London, 1966)

Mayes, A. C. D., *Carl Dolmetsch and the Recorder Repertoire of the Twentieth Century* (Aldershot, 2003)

McCabe, J., *Alan Rawsthorne* (Oxford, 1999)

Mellers, W., *Francis Poulenc* (Oxford, 1993)

Meredith, A., and P. Harris, *Malcolm Williamson: a Mischievous Muse* (London, 2007)

—— *Richard Rodney Bennett: the Complete Musician* (London, 2010)

Milhaud, D., *Notes without Music*, trans D. Evans (London, 1952)

—— *My Happy Life: an Autobiography* (London/New York, 1995)

Mitchell, D., *Britten and Auden in the Thirties* (London, 1981)

Mitchell, D., with J. Evans, *Benjamin Britten: Pictures from a Life, 1913–1976* (London, 1978)

Mitchell, D., with H. Keller, eds., *Benjamin Britten: a Commentary on his Works from a Group of Specialists* (London, 1952)

Montsaingeon, B., *Mademoiselle: Conversations with Nadia Boulanger* (Manchester, 2001)

Nichols, R., *Ravel Remembered* (London, 1987)

—— *The Harlequin Years: Music in Paris, 1917–1929* (London, 2002)

—— *Ravel* (New Haven, 2011)

Oman, C., *Nelson* (London, 1947

Orledge, R., *Gabriel Fauré* (London, 1983)
—— *Charles Koechlin (1867–1950): his Life and Works* (Chur, 1989)
Palmer, C., ed., *The Britten Companion* (London, 1984)
Potter, J., *Stephen Potter at the BBC: Features in War and Peace* (Orford, 2004)
Poulenc, F., *Correspondance, 1915–63* (Paris, 1967)
—— *My Friends and Myself*, ed. S. Audel, trans. J. Harding (London, 1978)
—— *Echo and Source, Selected Correspondence, 1915–1963*, ed. and trans. S. Buckland (Paris, 1994)
Rosenstiel, L., *Nadia Boulanger: a Life in Music* (New York, 1982)
Routh, F., *Contemporary British Music* (London, 1972)
Steegmuller, F., *Cocteau: a Biography* (London, 1986)
Stravinsky, I., *An Autobiography*, New York, 1936)
—— *The Poetics of Music* (London, 1947)
—— *Selected Correspondence*, ed. R. Craft, 3 vols. (London and New York, 1982–5)
Stravinsky, I., with R. Craft, *Conversations with Igor Stravinsky* (London and New York, 1959)
—— *Memories and Commentaries* (London and New York, 1960)
—— *Expositions and Developments* (London and New York, 1962)
—— *Dialogues and a Diary* (Garden City, NY, 1963)
—— *Themes and Episodes* (New York, 1966)
—— *Retrospectives and Conclusions* (New York, 1969)
Tear, R., *Tear here* (London, 1990)
Thomson, V., *Virgil Thomson* (London, 1967)
Tippett, M., *Those Twentieth-Century Blues* (London, 1991)
Vaughan, D., *Frederick Ashton and his Ballets* (London, 1977)
Walsh, S., *The Music of Stravinsky* (Oxford, 1988)
—— *Igor Stravinsky: a Creative Spring: Russia and France, 1882–1934* (London, 1999)
—— *Stravinsky: the Second Exile: France and America, 1934–1971* (London, 2006)
Walton, S., *Behind the Façade* (Oxford, 1988)
Whittall, A., *The Cambridge Introduction to Serialism* (Cambridge, 2008)

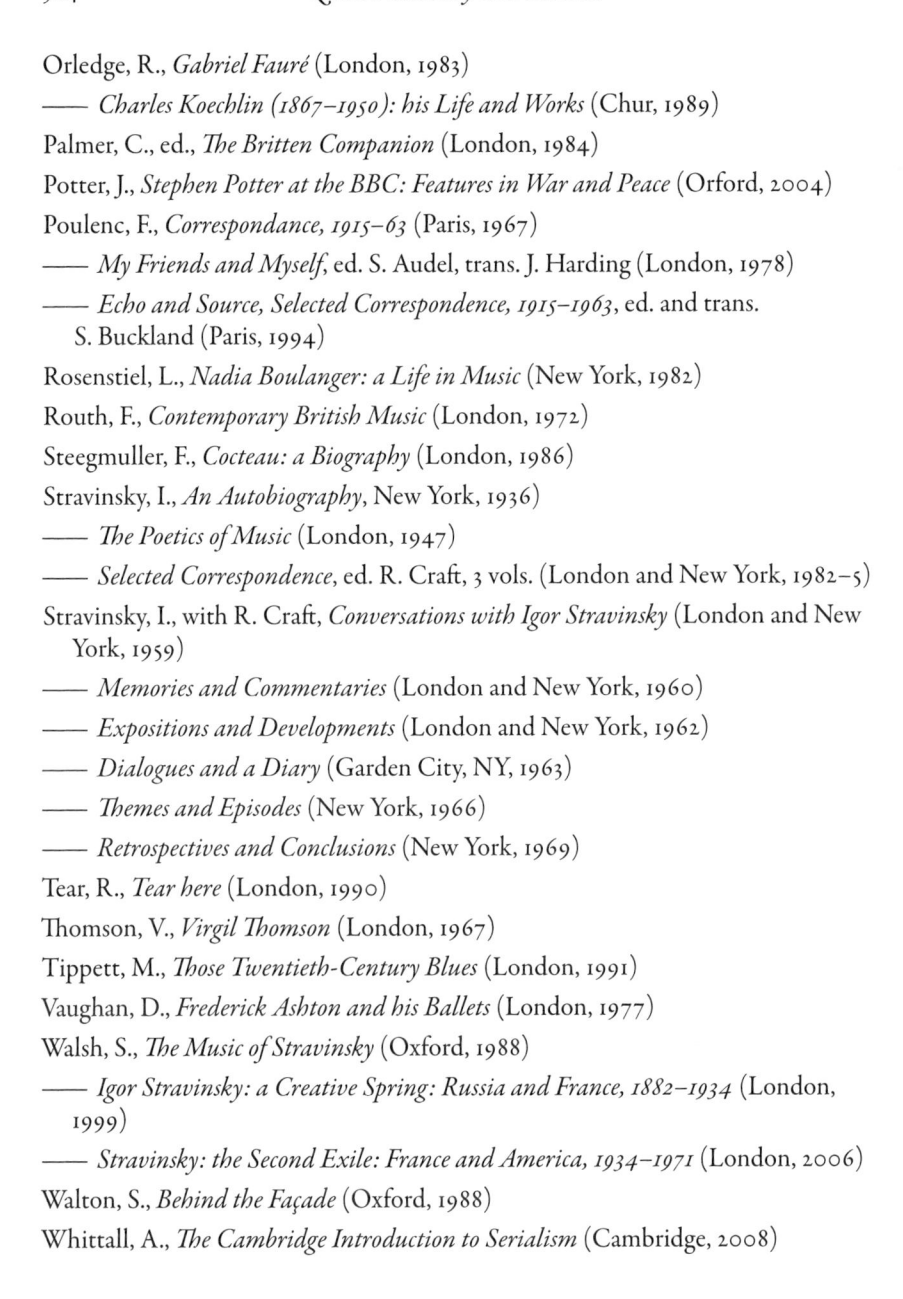

Index of Works by Berkeley

Andantino for cello and piano, op. 21/2a, 11
Andantino for organ, op. 21/2a, 11
Another Spring, op. 91/3, 10, 216
Antiphon, op. 85, 10, 202, 203, 219, 246
Auden, W. H., two songs to poems of (1926), lost, 155n5, 163
Automne, song, op. 60/3, 4, 143, 201n55
Autumn's Legacy, op. 58, 143, 202

Batter my heart, 174

Castaway, op. 68, 86, 174, 180, 274, 281
Concertino, op. 49, 244
Concerto for cello (1939), 13, 69, 247
Concerto for flute, op. 36, 160, 221, 240
Concerto for guitar, op. 88, 10, 13, 170, 205–7, 227–8, 279
Concerto for piano, op. 29, 2, 5, 9, 11, 17, 160, 174, 210, 237–40, 247, 249, 273
Concerto for piano and double string orchestra, op. 46, 8, 110, 239–40
Concerto for two pianos, op. 30, 2, 5, 11, 17, 77, 160, 172, 234, 240, 249, 273, 277
Concerto for violin, op. 59, 9, 192, 234, 254

Dialogue for cello and orchestra, op.79, 193–4, 196, 219, 234
Dinner Engagement, A, op. 45, 2, 5, 13, 83, 174, 188, 227, 233, 244–5, 262, 265, 269, 273, 274, 281
Divertimento in B flat, op. 18, 2, 3, 4, 73, 159, 172, 174, 191, 231–2, 235, 254, 262, 266, 269, 276
Domini est terra, op. 10, 56, 59, 60
D'un vanneur de blé aux vents (*The Thresher*) (1925), 143, 156, 201n55
Duo for cello and piano, op. 81/1, 194, 196, 281

Elegy and Toccata, violin and piano, op. 33/2–3, 212

Faldon Park, 179, 214, 222–4
Fantasia for organ, op. 92, 11, 215, 220
Festival Anthem, A, op. 21/2, 11
Fête étrange, La (Fauré), arr. for ballet, 90n4

First Gentleman, The (film), 230
Five Chinese Songs, op. 78, 4n10, 10, 143–4, 172, 189, 191, 192, 201n55
Five De la Mare Songs, op. 26, 5
Five Herrick Poems, op. 89, 171, 206
Five Poems of W. H. Auden, op. 53, 3, 4, 10, 88, 111, 143–4, 172, 185, 187, 250
Five Short Pieces, piano, op. 4, 241
Four Concert Studies, piano, op. 14/1, 66, 68, 70, 74n110, 236, 237, 241, 277
Four Piano Studies, op. 82, 196, 277
Four Poems of Saint Teresa of Avila, op. 27, 2, 4, 7, 79, 143, 169, 172, 174, 225, 246, 250, 262, 266–7, 269
Four Ronsard Sonnets, Set 1, op. 40, 217
Four Ronsard Sonnets, Set 2, op. 62, 197–8, 250

Glutton for Life, A (film), 159n16

Hill of the Graces, The, op. 91/2, 209, 211
Hotel Reserve (film, 1944), 72
How Love Came In (*c.* 1935), 88, 274

I carry your heart with me (1972), 171
Introduction and Allegro, for double bass and piano, op. 80, 194
Introduction and Allegro, for two pianos and orchestra, op.11, 69–95
Introduction and Dance (*c.* 1925), lost, 156

Jonah, op. 3, 7, 54, 55, 59, 158, 271, 273
Judica me, op 96/1, 220

Lord is my Shepherd, The, op. 91/1, 11, 257

Magnificat, op. 71, 11, 127–9, 181, 184, 186, 220
Magnificat and Nunc Dimittis, op. 99, 224
Mass for Five Voices, op. 64, 281
Missa Brevis, op. 57, 189, 203, 261
Mont Juic Suite, op. 9 (with Britten), 89, 158, 165, 174, 245, 267

Nelson, op. 41, 2, 4, 6, 82n142, 81, 83, 161, 168, 173, 201, 233, 240, 244, 255–6, 261, 265, 274–5, 278, 281

Night Covers up the Rigid Land, op.14/2, 254
Nocturne, op. 25, 5

Oboe Quartet, op. 70, 183, 223
Ode for SATB, trumpet and strings (*c.* 1932), 57
Ode du premier jour de mai, op. 14/2, 253
Overture (1947), 111
Overture, op. 8, 2, 51n14, 54, 63

Palm Court Waltz (*Diana and Actaeon Waltz*), op. 81/2, 9, 88, 174, 193
Partita, op. 66, 246
Pindar, deux poèmes de, SATB and orchestra (*c.* 1935), 54
Poulette grise, La, children's choirs, trumpet, 2 pianos (*c.* 1931), 58
Prelude, Intermezzo (Blues) and Finale (1927), 47n8

Quatre pièces pour la guitarre (*c.* 1928), 225n2
Quintet for piano and wind, op. 90, 10, 207–9, 211, 215, 240

Ruth, op, 50, 2, 9, 13, 174, 240, 244–5, 250, 262, 274, 278, 281

Scherzo for piano, op. 32/2, 239
Serenade for strings, op. 12, 2, 66–8, 172, 225, 231, 254, 256, 262, 266, 276
Sextet, op. 47, 6, 199, 202, 244
Signs in the Dark, op. 69, 181, 198
Sinfonia Concertante, oboe and orchestra, op. 84, 7, 9, 13, 172–3, 198, 201, 202
Sinfonietta, op. 34, 79n130, 231, 254
Six Preludes, piano, op. 23, 5, 104, 185, 236–7, 239, 241, 243, 248, 254–5, 263
Sonata for flute, op. 97, 10
Sonata for flute (Poulenc), orchestrated, 212–13
Sonata for piano, op. 20, 2, 4, 237, 240, 255
Sonata for viola and piano, op. 22, 223
Sonata for violin and piano no. 1 (1931), 50, 52
Sonata for violin and piano no. 2, op. 1, 51–3, 53n26
Sonatina for flute, op. 13, 280
Sonatina for guitar, op. 52/1, 170–1, 225–7
Sonatina for oboe and piano, op. 61, 9, 88, 223
Sonatina for piano duet, 88, 187, 196

Sonatina for two pianos, op. 52/2, 111
Sonatina for violin and piano, op. 17, 10, 73, 241, 263
Sonatina for violin solo (1927), lost, 48
Songs of the Half-Light, op. 65, 143
Stabat Mater, op. 28, 5, 7, 79, 219, 227, 233, 240, 242, 267, 277–8
String Quartet no. 1, op. 6, 55, 70, 173, 254
String Quartet no. 2, op. 15, 90n5
String Quartet no. 3, op. 76, 9, 173, 190, 246
String Trio, op. 19, 5, 7, 72, 73, 160, 223
Suite for orchestra (1927), 16, 158
Suite for string orchestra, op. 87, 170
Symphony no. 1, op. 16, 2, 4, 5, 6, 58, 71–2, 172, 173, 176, 230–1, 232–3, 235
Symphony no. 2, op. 51, 4, 6, 7–8, 9, 10, 172, 178, 211, 213
Symphony no. 3, op. 74, 9, 87, 172, 173, 176–7, 185, 190, 195, 202, 207, 246, 249, 266, 279
Symphony no. 4, op. 94, 11, 173, 176–8, 214, 219, 220
Symphony for string orchestra (*c.* 1930), lost, 51, 156n7

Tant que mes yeux, op. 14/2, 88, 143, 274
Theme and Variations, guitar, op. 77, 171, 200
Theme and Variations, piano duet, op. 73, 196
Thou hast made me, op. 55/1, 4
Three Greek Songs, op.38, 185
Three Latin Motets, op. 81/3, 196, 198, 201
Three Mazurkas, piano, op. 32/1, 5, 88, 157, 237, 241
Three Pieces, organ, op. 72/1, 11, 185, 281
Three Pieces, two pianos, op. 5 (Polka, Nocturne, Capriccio), 60&n60, 61–3, 65, 174, 273
Tombeaux (1926), 47
Trio for horn, violin and piano, op. 44, 4, 6, 202, 237, 269, 277

Ubi caritas et amor, op. 96/2, 224, 281
Una and the Lion, op. 98, 221

Voices of the Night, op. 86, 10, 203, 210, 220

Windhover, The, 19
Windsor Variations, 172, 186, 202, 231, 235, 246

General Index

Acton, Harold, 15
Alberni Quartet, 192
Aldeburgh, 86, 174, 180, 197, 204, 206, 209, 217, 245, 256, 261, 273
Alwyn, William, 104, 206, 243
Ambler, Eric, 72n105
American Conservatory, Fontainebleau, 15, 46
Apollinaire, Guillaume, 121, 180
Apostel, Hans Eric, 182
Arner, Leonard, 211
Astruc, Yvonne, 50n9
Auden, Wystan Hugh, 1, 3, 4n10, 10, 88, 92, 101n37, 105, 107, 144, 155, 155n5, 163, 171, 254
Auric, Georges, 37, 39, 95, 182

Bach, Johann Sebastian 2, 16, 24, 27, 38, 41, 45, 49, 78, 89, 103, 124, 126, 127, 155, 163, 277
Bachauer, Gina, 239
Baker, Janet, 135, 197, 216
Ballets Russes, *see* Diaghilev, Serge
Banfield, Stephen, 261
Barber, Samuel, 66n85, 211
Barbirolli, John, 79n132, 238
Bartlett, Ethel, 62, 273
Bartók, Bela, 4, 70, 114, 133, 201
Bate, Jennifer, 11
Bax, Arnold, 4, 99, 165, 235, 257
BBC (pre-war wave-lengths and, later, Third Programme and Radio 3), 55, 56n38, 59n54, 59n55, 63, 64nn77–8, 69n94, 72, 73, 76, 77, 79n132, 80, 81, 93, 111, 132–5, 138, 140–2, 143, 154, 158n14, 159, 176–8, 201, 225, 258, 261, 265, 271–3
BBC Northern Orchestra, 205
BBC Singers, 209, 211
BBC Symphony Orchestra, 63n71, 202, 210, 235n19, 239, 279n67
Bean, Hugh, 199
Bean, T. E., 117–18
Beatles, The, 12, 170, 181n8
Beck, Conrad, 18, 21, 24, 28, 30, 36, 182
Beckett, Garth, 205
Bedford, David, 252
Beecham, Thomas, 230–1
Beers, Jacques, 36

Beethoven, Ludwig van, 20, 22, 24, 28, 37, 41, 42, 49, 92, 133, 142, 154, 166, 212, 238
Bennett, Richard Rodney, 9, 88, 185, 188, 196, 213, 219, 252, 254, 265, 266
Berg, Alban, 12, 28, 158, 276
Berkeley, Aline (née Harris, LB's mother), 55, 60, 68, 72–3, 156n8, 259
Berkeley, Freda (née Bernstein, LB's wife, Lady Berkeley), 76, 229, 246, 252, 256, 258–64, 272–3, 279, 282
Berkeley, Hastings George FitzHardinge (LB's father), 1, 154, 156n8, 261
BERKELEY, SIR LENNOX RANDALL FRANCIS
  [for Berkeley's musical works, see separate index]
  Alzheimer's, onset of, 10, 97n26, 179, 223n102, 263
  America, plans to visit, 63
  audience, attitude to, 117–18, 162, 168, 172
  Australia, Hong Kong, visits for PRS, 211
  BBC, as staff member, 69, 72, 73, 236, 272
  Berkeley earldom missed, 156n8, 164, 184, 262
  bilingual, 16, 263,
  birthdays
    70th, 88, 154, 202
    75th, 219, 220
  Boulanger
    coaches her in English, 56
    conducts his works, 46, 67, 77
    congratulated on Legion d'honneur, 51
    misses seeing her, 66, 75, 78
    reunions with, 74, 85
    on her teaching, 48–50, 68–9, 156–7, 163–4, 168
    tries to convince her about Britten, 66n83, 82
    reaction to her death, 222
    veneration for, 1, 52, 58, 77, 87, 251, 259
  Britten
    comparison with, 12–13, 226–7, 233, 240, 253, 276
    first meets, 1, 51n14, 58, 165, 174
    praises Berkeley, 206n69, 227, 245

BERKELEY, LENNOX, *continued*
   Britten, *continued*
      response to, 12, 89, 91–2, 101–2, 105–7,
         119–20, 174, 180, 183, 193, 215, 223, 260,
         267, 272, 276
      shares house with, 62
   Buckingham Palace, visits, 182, 207n70
   CBE, response to award, 84
   Cheltenham Festival, as President, 246, 279,
      282
   Chequers, visits, 198
   Commandeur de l'ordre du mérite culturel
      (Monaco), 86n152
   Composer's Guild Award, 204
   composing routines, 127–9, 167, 169, 175,
      176–8, 188, 226, 260, 264
   conducting, own, 1–2, 7, 70n95, 71, 158n14,
      188, 190, 198, 203, 207–8, 220, 230n5,
      238–9, 263, 267, 271n59, 275
   criticism, attitude to, 140–2, 262
   diary, becomes an effort, 199, 205, 218, 221,
      224
   early life and music, 1, 47n8, 154–9, 163–5,
      177
   early music and its instruments, connections
      with, 1, 54n32, 221, 244n28
   Elgar, response to, 97, 170, 193
   English music and context, assessment of,
      48, 64, 75, 97–104, 117–18, 132–5, 165,
      166–7, 170
   Fauré, response to, 5, 58, 60, 112–14, 274, 277
   favourite composers, 247, 250, 259, 262–3,
      274
   film about his life, 224
   film music, his scores, 72, 159, 230
   forms, traditional, use of, 159, 177–8
   French influences, 18, 144, 156, 167, 227, 232,
      263, 270, 276, 278
   harmony, use of, 2, 9–10, 88, 160, 173, 229,
      240–1, 248–9
   humour, sense of, 263, 267
   hymn, favourite, 218
   jazz, attitude to, 39, 170, 241
   knighthood, 88, 206–7
   Lake District holiday, 79
   Latin, anger at loss in Mass, 174, 189, 209,
      264
   listener, attitude to, 117–18, 162, 168, 172
   liturgical music, demands of, 11, 129, 169, 174,
      196, 203

BERKELEY, LENNOX, *continued*
   Lord Mayor's Banquet, 216
   manuscripts left with Boulanger or lost,
      57&n46, 263
   marriage, 2, 76, 180, 229, 246, 252, 256, 271–3,
      279
   mother, veneration for, 55, 58, 63, 68, 214
   Mozart, favourite composer, 68, 191, 229, 263,
      250, 274
   New York, visits, 211–12, 263
   old age, on, 152–3
   Oslo, visits, 220
   own works, composer needs to hear, 55,
      110–11
   Oxford, honorary degree, 189
   pacifism and politics, 67–8, 165–6, 213, 263–4
   Paris, wartime visits, 65–6, 263
   Parisian concert life, on, 31; his reports,
      15–44
   performance problems in his music, 231–2,
      236–7, 241
   Performing Right Society, as President, 210,
      246, 262, 279, 282
   pianist, as, 47n8, 69, 88, 104n53, 187, 196, 236,
      254n38, 263, 274
   piano, attitude to, 66, 157, 241, 282
   popular music, on, 169–70, 179
   popularity, obstacle to, 227, 231, 238, 249
   Poulenc, response to, 85, 108, 121–2, 164, 181,
      184, 191, 213
   pupils and influence, 3, 9, 84, 86, 157, 244,
      247, 248–9, 252, 254, 261, 268–9, 274–5
   Ravel, friendship with and estimate of, 1, 17,
      60, 145–8, 160–1, 185
   Rawsthorne, response to, 102, 138–9, 195
   reading, choice of books, 81, 115–16, 171, 182,
      195, 199–200, 217, 219, 226
   religion and contemporary composers, 123–5,
      127, 129
   repetition, eschews in composing, 7, 11, 144,
      177, 247, 250
   reputation, 3–13, 81–2, 219, 227, 232, 240, 246,
      249, 253–4, 262, 265
   reservations about own work, 12, 58, 60–1, 77,
      82, 217, 228, 231–2, 256–67
   Roman Catholic, as, 1, 97n25, 125, 153, 169,
      174, 209, 226, 250, 256, 259, 267, 273, 278
   serial music and atonality, attitude to, 9, 90,
      161, 167–8, 221, 279, 280n68
   sexuality, 2, 227, 270–1, 279

BERKELEY, LENNOX, *continued*
  song-writer and melodist, as, 143–4, 167n26, 169, 245, 280, 281–2
  Stravinsky
    admiration for, 52, 59, 73, 74, 75, 77, 78, 150, 203, 220–1, 262, 277, 280n68
    meetings with, 59, 200
  teacher, as, 3, 157, 168, 243–4, 247, 252, 254–5, 266
  temperament, 226, 228, 236, 245, 249–50, 265–6, 268, 270–1, 275–6
  war work, 65, 68, 217, 258
  Warwick Avenue, no. 8 (Berkeley home), 3, 229, 243–4, 259–60, 282
Berkeley, Michael FitzHardinge (LB's son), 6n22, 76, 181, 219, 219n94, 224n104, 256, 259, 265–70, 282
Berkeley Castle, 184, 262
Berlioz, Hector, 20, 42, 186, 199, 224
Bernac Pierre, 4, 56, 122, 191
Bernard, Anthony, 47n8, 51n13, 51n15, 79n130, 150, 156
Berners, Lord, 53, 64, 70–1, 268
Bernstein, Freda, *see* Berkeley, Freda
Bizet, Georges, 37
Bliss, Arthur, 23, 99, 155, 165, 202n58, 210
Bonham-Carter, Charlotte, 203n60
Booker Prize Dinner, 218
Boosey & Hawkes, 63n75, 66n83, 106, 255
Boulanger, Ernest (Nadia's father), 45
Boulanger, Lili, 15, 45, 59, 61, 89, 130–1
Boulanger, Nadia, 1, 3, 5, 6, 15, 16, 21, 31, 45–88, 89, 111, 132, 156–8, 160, 163–4, 168, 172, 181, 182, 188, 196, 222, 232, 244, 245, 248, 251, 251–3, 257, 259, 271, 276–8, 282
Boulanger, Raïssa (Nadia's mother), 47, 51, 53, 73
Boulez, Pierre, 12, 110, 121, 187, 212
Boult, Adrian, 186, 191, 210, 235n19, 272, 279n67
Bowman, James, 204
Bowra, Maurice, 183
Boys, Henry, 67n86
Bradshaw, Susan, 88, 217
Brahms, Johannes, 20, 38, 42, 212, 232, 237
Brain, Dennis, 237n23, 262, 269
Braithwaite, Nicholas, 8, 213
Braque, Georges, 16
Bream, Julian, 11, 12, 170, 200, 205–6, 208, 225–9, 262, 269
Brendel, Alfred, 133

Breton, André, 16
Breughel, Pieter, 105
Bridge, Frank, 33
British Council, 76, 97, 111, 220, 223
British Institute of Recorded Sound, 196
British Music Information Centre, 204n64
British Music Society, 51n13
Britten, Benjamin, 1–2, 4, 5–6, 9, 11–13, 18, 57n42, 58n48, 59nn53–5, 61, 62, 63, 70, 71, 75, 76, 82, 83, 89, 91–2, 107, 111, 117, 119–20, 124, 158, 159, 165–6, 174, 197, 203, 208, 209, 215, 225–8, 240, 245, 247, 249, 251, 253, 255–7, 258–9, 265, 266–7, 269–71, 276, 277, 278
  Albert Herring, 100, 119, 189, 204, 272
  characters in operas, 119–20
  Death in Venice 204, 210
  Illuminations, Les, 66n83, 189, 231
  Midsummer Night's Dream, A, 180, 204, 223
  Peter Grimes, 100, 101, 119, 124, 183, 193, 215, 231, 258
  Rape of Lucretia, The, 100, 101, 119, 272
  Spring Symphony, 89, 105–7
  String Quartet no. 1, 91–2
  Turn of the Screw, The, 9, 11, 82, 119, 120, 180, 222, 255
  War Requiem, 180, 218, 228
Brosa, Antonio, 2
Browning, John, 211, 215
Buckland, Sidney, 4
Bruckner, Anton, 250
Bryan, Gordon, 48n8, 156n6
Bryans, Gladys Sophia, 58n51
Bryanston Summer School (later Dartington) 77
Brymer, Jack, 199
Buckingham Palace, 182, 207n70
Buckle, Richard, 193
Burkhard, Willi, 61
Burney, Charles, 136
Bush, Alan, 104, 166, 193
Byrd, William, 181

Cage, John, 154, 170
Cameron, Basil, 51n13, 238
Capdevielle, Pierre, 179–80
Capel, Richard, 18
Cardew, Cornelius, 154, 166
Carl Flesch competition, 219
Cartan, Jean, 36

Carter, Elliott, 45,
Casals, Pablo, 37
Casella, Alfredo, 27, 37, 41,
Catholic Musicians Guild, 253, 257
Cézanne, Paul, 97
Chabrier, Emmanuel, 37
Chaliapin, Feodor, 27, 37,
Chaplin, Alvide, 74
Chaplin, Anthony, 3rd Viscount, 71
Chardin, Teilhard de, 116
Charpentier, Gustave, 80
Cheltenham Festival, 87, 154, 185, 186, 201–2, 219, 222, 243, 246, 279, 282
Chequers, 198
Chester, J. & W., 51n17, 53n25, 62, 64, 67, 73, 77n125, 232n9
Cholmondeley, Sybil Sassoon, Marchioness of Cholmondeley, 189
Chopin, Frédéric, 28, 112, 157, 199, 209, 237
Cimarosa, Domenico, 166
Civil, Alan, 199
Clark, Kenneth, 142
Clarke, Ashley, 111
Claude (Claude Lorrain), 105
Cocteau, Jean, 15, 17, 18, 26, 47n8, 95
Cœuroy, André, 101
Colefax, Sybil, Lady, 73
Coleridge, Samuel Taylor, 142
Colette, Sidonie-Gabrielle, 148
College of St Mark and St John, Chelsea, 4
Composer's Guild, 204, 208, 282
Contemporary Music Centre, London, 52n19
Cooke, Arnold, 67n86, 208
Coolidge, Elisabeth Sprague, 23, 33, 91, 147
Cooper, Martin, 7, 142
Copland, Aaron, 9, 11, 15, 21, 45, 46, 61, 85n148, 160, 214, 269, 278
Cortot, Alfred, 31, 35, 37, 38
Covent Garden, 183, 186, 187, 188, 190, 193, 194, 204, 210, 213, 214, 223
Crabbe, George, 100
Craft, Robert, 125, 200
Crane, Hart, 16
Craxton, Essie, 218
Craxton, Janet, 88, 183, 202, 262, 269
Crichton, Ronald, 147, 195
Croisa, Claire, 40
Cuénod, Hughes, 80, 217
Cummings, E. E., 16, 171
Curzon, Clifford, 60n60, 198, 255

Damrosch, Walter, 46,
D'Annunzio, Gabriel, 46
Dartington Summer School, and Quartet, 75, 77n114, 190, 192
Davenport, John, 67
Davies, Meredith, 205
Davies, Peter Maxwell, 132, 222
Davis, Andrew, 220
Davis, Colin, 274
Davis, Hugh, 3
De la Mare, Walter, 10
Dean, Winton, 142, 179, 214, 222, 280n68
Debussy, Claude, 15, 17, 27, 28, 30, 42, 49, 92, 97, 99, 112–14, 131, 146, 155, 161, 163, 164, 187, 189, 199, 201, 247, 259, 270, 274
memorial unveiled, 35–6
Dehn, Paul, 174, 188, 274
Del Mar, Norman, 12, 205, 230–5
Delius, Frederick, 64, 156, 230–2, 234, 253
Delvincourt, Claude, 41
Desormière, Roger, 27
Diaghilev, Serge, 15, 17, 19n14, 21, 22, 26, 27, 37, 53n23, 93, 95, 146, 150, 203
Dickinson, Peter, 2–5, 88, 143, 185, 191, 192, 196, 201, 201n57, 219
Dickinson, Meriel, 3n19, 88, 143, 185, 191, 192, 201, 219
Dieudonné, Annette, 52, 64, 82
D'Indy, Vincent, 29
Dolmetsch, Carl, 221, 244n28
Domingo, Placido, 223
Donne, John, 126
Douglas, Basil, 83, 93, 256n45, 258, 271–5
Dreier, Per, 220
Drewry, Val, 236, 237
Dukas, Paul, 31, 42, 95
Dushkin, Samuel, 33, 39, 40, 50, 52, 53
Dutilleux, Henri, 179, 216

Eathorne, Wendy, 205
Edinburgh Quartet, 207
Einstein, Alfred, 142
Eisenberg, Maurice, 69
Elgar, Edward, 51n13, 97–8, 132, 167, 170, 193, 246, 253, 257
Eliot, T. S., 16
Elizabeth II, Queen, 182–3
Ellis, Osian, 135, 171, 206
Elman, Mischa, 22, 38
English Chamber Orchestra, 196, 202

English Opera Group, 76n121, 83, 101, 174,
    206n68, 230, 233, 255, 271–2, 274
Ernst, Max, 16
Esty, Alice Swanson, 3n1, 4
Evans, Edwin, 72
Evans, Geraint, 183
Evans, Nancy, 256

Fairchild, Blair, 53
Falla, Manuel de, 25, 39, 46,
Fauré, Gabriel, 5, 31, 40, 45, 89, 97, 112–14, 131,
    143, 157, 170, 227, 229, 247, 266, 274, 277
  Requiem, 58, 60, 196, 251, 259
Ferguson, Howard, 248
Ferneyhough, Brian, 252
Ferrier, Kathleen, 79n132, 80, 143
Fine Arts Orchestra, 203
Finzi, Gerald, 104
Fistoulari, Anatole, 238
Fitzgerald, Scott, 16
Forbes, Sebastian, 187
Ford, Ford Madox, 16
Françaix, Jean, 38, 57, 60n60, 63–5, 69, 75
Francis, John, 160, 240
Franck, César, 212, 239
Fraser, Peter, 271, 279
Furtwängler, Wilhelm, 20, 30

Galway, James, 10, 212, 219, 221, 262, 269
Gendron, Maurice, 193–4
Gibson, Douglas, 77, 78, 84, 79n130, 84
Gide, André, 16, 43, 115
Gieseking, Walter, 24, 28, 47
Gilardino, Angelo, 225n2
Glock, William, 67n86, 69, 75, 118, 202
Gluck, Christoph, Willibald, 43
Glyndebourne, 183, 189, 197, 212
Goethe, Johann Wolfgang von, 169
Goldsbrough, Arnold, 79n132
Golschmann, Vladimir, 38
Gomez, Jill, 4, 190
Goodwin, Noel, 7
Goossens, Eugene, 63, 238, 253, 254
Goulden, Oliver, 46, 97
Green, Julian, 81, 115, 182, 192, 195
Greenidge, John, 47, 69n93, 80, 259
Gresham's School, 1, 155
Grinke, Frederick, 263
Groves, Charles, 202, 219, 222, 238
Grovlez, Madeleine, 50

Guest, George, 132
Gunson, Ameril, 187

Hacker, Alan, 187
Haief, Alexei, 85n148
Hall, Peter, 197
Hamburger, Paul, 248
Hamilton, William, 137
Handel, George Frideric, 142
Hardy, Thomas, 115, 203–4
Harewood, Countess of (later Marion Thorpe),
    180
Harewood, George, 7th Earl, 214, 222
Harris, Roy, 21,
Harris, W. H., 155
Harsányi, Tibor, 21, 36
Hawkes, Ralph, 63
Haydn, Joseph, 27, 35, 60n56, 109
Hays, Roland, 29
Hazlitt, William, 142
Heath, Edward, 197–8
Hemingway, Ernest, 16
Henze, Hans Werner, 181, 207, 213
Heyworth, Peter, 208
Hickox, Richard, 1, 2, 8, 213n81, 221
Hindemith, Paul, 2, 24, 25, 26, 27, 32, 33, 70, 101,
    103, 208n72
Holmboe, Vagn, 182, 186, 197
Honegger, Arthur, 17, 19, 22, 23, 26, 29, 30–1, 40,
    43, 44, 124
Hopkins, Gerard Manley, 10
Horowitz, Vladimir, 38, 66
Horsley, Colin, 8–9, 12, 110, 160, 208n73,
    236–42, 243, 254, 262, 269
Howard, Michael, 181
Howarth, Elgar, 201n57
Howells, Herbert, 2, 124
Howes, Frank, 5
Hügel, Friedrich von, 116
Hull, Robin, 6
Hunt, Donald, 220
Hunter, Ian, 227
Hüttel, Joseph, 23
Huysmans, J. K., 115

Ibert, Jacques, 38, 44, 95, 160
International Society for Contemporary Music,
    1, 21, 38n39, 51, 51n14, 54n30, 56n35, 59, 60,
    61, 62n64, 64n80, 158, 161, 238
Ireland, John, 4, 64, 99
Isaacs, Leonard, 80–1

Isnard, Jeanne, 48n8
Ives, Charles, 235

Jackson, Sybil (LB's god-mother), 276
Janacopoulos, Vera, 25
jazz, 15, 17, 18, 21, 39, 46, 145, 170, 190
John Radcliffe Trust, 217
Johnston, David, 101n57
Joyce, James, 16

Kahn-Casella, Hélène, 67
Kammerchor of Basle, 42
Kanawa, Kiri te, 214
Keele University, 208, 214
Keller, Hans, 5
Kipling, Rudyard, 40
Knox, Msgr Ronald, 116
Kochno, Boris, 37
Koechlin, Charles, 31, 40, 160
Koussevitsky, Serge, 46, 105
Krenek, Ernst, 61
Kynaston, Nicholas, 215

Labunski, Felix, 36
Lajtha, László, 40
Laks, Simon, 21
Lambert, Constant, 20, 165, 238
Landowska, Wanda, 20, 35
Larkin, Philip, 218
Lee, Laurie, 181, 198
Lees-Milne, James, 217
Leppard, Raymond, 194, 196, 197, 202, 220
Lewis, C. Day, 155, 163
Lewis, C. S., 116
Lewis, Richard, 143
Ley, Henry, 163
Lincoln Center, Chamber Music Society, 208n73, 211, 240n27
Lipatti, Dinu, 79
Liszt, Franz, 24, 112, 133, 147
Litvin, Natasha, 76
London Chamber Orchestra, 51n15, 79n130, 156
London Philharmonic Orchestra, 70n95, 71n102, 190, 195, 201, 238
London Sinfonietta, 198
London Symphony Orchestra, 56n40, 77n126, 79n132, 127, 238n24
Long, Kathleen, 52n19
Lott, Felicity, 218, 222
Lotti, Antonio, 42
Loveday, Alan, 243

Lully, Jean-Baptiste, 34, 93
Lutoslawski, Witold, 170, 200
Lutyens, Elisabeth, 12, 104, 194, 195, 253–4, 255

MacCrindle, Sheila, 256
Maconchy, Elisabeth, 104, 187, 194, 195, 217
Maggini Quartet, 55n33
Mahler, Gustav, 18, 30, 208, 220, 232, 272
Malcolm, George, 132, 198, 257
Malipiero, Gian Francesco, 23, 27, 33
Mallarmé, Stéphane, 135
Manduell, John, 203n63, 243–7, 281–2
Manduell, Renna, 185
Mann, William, 195
Maréchal, Maurice, 26
Marescotti, André-François, 180
Margaret, Princess, 268
Marie José, Queen of Belgium, 179
Markevitch, Igor, 18, 26, 27, 28, 33, 37
Marriner, Neville, 202, 203n62
Martenot, Maurice, 44
Martinon, Jean, 87n156, 186, 246
Martinů, Bohuslav, 18, 23, 36
Massimo, Leone, 33
Maupassant, Guy de, 159
Mauriac, François, 195
Maw, Nicholas, 84, 189, 248–52
Mawby, Colin, 201
Mayer, Robert, 56n39
McDonald, Boyd, 205
Mellers, Wilfrid, 6
Melos Ensemble, 214
Memorial Requiem Mass, 264, 281–2
Mengelberg, Willem, 22, 30
Menuhin, Yehudi, 39, 185, 186, 192, 234, 251, 262, 269
Messiaen, Olivier, 45, 125
Meyer, Krzysztof, 188
Mihalovici, Marcel, 36, 186
Milhaud, Darius, 15, 17, 18, 22, 23, 26, 30, 33, 34, 38, 95, 160, 274–5
Milner, Anthony, 124, 134
Milton, John, 106, 107
Mitchell, Donald, 5
Mitford, Nancy, 115
Mitropoulos, Dimitri, 41–2
Modrakowska, Maria, 35
Monaco, 83–6, 179, 182, 186, 197, 216, 259
Montani, Pietro, 182
Monteux, Pierre, 20, 22, 28, 38

Monteverdi, Claudio, 16, 34, 45, 60n56, 64, 80, 127, 197
Monthly Musical Record, 1, 18, 19–44, 47, 48, 90
Mozart, Wolfgang Amadeus, 20, 22, 43, 68, 109, 126, 137, 142, 146, 166, 174, 180, 189, 190, 191, 197, 212, 214, 224, 229, 237, 238, 247, 250, 257, 259, 263, 265, 268–70, 274
Munch, Charles, 67, 108
Musgrave, Thea, 132, 197, 206
Mussorgsky, Modest, 27

Nabokov, Nicholas, 19, 37
Nashe, Thomas, 106
Naylor, Bernard, 124
New York, 4, 21n20, 62n67, 63n75, 68, 211, 212n79, 215, 216, 250n33, 263
Newman, Ernest, 142
Nieman, Alfred, 134
Nijinksa, Bronislava, 27, 37
Nijinsky, Vaslav, 146
Noalles, Vicomte de, 37
Nono, Luigi, 252
Nostradamus (Michel de Nostradame), 81

O'Donnell, James, 281
Oliver, Michael, 11, 154, 176–8
Oman, Carola, 261
Opéra Russe à Paris, 27
Orchestre symphonique de Paris, 19, 22, 23, 26, 27
Organ Club, 215
Orr, Robin, 3
Osborne, Nigel, 217
Owen, Wilfred, 124
Oxford, 1, 18, 54n32, 85, 87, 115n57, 155n5, 156, 160, 163, 184, 187, 189, 217, 245, 251, 259, 276

Paderewski, Ignacy, 30
Palestrina, Giovanni Pierluigi, da, 10, 42, 127, 247, 256
Panufnik, Andrzej, 7
Parikian, Manoug, 234
Paris, 1, 15–44, 45–68, 73, 74, 76, 77, 79, 80, 82–4, 90, 93, 95, 97, 117, 136, 145, 146, 150, 155, 156, 160, 161, 163, 179, 180, 182, 197, 203, 223, 245, 259, 262, 263, 282
Park Lane Group, 219
Parny, Evariste, 147
Partridge, Frances, 219
Pathé-Nathan film company, 37

Pavlova, Anna, 26
Pears, Peter, 70n97, 143, 171, 189, 197, 198, 206, 215, 217, 218, 222, 261, 273
Peele, George, 106
Performing Right Society, 208, 210, 211, 246, 262, 279, 282
Pernel, Orea, 52n19
Pernet, André, 34
Petit, Raymond, 33
Peyer, Gervaise de, 211
Phillip, Isidore, 31
Picasso, Pablo, 15, 16, 82n139
Pilkington, Vere, 1, 54
Pindar, 54
Pipkov, Lyubomir, 21
Piston, Walter, 45, 85n148
Pizzetti, Ildebrando, 42
Polignac, Countess Jean de (née Marie-Blanche Lanvin), 71, 73
Polignac, Princess Edmond de (née Winaretta Singer), 55, 56n40, 69, 70, 71, 72–3
Ponsonby, David, 74
Ponsonby, Robert, 219
Porter, Andrew, 7, 216
Porter, Quincy, 48n8
Poulenc, Francis, 1, 4, 17, 18, 27, 31, 35n34, 36, 56, 69, 75, 85, 89, 95, 96, 108–9, 114, 125, 143, 160, 164, 167, 181, 191, 212–13, 215, 229, 231, 232, 247, 251, 257, 259, 270, 273–4
    Aubade, 24
    Bal masqué, Le, 37
    Concert champêtre, 20
    Flute Sonata, 212–13
    La Grenouillière 184
Pound, Ezra, 16
Poussin, Nicholas, 105
Powell, Anthony, 115
Préger, Louis, 75, 80
Preston, Simon, 196
Previn, André, 185
Princeton University, 211
Pritchard, John, 202
Pro Arte Quartet, 55
Prokofiev, Serge, 21, 33, 38, 40, 53, 66n85, 164, 236
Proust, Marcel, 16
Prunières, Henri, 34
Puccini, Giacomo, 13

Pugno, Raoul, 45–6
Purcell, Henry, 22, 78, 83, 103, 123, 189, 215

Quirk, John Shirley, 218

Rachmaninov, Sergei, 38, 46, 236, 238, 239
Radcliffe, Philip, 3
Radio Times, 210
Raffalli, José, 57, 67n87, 263
Rainier III, Prince of Monaco, 83–4, 86nn151–2
Rainier, Priaulx, 104
Rameau, Jean Philippe, 15, 26, 60n56, 80
Ravel, Maurice, 1, 15, 17, 21, 24, 25, 27, 28–9, 35, 38, 40, 42, 43, 44, 47n8, 49, 60, 89, 96, 97, 99, 114, 145–9, 155, 160–1, 163, 170, 180, 185, 201, 227, 229, 237, 247, 250, 251, 259, 270, 282
  Daphnis et Chloé, 93–4, 146–7, 149
  L'Enfant et les sortilèges, 148
  L'Heure espagnole, 148
  Introduction and Allegro, 146
  String Quartet, 146, 163, 207
  Valse, La, 147
Rawsthorne, Alan, 5, 6, 11, 89, 102, 138–9, 159, 167, 193, 196, 208, 241
Read, Herbert, 142
Redlich, Hans, F, 5
Renoir, Pierre-Auguste, 97
Respighi, Otto, 42
Richardson, Alan, 88
Rieti, Vittorio, 22, 33
Rignold, Hugo, 79n132
Rimsky-Korsakov, Nikolay Andreyevich, 150
Robbins, Jerome, 199
Robertson, Alec, 123
Robertson, Rae, 62, 273
Rodrigo, Joaquin, 226, 228
Roet, Janet de, 88
Roland-Manuel, Alexis, 179, 185
Rolf-Johnson, Anthony, 205
Rossini, Gioachino, 21, 27
Rostal, Max, 241
Rostropovitch, Mstislav, 180
Roussel, Albert, 20, 23, 36, 40, 95, 160, 250, 251
Rowlands, Alan, 4
Rowse, A. L., 216
Royal Academy of Music, 2, 84, 168, 243, 248, 254, 260, 261, 265, 266, 282
Royal College of Music, 2, 199, 225
Royal Northern College, 220, 243

Royal Philharmonic Orchestra, 54n29, 207, 208, 214, 220, 230n4, 256
Rubbra, Edmund, 66n83, 103, 124, 187, 253
Rubinstein, Ida, 43–4, 95

Sackville-West, Edward, 5th Baron Sackville, 276
Sadlers Wells, 2, 90n4, 99, 100, 110, 183, 244, 255, 274
Saint-Beuve, Charles Augustin, 142
Saint-Säens, Camille, 27
Sammonds, Albert, 51n13
Satie, Erik, 15, 17, 26, 27, 95, 114
Sandringham, 189
Sauguet, Henri, 27, 33, 37, 95, 160
Sautelet, Charles, 47,
Scarlatti, Alessandro, 44
Schaffer, Murray, 9, 154
Schmitt, Florent, 95, 180
Schnittke, Alfred, 235
Schoenberg, Arnold, 4, 9, 10, 12, 32, 42, 45, 135, 161, 168, 274
Scholes, Percy, 137
Schöne, Lotte, 25
Schott & Co., 68
Schubert, Franz, 20, 29, 169, 189, 198, 215, 274
Schumann, Robert, 20, 47, 112, 254
Schütz, Heinrich, 42
Schwartz, Rudolph, 239
Scofield, Paul, 182
Scotland, Tony, 2, 60n60, 69n93
Sculthorpe, Peter, 187
Searle, Humphrey, 12, 67n86, 104, 134, 193, 195
Segovia, Andrés, 29–30, 38,
Sellick, Phyllis, 77n126, 160, 273,
Shakespeare, 12, 103, 166, 191, 193, 216, 223
Shaw, George Bernard, 12
Shawe-Taylor, Desmond, 6, 12, 257, 276–80
Shelley, Howard, 215
Sherlaw Johnson, Robert, 187
Shirley, George, 187
Shostakovich, Dimitri, 134n64, 208, 227
Sibelius, Jean, 64
Siegfried, André, 32
Silver, Millicent, 57n42
Sitwell, Edith, 20
Six, Les, 15, 17, 31, 95, 232
Slatford, Rodney, 194
Smith, Cyril, 77n126, 160, 273

Société musicale indépendente, 16, 20, 35, 47n8, 50n9, 50n12, 53n26, 67n89
Soetans, Robert, 53
Solti, George, 201
Spender, Stephen, 76
Stein, Erwin, 255
Stein, Gertrude, 16
Stephenson, Ronald, 134
Stevens, Bernard, 104
Stockhausen, Karlheinz, 12, 187
Stoker, Richard, 8, 193
Straram, Walter, 16, 24, 30, 41, 42, 95, 96
Strauss, Johann, 25, 49
Strauss, Richard, 13, 18, 37, 212, 232, 278
Stravinsky, Igor, 1, 4, 6, 11, 12, 15, 18–24, 27, 28, 33, 39–40, 41–4, 45, 46, 52–3, 59, 70, 73, 74, 75, 78, 85n148, 90, 92, 93n11, 96, 101, 111, 114, 117, 124–6, 135, 141, 147, 150–1, 155, 164, 199, 200, 214, 220–1, 222, 227, 232, 239, 241, 251, 257, 262, 277
  Duo Concertant, 39, 53, 221, 241
  Les Noces, 17, 19, 21, 49, 153, 203
  Perséphone, 17, 18, 43–4
  Rite of Spring, The, 17, 28, 141, 150, 220–1
  Symphony of Psalms, 18, 28, 125, 221, 257
Stravinsky, Soulima, 76, 78, 150, 200, 262
Sutherland, Margaret, 254
Szalowski, Anton, 64
Szymanovski, Karol, 36, 236

Tailleferre, Germaine, 25
Tansman, Alexandre, 33
Tavener, John, 86, 181,
Tchaikovsky, Pyotr Ilyich, 147, 183
Teresa, St of Avila, 116, 169
Thibaud, Jacques, 37
Thill, Georges, 38
Thomas, Dylan, 67n86, 171
Thomson, Virgil, 16, 212, 216
Three Choirs Festival, 203, 220
Tippett, Michael, 71, 102, 167, 190, 193, 228, 231, 245, 249, 266, 274, 278
Toscanini, Arturo, 36, 42
Toumanova, Tamara, 37
Turina, Joaquin, 29, 200

Twiner, Anthony, 199
Tzara, Tristan, 16

Valéry, Paul, 54
Van Wyck, Arnold, 56
Vatican Council, Second, 209
Vaughan Williams, Ralph, 18, 22, 64, 98–9, 123–4, 165, 167, 170, 204n64, 239, 249, 253, 257
Verdi, Guiseppe, 120, 127, 179, 183, 193–4, 213, 221, 263, 265, 269
Verlaine, Paul, 113
Vines, Ricardo, 25
Vivaldi, Antonio, 27
Vivian, Jennifer, 222

Wagner, Richard, 5, 17, 30, 42, 97, 112, 142, 194, 208
Waley, Arthur, 189
Walter, Bruno, 24, 30
Walton, William, 5, 11, 20, 58, 99–100, 132, 158, 165, 188, 195, 214, 266
Warwick Avenue, no. 8, *see under* Berkeley, Lennox
Waugh, Evelyn, 115
Webster, Beveridge, 50
Weill, Kurt, 39
Wellesz, Egon, 187, 253, 257
Welsh, Moray, 69n92
Westergaard, Peter, 211
Westminster Cathedral, 127, 128, 170, 184, 198, 218, 221, 224, 226, 257, 261, 264, 265, 278, 281–2
Whittall, Arnold, 12
Wilde, David, 210
Williamson, Malcolm, 195, 253–7
Wittgenstein, Paul, 40
Wolf, Hugo, 5
Wood, Henry, 22, 63n71
Woodhouse, Violet Gordon, 54n32
Woolf, Virginia, 199
Wordsworth, William, 142
Wyss, Sophie, 48n8

Zeffirelli, Franco, 183